A Dictionary of Lost East London
Copyright © Mick Lemmerman 2017

CW01513320

Dedicated to
Angela Lemmerman and John Lemmerman

Also by Mick Lemmerman:

The Isle of Dogs During World War II, ISBN 9781507746110

The (Old) Isle of Dogs from A to Z, ISBN 9781503056121

Edited by Mick Lemmerman:

Heavy Duty Rescue Squad on the Isle of Dogs – Bill Regan's Second World War Diaries, Ann Regan-Atherton, ISBN 9781519610867

Introduction

In terms of the long history of London, the East End is a relatively new place. Take a look at a map of London in, say, 1600, and the area to east of the City walls is mostly farmland, punctuated with the odd village, such as Stepney, Poplar or Bow, connected by country lanes. In 1700, the area immediately outside of the walls had seen some development (Spitalfields, Goodmans Yard, for example) as had a strip of land along the river, but still there was nothing that could be described as East London.

By the end of the 1700s, however, the Industrial Revolution had caused an explosive growth in industry and house building, London spilled out of its old borders (from a population of 1 million in 1800 to more than 6 million in 1900), and East London was a fact.

Until the 19th century there were few rules regarding how places and streets should be named or spelled; the names developed organically and according to popular, local convention. The Metropolitan Board of Works, established in the mid-19th century sought to bring order to this situation. Not only did they take official responsibility for new names, they also carried out an extensive renaming, in order to facilitate their administration of London and to support accurate delivery of post by the General Post Office.

Fifty years later, much of the administration was delegated to newly-formed borough councils who mostly endeavoured to make sure that 'their' street names were unique and easily located. When, for example, a council was confronted with four of five separate Cross Streets within its area, it would likely rename four of them. When widening roads, or creating major new routes, it made sense to amalgamate multiple, differently-named road sections into one (take The Highway as an example, whose original names are mentioned later in this chapter).

A further, major influence on London street names was World War II, which caused the obliteration of many streets, with large numbers being buried under new council estates during the post-war rebuilding.

The frequent name-changing is a challenge to an avid family tree researcher and amateur historian like myself, and I am always interested in (old) documents which allow me to better identify the location of old addresses or buildings. Among the useful publications I have come across is "Lockie's Topography of London" by John Lockie, published in 1810. Lockie spent seven years preparing the book, which he created for the insurers Phoenix Fire-Office off Lombard Street, for whom he was the Inspector of Buildings.

i

The topography accurately describes itself as providing "a concise local description of, and accurate direction to, every square, street, lane, court, dock, wharf, inn, public-office, &c. in the metropolis and its environs, including the new buildings to the present time, upon a plan never hitherto attempted." The descriptions are short, clear, and indeed accurate; it takes little effort to identify the present-day location.

> Bethnal-Green-Workhouse,—the E. end of Hare-st. by the fields; about ⅔ of a mile on the R. in it from 110, Brick-lane.
>
> Betts-Place, Betts-Street, Ratcliffe-highway,—is four doors on the L. from 164, Ratcliffe-highway towards the New-road or Back-lane.

In the decades that followed its publication, books in a similar vein were published, including "A Topographical Dictionary of London and its Environs" by James Elmes, published in 1831. Elmes was born in Greenwich and was an architect of some note, as is apparent from his ample architectural descriptions of many of the buildings. Although not as comprehensive as Lockie's Topography (nor did it claim to be), it was a welcome addition to my reference "library". Both works are abundantly quoted in this book.

After finding other books of the same ilk, I started to think about combining them all, along with the readily-available street name change information on the internet, to provide myself with a handy list of everything in one place. I wasn't planning to publish a book, it was meant to be for just my own use. The idea of making a book from it grew gradually, along with my realisation that it could be of use to other people too. I also thought I'd be finished in a few weeks.

That was 18 months ago! Once I had started, there seemed no end to it, apart from the obvious geographical boundaries. Mind you, the earliest drafts also included what is now Newham and Stratford and the north half of Hackney, before I decided that it was just too much (and also because these areas have seen nothing like the extent of the changes by areas clser to the City).

I would not dare to state that the end result is complete and comprehensive, there is always new research and information cropping up from somewhere, but in the same way that I drew geographical lines as a practical necessity, the law of diminishing returns meant calling an end to the research after much longer than the 'few weeks' I had in mind. Oh to have had Lockie's seven years' research time.

How to use this book and other notes

In almost all cases (where possible, practical and known), each entry is followed by:

- the street in which, or off which, it was located
- its area
- the year of the record or map which refers to the entry
- extra information, for example about the location or history

If an obsolete street name is presented, the modern equivalent (or closest) is included immediately afterwards in brackets.

By way of example, consider the following entry:

> **Albert Villas**, Albert Road (Albion Drive), Hackney, 1868, between Queens Road (Queensbridge Road) and Malvern Road.

This states that Albert Villas were in Albert Road (which is named Albion Drive these days) in Hackney. Albert Villas were referred to in an 1868 document. They were located between Queens (now Queensbridge) Road and Malvern Road.

If there were multiple streets (or pubs, schools, etc.) with the same name then these are presented in a numbered list, for example:

> **Adams Place**, 1. Salmon Lane, Limehouse. 2. Three Colts Lane, Bethnal Green, 1891. 3. Wentworth Street, Whitechapel, 1891.

Alternative references to the same place, due to – for example – street name changes are included for the sake of completeness, and to aid readers who are searching for a specific address.

Spelling was not consistent until recent centuries, and although this book attempts to present the alternative spellings over time, you may need to try different spellings before you can find a particular street or place.

Punctuation – and in particular the use of apostrophes – was also not consistently applied in the past. As an aid to searching and sorting, this book uses no apostrophes in street or place names.

When considering street numbers, bear in mind that many were changed in Victorian times. Before then, the so-called "horseshoe" number system was applied, whereby the numbers increased sequentially along one side of the street before continuing on the other side of the street in the reverse direction. In the mid-19th century the current street numbering, with odd and even numbers on opposite sides of the road, became prevalent.

East London Defined

For the purposes of this book, East London is defined as the area bounded approximately by the Thames in the south, the River Lea in the east, the North London Railway Line in the north, and the A10 and the City in the west.

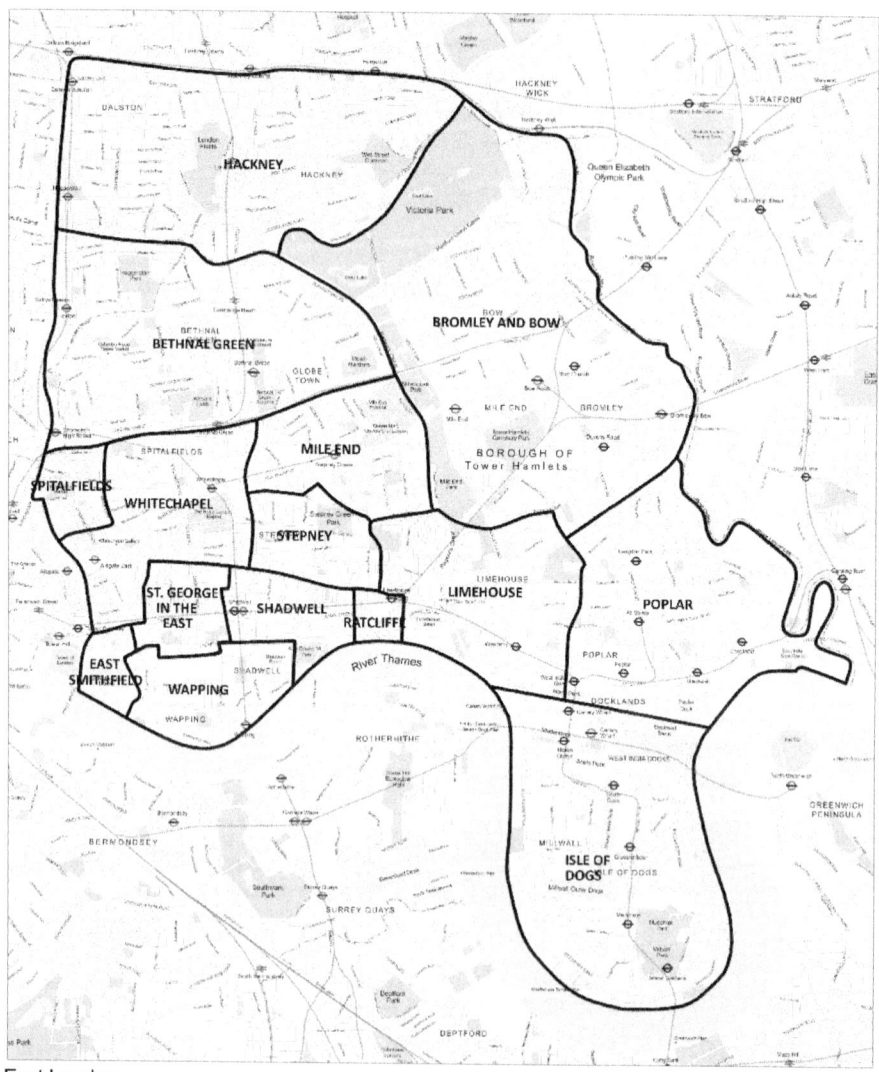

East London

There are of course arguments that some places outside of this area could also be classed as East London, or perhaps that Hackney is more North London than East London, but - being confronted with the practical need to draw the line somewhere – I chose for the convenient natural borders of the Lea and the Thames, and was guided by the physical extents of London a century ago, when East and West Ham, for example, were administratively a part of Essex.

Significant Thoroughfares and Places

Bethnal Green

The area now occupied by Bethnal Green Library, the V&A Museum of Childhood and St John's Church. Bethnal Green is derived from the Anglo-Saxon *Blithehale*, meaning 'Blitha's corner of land', and which would later became *Blethenalegrene*.

Boundary Street Estate

The Old Nichol (aka The Nichol or The Old Nichol Street Rookery) was a notorious slum area north of Bethnal Green Road close to its junction with Shoreditch High Street. After slum clearance, the Boundary Estate was built on it site (opened in 1900).

Bow Common Lane

Bow Common was south of the present day Tower Hamlets Cemetery. Bow Common Lane was the main route across the common from Mile End to Poplar.

Bow Road

The main road from Mile End Road to the place *Stratford-atte-Bow* or *Stratford-le-Bow* (where 'Bow' is derived from the Old English *boga*, meaning 'bridge') on the west side of the River Lea, distinct from the present day Stratford on the east side of the river.

Brick Lane

Formerly called Whitechapel Lane, Brick Lane was named after the brick manufacture that took place in the area from the 15th century. Sections of the road were (re)named over the following centuries as follows:

1746, Whitechapel Road to (what would become) Bethnal Green Road.

1775, south section, Whitechapel Road to Wentworth Street, renamed Osborn Street. North end extended to Virginia Road (but not yet named Brick Lane)

1890, extended northwards across Bethnal Green Road as far as Columbia Road, absorbing Tyssen Street and Turk Street.

1950s, north section truncated to just south of present day Chambord Street.

Burdett Road

Road from Limehouse to Mile End Road constructed in the mid-19th century, named after Victorian philanthropist Angela Burdett-Coutts (b1814).

Cable Street

Originally a straight path along which hemp ropes were twisted into ships' cables (i.e. ropes). The current Cable Street is an amalgamation of a number of earlier roads, from west to east: Cable Street, Knock Fergus, New Road, Back Lane, Blue Gate Fields, Sun Tavern Fields, and Brook Street.

Cambridge Heath Road

Cambridge Heath was at the present day junction of Old Bethnal Green Road and Cambridge Heath Road. The earliest recorded use of the name is as *Camprichthesheth* in 1275, thought to mean 'Cantbeorth's Heathland'. The section of the road from Whitechapel to just south of Bethnal Green, was originally named Dog Row.

Cannon Street Road

New Road was a new road from Whitechapel Road to the present day Cable Street. The existing street from there to the present day Highway was named Cannon Street, in reference to the artillery practice ground in the area. Hence a section of New Road being named Cannon Street Road.

Chrisp Street

One of a few streets that were developed north of East India Dock Road in the 1830s (in 1836 the street was less than 100 feet long) on the former estate of Mary Wade, who had divided the land among her five daughters. Early streets were named after the daughters and their husbands: husbands: Sarah and William Kerbey, Sophia and James Duff, Susannah and James Grundy, Elizabeth Chrisp Willis, widow of William Willis, and Catherine Wade, who remained unmarried.

Columbia Road

In 1864, Angela Burdett-Coutts, also responsible for the construction of Burdett Road, donated £20,000 for the building of Columbia Market in Bethnal Green, which was intended to provide locals with jobs and affordable food. Columbia Square and Road were named after the market, which was not a success and closed in 1886.

Commercial Road

Commercial Road was constructed in 1802–6 as a direct route to link dock traffic between the West India Docks and East India Docks to the City of London. An Act of Parliament awarded construction to the Commercial Road Company, whose trustees were allowed to raise money and levy tolls. The road originally began at Back Church Lane and cut a path across fields north of Ratcliffe Highway. It was c1870 before the section between Gardiners Corner and Back Church Lane was constructed.

Commercial Street

The southern section of Commercial Street was created in 1843–5 as part of a slum clearance programme, and to connect Whitechapel with Spitalfields Market. It followed approximately the route of the (demolished) streets: Essex Street, Rose Lane and Red Lion Street. The later northern extension was opened in 1858.

Devons Road

Previously named Bromley Lane, the road may have gained its present name from former landowner Thomas Devon.

East India Docks

Opened in 1806 to the north east of West India Docks. It was, in 1967, the first of the London Docks to close.

East India Dock Road

Main road connecting Commercial Road to the East India Docks, created north of Poplar High Street in the early 1800s.

Grove Road

Formerly Grove Street, and likely named after the 14th century Richard atte Grove.

Hackney Road

Hackney is derived from the Old English *Hakeneia*, meaning 'Haca's Island' (where 'Island' was a reference to dry land within Hackney Marshes).

King Edward Memorial Park

More commonly known as Shadwell Park, opened in 1922 by King George V and Queen Mary.

Kingsland Road

The road to Kingsland, an old settlement that has been absorbed by modern Dalston. It is one of the oldest roads in England and is thought to follow the route of the Roman Ermine Street, later known as the Old North Road.

Leman Street

Named after William Leman, whose great-uncle, John Leman had bought Goodman's Fields earlier in the seventeenth century.

London Docks

The London Docks were constructed in Wapping between 1799 and 1815 and occupied an area of about 30 acres. The construction of the docks was preceded by demolition of streets and houses, but not to the extent of St. Katharine Dock due to significant areas being occupied by orchards and other farmland at the time.

Manchester Road

Road created in the east of the Isle of Dogs by William Cubitt in the 1840s, providing a main road from the Greenwich Ferry in the south, through his 'Cubitt Town' to Blackwall in the north.

Mansell Street

Named after a relative of William Leman (see 'Leman Street').

Middlesex Street

Originally known as Hogs Lane (in Tudor times), before being renamed *Peticote Lane* in the early 1600s, possibly due to its second-hand clothes market.

Mile End Road

Mile End was first mentioned in 1288 as *La Mile ende*, meaning 'the hamlet a mile away' – a mile from the City (the junction of Whitechapel Road, Cambridge Heath Road and Mile End Road).

Millwall Docks

Opened in 1868. Few streets or houses were lost in its construction (nor during the construction of the West India Docks), due to the Isle of Dogs being sparsely populated grazing land at the time, with the small population that there was occupying premises along the river.

Old Ford Road

Old Ford was the oldest, most downstream place to cross the River Lea, on the ancient route from London to Colchester.

Poplar Dock

Opened in 1828, and was based on a series of reservoirs that belonged to the West India Dock Company. It had water connections with the West India Docks and Blackwall Basin, but no direct connection to the Thames. Today, much of the docks is named Poplar Dock Marina.

Rhodeswell Road

Named after Rhodes Well, a spring or pond at the present day corner of Copperfield Road and Rhodeswell Road,

Roman Road

Created in 1855 by the Metropolitan Board of Works. There is no evidence that it is based on a route followed by the Romans. The westernmost end of the road, as far as Bethnal Green, was named Green Street until the 1930s.

Salmon Lane

The main route from Limehouse to Stepney parish church, Salmon Lane has been a public highway since at least the 15th century. The road was originally named 'Salmon's Lane' and was sometimes known as 'Sermon Lane'.

St. Katharine's Dock

Named after the 12th century hospital of St Katharine's by the Tower, which stood on the site. A large number of streets, alleys and lanes were lost due to the dock's construction (1827-1828), including the demolition of 1250 houses.

St. Leonards Road

The road to Bromley, which was formerly known as Bromley – St. Leonards, after St. Leonard's Priory, a Benedictine nunnery founded in the time of William the conqueror.

Stepney Green

Stepney developed around the church of St Dunstan's (founded in 923) and was known as *Stybbanhyð*, 'Stybba's landing-place'. Until the 19th century, it was a largely rural location, centred on the church and adjoining green.

The Highway

The main route east from the City, made up of former roads variously named, from west to east, Ratcliffe Highway (later St. George Street), Upper Shadwell (later High Street, Shadwell), Cock Hill and Broad Street.

Vallance Road

Main road north from Whitechapel Road to Old Bethnal Green Road, constructed in the late 1800s on the path of the former roads (from south to north): Bakers Row, Charles Street, New Charles Street, Wellington Street, Nottingham Street and White Street. It received its present name in 1896, named after W. Vallance, clerk to the Metropolitan Board of Guardians.

Victoria Park

Victoria Park was opened in 1845, constructed on an area of former parkland (which had been spoiled by gravel and clay excavation) known as Bonner Fields.

West India Docks

The northern West India Docks were constructed between 1800 and 1802, and the South Dock in the 1860s, on the site of the former City Canal (opened in 1806).

Westferry Road

Main road from Cuba Street in the north west of the Isle of Dogs to the Greenwich Ferry in the south of the Island. Opened around 1817 and variously named New Road, Deptford and Greenwich Road, Mill Wall Road, and West Ferry Road (from 1862 to the 1950s). The roads north of West Ferry Road in the direction of Limehouse, Ord Street and Bridge Road respectively, became part of Westferry Road.

White Horse Road

White Horse Street was the main street from the medieval village of Stepney connecting with Brook Street (The Highway) and Butcher Row in the south. On the creation of Commercial Road, the southernmost section of White Horse Street became part of an extended Butcher Row, and the remainder of the street renamed White Horse Road.

Whitechapel Road The village of White Chapel was named after a 13th century 'chapel of ease' which was later replaced by the St Mary Matfelon church, popularly known as St Mary's.

A

Abbey Place, Essex Street (Blythe Street), Bethnal Green, 1841.

Abbey Street, Off Bethnal Green Road, Bethnal Green, "at 92 the first on the right below the turnpike about ½ a mile from 65 Shoreditch" (Lockie), renamed Buckfast Street.

Abbots Yard, Pollard Street, Bethnal Green, 1891.

Abbotsham Villas, Brookfield Road, Hackney, 1891.

Abbotts Cottages, Victoria Road (Usher Road), Bethnal Green, 1851.

Abel Court, Rosemary Lane (Royal Mint Street), East Smithfield, 1746.

Abels Buildings, Rosemary Lane (Royal Mint Street), East Smithfield, 1746.

Aberdeen Terrace, 181 Grove Road, Bromley and Bow, site of Earl of Aberdeen Public House.

Aberdeen Wharf, Emmett Street, Limehouse, 1950.

Aberfeldy Tavern Public House, 357-359 East India Dock Road, Poplar, address also 26 Aberfeldy Street.

Abernant Place, Old Ford Road, Bromley and Bow, 1851.

Abingdon Court, Abingdon Street (Herald Street), Bethnal Green, 1851, became part of Herald Road.

Abingdon Street, Off Three Colts Lane, Bethnal Green, renamed Herald Street.

Acacia Villas, Grange Road (Gayhurst Road), Hackney, 1868, between Malvern Road and Lansdowne Road.

Accidental Place, Bath Street (Darling Row), Whitechapel, 1851.

Acland Street, Off St. Pauls Way, Bromley and Bow, 1891, east of Wallwood Street.

Acorn Public House, 149 Great Cambridge Street (Queensbridge Road), Bethnal Green, 1874.

Acorn Wharf, Wapping High Street, Wapping, 1895, south of Orange Court.

Acton Arms Public House, 296 Kingsland Road, Hackney, 1874.

Acton Mews, Dunston Street, Hackney, 1950, west of railway line.

Acton Place, Kingsland Road, Hackney, 1827.

Acton Street, Off Kingsland Road, Hackney, 1868.

Adam & Eve Public House, 118 Bethnal Green Road, Bethnal Green, 1874.

Adam & Eve Yard, Ratcliffe Highway (The Highway), St. George in the East, 1812.

Adams Place, 1. Salmon Lane, Limehouse. 2. Three Colts Lane,

Bethnal Green, 1891. 3.
Wentworth Street, Whitechapel,
1891.

Adderley Street, Off Lodore
Street, Poplar, 1950.

Adelaide Buildings, Ann Street
(East India Dock Road), Poplar.

Adelaide Cottages, Grundy
Street, Poplar, 1851.

Adelaide Place, 1. Forest Row,
Hackney, 1841, immediately east
of Holly Street. 2. Heneage
Street, Whitechapel, renamed Ivy
Yard. 3. Westferry Road, Isle of
Dogs, 1851.

Adelphi Chapel, Hackney Road,
Bethnal Green, 1860, on the
corner of St. Peter Street.

Adelphi Terrace, Old Ford
Road, Bromley and Bow, 1891.

Adler Buildings, Adler Street,
Whitechapel.

**Admiral Blakeneys Head
Public House**, 56 Cable Street,
St. George in the East, aka
Blakeneys Head, aka American
Stores Public House.

**Admiral Denham Public
House**, 47 St. Thomas Road,
Bromley and Bow.

Admiral Napier Public House,
94 Canrobert Street, Bethnal
Green.

Admiral Public House, 221 East
India Dock Road, Poplar.

Admiral Vernon Public House,
8 New Nichol(s) Street
(Boundary Estate), Bethnal
Green.

**Admiralty Merchant Navy
Signalling School**, 133 East
India Dock Road, Poplar, 1936.

Africa Tavern Public House,
Grundy Street, Poplar, 1891,
corner of Duff Street, renamed
African Queen.

Agatha Street, Off Pearl Street,
Wapping, partially followed by
Agatha Close.

Agra Buildings, Agra Place,
Lower Chapman Street (Bigland
Street), Shadwell.

Agra Place, Lower Chapman
Street (Bigland Street), Shadwell,
1891.

Ainsworth Street, Off Club
Row, Bethnal Green, 1912.

Albany House, Albany Street
(Bromley Street), Stepney, 1891.

Albany Place, Commercial
Road, Stepney, 1868, Bromley
Street to White Horse Street.

Albany Street, Off Bromley
Street, Stepney, 1851, renamed
Chudleigh Street.

Albany Terrace, Old Ford Road,
Bromley and Bow.

Albert Arms Public House, 1.
239 Bancroft Road, Mile End. 2.
6 Railway Place (Malcolm
Place), Bethnal Green.

Albert Cottages, 1. Lyme
Grove, Hackney, 1891, Mare
Street. 2. Pelham Street
(Woodseer Street), Whitechapel,
1891.

Albert Dwellings, Old Ford
Road, Bromley and Bow, 1891.

Albert Family Dwellings aka Albert Street Metropolitan Buildings, Albert Street (Deal Street), Spitalfields, 1891, corner of Albert Street and Underwood Road.

Albert Grove, Morpeth Road, Hackney, 1891.

Albert Mews, Bromley and Bow, now part of Haven Mews.

Albert Place, 1. Albert Street (Deal Street), Spitalfields, 1891. 2. Westferry Road, Isle of Dogs, 1851, between Thomas Street and Tooke Street.

Albert Road, 1. Mile End, combined with Albert Street to become Moody Street. 2. Off Bonner Road, Bethnal Green, renamed Waterloo Road (now Gardens). 3. Off Queensbridge Road, Hackney, 1895, renamed Albion Drive, became the eastern half of Middleton Road.

Albert Square, Commercial Road, Shadwell, 1891, renamed Albert Gardens.

Albert Street, 1. Off Bromley High Street, Bromley and Bow, Bromley High Street to Bow High Street, Bow Bridge Estate built over street. 2. Off Cable Street, Shadwell, 1891, Cable Street to The Highway, east of Dellow Street, renamed Solander Street, Solander Gardens is close to its route. 3. Off East Street (Bishops Ways), Mile End, became part of Moody Street. 4. Off Fremont Street, Hackney,

renamed Gotha Street, became part of Warneford Street. 5. Off Great Cambridge Street (Queensbridge Road), Bethnal Green, became the easternmost end of Laburnum Street. 6. Off Pelham Street (Woodseer Street), Whitechapel, became part of Deal Street. 7. Off Railway Place (Malcolm Place), Bethnal Green, 1891, renamed Entick Street, close to Bancroft Road. 8. Off St. Leonards Road, Poplar, 1891, St. Leonards Road to Brunswick Road, close to Blair Street.

Albert Terrace, 1. Alpha Road (Alpha Grove), Isle of Dogs, 1891. 2. Bow Common Lane, Bromley and Bow, 1851. 3. 186 Bow Road, Bromley and Bow, 1891, close to 186 Bow Road. 4. Bromley High Street, Bromley and Bow, 1891.

Albert Victor Public House, 35 Grace Street, Bromley and Bow.

Albert Villas, Albert Road (Albion Drive), Hackney, 1868, between Queens Road (Queensbridge Road) and Malvern Road.

Alberta House, Blackwall Way, Poplar, 1950, close to St. Lawrence Street.

Albion Academy (School), Oxford Street (Wingham Street), Bethnal Green, 1851.

Albion Baths, Albion Drive, Hackney, 1851.

Albion Brewery, Whitechapel Road, Whitechapel, "at 170 a few doors north from Mile End turnpike" (Lockie).

Albion Buildings, 1. Clare Street, Bethnal Green, 1891, Hackney Road. 2. Elbow Lane (Newlands Quay), Shadwell, 1851.

Albion Cottages, 1. Hollybush Gardens, Bethnal Green, 1851. 2. Mercer Street (Cable Street), Shadwell, 1891. 3. Queens Road (Queensbridge Road), Hackney, 1851, south of Temple Street. 4. Redmans Road, Mile End, renamed Redmans Cottages.

Albion House, 214 East India Dock Road, Poplar, 1839.

Albion Place, 1. Ducal Street, Bethnal Green, 1891. 2. Felix Street, Bethnal Green, 1851. 3. Morning Lane, Hackney, 1851, next to its corner with Paragon Road. 4. Tait Street, St. George in the East, 1891.

Albion Public House, 1. 43 Duckett Street, Mile End. 2. 36 Lauriston Road, Hackney. 3. 41 London Street (Bekesbourne Street), Ratcliffe. 4. 28 Lower East Smithfield (St. Katharines Way), East Smithfield, 1874. 5. Old Ford Road, Bromley and Bow. 6. 7 Redmans Road, Mile End, renamed Rose and Punchbowl. 8. 101 Salmon Lane, Limehouse. 9. 211-212 Shadwell High Street (The Highway), Shadwell, aka Ship and Shears. 10. 25 St. Pauls Way, Bromley and Bow. 11. 66 Three Colt Street, Limehouse.

Albion Road, Off Morning Lane, Hackney, 1868, renamed Stockmar Road.

Albion Street, 1. Off Artillery Street (Peace Street), Whitechapel, 1851. 2. Off Bridge Street (Hamlets Way), Bromley and Bow, renamed English Street, now named Hamlets Way. 3. Off Commercial Road, Shadwell, 1820, renamed Winterton Street. 4. Whitechapel, renamed Hemming Street.

Albion Terrace, 1. Commercial Road, Limehouse, 1860, south side of Commercial Road, west of Mill Place. 2. Derby Road, Hackney, 1841. 3. Haggerston Road, Hackney, 1891. 4. Rhodeswell Road, Limehouse, close to Copenhagen Place.

Albion Wharf, Wapping High Street, Wapping, 1950, west of corner with Knighten Street.

Alderman Parsons Stairs, St. Catherines Way (St. Katharines Way), East Smithfield, "a public landing place on the north bank of the Thames, at Shadwell named after a former owner, it is also called Lady Parsons Stairs" (Elmes), now named Parsons Stairs.

Alderney Place, Alderney Road, Mile End, 1891.

Aldgate (East) Tavern Public House, 1 Goulston Street, Whitechapel, aka Aldgate Tavern, Aldgate East Wine Stores, aka Aldgate Distillery.

Aldgate Exchange Public House, 133 Whitechapel High Street, Whitechapel.

Alexandra Buildings, Commercial Street, Whitechapel, 1891.

Alexandra Public House, 25 Upper North Street, Poplar.

Alexandra Tavern Public House, 162 Victoria Park Road, Hackney, 1874.

Alexandra Yard, Victoria Park Road, Hackney, rear of Alexandra Tavern Public House.

Alfred Buildings, Cartwright Street (Royal Mint Street), East Smithfield, 1891.

Alfred Place, 1. Cester Street, Bethnal Green, 1950, Whiston Road. 2. Mill Street (Old Ford Road), Bromley and Bow, 1851. 3. Westferry Road, Isle of Dogs, "is about a furlong south of the Limehouse entrance of the City Canal" (Elmes), West India Docks Impounding Station Westferry Road is on site of City Canal entrance. 4. Russia Lane, Bethnal Green, 1891, renamed Russia Place.

Alfred Place & Terrace, Hardinge Street, Shadwell, 1851.

Alfred Row, Charles Street (Vallance Road), Bethnal Green, "Bethnal Green Road, the second on the left opposite Wilmot Square, is about ¾ of a mile on the right from 65 Shoreditch" (Lockie), now part of Derbyshire Street.

Alfred Street, 1. Off Bow Road, Bromley and Bow, 1891, now includes Lucas Terrace. 2. Limehouse, renamed Cotall Street. 3. Mile End, renamed Shandy Street. 4. Off Westferry Road, Isle of Dogs, 1851, renamed Manilla Street.

Alfred Terrace, 1. Alpha Road (Alpha Grove), Isle of Dogs, 1891. 2. Cambridge Road (Cambridge Heath Road), Bethnal Green, 1851. 3. Dora Street, Limehouse, 1891, later part of Spenlow Street.

Alfred Villas, Albert Road (Albion Drive), Hackney, 1868, between Queens (now Queensbridge) Road and Malvern Road.

Alfreds Head Public House, 1. 15 Brushfield Street, Spitalfields. 2. 49 Gold Street (Stepney Green), Stepney. 3. 67 Shandy Street, Mile End.

Alice Place, 1. Berger Road, Wick Road, Hackney, 1891. 2. Mead Place, Retreat Place, Hackney, 1891.

Alie Place, Great Alie Street (Alie Street), Whitechapel, 1891, became part of St. Marks Street.

Alie Street, Off Tenter Street, Whitechapel, 1881.

Alie Street Chapel, Alie Street, Whitechapel, 1891.

Alie Street Synagogue, Alie Street, Whitechapel, 1896-1969.

All Hallows Church, East India

Dock Road, Poplar, 1880-1952, opposite Orchard Street.

All Saints Church, Westferry Road, Isle of Dogs, between Tooke Street and Charles Street. Site of later Millwall Independent (Congregational) Church late 1800s.

All Saints Church & School, Buxton Street, Whitechapel, 1895, opposite Hunton Street.

All Saints Institute & School, All Saints Church Rectory Garden, East India Dock Road, Poplar, 1850.

All Saints Stonebridge Church & School, Stonebridge Road (Haggerston Road), Hackney, 1868.

Allanmouth Road & Terrace, Wansbeck Road, Bromley and Bow, 1891.

Allas Road, Off Portman Place, Bethnal Green, 1891, east of Bethnal Green Road Globe Road north of Railway Line.

Allenbury Street, Off Three Colts Lane, Bethnal Green.

Allens Brewhouse, Off Nightingale Lane (Thomas More Street), East Smithfield, 1800, St. Katharine Dock is on its site.

Allens Court, Harrow Alley (Middlesex Street), Spitalfields, 1812, Middlesex Street.

Aller Street, Off Wear Street, Bethnal Green, 1912.

Allington Place, Back Road (Cable Street), St. George in the East, 1860, north side of Back Road, opposite Prospect Place.

Allsopps Buildings, Back Road (Cable Street), St. George in the East, 1860, south side of Back Road, Cable Street, east of the Wesleyan Chapel.

Alma (Arms) Public House, 16 West India Dock Road, Limehouse, corner of Rich Street.

Alma Place, Cartwright Street (Royal Mint Street), East Smithfield.

Alma Public House, 1. 27 Cobden Street (Langdon Park School is on the site), Poplar. 2. 96 Grundy Street, Poplar, corner of Woollett Street. 3. 41 Spelman Street, Whitechapel. 4. 1 Tyssen Street (Brick Lane), Bethnal Green.

Alma Road, 1. Off Burdett Road, Bromley and Bow, renamed Portia Road. 2. Off Dalston Lane, Hackney, renamed Ritson Road. 3. Off Doric Road (Cranbrook Estate), Bethnal Green, 1895.

Alms Alley, Off Harrow Alley (Middlesex Street), Spitalfields, 1812.

Alpha & Hope Cottages, Douro Street, Bromley and Bow, 1851.

Alpha House, Lucas Place (Commercial Road), Shadwell, "Commercial Road, a few yards east on the right from the half way house" (Lockie), immediately east of Sutton Street.

Alpha Place, 1. Chrisp Street, Poplar, 1851. 2. Collingwood Street, Whitechapel, 1851. 3. Grange Road (Gayhurst Road), Hackney, 1868, between Mayfield Street and Holly Street.

Alpha Road, Isle of Dogs, 1891, renamed Alpha Grove.

Alpha Terrace, Three Colts Lane, Bethnal Green, 1851, close to corner of Collingwood Street.

Alpha Wharf, Saunders Ness Road, Isle of Dogs, 1950, close to Grosvernor Wharf Road.

Alpine Cottages, St. Stephens Road, Bromley and Bow, 1871.

Amber Place, William Street (Ponler Street), St. George in the East, 1891.

Amberston Street, Off Commercial Road, St. George in the East, 1860, later north half of Umberston Street.

Amble Close, Wellclose Square, St. George in the East, 1812.

American Stores Public House, 56 Cable Street, St. George in the East, aka (Admiral) Blakeneys Head.

Ames Street, Off Roman Road, Bethnal Green, Cranbrook Estate is on the site.

Amias Almshouses, George Yard (Gunthorpe Street), Whitechapel, "at 108 Old Street St. Lukes near Brick Lane" (Lockie).

Ammiel Street, Off Devons Lane (Devons Road), Bromley and Bow, 1851.

Amors Dock & House, Three Colt Street, Limehouse, 1891.

Amos Court, Wapping High Street, Wapping, 1950, former Church Court.

Amy Villas, Shrubland Grove (Mapledene Road), Hackney, 1868, close to its corner with Lansdowne Road.

Amys Place, Bath Street (Darling Row), Whitechapel, 1841.

Anchor & Crown Public House, 1 High Street (Greatorex Street), Stepney.

Anchor & Hope Alley, Wapping, 1790, renamed Red Lion Street (Reardon Street).

Anchor & Hope Public House, 1. 41 Brook Street (Cable Street), Ratcliffe. 2. 90 Duckett Street, Mile End. 3. Horse Ferry Branch Road (Branch Road), Ratcliffe. 4. 8 Jamaica Street, Stepney. 5. 75 Mape Street, Bethnal Green. 6. 68 Myrdle Street, Whitechapel. 7. 198 New Crane (New Crane Place), Wapping, 1874, address also 168 Wapping High Street. 8. 31 Pekin Street (Canton Street), Limehouse, address also 32 Evans Street. 9. 81 Poplar High Street, Poplar. 10. 97 Redmans Road, Mile End. 11. 8 Shadwell Dock Street, Wapping, aka, Hope & Anchor, address also 168 New Street. 12.

224 St. George Street (The Highway), St. George in the East. 13. 50 Upper East Smithfield, East Smithfield, 1874, renamed New York Stores. 14. 57 Watney Street, Shadwell. 15. 41 Westferry Road, Isle of Dogs, 1851.

Anchor Brewery, Mile End Road, Mile End, "Charringtons, Mile End Road a little above ¾ of a mile on the left east from the turnpike opposite Stepney Green" (Lockie).

Anchor Public House, 1. 162 Chrisp Street, Poplar. 2. 45 Grove Street (Golding Street), St. George in the East. 3. 31 Pekin Street, Limehouse. 4. 7 Turner Street, Whitechapel.

Anchor Street, 1. Off Club Row, Bethnal Green, 1860, became westernmost section of Bethnal Green Road. 2. Off Lanyard Street (Whitehorse Road Park), Stepney. 3. Off Maroon Street, Limehouse, 1891. 4. Off Mile End Road, Mile End, "on the west side of Charringtons Brewery about ¼ of a mile on the left east from the turnpike opposite Stepney Green" (Lockie). 5. Off Poplar High Street, Poplar, "is in Catherine Street a new street in the East India Dock Road nearly opposite Poplar Church" (Elmes).

Anchor Wharf, Limekiln Dock, Narrow Street, Limehouse, 1950.

Ancient Britain Public House, 22 Glaucus Street, Bromley and Bow.

Andrew Street, Off St. Leonards Road, Poplar, 1891.

Andrewes House, Wapping Lane, St. George in the East, 1950.

Angel & Crown Public House, 1. 47 Brushfield Street, Spitalfields, address also 6 Crispin Street. 2. 180 Green Street (Roman Road), Bethnal Green. 3. 19 Ship Alley (Wellclose Square), St. George in the East. 4. 5 Whitechapel Road, Whitechapel, 1874.

Angel & Trumpet Public House, 2 Stepney High Street, Stepney.

Angel Alley, 1. Nightingale Lane (Thomas More Street), Wapping, 1746. 2. Ratcliffe Highway (The Highway), St. George in the East, 1746. 3. Whitechapel Road, Whitechapel, "at 84 near the church the first west parallel to Osborn Street leading into Wentworth Street" (Lockie), just west of present-day Whitechapel Art Gallery.

Angel Court, 1. Back Lane (Cable Street), Shadwell, "four doors east on the right from Bluegate Fields by the Angel Public House" (Lockie). 2. Close to 273 Poplar High Street, Poplar, 1851. 3. Red Lion Street (Commercial Street), "on the west side of Spitalfields Church nearly opposite Dorset Street" (Lockie). 4. Upper East Smithfield, East Smithfield, "the continuation of Angel Alley from 22 Nightingale Lane leading to Sun Yard" (Lockie).

Angel Gardens, Back Lane (Cable Street), Shadwell, "eight doors east on the right from Bluegate Fields by the Angel Public House about $^1/_5$ of a mile east from Cannon Street turnpike" (Lockie).

Angel Place, Back Road (Cable Street), St. George in the East, 1851.

Angel Public House, 1. 40 Broad Street (The Highway), Ratcliffe. 2. 268 Cable Street, Shadwell. 3. 76 Old Gravel Lane (Wapping Lane), Wapping. 4. 275-279 Poplar High Street, Poplar, 1874, aka Queens Arms. 5. 85 Whitechapel High Street, Whitechapel, aka Ye Olde Angel Public House.

Angela Street, Off Columbia Road, Bethnal Green, renamed Pelter Street.

Anglesea Street, Off Selby Street, Whitechapel, 1950, Fakruddin Street is partially on the site.

Angrave Terrace, Queensbridge Road, Hackney, 1950, opposite Broke Road.

Ann Street, 1. Off Devonport Street, Shadwell, renamed Barnardo Street in 1911. 2. Off East India Dock Road, Poplar,

renamed Oceana Close. 3. Off James Street (Chilton Street), Bethnal Green, 1827, renamed Hadleigh Street. 4. Mile End, became part of Mantus Road. 5. Off Pollard Row, Bethnal Green, 1891, became the easternmost end of Florida Street. 6. Off Upper Chapman Street (Chapman Street), St. George in the East, "the third east parallel to Cannon Street New Road, extending from Upper Chapman Street to Lower Chapman Street" (Lockie).

Annabel Street, Off Ricardo Street, Poplar, ran from Cordelia Street to Ricardo Street just east of Bygrove Street.

Anne Court & Street, Off Bath Street (Poplar Bath Street), Poplar, 1891.

Anne Street, Stepney, became part of Apsley Street (Wickham Close).

Annes Court, Well Street, Wapping.

Annes Court or Place, Salmon Lane, Limehouse, 1891, behind number 142.

Annes Road, Off Cassland Road, Hackney, 1870, renamed Queen Annes Road.

Anns & Halls Cottages, Old Ford Road, Bromley and Bow, 1851.

Anns Place, 1. Arundel Street (Peace Street), Whitechapel. 2. Bath Street (Poplar Bath Street), Poplar. 3. Orchard Place, Poplar,

1891. 4. Pritchards Road, Bethnal Green.

Anns Place & Street, Off Wentworth Street, Spitalfields, 1891, north of Wentworth Street, just west of Commercial Street.

Anns Place School, Pritchards Road, Bethnal Green.

Anns Row, Ann Street (East India Dock Road), Poplar, 1891.

Anns Terrace, 1. Cubitt Town (precise location unknown), Isle of Dogs, 1888. 2. Mary Street (Bigland Street), St. George in the East, 1871.

Ansels Rents, Three Colt Street, Limehouse, "at the back of 34 in the said street nearly opposite Ropemakers Fields" (Lockie).

Antcliff Street, Off Bromehead Street, Stepney, 1950, Bromehead Street to Bromehead Road.

Anthony Street, Off Commercial Road, St. George in the East, originally extended as far south as Chapman Street.

Antigallican Public House, Limehouse Hole (Three Colt Street), Limehouse, 1800.

Antigua Place, Salmon Lane, Limehouse, "the continuation of Wilson Place entrance by the first on the left from the Commercial Road towards Stepney" (Lockie), corner at 146 Salmon Lane.

Antiquarian Hall, Old Ford Road, Bromley and Bow, 1851.

Antwerp Street, Off Ada Street, Hackney.

Appian Road, Off Old Ford Road, Bromley and Bow, 1891, diagonally opposite Parnell Road.

Approach Tavern Public House, 47 Approach Road, Bethnal Green.

Apsley Street, Off Redmans Road, Mile End, 1891, Redmans Road to the south end of Wellesley Street.

Arabella Place, Pollard Street, Bethnal Green.

Arabian Arms Public House, 234 Cambridge Heath Road, Bethnal Green, 1874.

Arbour Gardens, Fair Place (Dunelm Street), Stepney, 1862, west of and parallel with Heath Street.

Arbour Square Police Station & Court, Aylward Street, Stepney, 1950.

Arbour Terrace, Commercial Road, Stepney, 1865, south of Arbour Square.

Archer Place, East India Dock Road, Limehouse, 1851.

Archer Street, Off Lucas Street (Newcourt House), Bethnal Green, 1841.

Archer Terrace, East India Dock Road, Limehouse, 1864, 12-50 East India Dock Road.

Archers Place, Mill Street (Old Ford Road), Bromley and Bow, 1851.

Archers Public House, 24 Osborn Street, Whitechapel, 1874.

Archers Tavern Public House, 24 Osborn Street, Whitechapel.

Archers Terrace, Old Ford Road, Bromley and Bow, 1851.

Archibold Street, Off Campbell Road, Bromley and Bow, renamed Arnold Road.

Arline Street, Off Hassard Street, Bethnal Green, 1891, previously named Queen Street.

Armenian Chapel, Princes Row (Old Montague Street), Whitechapel, 1799.

Arno Place, Jamaica Place (Beccles Street), Limehouse, 1890, near corner with Gun Lane.

Arnolds Buildings, Emmett Street, Limehouse, close to corner with Westferry Road.

Arran Terrace, Sewardstone Road, Bethnal Green.

Arthur Street, 1. Off Bonner Lane (Bonner Street), Bethnal Green. 2. Became part of Lawless Street, Poplar. 3. Became part of Pixley Street, Limehouse. 4. Off St. Leonards Road, Poplar, renamed Chadbourn Street. 5. Off Well Street, Hackney, path partially now followed by Brooksbank Street.

Arthur Terrace, Old Ford Road, Bromley and Bow.

Arthur Villas, Lansdowne Road (Lansdowne Drive), Hackney, 1868, between Richmond Road and Grange Road.

Artichoke Lane, Redmaid Lane (Redmead Lane), Wapping, 1790, north of, and parallel with, Red Maid Lane, London Docks Western Dock was built on site.

Artichoke Public House, 1. 93 Cambridge Road (Cambridge Heath Road), Whitechapel, aka Foresters. 2. 143 Jubilee Street, Stepney, address also 91 Stepney Way. 3. 50 The Highway, St. George in the East, aka St. George's Tavern, aka Caxton.

Artichoke Row, Mile End Road, Mile End, "part of the south side of the road opposite the Bell and Mackerel about $1^{1}/_{3}$ of a mile on the right from Aldgate Pump" (Lockie).

Artichoke Tavern Public House, 1. Blackwall (Raleana Road), Poplar, 1840, Old Blackwall riverside. 2. 19 St. George Street (The Highway), St. George in the East, 1874.

Artillery Lane Chapel, Artillery Lane, Spitalfields, became Artillery Lane Synagogue.

Artillery Place, Artillery Lane, Spitalfields, "is the continuation of Artillery Lane and Street from Bishopsgate, this place is better known by the name of Smock Alley" (Lockie).

Artillery Street, 1. Off Artillery Lane, Spitalfields, 1950, became part of Artillery Lane. 2. Off Arundel Street (Peace Street), Whitechapel, 1891, renamed Peace Street.

Artillery Tavern Public House, 1 Gun Street, Spitalfields, aka Cock & Hoop, address also 17 Artillery Street.

Artizan Villas, Maria Street (formerly north of Janet Street), Isle of Dogs, 1865.

Arundel Street, Off Winchester Street (Dunbridge Street), Bethnal Green, 1891, renamed Hemming Street.

Ashfield Place, Ocean Row (Ocean Street), Stepney, 1891, "at the north east corner of Stepney Church Yard by the Walnut Tree in Ocean Row, Cow Lane" (Lockie), later part of Ben Jonson Road.

Ashford House, Red Lion Court (Commercial Street), Spitalfields, 1891.

Ashley Place, Stepney Causeway, Ratcliffe, now part of Pitsea Place.

Ashwell Road, Off Roman Road, Bromley and Bow, 1891, Mile End Park is on site.

Askew Street, Off Frampton Park Road, Hackney, Woolridge Way Estate is on the site.

Assembly Mews, Assembly Passage, Mile End, 1895.

Assembly Row, Mile End Road, Mile End, "art of the south side of the road commencing about ¹/₈

of a mile on the right below the turnpike and is nearly ¹/₈ of a mile in length" (Lockie), close to Assembly Passage.

Association Home, 4 The Terrace (Old Ford Road), Bromley and Bow, Old Ford Road.

Asylum for the Orphans of Merchant Seamen, 4 Clarkes Terrace (Cannon Street Road), St. George in the East.

Athelstane Road, Off St. Stephens Road, Bromley and Bow, 1891, renamed Athelstane Grove.

Athol Street, Poplar, Athol Square is on the site.

Atkins Gardens, Bethnal Green Road, Bethnal Green, "on the north side of Thorold Square about half a mile on the left from No 65 Shoreditch" (Elmes).

Atlas Arms, 37 Roman Road, Bethnal Green, 1930.

Atlas Place, Cotton Street, Poplar, "opposite the south end of Cotton Street and is the second turning on the right from the East India Docks" (Elmes).

Atlas Public House, 37 Green Street (Roman Road), Bethnal Green.

Atlas Wharf, Westferry Road, Isle of Dogs, 1950, north of Arnhem Place.

Atley Road, Bromley and Bow, became part of Dace Road.

Atley Road School, Atley Road (Dace Road), Bromley and Bow.

Atworth Street, Off Strattondale Street, Isle of Dogs, previously connected Strattondale Street and Galbraith Street and has since become part Galbraith Street.

Auckland Road, Off Roman Road, Bromley and Bow, 1891, renamed Zealand Road.

Austin Court, Austin Street, Bethnal Green, "Bethnal Green Road, is the first on the left in it from Hackney Road by Shoreditch Church" (Lockie).

Australian Arms Public House, 1. 40 Brick Lane, Spitalfields. 2. 18 Lower Chapman Street (Bigland Street), St. George in the East.

Austrian Dzikower Synagogue, 30 Dunk Street (Hanbury Street), Spitalfields, 1915, also known as Dunk Street Synagogue or Dzikower Synagogue.

Avenue House, Gore Road, Hackney.

Avenue Road, 1. Off Bow Road, Bromley and Bow, renamed Kitcat Terrace. 2. Off Old Ford Road, Bromley and Bow, renamed Autumn Street.

Axe Court or Place, Hackney Road, Bethnal Green, "is about $^1/_5$ of a mile on the left from Shoreditch Church at the back of the Axe Public House and opposite the Green Gate" (Lockie), opposite Baroness Road.

Aylward House, Dupont Street (Shaw Crescent), Stepney, 1950, Limehouse Fields Estate.

Ayshford House, Viaduct Street, Bethnal Green, 1950.

B

Back Change, Royal Mint Street, East Smithfield, 1870, rear of Royal Mint Street, opposite Cartwright Street.

Back Lane or Road, Shadwell, early name for the section of Cable Street through St. George in the East and Shadwell.

Back Lane, 1. Globe Lane (Globe Road), Mile End, "Mile End Road, is the first east parallel to the green also the north continuation of Globe Lane" (Lockie). 2. Ming Street, Limehouse, "is on the south side of the main road or street extending from the Commercial Road by the West India Docks to nearly opposite North Street" (Lockie), renamed King and then Ming Street.

Back Street, 1. Off Bromley High Street, Bromley and Bow, 1851. 2. Off Wades Place, Poplar, "the first north parallel to the main road or street extending from Wades Place to Finch Yard is nearly opposite Dolphin Lane and about one third of a mile east from the Commercial Road" (Lockie).

Baden Place, Andrews Road, Hackney, 1891.

Baffin Buildings, Prestons Road, Poplar, 1900.

Baggally Street, Off Burdett Road, Bromley and Bow, 1891, south of Sarum Road.

Bahama House, Limehouse Causeway, Limehouse, St. Vincent Estate.

Bailey Street, Off Whitechapel Road, Whitechapel, "off Whitechapel Road near no 75" (Elmes).

Baker & Basket Public House, 16 Leman Street, Whitechapel.

Baker & Friend Public House, 119 Brick Lane, Spitalfields.

Baker Street, 1. Off Damien Street, Whitechapel. 2. Off Green Street (Roman Road), Bethnal Green, 1851, renamed Bacton Street.

Baker Street School, Baker Street (Damien Street), Whitechapel, 1880.

Baker Terrace, St. Leonards Avenue (St. Leonards Road), Poplar, 1862, between St. Leonards Avenue and Tapley Street.

Baker(s) Arms Gardens, Wellington Row, Bethnal Green, 1841.

Bakers Alley, Bow High Street (Bow Road), Bromley and Bow, 1851, next to 178 Bow High Street.

Bakers Almshouses, 1. Lyme Grove, Hackney, 1891. 2. Oxford Street (Stepney Way), Whitechapel, 1895, south of London Hospital.

Bakers Arms Alley, Royal Mint Street, East Smithfield, 1851.

Bakers Arms Public House, 1. 13 Devonshire Street (Colebert Avenue), Mile End. 2. 75 North Street (Northiam Street), Hackney. 3. 44 Warner Place, Bethnal Green.

Bakers Buildings or Rents, Hackney Road, Bethnal Green, 1851.

Bakers Court, Old Castle Street, Bethnal Green, "is six doors on the left in it from the east end of Austin Street the back of Shoreditch Church" (Lockie).

Bakers Row, 1. Whitechapel Road, Whitechapel, 1891, Whitechapel Road to Selby Street, now southern end of Vallance Road. 2. Wick Lane, Bromley and Bow, 1841.

Bale Street, Off Harford Street, Mile End, 1891, west of gasworks.

Ball Court, Butcher Row, Ratcliffe, "at 3 the first on the left from Butcher Row towards the Commercial Road" (Lockie).

Balls Buildings, White Horse Street (Butcher Row), Ratcliffe, 1851, opposite St. James Church.

Balls Place, Shakespeare(s) Walk (Shadwell Basin), Shadwell, 1851.

Balnagaith House, 79 East India Dock Road, Limehouse, 1860.

Baltic Wharf, Wapping High Street, Wapping, 1895, south east of Sampson Street.

Bancroft Arms Public House, 1. 410 Mile End Road, Mile End. 2. 1 Moody Street, Mile End.

Bancroft Road Jewish Cemetery, Bancroft Road, Mile End.

Bancrofts or Bencrofts Almshouses, Mile End Road, Mile End, 1827, east of present-day Bancroft Road.

Bancrofts or Bencrofts Place, Mile End Road, Mile End, "is opposite the Almshouses, leading towards Stepney "(Lockie).

Bandon Road, Off Sewardstone Road, Bethnal Green, 1891.

Bank of Friendship Tavern Public House, 22 Harford Street, Mile End.

Barbers Yard or Alley, Hanbury Street, Spitalfields, 1891, North of Hanbury Street, just west of Brick Lane.

Barclay Place, Sheep Lane, Hackney, 1851.

Bardsey Place, Mile End Road, Mile End, 1895, just east of Vintners Almshouses.

Barford Terrace, Johnson Street, Wapping, Bridge Street to Skidmore Street.

Barkfields Terrace, King Edwards Road, Hackney, 1868, at its corner with Thomas Road.

Barley Mow Brewery, Northey Street, Limehouse, 1950,

between Northey Street and Narrow Street, Ropemakers Field park is on the site.

Barley Mow Court, Red Lion Street (Leman Street), Whitechapel, "at 39, nine doors east on the right from Red Lion Street" (Lockie).

Barley Mow Public House, 1. 46 Boundary Street, Bethnal Green. 2. 38 Cannon Street Road, St. George in the East. 3. 104 Commercial Road, St. George in the East. 4. 127 Eastfield Street, Limehouse. 5. 15 Hague Street, Bethnal Green. 6. 133 Narrow Street, Limehouse, 1874. 7. 86 New Gravel Lane (Garnet Street), Wapping, aka Ship. 8. 42 Northampton Street (Headlam Street), Bethnal Green. 9. 59 Vallance Road, Whitechapel, Bakers Row.

Barn Cottages, Westferry Road, Isle of Dogs, 1851, close to Moiety Road.

Barn Place, Old Ford Road, Bromley and Bow, 1851.

Barnaby Cottages, Cubitt Town (precise location unknown), Isle of Dogs, 1888.

Barnardo House, Stepney Causeway, Ratcliffe, 1950.

Barnes Alley or Place, Mile End Road, Mile End, "part of the south side of the road and adjoining the east side of the turnpike It extends from Epping Place to Harlow Place" (Elmes).

Barnes or Barns Buildings, 1. Castle Lane (Old Castle Street), Whitechapel, "is the first on the left from 124 Whitechapel leading into Tusons Buildings and Wentworth Street" (Lockie). 2. Nightingale Lane (Thomas More Street), Wapping, 1871.

Barnet Cottage, Barnet Grove, Bethnal Green, 1841.

Barnet Place, Nova Scotia Gardens (Barnet Grove), Bethnal Green, 1841.

Barnet(t) Street, 1. Off Ravenscroft Street, Bethnal Green, 1841, continuation of Birdcage Walk to Crabtree Row. 2. Off Rampart Street, St. George in the East, 1950.

Barnleys Buildings, Avenue Road (Kitcat Terrace), Bromley and Bow, 1851.

Baroda Place, Shadwell High Street (The Highway), Shadwell, became part of Shadwell High Street.

Baroness Street, Bethnal Green, renamed Baroness Road.

Barque Street, Off Manchester Road, Isle of Dogs, 1891, opposite its corner with Stebondale Street George Greens School was built on the site.

Barretts Buildings or Rents, Royal Mint Street, East Smithfield, 1851.

Barrossa Terrace, Cambridge Road (Cambridge Heath Road), Bethnal Green, 1851, between Old Bethnal Green Road and Hackney Road.

Barrows Buildings or Almshouses, Devonshire Street (Bancroft Road), Mile End, 1891, close to present-day Lang Street.

Bartholomew Place, Collingwood Street, Whitechapel, 1891, now part of Cudworth Street.

Bartholomew Terrace, Essex Street (Blythe Street), Bethnal Green.

Bartlett Street, Off St. Leonards Road, Poplar, 1891, near Venue Street.

Basil House, Berner Street (Henriques Street), St. George in the East, 1950, behind 19 Berner Street.

Basket Terrace, Three Colts Lane, Bethnal Green, 1851.

Bassets Court, Bromley High Street, Bromley and Bow, 1851.

Bastin Terrace, British Street, Bromley and Bow, 1891.

Bates Place, Old Ford Road, Bromley and Bow, 1841.

Batsons & Regents Wharves, Westferry Road, Isle of Dogs, 1950, Edison Building is on their site.

Bath Arms Public House, 48 Devonport Street, Shadwell.

Bath Cottages, Bath Street (Poplar Bath Street), Poplar, 1891.

Bath Place, 1. Bath Street (Darling Row), Whitechapel, 1851. 2. Dalston Lane, Hackney, 1862, east of Bath Row. 3. Gloucester Street (Mansfield Street), Hackney, 1868. 4. Bath Street (Poplar Bath Street), Poplar, 1891.

Bath Row, 1. Brady Street, Whitechapel, 1891. 2. Tyssen Passage, Hackney, 1891, Dalston Lane, renamed Ramgate Street. 3. Bird Cage Walk (Columbia Road), Bethnal Green, 1841.

Bath Street, 1. Off Brady Street, Whitechapel, 1891, became part of Darling Row. 2. Off Cambridge Road (Cambridge Heath Road), Bethnal Green, "the first turning on the right from the Salmon and Ball towards Belvidere (sic) Place in the new Cambridge Road formerly called the Dog Road" (Elmes), renamed Birkbeck Street. 3. Off East India Dock Road, Poplar, 1891, renamed Poplar Bath Street. 4. Off Hardinge Street, Shadwell, 1851, renamed Thirza Street. 5. Off Ravenscroft Street, Bethnal Green, renamed Shipton Street.

Bath Terrace, New Road, Whitechapel, "is part of the north side of the New Road or Back Lane near Cannon Street turnpike at the corner of Anthony Street" (Lockie).

Batsons Street, Off Three Colt Street, Limehouse, "at No. 34 on

the east side of the church" (Elmes), renamed Bates Street.

Batts Yard, Whitechapel High Street, Whitechapel, 1851.

Batty Place, Batty Street, St. George in the East, 1891.

Battys Gardens, Back Church Lane, St. George in the East, 1891, Harry Gosling School is on the site.

Baxendale Arms Public House, 164 Columbia Road, Bethnal Green.

Baxters Court, Church Street (Mare Street), Hackney, 1895, opposite and slightly to the north of Hackney Town Hall.

Bay Street, Off Holly Street, Hackney, 1891.

Bay Tree Public House, 112 Roman Road, Bethnal Green.

Bayard Street, Off Ullin Street, Poplar, 1929.

Bayst Terrace, Russia Lane, Bethnal Green, 1891, now part of Russia Lane.

Bazaar Street, Off Hessel Street, St. George in the East.

Beachcroft or Beechcroft Buildings, Brook Street (Cable Street), Ratcliffe, 1915, east of Collingwood Street.

Beadles House, William Street (Ivimey Street), Bethnal Green.

Beagle Street, Off Leman Street, Whitechapel, 1950, renamed Braham Street.

Bearbinder Lane, Coborn Road, Bromley and Bow, 1851, later Tredegar Road.

Beards Court, Eastfield Street, Limehouse, 1851.

Beards Place, Eastfield Street, Limehouse, "in Eastfield Street opposite the church" (Elmes).

Beast or Bull Lane, Stepney Way, Stepney, 1881, "on the west side of the church and last towards Whitechapel" (Elmes), later renamed Spring Garden Place then became the easternmost part of Stepney Way.

Beatrice House, Philip Street (Ellen Street), St. George in the East.

Beaumont Arms Public House, 52 White Horse Lane, Mile End.

Beaumont Cottage, Lark Row, Bethnal Green.

Beaumont Court, Poplar High Street, Poplar, 1880, between 289 and 291 Poplar High Street.

Beaumont Square Hall, Beaumont Square, Mile End, 1891, Beaumont Street.

Beaumont Street, Mile End, 1891, became part of Beaumont Grove.

Beaumonts Buildings, Cannon Street Road, St. George in the East, "is part of the eastside of it commencing at Lower Chapman Street and extending towards the Commercial Road" (Lockie).

Beavers Almshouse, Oxford Street (Stepney Way), Whitechapel.

Beazley Crescent, Old Ford Road, Bromley and Bow, 1851.

Beckford Row, Bethnal Green Road, Bethnal Green, "Mape Street is the first on the right from the road nearly opposite Wilmot Square and about ¾ of a mile from 65 Shoreditch" (Lockie), renamed Bedford Place.

Becks Rents, Royal Mint Street, East Smithfield, 1891.

Beckton Arms Public House, 22 Bedford Street (Cavell Street), Whitechapel.

Bede Road, Off Burdett Road, Bromley and Bow, parallel with and north of railway line.

Bedford Arms Public House, 1. 22 Bedford Street (Cavell Street), Whitechapel. 2. 1 Susannah Street, Poplar. 3. 79 Wapping Wall, Wapping.

Bedford Cottage, Bedford Street (Prestons Road), Poplar, 1891.

Bedford Hotel (& Public House), 220 Victoria Park Road, Hackney.

Bedford House, 1. 58 Christian Street, St. George in the East, 1950. 2. Bedford House, Oxford Street (Stepney Way), Whitechapel, 1891.

Bedford Institute, Wheler Street, Spitalfields, 1891, Corner of Wheler Street and Quaker Street, renamed Bedford House.

Bedford Place, Commercial Road, Whitechapel, 1860, Philpot Street to Sidney Street.

Bedford Square, Whitechapel, renamed Ford Square.

Bedford Street, 1. Off Brunswick Street, Poplar, "turns off at No 10 Brunswick Street Blackwall Causeway at the corner of Poplar High Street" (Elmes). 2. Whitechapel, renamed Cavell Street.

Bedford Street Buildings, Ditchburn Street, Poplar, early name for Ditchburn House.

Bedford Terrace, 1. Old Ford Road, Bromley and Bow. 2. Prestons Road, Poplar, 1891.

Bedford Villas, Malvern Road, Hackney, 1868, between Lavender Grove and Albert Road.

Beehive Home Public House, 1. 273 Mare Street, Hackney. 2. 31 Blount Street, Poplar. 3. 71 Christian Street, St. George in the East, address also 107 Christian Street. 4. 104 Empson Road (Empson Street), Bromley and Bow. 5. 36 Holly Street, Hackney. 6. 3 Maplin Street, Bromley and Bow. 7. 141 Narrow Street, Limehouse. 8. 1 Preston Street (Roman Road), Bethnal Green. 9. 46 Rhodeswell Road, Limehouse. 10. 12 Robin Hood Lane, Poplar. 11. 230 Roman Road, Bethnal Green, 1990. 12. 28 Sutton Street, Shadwell. 13. 22 Venice Street (Somerford Street), Bethnal Green.

Bekesbourne Buildings, Bekesbourne Street, Ratcliffe.

Belgrave Terrace, Queensbridge Road, Hackney, 1895, opposite Broke Road, renamed Angrave Terrace.

Belhaven Street, Off Grove Road, Bromley and Bow, Mile End Park is on site.

Bell & (Three) Mackerel Public House, 333 Mile End Road, Mile End, aka Old Bell and Mackerel.

Bell & Crown Public House, 181 Kingsland Road, Hackney, 1874.

Bell & Mackerel Public House, 1. 333 Mile End Road, Mile End, 1874. 2. Shadwell High Street (The Highway), Shadwell, aka Old Bell and Mackerel. 3. 116 St. George Street (The Highway), St. George in the East, aka Blue Bell Public House.

Bell Alley, Lamb Street, Spitalfields, 1746.

Bell Court, Wheler Street, Spitalfields, "at 43 opposite Webb Square from 47 Shoreditch leading into Farthing Street" (Lockie), railway line is on the site.

Bell Lane, Petticoat Lane (Middlesex Street), Spitalfields, "the first east parallel to Petticoat Lane extending from Wentworth Street to Raven Street" (Lockie).

Bell Place, 1. Five Bell Place (Three Colt Street), Limehouse. 2. Princes Row (Old Montague Street), Whitechapel, "is the first on the left from Bakers Row entering at 94 Whitechapel Road" (Lockie).

Bell Public House, 1. 205 Bethnal Green Road, Bethnal Green. 2. 40 Brick Lane, Spitalfields, 1874, address sometimes given as 20 Osborn Place. 3. 15 Dean Street (Deancross Street), Shadwell. 4. 10 Garden Street, Stepney. 5. 12 Homerton Terrace, Hackney. 6. 106 Middlesex Street, Spitalfields, 1874. 7. 157 Wapping High Street, Wapping, aka Steam Ferry Tavern, address also 123 Wapping High Street.

Bell Road, Off St. Leonards Street, Bromley and Bow, 1891.

Bell Wharf Hill, Shadwell High Street (The Highway), Shadwell, 1851, Shadwell Park is on the site.

Bell Wharf Stairs, Shadwell High Street (The Highway), Shadwell, "by Bell Wharf the east end of Shadwell High Street and west end of Cock Hill" (Lockie), Shadwell Park is on the site.

Belle Vue Place, Cleveland Street (Cleveland Way), Mile End, 1891.

Belloc House, Carr Street, Limehouse, 1950, Limehouse Fields Estate.

Belmont Mansions, Goldsmiths Row, Bethnal Green, 1950.

Belmont Row, Bethnal Green (Patriot Square), Bethnal Green, "nearly opposite Patriot Square the first turning on the right going from the Green towards Hackney" (Elmes).

Belmont Terrace, Gardners Road (Mile End Park), Bromley and Bow, Roman Road.

Belvedere & Belvedere Place, part of Dog Row (Cambridge Heath Road), Whitechapel, 1841.

Bempton Street, near St. Peters Church (St. Peters Avenue), Bethnal Green, west of St. Peters Church, renamed St. Peters Avenue.

Ben Jonson Public House, 1. 83 Ben Jonson Road (Stepney Green), Stepney, 1851. 2. 22 Goodmans Yard, Whitechapel, aka Ben Jonsons Head. 3. 26 Pelham Street (Woodseer Street), Whitechapel.

Bengal Place or Terrace, 253-263 East India Dock Road, Poplar, "is in the East India Dock Road between the turnpike and the dock gates" (Elmes).

Benledi Street, Off East India Dock Road, Poplar, 1891, renamed Benledi Road.

Benledi Street School Chapel, Benledi Street, Poplar, 1933-1940.

Benn Road, Hackney, renamed Benn Street.

Bennet(t)s Place, Bethnal Green Road, Bethnal Green, "being the first turning to the east parallel to Pollards Row at the north end of Pollard Street about half a mile on the left hand from Shoreditch" (Elmes).

Bennets Court, George Street (Code Street), Whitechapel, "is two doors south from Spicer Street Brick Lane" (Lockie).

Bennetts Court & Place, Browns Lane (Hanbury Street), Spitalfields, 1851.

Bentham Road, Off Kenton Road, Hackney, 1891.

Bentley Terrace, Chrisp Street, Poplar, 1851.

Bere Place, Brook Street (Cable Street), Ratcliffe, 1851.

Bermuda Street, Off Jamaica Street, Stepney, 1950, east of Jamaica Street, close to Commercial Road.

Berner Street, Off Commercial Road, St. George in the East, "the first on the right, east of the one mile stone from the Royal Exchange opposite Plumbers Row" (Lockie), part renamed Henriques Street part renamed Boyd Street.

Berner Street School, Berner Street (Henriques Street), St. George in the East, 1889.

Bernhard Baron St. Georges Jewish Settlement, Berner Street (Henriques Street), St. George in the East, corner of Fairclough Street.

Berry Place, Pundersons Gardens (Bethnal Green Road), Bethnal Green.

Besant House, Carr Street, Limehouse, 1950, Limehouse Fields Estate.

Bessarabia Kiev Synagogue, Fashion Street, Spitalfields, 1899.

Beth Aharon Synagogue, 181 Bow Road, Bromley and Bow, 1946.

Beth Jacob Synagogue, 22 Sidney Square, Whitechapel, 1935.

Beth Sholom Synagogue, 67 Chicksand Street, Whitechapel, 1940.

Bethel Baptist Chapel, 165 Poplar High Street, Poplar.

Bethel Oak Chapel, Sidney Street, Whitechapel, south end of Sidney Street.

Bethnal Green British School, Abbey Street (Buckfast Street), Bethnal Green, 1868.

Bethnal Green Hospital, Cambridge Heath Road, Bethnal Green, 1895, south of Parmiter Street.

Bethnal Green Mission to the Jews, 55 Bethnal Green Road, Bethnal Green.

Bethnal Green Old Town Hall, Church Row (Bethnal Green Road), Bethnal Green, 1860, opposite St. Matthews Church.

Bethnal Green Workhouse,

Bishops Way, Bethnal Green, 1827.

Bethnal Green Workhouse, Hare Street (Cheshire Street), Whitechapel, "at the east end of Hare Street by the fields about $\frac{1}{5}$ of a mile on the right in it from 110 Brick Lane" (Lockie).

Bethnal House Lunatic Asylum, Green Street (Roman Road), Bethnal Green, 1891, immediately east of Bethnal Green Gardens.

Betton Place, Pearson Street, Bethnal Green, 1950.

Bettons Terrace, Westferry Road, Isle of Dogs, 1820, opposite Ingelheim Place.

Betts Place, Betts Street, St. George in the East.

Betts Street, Off Ratcliffe Highway (The Highway), St. George in the East, "at 164 on the east side of Princes Square extending to 35 New Road or Back Lane about $\frac{1}{8}$ of a mile in length" (Lockie), joined The Highway at present-day St. Georges Baths.

Beulah Cottage(s), Bonner Lane (Bonner Street), Bethnal Green, Bonner Lane.

Beulah Place, Cambridge Road (Cambridge Heath Road), Bethnal Green, 1851.

Bickmore Street, Off Poplar High Street, Poplar, 1891, formerly Queen Street entrance street to Poplar Workhouse.

Bigland Place, Bigland Street, St. George in the East, 1950.

Bird Cage (or Birdcage) Fields & Walk, Crab Tree Row (Columbia Road), Bethnal Green, "the continuation of Crab Tree Row, Hackney Road near Shoreditch Church to Hackney Road again by the Nags head" (Lockie), renamed Columbia Road.

Bird in Bush Terrace, Salmon Lane, Limehouse, 1851.

Bird in Hand Court, Bromley High Street, Bromley and Bow, 1891.

Bird in Hand Public House, 1. 21 Bonner Street, Bethnal Green, 1874. 2. 126 Bow Road, Bromley and Bow.

Bird Street, Off Green Bank, Wapping, 1860, heads north from the western end of Green Bank, now part of Tench Street.

Birdcage Place, Barnet Place (Barnet Grove), Bethnal Green, 1841.

Birds Cottages or Place, Old Ford Road, Bromley and Bow, 1851.

Birkbeck School, Bath Street (Darling Row), Whitechapel, 1860.

Bishop Bonner Public House, 1. 124 Wapping High Street, Wapping, also known as Black Boy. 2. 169 Mile End Road, Mile End, aka Black Boy. 3. 21 Bonner Street, Bethnal Green, 1874.

Bishop Road, Off Valentine Road, Hackney, 1891, renamed Killowen Road.

Bishops Road, Off Sewardstone Road, Bethnal Green, 1891, renamed Bishops Way.

Bishopsgate Road, Off Burdett Street (Purdey Street), Bromley and Bow, part renamed Burdett Street and part renamed Norris Road.

Bisterne Place, Prestons Road, Poplar, 1851.

Black Bell Alley, Petticoat Lane (Middlesex Street), Spitalfields, 1746, South of Wentworth Street.

Black Bird Alley, St. John Street (Grimsby Street), Bethnal Green, "the second on the right from 105 Brick Lane leading to Spicer Street" (Lockie).

Black Boy Court, Globe Road, Mile End, 1891.

Black Boy Lane, Poplar High Street, Poplar, "is about half a mile on the left from the Commercial Road opposite the Harrow leading to England Row and Meeting house Place" (Lockie).

Black Boy Public House, 1. 88 Bath Street (Poplar Bath Street), Poplar. 2. 88 Lower East Smithfield (St. Katharines Way), East Smithfield, 1874. 3. 169 Mile End Road, Mile End, 1874. 4. Well Street, Hackney, 1874.

Black Bull (& Star Public) House, 37 New Gravel Lane (Garnet Street), Wapping, 1874, address also 87 Wapping High Street.

Black Bull Alley, Petticoat Lane (Middlesex Street), Spitalfields, "is about 1/8 of a mile on the right from 41 Aldgate High Street or from Whitechapel, about 10 doors south from Wentworth Street leading into Goulston Street" (Lockie).

Black Bull Court, Brook Street (Cable Street), Ratcliffe, 1891, also called Black Thorne Place, behind Black Bull Court.

Black Bull Public House, 1. 35 Bacon Street, Bethnal Green. 2. 137 Brook Street (Cable Street), Ratcliffe, 1895, present-day corner of Cable Street and Butcher Row. 3. Haggerston Road, Hackney, 1950, corner with Lee Street. 4. 37 New Gravel Lane (Garnet Street), Wapping. 2. 20 Old Montague Street, Whitechapel. 3. 6 Thomas Street, Spitalfields, 1874.

Black Dog Public House, 1. 101 Bethnal Green Road, Bethnal Green. 2. Brick Lane, Spitalfields, 1874. 3. 13 Denmark Street (Crowder Street), St. George in the East, aka Old Black Dog Public House. 4. 101 Redchurch Street, Bethnal Green.

Black Eagle Public House, 1. 63 Brick Lane, Spitalfields, address also 140 Brick Lane.

Black Eagle Street, Off Brick Lane, Spitalfields, 1891, "is opposite 65 Brick Lane by Hanburys Brewery leading to Grey Eagle Street" (Lockie), subsumed by Trumans Black Eagle Brewery.

Black Eagle Wharf, Wapping High Street, Wapping, 1950, east of corner with Sampson Street.

Black Horse & Windmill Public House, 5 Fieldgate Street, Whitechapel, 1874, aka Black Horse Public House.

Black Horse Court, George Street (Code Street), Whitechapel, 1851.

Black Horse Public House, 1. 25 Abbey Street (Buckfast Street), Bethnal Green. 2. 52 Christian Street, St. George in the East, "The continuation of Princes Place, New Road" (Elmes). 3. 5 Fieldgate Street, Whitechapel, 1874, aka Black Horse & Windmill Public House. 6. George Yard (Gunthorpe Street), Whitechapel. 7. 67 Green Street (Roman Road), Bethnal Green. 8. 215 Kingsland Road, Hackney, 1874. 9. 40 Leman Street, Whitechapel. 10. 8 Middlesex Street, Spitalfields. 11. 168 Mile End Road, Mile End. 12. 72-74 Poplar High Street, Poplar. 13. 27 Ropemakers Fields, Limehouse, close to Narrow Street. 14. 10 Well Street (Ensign Street), St. George in the East, 1874.

Black Horse Yard, 1. Off Nightingale Lane (Thomas More Street), Wapping, 1790, St.

Katharine Dock is on its site. 2. Whitechapel Road, Whitechapel, "the first on the left from 88 Whitechapel Road near the church" (Lockie).

Black Lion Public House, 1. 63 Hanbury Street, Spitalfields. 2. 99 Middlesex Street, Spitalfields. 3. New Montague Street (Hanbury Street), Spitalfields, 1746.

Black Lion Yard, Whitechapel Road, Whitechapel, "at 39 a few doors on the left below the church leading into Old Montague Street" (Lockie), a footpath now follows part of its route.

Black Lion Yard Synagogue, 14 Black Lion Yard (Old Montague Street), Whitechapel, 1905-1955.

Black Lion Public House, 99 Middlesex Street, Spitalfields, 1874.

Black Swan Alley, Corbets Court (Hanbury Street), East Smithfield, 1746.

Black Swan Public House, 1. 148 Bow Road, Bromley and Bow. 2. 23 Hanbury Street, Spitalfields. 3. 16 Schoolhouse Lane, Shadwell.

Black(a)moors Head Public House, 5 Cartwright Street (Royal Mint Street), East Smithfield, 1874, Royal Mint Street.

Blackbird Alley, Fleet Street

24

(Pedley Street), Whitechapel, 1851.

Blacks (or Blocks) Court, Phoenix Street (Brick Lane), Spitalfields, "the first on the right and about 6 doors from 39 Wheler Street leading into Quaker Street" (Lockie).

Blacksmiths Arms Court & Place, Back Church Lane, St. George in the East, 1878, between Back Church Lane and Pinchin Street.

Blacksmiths Arms Public House, 1. 16 Back Church Lane, St. George in the East. 2. 110 Brook Street (Cable Street), Ratcliffe. 3. 2 Pinchin Street, St. George in the East. 4. 25 Westferry Road, Isle of Dogs.

Blackstone Road, Off Lansdowne Road (Lansdowne Drive), Hackney, 1891.

Blackwall Buildings, Thomas Street (Fulbourne Street), Whitechapel, 1891.

Blackwall Causeway, Naval Row, Poplar, "commences at the east end of Poplar by Naval Row extending to the Thames" (Lockie), became Brunswick Street.

Blackwall Cross, Robin Hood Lane, Poplar, 1851, area occupied by Robin Hood Lane and Naval Row.

Blackwall Railway Station, Brunswick Wharf (Jamestown Way), Poplar, 1840-1926.

Blackwall Stairs, Yabsley Street, Poplar.

Blackwall Yard, Brunswick Street, Poplar, 1851.

Blade Bone Public House, 185 Bethnal Green Road, Bethnal Green.

Blakeneys Head Public House, 1. 56 Cable Street, St. George in the East, aka Admiral Blakeneys Head, aka American Stores Public House. 2. 143 Poplar High Street, Poplar.

Blakes Court, Old Gravel Lane (Wapping Lane), Wapping, "at 150 near the middle of the west side" (Lockie), opposite Charles Street (Raine Street).

Blakesley Street, Off Sutton Street, Shadwell, Sutton Street to Watney Street.

Blanchard Road & Street, Off Lansdowne Road (Lansdowne Drive), Hackney, 1891.

Blatherwick Cottages & Villas, Shrubland Grove (Mapledene Road), Hackney, 1868, between Queens Road and Malvern Road.

Blenheim Cottages, Cassland Road, Hackney, 1851.

Blenheim House, Scouler Street, Poplar, 1880.

Blenheim Terrace, Morgan Street (Hessel Street), St. George in the East.

Blissett Street, Off Pundersons Place (Bethnal Green Road), Bethnal Green, "turns off at No 6

Pundersons Place on the north side near the Green" (Elmes).

Blo(o)mfield Street, Off Mapledene Road, Hackney, renamed Welbury Street.

Blomfield Street, Off Middleton Road (Freshfield Avenue), Hackney, parallel with Kingsland Road, close to railway, sometimes spelled Bloomfield Street.

Bloomfield Road, Off Burdett Road, Bromley and Bow, parallel with railway line north of Burdett Railway Station.

Bloomington Road, Off Burdett Road, Bromley and Bow, 1895.

Bloomsbury Street, Off St. Leonards Road, Poplar, 1885, St. Leonards Road to Brunswick Road, close to Grundy Street.

Blossom Place, Blossom Street, Spitalfields.

Blue Anchor Alley & Court, Brook Street (Cable Street), Ratcliffe, "at 106 nearly opposite Stepney Causeway" (Lockie).

Blue Anchor Lane, Bethnal Green (Russia Lane), Bethnal Green, "commences near the north-east corner of the green leading to Hackney Road" (Lockie), renamed Russia Lane.

Blue Anchor Public House, 1. 67 Bromley High Street, Bromley and Bow. 2. 102 Brook Street (Cable Street), Ratcliffe, 1874. 3. 80 Cable Street, St. George in the East, 1874. 4. 2 Chance Street, Bethnal Green. 5.

21 Dock Street, Shadwell, Shadwell Basin is on the site, address also 1 The Highway, also 1 Dock Street, also 43 St. George Street, also 43 Parsons Street. 6. 1 Middlesex Street, Spitalfields, 1874. 7. 225 Mile End Road, Mile End, 1874. 8. 48 Royal Mint Street, East Smithfield. 9. 1 the Highway, St. George in the East. 10. 140 White Horse Street (White Horse Road), Stepney, 1874. 11. 133 Whitechapel Road, Whitechapel, 1874.

Blue Anchor Yard, Royal Mint Street, East Smithfield, 1851.

Blue Ball Court, Artichoke Lane (Spirit Quay), Wapping, 1746.

Blue Bell Public House, 116 St. George Street (The Highway), St. George in the East, aka Bell (Tavern) Public House.

Blue Boar Court, Rosemary Lane (Royal Mint Street), East Smithfield, 1746.

Blue Coat Boy Public House, 32 Duval Street (Crispin Street), Spitalfields.

Blue Gate Fields, Shadwell High Street (The Highway), Shadwell, 1800, renamed Dellow Street.

Blue Last Court, Three Colt Street, Limehouse, "turns off at No 31 on the east side of Limehouse Church" (Elmes), close to Church Institute.

Blue Lion Public House (or Temperance Hotel), 9 Ames Street (Roman Road), Bromley and Bow, address also Green Street.

Blue Peter Public House, 61 Royal Mint Street, East Smithfield, 1874, aka City of Carlisle.

Blue Posts Tavern Public House, Limehouse Causeway, Limehouse, c1800 moved to 73 and 75 West India Dock Road, renamed Buccaneer in the 1970s.

Blyths Wharf, Narrow Street, Limehouse, 1950, close to junction with Ropemakers Fields.

Board of Trade Mercantile Marine Offices, 133 East India Dock Road, Poplar, 1921.

Boarded Entrance, Ship Street (Wapping High Street), Wapping, the second turning on the left from Wapping, it leads into Ship Street and Prussian Island" (Elmes).

Boars Head Court & Yard, Petticoat Lane (Middlesex Street), Spitalfields, "the first on the right and a few doors from 41 Aldgate High Street" (Lockie).

Bohn Street, renamed Bohn Road, Mile End.

Bohola House Public House, 423 Bethnal Green Road, Bethnal Green, aka Albion.

Boltwrights or Botwrights Court, Mount Street (Swanfield Street), Bethnal Green, "the third turning on the left in Mount Street going from Church Street by the Charity School" (Elmes).

Bolwright(s) Buildings, Hackney Road, Bethnal Green, 1860, opposite King Street.

Bombay Grab Public House, 246 Bow Road, Bromley and Bow.

Bonds Buildings, Chamber Street, Whitechapel, 1851.

Bonner Arms Public House, 1 Tagg Street (Cranbrook Estate), Bromley and Bow.

Bonner Road Chest Hospital, Bonner Road, Bethnal Green, 1891, Old Ford Road.

Bonner(s) Lane, Bonner Street, Bethnal Green, 1841, later part of Bonner Street.

Bonners Hall, Bonner Road, Bethnal Green, "a detached parcel of houses situated about $^1/_3$ of a mile north-east from the green, and about the same distance east from Cambridge Heath turnpike" (Lockie).

Bonwell Street, Off Knottisford Street, Bethnal Green, 1891, diagonally opposite Butler Street.

Booth Court, Brick Lane, Spitalfields, "at 18 the second on the right in it from 49 Brick Lane" (Lockie).

Booth Street, Off Brick Lane, Whitechapel, "commences at 50 Brick Lane about $^1/_5$ of a mile on the right from Osborn Street Church leading to Well Street and church Street Mile End New town" (Lockie) became the eastern half of Princelet Street.

Booth Street Buildings, Booth Street (Princelet Street), Whitechapel, 1891, renamed Perrys Avenue.

Bor(e)ham Street, 1. Off Peter Street (Rhoda Street), Bethnal Green, 1881, "turns off No 16 Peter Street near Tyssen Street" (Elmes). 2. Hackney, 1851, renamed Arthur Street (Brooksbank Street).

Bortons Buildings, Nelson Street (Boundary Estate), Bethnal Green, 1891, now part of Nelson Street.

Bortons Yard, St. Peter Street (St. Peter Square), Bethnal Green, 1891.

Bostock Place, Bostock Street (Chandler Street), Wapping.

Bostock Street, Off Old Gravel Lane (Wapping Lane), Wapping, Chandler Street approximately follows its route.

Boston Street, Off Hackney Road, Bethnal Green, 1891, west of Goldsmiths Row.

Botany Bay, Hackney Terrace (Well Street), Hackney, 1827, Well Street.

Botolph Passage, Campbell Road, Bromley and Bow, Campbell Road to Botolph Road.

Botolph Road, Off Devons Road, Bromley and Bow, 1891, close to corner with Bromley High Street.

Botwrights or Bol(t)wrights Court, Mount Street (Swanfield Street), Bethnal Green, "the third turning on the left in Mount Street going from Church Street by the Charity School" (Elmes).

Boundary Cottage, Kerbey Street, Poplar, 1851.

Boundary Court, St. John Street (Grimsby Street), Bethnal Green, "turns of at No 13 John Street" (Elmes).

Boundary Tavern Public House, 62 Commercial Road, St. George in the East.

Bow Baptist Chapel House, Old Ford Road, Bromley and Bow, 1891.

Bow Brewery, Bow High Street, Bromley and Bow, 1891, opposite St. Mary's Church.

Bow Bromley & Mile End Synagogue, 56 Bow Road, Bromley and Bow, 1920.

Bow Creek Council School, Old School Wharf (Orchard Place), Poplar, 1895, Orchard Place.

Bow Creek Mills, Orchard Place, Poplar, 1950.

Bow High Street, Off Bow Road, Bromley and Bow, section of present day Bow Road near St. Marys Church.

Bow Lane, Poplar High Street, Poplar, until the construction of the East India Docks in the early 19th century the main road from the east end of Poplar High Street to Bow, in 1950 its route was marked by Bazely Street Follett Street and Brunswick Road.

Bow Lane Buildings & Cottages, Bow Lane (Bazely Street), Poplar, 1851, Poplar High Street.

Bow Lane School, Bow Lane (Bazely Street), Poplar, 1870.

Bow Railway Station, Bow Road, Bromley and Bow, 1850-1944, Bow Church DLR is across the road to the site.

Bow Road Railway Station, Bow Road, Bromley and Bow, 1876-1949, at corner with Addington Road.

Bowbells Public House, 116 Bow Road, Bromley and Bow.

Bowen Street, Off Chrisp Street, Poplar, Chrisp Street to Kerbey Street.

Bower Road, Off White Post Lane, Hackney, 1891, A12 is on the site.

Bowles Wharf, Broad Street (The Highway), Shadwell, 1895, east of Shadwell Park, became part of Charringtons Wharf.

Bowley Street, Off Emmett Street, Limehouse, 1891, between Emmet Street and Westferry Road.

Bowleys Public House, 377 Manchester Road, Isle of Dogs, aka Dorset Arms.

Bowyers or Boyers Buildings, James Street (Burslem Street), St. George in the East, "the first turning on the right in James Street from Cannon Street Road", (Elmes).

Box Street, Off Furze Street, Bromley and Bow.

Boys Refuge & Industrial School, 28 Commercial Street, Whitechapel.

Braces Buildings, Blue Anchor Yard (Royal Mint Street), East Smithfield, 1851.

Bradfield Street, Off East Ferry Road, Isle of Dogs, north end of East Ferry Road, combined with Rushbrook Street to form Chipka Street.

Bradlaugh Street, Off Smart Street, Bethnal Green

Bradshaws Cottages, Westferry Road, Isle of Dogs, 1851, parallel with and just west of Cahir Street.

Brady Place, Brady Street, Whitechapel, between 84 and 86 Brady Street.

Brady Street Dwellings, Brady Street, Whitechapel, 1891.

Brady Street Jewish Cemetery, Brady Street, Whitechapel, 1761-1858.

Brady Street Mansions, Brady Street, Whitechapel, 1911.

Bradys Buildings, Barnet Grove, Bethnal Green, 1950, behind 34 Barnet Grove.

Braemar Street, Off Usk Street, Bethnal Green, 1950, between Usk Street and Smart Street.

Brampton Road, Off Cassland Road, Hackney, 1891, renamed Bramshaw Road.

Branch Court, Narrow Street, Limehouse, in Narrow Street which leads from Ratcliffe Cross to Fore Street (Elmes).

Brantridge Street, Off Bridge Street (Hamlets Way), Bromley and Bow, 1891, later became part of Eric Street.

Brassfounders Arms Public House, 255 Whitechapel Road, Whitechapel.

Bremen Street, Hackney, renamed Dericote Street.

Brenans (or Brennans) Buildings, Gibraltar Row (Gibraltar Walk), Bethnal Green.

Brent House Maternity Home, 27-29 Devonshire Road (Brenthouse Road), Hackney, 1888-1926.

Brethren Mission Hall, Paragon Road, Hackney, 1921.

Bretts or Britts Alley or Building, Whitechapel High Street, Whitechapel, 1881, "in Osborne Street" (Elmes).

Brewer Street, Off, Shadwell, 1881, Turns off at No 75 High Street" (Elmes).

Brewers Almshouses, Oxford Street (Stepney Way), Whitechapel, 1891, immediately east of St. Philips Church.

Brewers Arms Public House, 100 Maroon Street, Limehouse.

Brewers Hall Public House, 414 Commercial Road, Shadwell.

Brewers or Brewhouse Court, New Gravel Lane (Garnet Street), Wapping, 1851, just south of corner of Prusom Street.

Brewers or Brewhouse Lane, Wapping High Street, Wapping, "at 128 Wapping Street by Pickards brewery leading to New Market Street and Old Gravel Lane" (Lockie).

Brewers Wharves, Wapping High Street, Wapping, 1950, east of corner with Sampson Street.

Brewery Lodge, Northey Street, Limehouse, 1891, eastern end of street Ropemakers Field is now on the site.

Brewery Tap Public House, 1. 500 Commmercial Road (Commercial Road), Shadwell, aka Commercial Brewery Tap. 2. 505-507 Hackney Road, Bethnal Green. 3. 525 Kingsland Road, Hackney.

Brewery Yard, 1. Bromley High Street, Bromley and Bow, 1851. 2. Commercial Street, Spitalfields, 1851.

Brewery Wharf, Limekiln Dock, Narrow Street, Limehouse, 1950.

Brewhouse Street, Off Labour in Vain Street (Shadwell Park), Shadwell, "the first on the right in Labour in Vain Street from the south east corner of Shadwell market by the Water Works" (Lockie), Shadwell Park is on the site.

Brewhouse Yard, 1. Foxes Lane (Shadwell Basin), Shadwell, "Lower Turning at the bottom of Foxes Lane from the church on the right by the New Road to the Dock" (Lockie), Shadwell Basin is on the site. 2. Princes Street (Princelet Street), Whitechapel.

Brewster Road Bromley and Bow, 1929, renamed Priscilla Road (Bow Road).

Brickfield Cottage, Chrisp Street, Poplar, 1891, East India Dock Road.

Bricklayers Arms Public House, 1. 26 Cable Street, St. George in the East. 2. 389 Cable Street, Shadwell, address also 1 Parnham Place. 3. 319 Cambridge Road (Cambridge Heath Road), Bethnal Green. 4. 92 Collingwood Street, Whitechapel. 5. 145 Devons Road, Bromley and Bow. 6. 92 Fairfield Road, Bromley and Bow. 7. 20 Gloucester Street (Settles Street), Whitechapel. 8. 36 Hassard Street, Bethnal Green. 9. 38-40 Lowell Street, Poplar. 10. 59 Minerva Street, Bethnal Green. 11. 65 Narrow Street, Limehouse, on corner of Limehouse Cut Entrance Lock now Albert Mews. 12. 71 Redmans Road, Mile End. 13. 34 Settles Street, Whitechapel. 14. 12 Union Street (Bullivant Street), Poplar, corner of Ashton Street. 15. 15 Upper Fenton Street (Fenton Street), St. George in the East. 16. 236 Vallance Road, Bethnal Green. 17. Westferry Road, Isle of Dogs, 1830, in short row of houses on marsh wall close to Moiety Road.

Bridge Dock, Narrow Street, Limehouse, "at the east end of Narrow Street by the drawbridge" (Lockie).

Bridge House, Stonebridge Lane (Haggerston Road), Hackney, 1841.

Bridge House Public House, 1. 14 Bow Common Lane, Bromley and Bow. 2. 187 Tredegar Road, Bromley and Bow.

Bridge Houses, Cambridge Heath (Mare Street), Hackney, 1851, later part of Mare Street.

Bridge of Hope Mission Refuge, 28 Betts Street, St. George in the East.

Bridge of Hope Mission Training Home, Ashburton House (Globe Road), Mile End, Globe Road.

Bridge Place, Wallis Road, Hackney, 1891, White Post Lane.

Bridge Road, 1. Off Garford Street, Limehouse, 1891, between Garford Street and Westferry Road (near City Arms pub), became part of Westferry Road. 2. Off Roman Road, Bromley and Bow, later part of Roman Road.

Bridge Street, 1. Off Harford Street, Mile End, 1891, part renamed Solebay Street and part (eastern end) renamed Hamlets Way. 2. Off Solebay Street, Mile

End, section west of canal renamed Solebay Street (Mile End) and section east of Mile End Park renamed Hamlets Way (Bromley and Bow).

Bridge Terrace, Queens Road (Queensbridge Road), Hackney, 1862, immediately north of the canal.

Bridge Terrace & Lock House, Parnham Street, Limehouse, 1891.

Bridge Wharf, Westferry Road, Isle of Dogs, 1950, on the riverfront west of present-day Westferry Circus.

Brierly Street, Off Royston Street, Bethnal Green, Brierly Gardens is part on the site.

Brig Street, Off Manchester Road, Isle of Dogs, 1891, George Greens School was built on the site.

Brightlingsea Buildings, Ropemakers Fields, Limehouse, western end of Ropemakers Fields, backing on to Brightlingsea Place.

Brighton Place, Hackney Road, Bethnal Green, 1860, immediately east of Coleharbour Street.

Brighton Terrace, Bishops Road (Bishops Way), Bethnal Green, 1862, corner with Waterloo Road.

Brimstone Court, Rosemary Lane (Royal Mint Street), East Smithfield, 1746.

Brinsley Street, Off Sutton Street, Shadwell, 1950, north of Martha Street.

Britannia Dry Dock, Westferry Road, Isle of Dogs, 1891.

Britannia Place, 1. Commercial Road, Limehouse, "is in the Commercial Road on the west side of the turnpike near the bridge" (Elmes), opposite Limehouse Town Hall. 2. Three Colts Lane, Bethnal Green, 1851.

Britannia Public House, 1. 185 Bow Common Lane, Bromley and Bow. 2. 232 Cable Street, St. George in the East, aka Old Britannia. 3. 29 Cambridge Road (Cambridge Heath Road), Whitechapel. 4. 12 Chilton Street, Bethnal Green. 5. 279 Church Street (Mare Street), Hackney, 1874. 6. 759 Commercial Road, Limehouse, opposite Limehouse Town Hall. 7. 87 Commercial Street, Spitalfields. 8. 2 Digby Street, Bethnal Green. 9. 209 Globe Road, Bethnal Green. 10. 212 Kingsland Road, Hackney, 1874. 11. 279 Mare Street, Hackney. 12. 11 Martha Street (Wadeson Street), Hackney. 13. 254 Mile End Road, Mile End. 14. 44 Morris Street, Shadwell. 15. 33 Ocean Street (Ben Jonson Road), Mile End. 16. 106 St. Anns Road (Mile End Stadium), Bromley & Bow. 17. 54 Wadeson Street, Hackney.

Britannia Tavern Public House, Blackwall (Raleana

Road), Poplar, 1840, Old Blackwall riverside.

British & Foreign Wharf, St. Katharines Way, East Smithfield, 1950, south of corner with Burr Close.

British Flag Public House, 108 Duckett Street, Mile End, aka Prince of Wales, address also 14 Waley Street.

British Lion Public House, Oxford Street (Stepney Way), Whitechapel, 1874.

British Oak Public House, 1. 16 Old Castle Street, Bethnal Green. 2. 28 Oxford Street (Stepney Way), Whitechapel. 3. 60 Robin Hood Lane, Poplar, address also 28 Robin Hood Lane.

British Penitent Female Refuge, 1. Cambridge Heath Bridge (Cambridge Heath Road), Bethnal Green, 1868. 2. 10 North Side (Old Ford Road), Bethnal Green, north of Bethnal Green.

British Prince Public House, 49 Bromley Street, Stepney, 1874.

British Queen Public House, 1. 134 Cannon Street Road, St. George in the East. 2. 51 Globe Road, Mile End. 3. 114 New Gravel Lane (Garnet Street), Wapping. 4. 31 White Horse Lane, Mile End.

British School, 1. Abbey Street (Buckfast Street), Bethnal Green, 1841. 2. Princes Square (Swedenborg Square), St. George in the East.

British Street, Off Westferry Road, Isle of Dogs, 1891, renamed Harbinger Road.

British Street School aka Millwall British School, British Street (Harbinger Road), Isle of Dogs, originally on the east side of the street moved in 1872 to a new building across the road which was renamed Harbinger School in the 1930s.

British Tar Public House, 29 St. George Street (The Highway), St. George in the East.

Brits or Britt Street, Off Sampsons Gardens (Sampson Street), Wapping, "the second on the right in Globe Street from 60 Wapping Street leading to the London Docks" (Lockie).

Brittens Court, Swedenborg Square (Swedenborg Gardens), St. George in the East, between Swedenborg Square and the Highway.

Broad Bridge, 1. Old Castle Street, Whitechapel, 1851. 2. Shadwell High Street (The Highway), Shadwell, "at 87 the fifth on the right below the church leading to Dean Street" (Lockie), Shadwell Park is on the site.

Broad Place, Flower and Dean Street, Spitalfields, 1746.

Broad Street, 1. Off The Highway, Ratcliffe, "the east continuation of Ratcliffe Highway and Shadwell High Street extending from Cock hill to Ratcliffe Cross" (Lockie), now part of The Highway. 2. Off Worcester Street (Reardon Street), Wapping, 1860, Worcester Street to Tench Street, became part of Red Lion Street.

Broadbridge or Broadway, Austin Street, Bethnal Green, 1841, rear of St. Leonards Church, now part of Boundary Street.

Broadway London Fields, West Street (Westgate Street), Hackney, 1895, renamed Broadway Market.

Broadway Wharf, Narrow Street, Limehouse, 1950, close to Narrow Street junction with Ropemakers Fields.

Brocks Cottage, Devonport Street, Shadwell, 1871.

Broke Road, Off Queensbridge Road, Hackney, 1895, route largely followed by Broke Walk.

Bromehead Road, Off Commercial Road, Stepney, 1950, east of and parallel with Bromehead Street.

Bromehead Street, Off Commercial Road, Stepney, 1950, opposite Dean Street.

Bromley Arms Public House, 51 Fairfield Road, Bromley and Bow.

Bromley Cottages, St. Leonards Road, Poplar, 1891.

Bromley Hall, Quay Lane (Brunswick Road), Poplar, 1851, later Brunswick Road.

Bromley Hall (Tavern) Public House, 211 Brunswick Road, Poplar.

Bromley House & Excise Office, Bromley High Street, Bromley and Bow, 1851.

Bromley Lane, early name for Devons Road, Bromley and Bow.

Bromley Lock, St. Leonards Street, Bromley and Bow, 1891.

Bromley Marsh Farm, Quay Lane (Brunswick Road), Poplar, 1851, later Brunswick Road.

Bromley National School, St. Leonards Street, Bromley and Bow, 1891.

Bromley Place, Ann Street (East India Dock Road), Poplar, 1851.

Bromley Terrace, 1. Bromley High Street, Bromley and Bow, 1851. 2. St. Leonards Road, Poplar, 1862, between Andrew Street and Bloomsbury Street.

Brook Street, 1. Off Devonport Street, Shadwell, 1891, south end of Devonport Street in the west, to Butcher Row in the east, now the easternmost part of Cable Street. 2. Off Old Ford Road, Bromley and Bow, 1891, renamed Ranwell Street, Ranwell Close is on the site.

Brooklyn Cottages, Rhodeswell Road, Limehouse, 1891, later part of Lydbrook Street.

Brooks Terrace, Rhodeswell Road, Limehouse, 1891.

Broom Alley, Whitechapel Road, Whitechapel, "turns off at

No 53 two houses eastward of Great Garden Street" (Elmes).

Brougham Arms Public House, 13 Queen Street (Clegg Street), St. George in the East, 1874.

Broughton Place, Hackney Road, Bethnal Green, 1841, opposite Temple Street.

Brown Bear Alley, Upper East Smithfield, East Smithfield, 1851, opposite Thomas More Street.

Brown Bear Public House, 1. 139 Leman Street, Whitechapel. 2. 43 Upper East Smithfield, East Smithfield.

Brown Horse Public House, 16 Tetley Street (Chrisp Street), Poplar.

Brownings Court, Upper Chapman Street (Chapman Street), St. George in the East, 1891.

Brownlow Place, Queens Road (Queensbridge Road), Hackney, 1862, opposite Brownlow Road.

Browns Cottages, Russia Lane, Bethnal Green, 1891, now part of Russia Lane.

Browns Court, Goodmans Fields (Alie Street), Whitechapel, "Great Ayliff Street Goodmans Fields at 49 the first on the right four doors west from Red Lion Street" (Lockie).

Browns Lane, Commercial Street, Spitalfields, 1792, Commercial Street to Brick Lane, became western end of Hanbury Street.

Browns Quay, Wapping High Street, Wapping, "opposite No 7 Wapping Street by Hermitage Bridge" (Elmes).

Brownsons Court, Great Alie Street (Alie Street), Whitechapel, 1851.

Brunehild Street, Off Fairclough Street, St. George in the East, 1950.

Brunswick Arms Public House, 1. 78 Brunswick Street, Poplar, address also 78 Blackwall Way. 2. 3 Hooper Square, Whitechapel, 1874, Leman Street. 3. 237 Well Street, Hackney.

Brunswick Buildings, New Goulston Street, Whitechapel, 1891.

Brunswick Chapel & Sion Chapel, 192-194 Whitechapel Road, Whitechapel, 1883-1900, now site of the Whitechapel Mission Methodist Church.

Brunswick Hotel & Tavern, Brunswick Pier (Jamestown Way), Poplar, 1851, Blackwall Railway Terminus.

Brunswick Place, Back Church Lane, St. George in the East, 1851, north end and west side of Back Church Lane.

Brunswick Place, 1. Caroline Street, Ratcliffe, 1891, Caroline Street to Dorset Street, immediately south of railway line. 2. Four Mills Street (St.

Leonards Street), Bromley and Bow, 1851. 3. Hackney Road, Bethnal Green, 1860, immediately west of Caroline Street. 4. Mile End Road, Mile End, just west of Cleveland Way, renamed Bardsey Place. 5. Stevens Acre (Brunswick Street), Poplar, 1891, Brunswick Street, later Blackwall Way.

Brunswick Road, Off Well Street, Hackney, renamed Cressett Street.

Brunswick Road Board School, 299-301 East India Dock Road, Poplar, 1875, formerly a ragged school, renamed Day Industrial School in 1899.

Brunswick Square, Brunswick Street (Haggerston Road), Hackney, 1827, east of Hows Street.

Brunswick Street, 1. Off Fairclough Street, St. George in the East, renamed Brunehild Street. 2., Off Hackney Road, Bethnal Green, became the southern half of Haggerston Road later renamed Thurtle Road. 3. Off Poplar High Street, Poplar, 1851, Poplar High Street to Blackwall Stairs, renamed Blackwall Way. 4. Off Well Street, Hackney, 1841, renamed Cresset Road.

Brunswick Tavern Public House, Brunswick Wharf (Jamestown Way), Poplar, renamed Brunswick Buildings.

Brunswick Terrace, 1. Brunswick Street, Poplar, 1851. 2. Well Street, Hackney, 1841.

Brunswick Wesleyan Methodist Chapel, Three Colt Street, Limehouse, 1819-1965, opposite corner with Newell Street.

Bruntons Cottages & Factory, Brunton Place, Limehouse, 1851, Commercial Road.

Brush Court, Upper East Smithfield, East Smithfield, "at 60 the third on the right about sixteen doors east from Tower Hill" (Lockie).

Brushwood Street, Off Uamvar Street, Poplar, opposite Yattan Street.

Bryant House, Whiston Road, Bethnal Green, 1950, corner of Shaps Street.

Bryce Street, Stepney, renamed Senrab Street.

Buccaneer Public House, West India Dock Road, Limehouse, former Blue Posts Public House.

Buckeridge Street, Off Longnor Road, Mile End, 1950.

Buckingham Terrace, Bonner Road, Bethnal Green.

Buckle Street, Off Red Lion Street (Leman Street), Whitechapel, 1746.

Buckle Street Buildings, Leman Street, Whitechapel.

Bucks Head Public House, 26 Chilton Street, Bethnal Green.

Bucks Row, Thomas Street (Fulbourne Street), Whitechapel, 1891, later part of Durward Street.

Builders Arms Public House, 1. 162 Grundy Street, Poplar, corner of present-day Lodore Street and Brownfield Street. 2. 424 Old Ford Road, Bromley and Bow. 3. 99 Stebondale Street, Isle of Dogs.

Bull Alley, George Yard (Gunthorpe Street), Whitechapel.

Bull Court, 1. Nightingale Lane (Thomas More Street), Wapping, "the first on the left from Ropemakers Fields towards the New Cut" (Lockie), Brightlingsea Place is on the site. 2. Sandys Row, Spitalfields, 1891, east of Sandys Row, and north of Wentworth St. 3. Whitechapel High Street, Whitechapel, "the first west from Osborn Street nearly opposite the church" (Lockie).

Bull or Beast Lane, Stepney High Street, Stepney, "on the west side of the church and least towards Whitechapel" (Elmes), renamed Spring Garden Place, now the easternmost section of Stepney Way.

Bull Stake Court, Whitechapel High Street, Whitechapel, 1851, just east of Red Lion Street.

Bullivants Wharf, Westferry Road, Isle of Dogs, 1895, opposite Havannah Street.

Bulls Head Public House, 1. 31 Ben Jonson Road, Mile End. 2. 1 New Market Street (Wapping Lane), Wapping, address also 84 Old Gravel Lane. 3. 1 Shadwell High Street (The Highway), Shadwell. 4. 58 St. Katharines Way, East Smithfield. 5. 13 Well Street (Hanbury Street), Spitalfields, 1874, address also 103 Hanbury Street. 6. 148 Whitechapel High Street, Whitechapel.

Bully Rag Row, Green Street (Roman Road), Bethnal Green, "is about $^1/_8$ of a mile east from the green, at the back of the corner formed by Green Street and Globe Street" (Lockie).

Bulwery House, Woodseer Street, Whitechapel, 1950.

Bunch of Grapes Public House, 69 St. George Street (The Highway), St. George in the East, 1874, aka United States Public House.

Bunches Alley, Thrawl Street, Spitalfields, "at 22 the first on the right from 208 Brick Lane about $^1/_5$ of a mile north from Whitechapel Church" (Lockie).

Burdett Dormitory (Barnados), 317 Burdett Road, Limehouse, close to corner of Dod Street.

Burdett Road Congregational Chapel, Burdett Road, Bromley and Bow, 1855-1939.

Burdett Road Railway Station, Burdett Road, Bromley and Bow, 1871-1941.

Burdett Street, Off Devons Road, Bromley and Bow, 1891, renamed Purdy Street.

Burdett Terrace, Burdett Road, Limehouse, 1871.

Burford House, Lyme Grove, Hackney, 1891, Mare Street.

Burford Lane, Mare Street, Hackney, 1851.

Burfords Court & Terrace, East India Dock Road, Poplar, 1890, corner of Robin Hood Lane.

Burgin Terrace, Grove Road, Bromley and Bow.

Burgoyne Road, Off Conyer Street, Bromley and Bow, 1891.

Burlington Place, Broad Street (The Highway), Ratcliffe, 1851, east of Collingwood Street.

Burlington Terrace, Sewardstone Road, Bethnal Green, 1895.

Burmans Row, Green Street (Roman Road), Bethnal Green, "is part of the south side of the Green and nearly opposite Chester Place" (Elmes).

Burn Street, Off Henry Street (Carr Street), Stepney, 1851, renamed Dupont Street.

Burnham Square, Globe Road, Bethnal Green, 1851.

Burnside Row, Bow Park, Bromley and Bow, Bow Park is on site.

Burnside Street, Off Grove Road, Bromley and Bow, 1891, Mile End Park is on site.

Buross Street, Off Commercial Road, St. George in the East, 1950, Commercial Road to Mariner Street.

Buross Street Synagogue, 47A Buross Street, St. George in the East, 1950, Commercial Road.

Burr Street, Off East Smithfield (St. Katharine Dock), East Smithfield, "is near ¼ of a mile east from the Tower extending from St. Catherines by Goodwins brewery to Nightingale Lane about $^1/_5$ of a mile in length" (Lockie), St. Katharine Dock is on the site.

Burton Ale House, 202 Brick Lane, Spitalfields.

Burton Buildings, Back Lane (Cable Street), Shadwell, "at the north end of Mercers Row" (Elmes).

Burtons Entry, White Horse Street (White Horse Road), Stepney, 1895, just south of Troon Street.

Bushell(s) Rents, Great Hermitage Street (Hermitage Wall), Wapping, "at 7 the second on the left below the Hermitage Bridge leading to Great Hermitage Street" (Lockie). Later Bushell Street.

Buss Yard, Green Street (Roman Road), Bethnal Green.

Busy Bee Public House, 22 Ben Jonson Road, Mile End.

Butcher Row, Lower East Smithfield (St. Katharines Way), East Smithfield, 1746, south to Red Cross Street, St. Katharine Dock is on its site.

Butchers Arms Public House, 4 South Street (Brushfield Street), Spitalfields.

Butler Street, Spitalfields, 1891, renamed Brune Street.

Butlers Arms Public House, 1. 19 Knottisford Street, Bethnal Green. 2. 414 Old Ford Road, Bromley and Bow.

Butlers Buildings, 1. George Street (Code Street), Whitechapel, "the first on the right north from Spicer Street near 82 Brick Lane" (Lockie), immediately east of Code Street. 2. Rosemary Lane (Royal Mint Street), "East Smithfield, leading into Cartwright Square and Rosemary Lane" (Lockie).

Buttress Gardens, Underwood Road, Whitechapel, 1891, opposite Buttress Street, Osmani primary school is on the site.

Buttress Street, Off Buxton Street, Whitechapel, 1891, west end of Buxton Street, south to Underwood Street.

Butts Lane, Poplar High Street, Poplar, occasional name for Dingles Lane.

Byce Court, Blue Anchor Yard (Royal Mint Street), East Smithfield, "the third on the right from 48 Rosemary Lane towards Upper East Smithfield" (Lockie).

Byde Street, Off Anchor Street (Boundary Street), Bethnal Green, "the north side of Anchor Street extending from Swan Yard to Club Row" (Lockie).

Bygrove Cottages, Upper North Street, Poplar, 1891.

Byng Street, Off Torrington Street (Kennet Street), Wapping, 1790, London Docks Western Dock was built on the site.

Byron Cottages, Bloomfield Street (Freshfield Avenue), Hackney, 1851.

Byrons Head Public House, 17 Railway Street (Hay Currie Street), Poplar.

C

Cadell Street, Off Hackney Road, Bethnal Green, 1891, Cadell Close is close to route.

Cadiz Street, Off White Horse Lane, Mile End, 1950, south of and parallel with Shandy Street.

Caesar Street, Off Kingsland Road, Hackney, 1950, rear of corner with Cremer Street.

Cains Court & Place, Church Lane (Back Church Lane), St. George in the East, "about six doors from 65 Cable Street Wellclose Square" (Lockie).

Calcutta Place or Terrace, East India Dock Road, Poplar, 1851, opposite Robin Hood Lane.

Calcutta Street, Off Farrance Street, Limehouse, renamed Silver Street.

Caledonia Arms Public House, Fairfield Road, Bromley and Bow, 1851.

Caledonia Place, Kerbey Street, Poplar, 1851.

Caledonian Arms Public House, 62 Fairfield Road, Bromley and Bow.

Caledonian Terrace, Jeremiah Street, Poplar, 1891.

Caledonian Wharf, Saunders Ness Road, Isle of Dogs, 1950, present-day street, also named Caledonian Wharf, is on its site.

Calverley Street & Walk, Mile End Road, Mile End, 1895, opposite Mile End Place.

Calvert Street, Off Old Gravel Lane (Wapping Lane), Wapping, 1891, renamed Watts Street.

Cambridge Arms Public House, 23 St. Peter Street (St. Peter Square), Bethnal Green.

Cambridge Buildings, Darling Row, Whitechapel, 1891.

Cambridge Castle Public House, 3 Essex Street (Blythe Street), Bethnal Green.

Cambridge Circus, Hackney Road, Bethnal Green, 1891.

Cambridge Heath, Cambridge Road (Cambridge Heath Road), Bethnal Green, 1827, south of Mare Street.

Cambridge Heath Brewery, Hackney Road, Bethnal Green, 1841, later Wiltshire Brewery.

Cambridge Lodge Villas, Mare Street, Hackney, 1891.

Cambridge Mansions, Key Street (Cambridge Heath Road), Mile End, 1950, Cambridge Heath Road.

Cambridge Place, 1. Hackney Road, Bethnal Green, 1860, opposite London Street. 2. Middleton Road, Hackney, 1868.

Cambridge Road, Bethnal Green, renamed Cambridge Heath Road.

Cambridge Stores Public House, 116 Tredegar Road, Bromley and Bow.

Cambridge Street, Off Grove Street (Ellsworth Street), Bethnal Green, 1860, heading south towards but not meeting Bethnal Green Road.

Cambridge Terrace, 1. Broke Road (Broke Walk), Hackney, 1862. 2. Cambridge Road (Cambridge Heath Road), Bethnal Green, 1827, north of its corner with North Road. 3. Middleton Road, Hackney, 1851.

Camden Cottages, Bethnal Green Road, Bethnal Green.

Camden Passage, Jersey Street, Bethnal Green.

Camden Street, Off Bethnal Green Road, Bethnal Green, 1841, renamed Ellsworth Street.

Camden(s) Place or Row, Bethnal Green Road, Bethnal Green, 1827, either side of Wilmot Street.

Camdens Garden, Bethnal Green Road, Bethnal Green, 1827, immediately east of Wilmot Street Corfield Street is on the site.

Camdens Head Public House, 456 Bethnal Green Road, Bethnal Green.

Camdens Head Public House, 19 Church Lane (Ropemakers Fields), Limehouse, address also 52 Church Row.

Camel Public House, 277 Globe Road, Bethnal Green.

Camel Row, Mile End Road, Mile End, 1746, Opposite and west of Stepney Green.

Cameron Place, Nelson Street, Whitechapel, 1891.

Canal Lock Houses, Old Ford Road, Bromley and Bow, 1851.

Canal Place, Mile End Road, Mile End, "near the Regents Canal Bridge in the Mile End Road" (Elmes).

Canal Road, Off Solebay Street, Bromley and Bow, 1891, immediately east of canal bridge south to Rhodeswell Road near Victory Bridge Mile End Park and Leisure Centre are on the site.

Canal Row, Manchester Road, Isle of Dogs, 1891, later part of Glen Terrace Manchester Road.

Canal Side, Andrews Road, Hackney, 1891, The Broadway to Mare Street.

Canal Villa, 412 Manchester Road, Isle of Dogs, 1876.

Cannings Head Public House, 63 Sidney Street, Whitechapel, 1874.

Cannon Place, Whitechapel Road Whitechapel, "the first on the left from the turnpike towards London, leading into Mile End Grove" (Lockie), renamed Maples Place.

Cannon Public House, 33 Cannon Street Road, St. George in the East.

Cannon Street, The Highway, St. George in the East, 1800, original name of the section of Cannon Street Road between Cable Street and The Highway. Later connected to Commercial Road by New Road.

Cannon Street New Road, Cable Street, The Highway, early alternative name for Cannon Street Road.

Canterbury Court, Phoenix Street (Brick Lane), Spitalfields, "at No 53 Phoenix Street" (Elmes).

Canterbury Place, Westferry Road, Isle of Dogs, 1868, opposite Tooke Street.

Canton Buildings, Canton Street, Limehouse, 1860, Canton Street to Gough Street.

Canton Cottage, 52 East India Dock Road, Limehouse, 1856, corner of Birchfield Street later National Westminster Bank.

Canton House, 47–49 East India Dock Road, Limehouse, rebuilt in 1863 as the Stainsby Tavern.

Canton Place, East India Dock Road, Limehouse, "forms part of the north side of it opposite Pennyfields near ¼ of a mile on the left east from Limehouse Church towards Blackwall" (Lockie).

Canton Villa, Stainsby Road, Limehouse, 1851.

Cape of Good Hope Public House, 787 Commercial Road, Limehouse, at the corner with St. Annes Street.

Capel Terrace, Bromley and Bow, renamed Tredegar Terrace.

Captain Cook Public House, 45 Umberston Street, St. George in the East.

Captain Cooks Almshouses, Mile End Road, Mile End, "about $2^1/_8$ miles on the left from Aldgate Pump opposite York Place" (Lockie), opposite Burdett Road on the corner of Grove Road.

Captain Cooks Passage, James Street (Burslem Street), St. George in the East, "is in Patriot Street, James Street" (Elmes).

Captain Man-of-War Public House, 324 Poplar High Street, Poplar.

Carlisle Street, Off Dunbridge Street, Bethnal Green, renamed Stonehouse Street.

Carlisle Tavern Public House, 26 Musty Grove, Bromley and Bow.

Carlisle Terrace, Fairfield Road, Bromley and Bow, 1851.

Carlton Arms Public House, 238 Devonshire Street (Bancroft Road), Mile End.

Carlton Place, Cudworth Street, Whitechapel, 1891, renamed Caslon Place.

Carlton Road, Off Devonshire Street (Bancroft Road), Mile End, 1891, Portlet Road follows some of its path.

Caroline Court or Place, Hunt Street (Hunton Street), Whitechapel, 1851.

Caroline Place, 1. Carr Street, Limehouse, renamed Carr Place. 2. Wells Street (Cotton Street), Poplar, 1851.

Caroline Square, Four Mills Street (St. Leonards Street), Bromley and Bow, 1851.

Caroline Street, renamed Cadell Street (Cadell Close), Bethnal Green.

Caroline Terrace, Dalston Lane, Hackney, 1868, opposite Holly Street.

Carpenters Arms Public House, 1. 94 Ben Jonson Road, Mile End. 2. 151 Cambridge Road (Cambridge Heath Road), Whitechapel. 3. 38 Grenade Street, Limehouse. 4. 73 Hare Street (Cheshire Street), Whitechapel. 5. 121 Kingsland

Road, Hackney, 1874. 6. 5 Mape Street, Bethnal Green. 7. 51 Pritchards Road, Bethnal Green. 8. 169 St. Leonards Road, Poplar, aka Victory. 9. 57 Wentworth Street, Spitalfields, address also 103 Wentworth Street.

Carron Wharf, St. Katharines Way, East Smithfield, 1950, west of corner with Thomas More Street.

Carrons Buildings, Suffolk Street (Walden Street), Whitechapel, 1891, now part of Coventry Street.

Carrs Almshouses, Sun Tavern Row (Juniper Street), Shadwell, 1871.

Carter Street, 1. Off Chrisp Street, Poplar, 1891, now part of Carmen Street. 2. Bromley and Bow, renamed Treby Street. 3. Of Weaver Street, Whitechapel, 1860, between Weaver Street and Selby Street, a railway shed was built on the site.

Carters Rents, Spital Street, Spitalfields, 1851, connected Spital Street to Carter Street.

Carters Terrace, Jeremiah Street, Poplar, 1891, East India Dock Road.

Cartwright Square, Royal Mint Street, East Smithfield, 1851.

Cartys Free House, 68 Poplar High Street, Poplar, former Green Man.

Cassland Hotel & Public House, 295 Victoria Park Road, Hackney, 1874.

Castalia Street, Off East Ferry Road, Isle of Dogs, 1891, now part of Castalia Square.

Casterton Arms Public House, 43 Casterton Street, Hackney, Wilton Way.

Casterton Terrace, Pigwell Path (Wilton Way), Hackney, 1891.

Castle Alley, Whitechapel High Street, Whitechapel, 1851, renamed Old Castle Street.

Castle Lane, Whitechapel Road, Whitechapel, "at 124 about three quarters of a mile on the left below Aldgate Pump leading to Old Castle Street and Wentworth Street" (Lockie).

Castle Place, New Castle Street (Tyne Street), Whitechapel, "the first on the right from 120 Whitechapel leading to Old Castle Street and Wentworth Street" (Lockie).

Castle Public House, 1. 44 Commercial Road, Whitechapel. 2. Little Alie Street (Alie Street), Whitechapel, 1874. 3. 19 Quaker Street, Spitalfields, 1874.

Castle Street, 1. Off Cock Lane (Boundary Street), Bethnal Green, "extends from Cock Lane behind Shoreditch Church to Gascoigne Place it is continued by Virginia Row to Bird cage walk and Hackney Road" (Lockie), renamed Epworth

Street. 2. Off Whitechapel High Street, Whitechapel, 1891.

Castor Place, Commercial Road, Limehouse, "in the Commercial Road near Pennyfields" (Elmes).

Castor Street, Off Birchfield Street, Limehouse, 1950, close to West India Dock Road.

Cat & Mutton Bridge, Pritchards Road, Bethnal Green.

Cat & Mutton Public House, 76 Broadway Market, Hackney.

Catherine or Katharine Wheel Public House, 50 St. Peters Road (Cephas Avenue), Mile End, 1874.

Catherine Place, 1. Bird Cage Walk (Columbia Road), Bethnal Green, 1851, at the corner of Catherine Street. 2. Henry Street (Carr Street), Stepney, 1851, became part of Dupont Street. 3. Wells Street (Cotton Street), Poplar, 1851.

Catherine Rents, Back Road (Cable Street), St. George in the East, 1851.

Catherine Street, 1. Off Commercial Road, St. George in the East, "the third on the right east from Cannon Street New Road extending to Lower Chapman Street" (Lockie), became the northern part of Anthony Street. 2. Off Durham Street (Teesdale Street), Bethnal Green, 1841, renamed Winkley Street. 3. Off East India Dock Road, Poplar, 1851, renamed Ida Street. 4. Off Hackney Road,

Bethnal Green, 1827, renamed Caroline Street (1862) and then Cadell Street. 5. Off Old Road (Maroon Street), Limehouse, 1851, renamed Maroon Street.

Catherine Terrace, 1. Catherine Street (Anthony Street), St. George in the East, 1851. 2. Fairfield Road, Bromley and Bow, 1851. 3. Henry Street (Carr Street), Stepney, 1851. 4. Wentworth Street, Whitechapel, 1891. 5. Westferry Road, Isle of Dogs, 1851, corner of Westferry Road and Cahir Street.

Catherine Wheel Public House, 1. 3 Essex Street (Commercial Street), Spitalfields. 2. 50 St. Peters Road (Cephas Avenue), Mile End, aka Katharine Wheel, address also 50 Cephas Avenue.

Cathcart Villas, Malvern Road, Hackney, 1868, between Grange Road and Shrubland Grove.

Catholic & National School, Spicer Street (Buxton Street), Whitechapel, 1851.

Causeway Court, Stepney Causeway, Ratcliffe, 1891.

Cawdor Street, Off St. Leonards Road, Poplar, 1891.

Cawley Road, Off Wetherell Road, Hackney, 1891.

Caxton Public House, 50 The Highway, St. George in the East, aka St. George's Tavern, aka Artichoke.

Caxton Street & Cottage, Addington Road, Bromley and

Bow, 1891, renamed Caxton Grove.

Cayley Street, Off White Horse Street (White Horse Road), Stepney, 1891.

Cayman House, Limehouse Causeway, Limehouse, St. Vincent Estate.

Cecil Street, Off Mile End Road, Mile End, 1891, opposite Vintners Almshouses.

Central Foundation School for Girls, Spital Square, Spitalfields.

Chad Street, Off Wrights Road, Bethnal Green, renamed Beale Road.

Chalk Stone Stairs, Cuba Street, Isle of Dogs, 1860, river end of Cuba Street, site of later West India Dock Pier.

Challis Court, John Street (Cannon Street Road), Stepney, John Street was immediately north west of railway line.

Chamber Court, Chamber Street, Whitechapel, 1851.

Chambers Square, Upper East Smithfield, East Smithfield, "at 95 nearly opposite the London Dock" (Lockie).

Champion Public House, 1. 61 Ben Jonson Road, Mile End. 2. 13 Weymouth Terrace, Bethnal Green, 1874, Hackney Road.

Chancellor Court, Church Street (Bethnal Green Road), Bethnal Green, "at 191 the first on the right a few doors from 65 Shoreditch" (Lockie).

Chancery Court, Walburgh Street, St. George in the East, "the corner of Upper Chapman Street" (Elmes).

Chancery Place, Lowood Street, Shadwell, 1851.

Chandlers Court, Martha Street (Wadeson Street), Hackney.

Chapel Court, Mill Yard, Whitechapel, 1851.

Chapel Court or Place, Holloway Street (Adler Street), Whitechapel, 1891.

Chapel House & Cottages, East Ferry Road, Isle of Dogs, 1851.

Chapel House Place, Chapel House Street, Isle of Dogs, originally a side road of Chapel House Street, renamed Julian Place.

Chapel Place, 1. Holloway Street (Adler Street), Whitechapel, 1912, renamed Synagogue Place. 2. Chapel Place, Victoria Street (Dellow Street), Shadwell, 1851.

Chapel Street, 1. Off Great Garden Street (Greatorex Street), Whitechapel, "the first on the right in Great Garden Street from 50 Whitechapel Road it is continued by Princes Row to Bakers Row" (Lockie). 2. Off Queen Street (Dorset Estate), Bethnal Green, renamed Arline Terrace. 3. Off Spital Square, Spitalfields, "the second on the left in the said square from 104 Bishopsgate Without" (Lockie). 4. Off Walbridge Street, St.

George in the East, "is parallel to and between Upper and Lower Chapman Streets, extending from Walbridge Street to Mary Street", (Lockie), renamed Tait Street. 5. Off Wheler Street, Spitalfields, 1891, behind St. Marys Church, renamed Drant St.

Chapel Yard, 1. Coopers Gardens (Hackney Road), Bethnal Green, 1851. 2. Cambridge Heath Road, Stepney, renamed Kerwin Place.

Chapman Arms Public House, 25 Lower Chapman Street (Bigland Street), St. George in the East.

Chapman Place, 1. Chapman Street, St. George in the East, "the third on the left from Cannon Street Road between Anthony Street and Ann Street leading in to Chapel Street" (Lockie). 2. Chrisp Street, Poplar, 1851.

Chapman Road, Off White Post Lane, Hackney, 1891.

Chapman(s) Gardens, Pritchards Road, Bethnal Green, 1841.

Charles Court, 1. Ann Street (East India Dock Road), Poplar, 1891. 2. Charles Street (Wapping Lane), Wapping, "the first on the left from 44 Old Gravel Lane" (Lockie). 3. Coke Street, Whitechapel, 1891. 4. King Street, Bethnal Green, 1851.

Charles Court or Terrace, Mace Street, Bethnal Green, 1891.

Charles Place, 1. Bethnal Green Road, Bethnal Green, "the northwest corner of Thorold Square about $3/8$ of a mile on the left from 65 Shoreditch" (Lockie). 2. East India Dock Road, Poplar, 1851. 3. Shadwell, renamed Glamis Place.

Charles Square, Bethnal Green, became part of Canrobert Street.

Charles Street, Stepney, renamed Aylward Street.

Charles Street, 1. Off "Back Road (Cable Street), St. George in the East, is about $1/6$ of a mile on the left east from Cannon Street turnpike nearly opposite the Bluegate Fields, leading to Albion Street and the Commercial Road" (Lockie), later part of Watney Street. 2. Whitechapel, "the north continuation of Bakers Row from 94 Whitechapel Road" (Lockie) later part of Vallance Road. 3. Off Bethnal Green Road, Bethnal Green, "about $3/4$ of a mile on the right from 65 Shoreditch opposite Wilmot Square" (Lockie), renamed Canrobert Street. 4. Off Chrisp Street, Poplar, 1891, renamed Scurr Street. 5. Off Dalston Lane, Hackney, 1841, renamed Martel Place. 6. Off Greenfield Street (Greenfield Road), Whitechapel, 1891, renamed Coke Street. 7. Isle of Dogs, renamed Malabar

Street. 8. Off Old Bethnal Green Road, Bethnal Green, 1841, renamed Hassard Street. 9. Off Old Gravel Lane (Wapping Lane), Wapping, 1891, now part of Raine Street. 10. Off Pedley Street, Whitechapel, renamed Bratley Street. 11. Bethnal Green, renamed Tuscan Street (Butler Street). 12. Off West Street (Malcolm Road), Mile End, West Street to James Street, became part of Sceptre Road. 13. Off Whiston Road, Bethnal Green, 1827, became part of Whiston Estate.

Charles Terrace, 1. Bishops Road (Bishops Way), Bethnal Green. 2. Mace Street, Bethnal Green, Cranbrook Estate is on the site. 3. Stewart Street, Isle of Dogs. 4. Tredegar Road, Bromley and Bow.

Charleton House, Twine Court, Shadwell, 1891, Cable Street.

Charlie Browns, West India Dock Road, Limehouse, informal but most used name for the Railway Tavern Public House, West India Dock Road, corner of Garford Street.

Charlies Bar, 124 Globe Road, Mile End, aka Prince of Wales.

Charlotte Buildings, Court & Street, Off Turville Street, Bethnal Green, 1891.

Charlotte Cottage, Grundy Street, Poplar, 1851.

Charlotte Court, 1. Black Lion Yard (Old Montague Street), Whitechapel, 1829. 2. Charlotte Street (Fieldgate Street), Whitechapel, 1851.

Charlotte de Rothschild Dwellings, Thrawl Street, Spitalfields, 1950.

Charlotte Place, Buxton Street, Whitechapel, 1891, became the westernmost part of Underwood Road.

Charlotte Street, 1. Off Globe Street (Globe Road), Mile End, 1851. 2. Off Great Hermitage Street (Hermitage Wall), Wapping, "at the west end of Great Hermitage Street by the dock leading towards Nightingale Lane" (Lockie). 3. Off Hope Town (Bethnal Green Road), Bethnal Green, 1841. 4. Off New Road, Whitechapel, 1895, now the eastern half of Fieldgate Street. 5. Off Union Street (Turin Street), Bethnal Green, 1891, renamed Helston Street.

Charrington Brewery Public House, Mile End Road, Mile End.

Charrington Row, George Gardens (Bethnal Green Road), Bethnal Green, "is behind the George Public House on the north from east side of Wilmot Square" (Lockie).

Charringtons Wharf, The Highway, Shadwell, 1950, east of Shadwell Park.

Chaurgur Row, Back Road (Cable Street), St. George in the

East, 1860, north side of Back Road, opposite the Wesleyan Chapel.

Chechanover Synagogue, 26 Old Montague Street, Whitechapel, more commonly spelled Tchechenover.

Cheesemans Court, George Street (Code Street), Whitechapel, "about six doors on the right from Carter Street 68 Brick Lane" (Lockie).

Chequers & Greenland Fishery Public House, 36 Wapping Wall, Wapping, aka Chequers.

Chequers Public House, 1. Limehouse Hole (Three Colt Street), Limehouse, 1770, renamed Horns and Chequers. 2. 36 Wapping Wall, Wapping, aka Chequers & Greenland Fishery.

Cherry Place, Redmans Road, Mile End, 1891, diagonally opposite Hannibal Road.

Cherry Tree Inn Public House, Bow Lane (Brunswick Road), Poplar, 1851, address also 321 Brunswick Road.

Cherry Tree Passage, Back Church Lane, St. George in the East, 1851, north end and west side of Back Church Lane.

Cherry Tree Public House, 1, 111 Back Church Lane, St. George in the East. 2. 321 Brunswick Road, Poplar. 3. 17 Green Bank, Wapping, aka Kings Arms. 4. 64 Kingsland Road, Hackney, 1874.

Cherubim Court, Glasshouse Street (John Fisher Street), East Smithfield, 1851.

Cheshire Buildings, 99-101 Cheshire Street, Whitechapel, 1950, rear of 99-101 Cheshire Street.

Chester Arms Public House, 35 Green Street (Roman Road), Bethnal Green.

Chester Place, Green Street (Roman Road), Bethnal Green, Green Street "the first Row on the left from the east side of the green leading to Green Street and the Rising Sun" (Lockie), Burnham Estate is on the site.

Chester Street, Bethnal Green, renamed Burnham Street.

Chestnut Walk, Green Street (Roman Road), Bethnal Green, renamed Cranbrook Road.

Cheves Court, Nightingale Lane (Thomas More Street), Wapping, "the first on the right in it from Rope makers fields towards the New Cut" (Lockie).

Chevra Bikkur Cholim Synagogue, Fashion Street, Spitalfields, 1858.

Chevra Mikrah Synagogue, New Court (Fashion Street), Spitalfields.

Chicksand Place, Chicksand Street, Whitechapel, 1851.

Chigwell Street, Off St. George Street (The Highway), St. George in the East, mostly lost to construction of London Docks, remaining section renamed Chigwell Hill.

Chilcot Street, Off Kerbey Street, Poplar, 1891.

Childe Harold Public House, 20 Railway Street (Hay Currie Street), Poplar, 1874.

Chimes Public House, 21 Woollett Street (Vesey Path), Poplar.

China Ship Public House, 4 Little Hermitage Street (Orton Street), Wapping, 1874.

Chinnocks Wharf, Narrow Street, Limehouse, 1950, west of Regent's Canal entrance.

Chivers Court, Nightingale Lane (Thomas More Street), Wapping, 1851.

Christ Church, Jamaica Street, Stepney, 1877-1940, corner of Smith Street.

Christ Church National School, Billson Street, Isle of Dogs, 1895.

Christ Church Rectory, 2 Fournier Street, Spitalfields.

Christ Church School, Watney Street, Shadwell, 1868, near corner with Upper Chapman Street.

Christian Buildings or Dwellings, Devons Road, Bromley and Bow, 1891.

Christian Place, Christian Street, St. George in the East, 1950, became part of Burslem Street.

Christian Street School, Christian Street, St. George in the East.

Christopher Court, Lambeth Street (Alie Street), Whitechapel, 1851.

Christopher Street, Off Sherwood Place, Bethnal Green, 1891.

Christophers Court, Cartwright Street (Royal Mint Street), East Smithfield, 1746.

Church Avenue, Brickfield Road, Bromley and Bow, 1891.

Church Court, High Street (Wapping High Street), Wapping, parallel with and immediately east of Church Street, renamed Amos Court.

Church Lane, 1. Church Row (Newell Street), Limehouse, at the railway line near Ropemakers Fields, later became part of Church Row. 2. From St. Marys Church, Whitechapel Road to Cable Street, following path of present day White Church Lane, a small section of Commercial Road, and Back Church Lane. 1740.

Church Lodge, Row & Yard, Church Street (Mare Street), Hackney, 1841.

Church Passage, 1. Charles Street (Aylward Street), Stepney, 1862, Charles Street to Spring Garden Place, became part of Charles Street. 2. Commercial Road, Limehouse, 1912, renamed Charles Street, renamed Scurr

Street. 3. White Lion Street (Folgate Street), Spitalfields, 1891, renamed Nantes Passage.

Church Path, 1. Morant Street, Limehouse, 1890, to south end of Oriental Street. 2. The Grove (Reading Lane), Hackney, 1895, The Grove to Richmond Road, renamed Hackney Grove. 3. Hackney, renamed Church Crescent.

Church Road, 1. Off Commercial Road, Stepney, 1868, opposite Stepney Causeway to St. Dunstans Church, Old Church Road follows some of its route. 2. Shadwell, renamed Sutton Street.

Church Row, 1. Bromley High Street, Bromley and Bow, 1851. 2. Church Street (Bethnal Green Road), Bethnal Green, "at 106 by the turnpike about ½ a mile on the right from 65 Shoreditch leading to 41 Hare Street about 1/7 of a mile in length" (Lockie), renamed St. Matthews Row. 3. Limehouse, renamed Newell Street. 4. Spring Garden Place (Durham Row), Stepney, "Stepney Church Yard, is about six houses at the north-east corner of it - there are a few houses on the west side of the church Yard from Spring Garden Place towards the green also called by the same name" (Lockie), renamed Durham Row.

Church Street, 1. Off Bakers Row (Vallance Road), Whitechapel, became eastern end of Hanbury Street. 2. Bethnal Green, 1851, became the westernmost section of Bethnal Green Road. 3. Off Brick Lane (Fournier Street), Spitalfields, "opposite 41 Brick Lane the fifth on the left from 74 Whitechapel is continued by Paternoster Row and Union Street to 69 Bishopsgate Without" (Lockie), Brick Lane to Commercial Street later Fournier Street. 4. Off Greatorex Street (Hanbury Street), Whitechapel, now Hanbury Street from Greatorex Street to Vallance Road. 5. Off Grundy Street, Poplar, 1891, renamed Lindale Street. 6. Off Manchester Road, Isle of Dogs, renamed Newcastle Street and now Glengarnock Avenue. 7. Hackney, now part of Mare Street. 8. Off Wapping High Street, Wapping, renamed Scandrett Street.

Church Terrace, Bonner Road, Bethnal Green.

Church Yard, Church Row (Bethnal Green Road), Bethnal Green, 1851.

Churchyard Alley, Rosemary Lane (Royal Mint Street), East Smithfield, 1746.

City Arms Public House, 1. 134 Devons Road, Bromley and Bow, 1874. 2. 6 Rose Lane (Ratcliffe Lane), Ratcliffe. 3. 1 Westferry Road, Isle of Dogs, 1874, formerly the City Arms and Canal Tavern later City Pride.

City Canal, Westferry Road, Isle of Dogs, ship canal built across the Isle of Dogs between 1800 and 1805 Absorbed into West India South Dock.

City of Canterbury Public House, 113 Hanbury Street, Spitalfields.

City of Canton Public House, 4 Upper North Street, Poplar, 1874.

City of Carlisle, 61 Royal Mint Street, East Smithfield, 1874, aka Blue Peter.

City of London Workhouse, 2A Bow Road, Bromley and Bow, site of later St. Clements Hospital.

City of Norwich Public House, 111 Wentworth Street, Spitalfields, 1874.

City of Paris Public House, 178 Old Ford Road, Bromley and Bow, 1874.

City of Quebec Public House, 70 Wapping Wall, Wapping.

Clare Hall Public House, 269 Stepney Way, Mile End, aka Pride of Stepney, corner of Diggon Street.

Claremont Cottages & Terrace, Durham Street (Teesdale Street), Bethnal Green, 1851.

Claremont Place, Redmans Road, Mile End, 1891, renamed Cherry Place.

Claremont Place or Square, New Gravel Lane (Garnet Street), Wapping, 1851.

Claremont Street, Off Durham Street (Teesdale Street), Bethnal Green, 1851, renamed Claredale Street.

Claremont Terrace, Alpha Road (Alpha Grove), Isle of Dogs, 1891.

Clarence Buildings, Hackney Road, Bethnal Green, 1851.

Clarence Cottages, Grundy Street, Poplar, 1851.

Clarence Place, 1. 128-134 East India Dock Road, Poplar, 1851. 2. Grafton Street (Grantley Street), Mile End, 1891, now part of Leatherdale Street. 3. Hackney Road, Bethnal Green, 1860, at its corner with Crab Tree Row (present-day Columbia Road). 4. Middleton Road, Hackney, 1851, between Mayfield Road and Holly Place.

Clarence Street, Off Anglesea Street (Fakruddin Street), Whitechapel, 1851, just west of Vallance Road, Fakruddin Street is partially on the site.

Clarence Terrace, Queensbridge Road, Hackney, 1895, renamed Denne Terrace.

Clarendon Arms Public House, 86 Balcorne Street, Hackney, 1874.

Clarendon Cottages, Poplar, 1912, renamed Denbigh Road.

Clarendon Place, Middleton Road, Hackney, 1851, between Mayfield Road and Holly Place.

Clarendon Public House, 119 Bow Road, Bromley and Bow, 1874.

Clarendon Terrace, Bow Road, Bromley and Bow, 1851.

Clarissa House, Clarissa Street, Hackney, 1950.

Clarks or Clarks Terrace, Cannon Street Road, St. George in the East, "is part of the east side of it, extending from the turnpike by Cannon Street to Mr Lindalls chapel" (Lockie).

Clarkes Place, 1. St. Stephens Road, Bromley and Bow, 1891. 2. Bromley and Bow, became part of St. Stephens Road.

Clay Corner, Turville Street, Bethnal Green, 1851.

Clay Hall Public House, 497 Old Ford Road, Bromley and Bow, 1874.

Clay Hall Road, Off Old Ford Road, Bromley and Bow, 1895, south of Blondin Street.

Claydons or Claydens Buildings, Salmon Lane, Limehouse, 1891.

Clayhall Place, Old Ford Road, Bromley and Bow, 1851.

Cleavers Rents, Great Ayliffe (Alie Street), Whitechapel, "at 29 the first on the left from Somerset Street Whitechapel" (Lockie).

Clerkason Street, Off Canrobert Street, Bethnal Green, 1860, early spelling of Clarkson Street.

Cleveland House, 211 East India Dock Road, Poplar.

Cleveland Street, Mile End, 1851, renamed Cleveland Way.

Cleveland Terrace, north end of East Ferry Road, Isle of Dogs, 1881.

Cleveland Villas, Albert Road (Albion Drive), Hackney, 1868, between Queens (now Queensbridge) Road and Malvern Road.

Clifford House, Wellclose Square, St. George in the East, 1915.

Clifton Cottages, Homerton Terrace, Hackney, 1891, Morning Lane.

Clifton House 44-45 Wellclose Square, St. George in the East, 1950.

Clifton Street, Off Cotall Street, Limehouse, 1890, Cotall Street to Hill Place Street, Bartlett Park is on the site.

Clifton Villas, Malvern Road, Hackney, 1868, between Shrubland Grove and Lavender Road.

Clifton Works, Old Ford Road, Bromley and Bow.

Clinton House, Pelham Street (Woodseer Street), Whitechapel, 1891.

Clive Street, Off Stepney Way, Mile End, 1950, north of Stepney

Way, between Apsley Street and Pole Street.

Clock House Public House, 140 Whitechapel High Street, Whitechapel, alternative name of Coach & Horses Public House.

Clyde Public House, 187 Commercial Road, Whitechapel.

Coach & Horses Public House, 1. 86 Back Church Lane, St. George in the East. 2. 259 Bow Road, Bromley and Bow. 3. 132 Chrisp Street, Poplar. 4. 129 Middlesex Street, Spitalfields, 1874. 5. 380 Mile End Road, Mile End, 1874. 6. 199 Shadwell High Street (The Highway), Shadwell, 1874, address also 335 The Highway. 7. 24 West India Dock Road, Limehouse. 8. 140 Whitechapel High Street, Whitechapel, 1874, also known as Clock House.

Coach House Yard, Love Lane (Brodlove Lane), Shadwell, 1851.

Coal Builders Arms Public House, 224 Rhodeswell Road, Limehouse.

Coal Meters or Coalmeters Arms Public House, 1. 62 Heath Street (Head Street), Stepney. 2. 46 Lower Shadwell (Shadwell Park), Shadwell.

Coal or Cole Stairs, Golds Hill (The Highway), Shadwell, 1746, "at the bottom of Golds Hill about two miles below London Bridge by the line of the river"

(Lockie), Shadwell Park is on the site.

Coat & Badge Public House, 10 Chrisp Street, Poplar.

Cobbold Road, renamed Suffolk Road (Pownall Road), Hackney, 1868.

Cobbs Court & Yard, Sandys Row, Spitalfields, 1891, east of Sandys Row, and north of Wentworth St, became part of Cobb Street.

Cobden Arms Public House, 28 Berger Road, Hackney.

Cobden Street, Off St. Leonards Road, Poplar, 1891, St. Leonards Road to Hay Curries Street.

Cobden(s) Head Public House, 189 St. Leonards Road, Poplar.

Cobleys Court, Essex Street (Commercial Street), Spitalfields, "the third on the left five doors from 107 Wentworth Street towards 105 Whitechapel it is nearly opposite Essex Court" (Lockie).

Cobleys Rents, Whitechapel Road, Whitechapel, "at the first turning northward of Cobleys Court" (Elmes).

Coborn Arms, 8 Coborn Road, Bromley and Bow.

Coborn New Road, Bromley and Bow, renamed St. Stephens Road.

Coborn Place, Bow Road, Bromley and Bow, 1851.

Coborn Road (former Old Ford) Railway Station, Coborn

Road, Bromley and Bow, 1865-1946, resited and renamed in 1883.

Coborn School, Fairfield Road, Bromley and Bow, 1851.

Coborn Terrace, Bow Road, Bromley and Bow, 1851.

Coburg Cottages, Grundy Street, Poplar, 1851.

Coburg Court, Bell Lane, Spitalfields, 1851.

Coburgh Court or Place, Cleveland Street (Cleveland Way), Mile End, 1891.

Cock & Castle Public House, 58 Mansford Street, Bethnal Green.

Cock & Hoop Public House, 1. 17 Artillery Street (Artillery Lane), Spitalfields, 1874. 2. 158 Hanbury Street, Spitalfields.

Cock & Key Public House, Old Montague Street, Whitechapel.

Cock & Lion Public House, 31 Lower East Smithfield (St. Katharines Way), East Smithfield, 1874.

Cock & Neptune Public House, 211 St. George Street (The Highway), St. George in the East.

Cock (or Cook) Hill, Love Lane (Brodlove Lane), Shadwell, from Brodlove Lane to Schoolhouse Lane, now part of the Highway.

Cock (or Old Cock) Lane, Bethnal Green, 1841, renamed Boundary Street.

Cock a Hoop Public House, 1 Gun Street, Spitalfields.

Cock Alley, 1. Cock Lane (Boundary Street), Bethnal Green, "at 75 the second on the right north from the turnpike leading into Cock Lane and Old Nichol Street" (Lockie). 2. Upper East Smithfield, East Smithfield, "is opposite 91 about $^1/_8$ of a mile on the left from Tower Hill leading to Cartwright Square" (Lockie).

Cock Hill, Anchor Street (Boundary Street), Bethnal Green, 1841, headed north from Anchor Street, path followed approximately by Boundary Street.

Cock Lane, Bethnal Green, 1841, also known as Old Cock Lane, renamed Boundary Street.

Cock Public House, 1. 3-5 Broad Street (The Highway), Ratcliffe, 1899, address also 433 The Highway, also 126 Cock Hill. 2. 315 Mare Street, Hackney, 1874. 3. 45 Whitechapel High Street, Whitechapel, 1874.

Coes Terrace, Chisenhale Road, Bromley and Bow.

Cohens Buildings, became part of Seven Stars Court (Royal Mint Street), Whitechapel.

Cohens Court, Baker Street (Damien Street), Mile End, 1891.

Colborn Place, Victoria Street (Dellow Street), Shadwell, 1851.

Colchester Street, Off Red Lion Street (Leman Street), Whitechapel, "at 29 about eight doors on the left from 32 Whitechapel High Street leading into Church Street or Lane" (Lockie), eventually bisected by Commercial Road, part renamed Braham Street, part renamed Manningtree Street.

Cold Street, Off Pearl Street, Wapping, Pearl Street to Ship Street, north of gasworks.

Cole Road, Off Well Street, Hackney, 1895, Frampton Park Estate is on the site.

Colebrook Terrace, Albert Street (Malcolm Place), Bethnal Green, 1891, Albert Road became part of Entick Street, once off Malcolm Place.

Coleharbour (or Coldharbour) Street, Off Hackney Road, Bethnal Green, 1860, became part of Ravenscroft Street.

Coleman Close, 1. Garnet Street, Wapping. 2. Harris Court (Cranford Street), Ratcliffe.

Coleman Street, Off New Gravel Lane (Garnet Street), Wapping, "extending from 150 New Gravel Lane under the arch to Star Street" (Lockie), part renamed Monza Place and part renamed Coleman Close.

Coles Street, Off Well Street (Woolridge Way Estate), Hackney, Woolridge Way Estate is on site.

Colet Arms Public House, 94 White Horse Street (White Horse Road), Stepney, 1874.

Colin Street, Off Empson Street, Bromley and Bow, 1891.

College Arms Public House, 99 Old Bethnal Green Road, Bethnal Green.

College Buildings, Wentworth Street, Whitechapel, 1891.

College Chapel, Stepney Green, Stepney, corner of Garden Street.

College Row or View, Wharf Road (Saunders Ness Road), Isle of Dogs, 1882.

Collen Bawn (or Collenbawn) Public House, 7 Bucks Row (Durward Street), Whitechapel.

Collet Place, White Horse Street (White Horse Road), Stepney, "White Horse Street at the north end of it by the workhouse near the south side of Stepney Church Yard" (Lockie).

Collets Yard, Off Nightingale Lane (Thomas More Street), Wapping.

Colliers Court, Fleet Street (Pedley Street), Whitechapel, "is two houses on the right hand in Fleet Street going from George Street Brick Lane" (Elmes).

Colliers or Collyers Place, Little George Street (Poyser Street), Bethnal Green, 1851.

Collin Court, Newcastle Street (Sunbury Workshops), Bethnal Green.

Colling Street, former Little Collingwood Street (Collingwood Street), Whitechapel, 1860, Collingwood Estate is on the site.

Collingwood Court & Place, Mount Street (Swanfield Street), Bethnal Green, "is nearly opposite Collingwood Street" (Lockie).

Collingwood Place, Broad Street (The Highway), Ratcliffe, "at 102 a few doors on the left from Cock hill and nearly opposite Stone Stairs" (Lockie).

Collingwood Street, 1. Off Brook Street (Cable Street), Ratcliffe, 1891, Brook Street to Broad Street, Heckford Street follows part of its route. 2. Off Mount Street (Swanfield Street), Bethnal Green, "the third on the left in it from 45 Church Street or the first on the right from Virginia Street behind Shoreditch Church" (Lockie), Boundary Estate is on the site. 3. Off Three Colts Lane, Bethnal Green, 1851, Three Colts Lane to Darling Row.

Collingwood Terrace, Bethnal Green, 1841.

Collins Court, Farmer Street (Shadwell Basin), Shadwell, "the first turning on the left in Farmer Street going from No 38 High Street" (Elmes).

Collins Court or Place, Poplar High Street, Poplar, 1851, between 191 and 193 Poplar High Street, Collins House was built on the site.

Collins Gardens, Preston Street (Roman Road), Bethnal Green.

Collins Place, Preston Street (Roman Road), Bethnal Green, renamed Surat Street.

Collyers Court, Pedley Street, Whitechapel, 1890.

Colmar Street, Off Alderney Road, Mile End, 1891.

Colnbrook Villas, Albert Road (Albion Drive), Hackney, 1868, between Queens (now Queensbridge) Road and Malvern Road.

Cologne Street, Off Rhodeswell Road, Limehouse, between East London Cemetery and Gas Works renamed Harford Street. A later section of Cologne Road ran east to west at Bohn Street and became part of Bohn Street.

Colonial Wharves, Wapping High Street, Wapping, 1950, south east of corner with Hellings Street.

Colquhoun Place, Garford Street, Limehouse, 1851.

Columbia Market, Columbia Road, Bethnal Green, on site of Columbia Square and surroundings.

Columbia Messenger & Shoeblack Brigade, 11 Wood Street (Wilkes Street), Spitalfields.

Columbia Square, Crab Tree Row (Columbia Road), Bethnal

Green, 1860, corner of Crab Tree Row and Charles Place (later named Columbia Road and Hassard Street).

Comboss Road, Off White Post Lane, Hackney, 1950.

Comet Public House, 20 Christian Street, St. George in the East.

Comfort Arms Public House, 51 Bridge Street (Solebay Street), Bromley and Bow.

Commercial Arms Public House, 142 Commercial Street, Spitalfields.

Commercial Brewery Public House, 500 Commercial Road, Ratcliffe, the Troxy is on the site, aka Brewery Tap.

Commercial Coffee House, Pennyfields, Limehouse, 1874.

Commercial Gas Company Works, Ship Street (Wapping High Street), Wapping, 1895, Bounded by Ship Street Boarded Entry New Gravel Lane Wapping High Street and Prusoms Island.

Commercial Place, Commercial Road, Shadwell, "part of the south side of it, about $^1/_8$ of a mile on the right east from the Half way house extending from Lucas Place to John Street" (Lockie).

Commercial Road Great Synagogue, 262 Commercial Road, Shadwell, 1968, corner of Winterton Street.

Commercial Road Synagogue, 90 Commercial Road, St. George in the East, 1915.

Commercial Street St. Leonards Road, Poplar, 1891, renamed Clutton Street.

Commercial Tap Public House, 66 Ben Jonson Road, Mile End.

Commercial Tavern Public House, 1 Pennyfields, Limehouse, 1874.

Commercial Terrace, 1. Commercial Road, Limehouse, "on the south side the road a few doors east of the church by the end of Gill Street" (Lockie). 2. St. Leonards Road, Poplar, between Joshua Street and Andrew Street, address changed to St. Leonards Road.

Commodore Court & Place, rear of 209 Poplar High Street, Poplar, 1851, Commodore House was built on the site.

Commodore Public House, 1. 52 Old Montague Street, Whitechapel, aka Old Commodore. 2. 209 Poplar High Street, Poplar.

Commodore Terrace, Cologne Street (Harford Street), Mile End, renamed Commodore Street.

Common(s) Street, Off Havannah Street, Isle of Dogs, connected Havannah Street and Strafford Street Lost on construction of the Barkantine Estate.

Compasses Court, Glasshouse

Street (John Fisher Street), East Smithfield, Royal Mint Street.

Conant Arms Public House, 41 Stainsby Road, Limehouse, 1874.

Conant Place, West India Dock Road, Limehouse.

Conants Place, Back Church Lane, St. George in the East, 1851.

Concordia Wharf, Cold Harbour, Isle of Dogs, 1950.

Conder Street, Off Salmon Lane, Limehouse, north of Raby Street.

Conduit Street, Off Old Bethnal Green Road, Bethnal Green, 1851, also known as South Conduit Street, renamed Viaduct Street.

Congregation of Jacob Synagogue, 351-353 Commercial Road, Stepney, 1920, west of Bromehead Road.

Connor Street, Off Morpeth Road, Hackney, 1891.

Conqueror Public House, 2 Austin Street, Bethnal Green.

Conrad Street, Off Loddiges Road, Hackney, 1950, Lodigges Road to Brenthouse Road.

Constable Row, Mile End Road, Mile End, in front of Drapers Almshouses.

Convent of Mercy, Crispin Street, Spitalfields, 1950, corner of Crispin Street and Artillery Lane.

Convent of our Lady of Dolours Ladies School, 83 East India Dock Road, Limehouse, 1921.

Cook & Hoop Public House, 1 Gun Street, Spitalfields, aka Artillery Tavern, address also 17 Artillery Street.

Cook (or Cock) Hill, Love Lane (Brodlove Lane), Shadwell, from Brodlove Lane to Schoolhouse Lane, now part of the Highway.

Cook Street, Off Ida Street, Poplar, 1891.

Cooks Almshouses, Shadwell Church Yard, Shadwell, 1800.

Coolhurst Villas, Devonshire Street (Bancroft Road), Mile End, 1891.

Coopers Almshouse(s), Brook Street (Cable Street), Ratcliffe, 1851.

Coopers Almshouses, Schoolhouse Lane, Shadwell, 1891.

Coopers Arms Public House, 1. 45 Cheshire Street, Whitechapel. 2. 5 Green Bank, Wapping. 3. 52 Oxford Street (Stepney Way), Whitechapel, aka Windsor Castle. 4. 309 Poplar High Street, Poplar, 1874, aka William IV. 5. 201 Salmon Lane, Limehouse. 6. 13 Sidney Street, Whitechapel. 7. 13 St. Leonards Road, Poplar. 8. 229 Stepney Way, Whitechapel, address also 229 Oxford Street, also 22 Wellington Place. 9. 15 Watney Street, Shadwell.

Coopers Buildings, Nightingale Lane (Thomas More Street), Wapping, 1851.

Coopers Court, Blue Anchor Yard (Royal Mint Street), East Smithfield, 1851, "Blue Anchor Yard, Rosemary Lane the last on the left from 48 Rosemary Lane and on the north side New Martin Street from 97 Upper East Smithfield" (Lockie).

Coopers Gardens, Hackney Road, Bethnal Green, "are the second turning on the right hand a few houses from Shoreditch church" (Elmes), Stepney Rents to Gasciogne Place.

Coopers Row, Upper East Smithfield, East Smithfield, 1851, renamed Minting Row.

Coopers Square, Schoolhouse Lane, Shadwell, "is a few doors on the right from Cock Hill towards Brook Street" (Lockie).

Copenhagen Tavern Public House, 183 Salmon Lane, Limehouse, 1874.

Copenhagen Yard, Salmon Lane, Limehouse, 1851.

Copley Street, Stepney Green to Aylward Street, 1950.

Corbet(t) s Court & Place, Hanbury Street, Spitalfields, 1891.

Corbets Court, Browns Lane (Hanbury Street), Spitalfields, 1891, "at 36 the third on the right from opposite 55 Brick Lane it is continued by Grey Eagle Street" (Lockie), renamed Corbets Place.

Cord Way, Tiller Road, Isle of Dogs, short street close to corner of Tiller Road and Alpha Grove.

Cordova Cottages, Grove Road, Bromley and Bow.

Cordova Road, Off Grove Road, Bromley and Bow, 1891.

Cordswainers Arms Public House, 16 Henrietta Street (Allgood Street), Bethnal Green.

Corea Place, Sandys Row, Spitalfields, 1891, east of Sandys Row, and north of Wentworth St.

Cornucopia Public House, 588 Mile End Road, Mile End, aka Horn of Plenty.

Cornwall Arms Public House, 161 Braintree Street, Mile End.

Cornwall Road, 1. Renamed Cornwall Avenue, Bethnal Green. 2. Off Victoria Park Road, Hackney, renamed Redruth Road.

Cornwall Terrace, Middleton Road, Hackney, 1851, east of Holly Street.

Coshs Buildings, Brook Street (Cable Street), Ratcliffe, 1891.

Cottage Court, Hayfield Passage, Mile End, 1891.

Cottage Grove Road, Bromley and Bow, renamed Rhondda Grove.

Cottage Place, 1. Adelina Grove, Mile End, 1891, Sidney Street. 2. Arthur Street (Brooksbank Street), Hackney, 1851. 3. East India Dock Road, Limehouse, "is about half a mile on the right in the East India Dock Road from Limehouse on the east side the East India Almshouses" (Lockie). 4. Salmon Lane, Limehouse, 1851. 5. Satchwell Road, Bethnal Green, 1841, renamed Darsham Place. 6. Victoria Street (Dellow Street), Shadwell, 1851. 7. Well Street, Hackney, opposite Cassland Road.

Cottage Row, 1. Cottage Street, Poplar, 1851, parallel with, and between, Cottage Street and Woodstock Terrace. 2. North Place (Globe Road), Bromley and Bow, 1841.

Cottages, The, Nightingale Lane (Thomas More Street), Wapping, 1891.

Cotton Arms, 92 St. Pauls Road (St. Pauls Way), Bromley and Bow, 1874.

Cotton Place, Cotton Street, Poplar, 1851.

Cotton Street, 1. Off Oxford Street (Stepney Way), Whitechapel, renamed Milward Street. 2. Off Turners Road, Bromley and Bow, renamed Locksley Street. 3. Baptist Chapel, Cotton Street, Poplar, 1864.

Cotton Yard, Poplar High Street, Poplar, "is about ¹/₂ a mile east from the Commercial Road on the left nearly opposite the Charity school and Town hall" (Lockie).

Cottons Arms Public House, 92 St. Pauls Way, Bromley and Bow.

Coutts Road, Off Burdett Road, Bromley and Bow, 1891, corner of Bow Common Lane to Rhodeswell Road Mile End Park and Leisure Centre are on the site.

Coventry Cross & Cottages, St. Leonards Street, Bromley and Bow, 1891.

Coventry Cross Estate, east of southernmost section of St. Leonards Street, Bromley.

Coventry Cross Public House & Row, Four Mills Street (St. Leonards Street), Bromley and Bow, 1851.

Coventry Place & Street, Off Three Colts Lane, Bethnal Green, 1841, renamed Coventry Road.

Cow Court, Hare Street (Cheshire Street), Whitechapel, "at 80 the first on the right a few doors from 108 Brick Lane" (Lockie).

Cow Lane, 1. Cow Lane, New Gravel Lane (Garnet Street), Wapping, south of West Gardens, Shadwell New Basin built on site. 2. Stepney High Street, Stepney, "the first north parallel to, and a few yards from the church yard extending from the south end of the green towards Rhodes Wells and Bow Common" (Lockie), later the westernmost section of Ben Jonson Road.

Cow Yard, Royal Mint Street, East Smithfield, 1851.

Cowley Gardens, Cable Street, Shadwell, Martineau Estate is on the site.

Cowley Street, Off Cable Street, Shadwell, 1891, renamed Cowley Gardens.

Cowpers Buildings, Nightingale Lane (Thomas More Street), Wapping, 1871.

Coxs Alley, east of Sandys Row, and north of Wentworth Street, Spitalfields, 1891.

Coxs Buildings, Mansford Street, Bethnal Green, 1891.

Coxs Court, Petticoat Lane (Middlesex Street), Spitalfields, "nearly opposite Stoney Lane about eight doors south from Wentworth Street and $1/8$ of a mile on the right north from 41 Aldgate" (Lockie).

Coxs Square, Wentworth Street, Spitalfields, "situated behind the corner formed by Wentworth Street and Petticoat Lane communicating to the former by Shorts Street to the latter by Cobbs Yard and Fishers Alley" (Lockie).

Crabtree (or Crab Tree) Row, Hackney Road, Bethnal Green, "Shoreditch Hackney Road the third on the right about $1/5$ of a mile from Shoreditch Church opposite Union Street extending to the Birdcage walk" (Lockie), became part of Columbia Road.

Cradle Court, Love Lane (Brodlove Lane), Shadwell, 1851.

Craft School, The, 37-39 Stepney Green, Stepney, 1910.

Crampton Cottages, Bow Common Lane, Bromley and Bow, 1891.

Cranberry Street, Off Anglesea Street (Fakruddin Street), Whitechapel, 1950, just west of Vallance Road, Fakruddin Street is partially on the site.

Cranbourne Public House, 50 Nairn Street, Poplar.

Cranbrook Place, Cranbrook Street, Bethnal Green, renamed Cranbrook Terrace.

Cranbrook Terrace, Roman Road, Bethnal Green, Cranbrook Estate is on the site.

Craster Place, Brook Street (Cable Street), Ratcliffe, 1851.

Craven Buildings, 1. Poyser Street, Bethnal Green, 1891. 2. Wansbeck Road, Bromley and Bow, 1891.

Crawcour Synagogue, Fieldgate Street, Whitechapel, 1890.

Crawford Court, Royal Mint Street, East Smithfield.

Crawfords Yard, 84-88 Poplar High Street, Poplar, 1851, rear of 86 Poplar High Street.

Creek Side or Creekside, Orchard Place, Poplar, 1891.

Crellin Street, Off Cannon Street Road, St. George in the

East, immediately north of railway line.

Crescent House, Cartwright Street (Royal Mint Street), East Smithfield, 1891, Royal Mint Street.

Crescent Place, Hackney Road, Bethnal Green, Hackney Road to Angela Street, renamed Cuff Place.

Creswick Road, Off Addington Road, Bromley and Bow, 1891, Lawrence Close is on its route.

Creswick Street, renamed Creswick Road (Lawrence Close), Bromley and Bow.

Cricketers Public House, 42 London Street (Bekesbourne Street), Ratcliffe.

Crispin Street, Dorset Street, Spitalfields, 1891, extended as far north as Lamb Street, subsumed by western expansion of Spitalfields Market.

Crobens or Crobers Cottages, Ditchburn Street, Poplar, 1851.

Crofton Street, Off Devonshire Street (Bancroft Road), Mile End, renamed Grantley Street.

Crombies Row, Commercial Road, Stepney, 1868, Bromehead Street to Bromehead Road.

Cromwell Terrace, Galbraith Street, Isle of Dogs, 1891, Manchester Road.

Crooked Billet Public House, 1. 1 Hermitage Street (Wapping High Street), Wapping. 2. 43 King David Lane, Shadwell,

address also 340 Cable Street. 3. 2 King Street (Royal Mint Street), East Smithfield.

Crooked Billet Tavern Public House, 32 St. George Street (The Highway), St. George in the East.

Cross Alley, Well Alley, St. George in the East, "two doors on the right in it from 105 Wapping Street leading into Upper Well Alley" (Lockie).

Cross Court, Dean Street (Deancross Street), Shadwell, 1891, east of Dean Street, south of Cornwall Street.

Cross Keys Public House, 125 Wentworth Street, Whitechapel, 1874.

Cross Place, Commercial Road, Stepney, 1868, Church Road to Grosvenor Street.

Cross Row, Stepney Green, Mile End, "the fourth on the right about $1/5$ of a mile from Mile End Road, extending to Saville Buildings south end of Pleasant Row" (Lockie).

Cross Row or Street, Off Periwinkle Street (Ratcliffe Cross Street), Ratcliffe, short street off Periwinkle Street immediately south of railway line, became part of Ratcliffe Cross Street.

Cross Street, 1. Off Abingdon Street (Herald Street), Bethnal Green, 1841, renamed Glass Street. 2. Off Back Road (Cable Street), St. George in the East, 1860, south half of later

Deancross Street. 3. Bethnal Green, renamed Bempton Street (St. Peters Avenue). 4. Off Bird Cage Walk (Columbia Road), Bethnal Green, 1851. 5. Off Church Street (Bethnal Green Road), Bethnal Green, "at 17 the second on the left from 65 Shoreditch extending to Old Nichol Street" (Lockie). 6. Off Coleharbour Street (Ravenscroft Street), Bethnal Green, 1851. 7. Off Coventry Street (Coventry Road), Bethnal Green, renamed Delta Street. 8. Off Devas Street, Bromley and Bow. 9. Off Digby Road, Hackney, 1891, renamed Daley Street. 10. Off Frampton Park Road, Hackney, 1891, renamed Askew Street. 11. Off Fulbourne Street, Whitechapel, renamed Trahorn Street. 12. Off Green Street (Roman Road), Bethnal Green, "the third on the left near $1/3$ of a mile from the green leading towards Bonners Hall" (Lockie), renamed Anne Street. 13. Off Hassard Street, Bethnal Green, 1891, renamed Hassard Place. 14. Off Hessel Street, St. George in the East, renamed Amazon Street. 15. Cross Street, Off Mape Street, Bethnal Green, renamed Kelsey Street. 16. Off Old Nichol(s) Street (Boundary Estate), Bethnal Green. 17. Off Rich Street, Limehouse, "is situated between the church and the West India Docks extending from Rich Street to Jamaica Place East" (Lockie). 18. Off Robert Street (Tobago Street), Isle of Dogs, 1862, between Robert Street and George Street, renamed Tobago Street. 19. Off Suffolk Street (Three Colts Lane), Bethnal Green, 1851. 20. Bethnal Green, renamed Viaduct Street. 21. Off Wade Street (Wades Place), Poplar, 1862, Wade Street to Shirbutt Street. 22. Off Wellington Row, Bethnal Green, 1841.

Crossed Guns Court, Rosemary Lane (Royal Mint Street), East Smithfield, 1746.

Crosskeys Public House, 125 Wentworth Street, Whitechapel.

Crossland Square, Sale Street, Bethnal Green, 1891.

Croucher Place, Railway Street (Hay Currie Street), Poplar, 1891.

Crown & Anchor Public House, 1. 44-46 Brook Street (Cable Street), Ratcliffe, 1874. 2. 71 Cheshire Street, Whitechapel, 1874. 3. 3 Hardinge Street, Shadwell, aka Mechanics Arms. 4. 49 Nelson Street, Whitechapel. 5. 72 St. George Street (The Highway), St. George in the East. 6. Storer Street (Nelson Street), Mile End, 1874. 7. 35 Temple Street, Bethnal Green.

Crown & Castle Public House, 564 Kingsland Road, Hackney.

Crown & Cushion Public House, 23 Farnfield Street (Kerbey Street), Poplar.

Crown & Dolphin Public House, 1. 56 Cannon Street Road, St. George in the East, 1874, aka Dolphin. 2. 10 Stepney High Street, Stepney, 1874.

Crown & Leek Public House, 6 Deal Street, Spitalfields, 1874, address also 11 Deal Street.

Crown & Queens Arms Public House, 32 Wapping High Street, Wapping, aka Queens Arms.

Crown & Sceptre Public House, 1. 84 Ben Jonson Road, Mile End. 2. Charles Street (Malcolm Road), Stepney, 1874, West Street. 3. 94 Sceptre Road, Bethnal Green. 4. 13 South Grove (Southern Grove), Bromley and Bow. 5. 20 Woolmore Street, Poplar, 1874.

Crown & Seven Stars Public House, 47 Royal Mint Street, East Smithfield, 1874.

Crown & Sheers Court, Rosemary Lane (Royal Mint Street), East Smithfield, 1746.

Crown (& Cushion) Public House, 12 Lion Street (Kerbey Street), Poplar.

Crown Court, 1. Cartwright Street (Royal Mint Street), East Smithfield, 1870. 2. Little Pearl Street (Calvin Street), Spitalfields, 1891. 3. New Gravel Lane (Garnet Street), Wapping, 1746.

Crown Hotel & Public House, 223 Grove Road, Bromley and Bow.

Crown Place, Mile End Road, Mile End, 1891, renamed Jewel Street.

Crown Public House, 1. 81 West Street (Usk Street), Bethnal Green. 2. 222 Bethnal Green Road, Bethnal Green. 3. 34 Church Street (Bethnal Green Road), Bethnal Green. 4. 184 Hackney Road, Bethnal Green. 5. 10 Butler Buildings (Upper East Smithfield), East Smithfield. 6. 40 Glasshouse Street (John Fisher Street), East Smithfield. 7. 667 Commercial Road, Limehouse, 1874. 8. 95 Rhodeswell Road, Limehouse, corner of Dora Street. 9. 12 Narrow Street, Limehouse, 1874. 10. 9 Orchard Place, Poplar. 11. 57 Alderney Road, Mile End. 12. 74 Mile End Road, Mile End. 13. 4 Grey Eagle Street, Spitalfields. 14. 4 North Street (Lamb Street), Spitalfields. 15. 182 Brick Lane, Spitalfields, aka Old Crown. 16. 172 Cable Street, St. George in the East. 17. 38 Lower Chapman Street (Bigland Street), St. George in the East. 18. 19 Mayfield Road, Hackney. 19. 223 Old Ford Road, Bromley and Bow, 1874. 20. 60 Shadwell High Street (The Highway), Shadwell. 21. 59 Wapping Wall, Wapping. 22. 128 White Horse Street (White Horse Road), Stepney. 23. 14 Goodman Street, Whitechapel. 24. 16 Cheshire Street, Whitechapel. 25. 14 Rupert Street (Goodman Street),

Whitechapel, 1874, Goodmans Fields.

Crown Row, Mile End Road, Mile End, "is nearly 1²/₃ mile on the right east from Aldgate Pump opposite the sign of the King Harry and the Jews hospital" (Lockie).

Crown Street, Off Wapping High Street, Wapping, 1891, renamed Hellings Street.

Crown Terrace, Mile End Road, Mile End, immediately next to Crown Place.

Crown Villas, Chisenhale Road, Bromley and Bow.

Crown Yard, Mile End, renamed Crown Works (Bancroft Road).

Crows Nest Public House, 14 Salmon Lane, Limehouse.

Cruden Place, Kerbey Street, Poplar, 1891.

Crystal Tavern Public House, 25 Burdett Road, Bromley and Bow.

Cubitt Arms Public House, 262 Manchester Road, Isle of Dogs.

Cubitt House, Roffey Street, Isle of Dogs, East Ferry Road.

Cubitt Town Wesleyan Chapel, Stebondale Street (Pier Street), Isle of Dogs, Pier Street destroyed during WWII.

Cubitt Town Wharf, Saunders Ness Road, Isle of Dogs, 1950, present-day street, at river end of Seyssel Street.

Cubitts Brickfields, Folly Wall, Isle of Dogs, 1851, Stewart Street.

Cumberland Place, Whitechapel, renamed Neath Place (Collingwood Estate).

Cumberland Street, Off Hackney Road, Bethnal Green, 1865, renamed Scawfell Street.

Curlings Dock, Limehouse Hole (Three Colt Street), Limehouse, "is between Limehouse Hole and the entrance to the West India Docks" (Lockie).

Cutside, Ropemakers Fields, Limehouse, 1891, renamed Oak Lane.

Cymon Street, Off Turin Street, Bethnal Green, 1891.

D

Dace Road, Off Monier Road, Bromley and Bow, 1746.

Dagger Court, Quaker Street, Spitalfields.

Dagmar Arms Public House, 1. 140 Commercial Road, St. George in the East. 2. Dagmar Arms Public House, 47 Danesdale Road, Hackney.

Dagmar Road, Off Cassland Road, Hackney, 1891, renamed Dale Road 1930s and now Danesdale Road.

Dagnall Place, Brady Street, Whitechapel, 1891, Collingwood Estate is now on the site.

Dahlia Cottages, Westferry Road, Isle of Dogs, 1868, east corner of Westferry Road and Chapel House Street.

Daintry Street, Off Osborne Road, Hackney, 1891, renamed Daintry Way.

Dakin Street, Off Cayley Street (Whitehorse Road Park), Stepney, 1891.

Dakley Place, Goldsmiths Row, Bethnal Green, 1862.

Dale Road, Off Cassland Road, Hackney, renamed Danesdale Road.

Dales Place, Flower and Dean Street, Spitalfields, 1851.

Dalgleish Place, Commercial Road, Limehouse, 1851, part of Dalgleish Street.

Dalston Distillery, Queensbridge Road, Hackney, 1895, corner of Pownall Road.

Dalston Green, Dalston Lane, Hackney, 1862, close to Kingsland High Street.

Dalston Presbyterian Church, Shrubland Grove (Mapledene Road), Hackney, 1868.

Dalston Terrace, Dalston Road (Dalston Lane), Hackney, was part of Dalston Lane between Dalston Road and Laurel Street.

Dame Colet Cottage Public House, 10 Duckett Street, Mile End.

Daniel Street, Off Gosset Street, Bethnal Green, 1851, west of and parallel with Turin Street.

Daniels Row, (Little) Union Place (Cressy Place), Stepney, 1891, behind the north side of Union Place

Danish Church, Wellclose Square, St. George in the East, "is the building which occupies the centre of the square It was erected in 1746 and is a commodious and handsome structure appropriated to the use of the Danes who reside in this neighbourhood" (Elmes).

Danish Lutheran Church St. Peters, King Street (Ming Street), Limehouse, 1890.

Daplyn Street, Off Woodseer Street, Whitechapel, 1950, Woodseer Street to Hanbury Street.

Darby Street, Off Cartwright Street (Royal Mint Street), East Smithfield, 1891, Royal Mint Street.

Dark Entry, Off Lower East Smithfield (St. Katharine Dock), East Smithfield, 1800, St. Katharine Dock is on its site.

Darling Place, Whitechapel Road, Whitechapel, "Corner of Dog Row the second on the left in Dog Row and about seventeen doors from Mile End turnpike right in Tothill Street from the abbey" (Lockie), Darling Row to Cambridge Heath Road, became part of Darling Row.

Darlington House, East Ferry Road, Isle of Dogs, 1891.

Darnley Crescent, Darnley Road, Hackney, became part of Darnley Road.

Darsham Place, Satchwell Road, Bethnal Green, 1950, west of present-day Hutton House.

Darts Alley, Whitechapel Road, Whitechapel, "at 47 the fourth on the left about twenty five doors west from the church" (Lockie).

Datchett Street, Off Commercial Street, Spitalfields, renamed Dorset Street.

Davenants School, Davenant Street, Whitechapel, Whitechapel Road.

Davey Road, Hackney, 1950, became part of White Post Lane.

David & Harp Public House, 54 Narrow Street, Limehouse, 1874.

David Place, Bow Lane (Bazely Street), Poplar, 1851.

Davies Buildings, Pennyfields, Limehouse, "is a few houses north from the High Street or Road near the Commercial Road" (Lockie).

Davis Buildings, 1. Gowers Walk, Whitechapel, 1891. 2. St. Johns Place (Priory Place), Hackney, 1851.

Davis Cottages, Priory Place (Frampton Park Estate), Hackney.

Davis Mansions, New Goulston Street, Whitechapel.

Davis Place, Moss Street (Smart Street), Bethnal Green, 1891.

Davis Street, Off Manchester Road, Isle of Dogs, 1891, was across Manchester Road to Marshfield Street.

Davis Terrace, North Street (Brady Street), Whitechapel.

Dawson Alley, Cottages or Court, Cuba Street, Isle of Dogs, 1851, south of Cuba Street river section.

Day Industrial School, 299-301 East India Dock Road, Poplar, formerly Brunswick Road Board School.

Day Place, Pell street (Swedenborg Gardens), St. George in the East, renamed Thomas Place.

Deacon(s) Court, Quaker Street, Spitalfields, "the second on the left from 29 Wheler Street leading into Woods Yard and Phoenix Street" (Lockie).

Deals Court, Flower and Dean Street, Spitalfields, "the first on the left about six doors from 200 Brick Lane near Whitechapel Church" (Lockie).

Deals Yard, Wells Street (Cotton Street), Poplar, 1851.

Dean Colet House, White Horse Street (White Horse Road), Stepney, 1851.

Dean Street, 1. Off Commercial Road, Shadwell, 1891, "south towards Cable Street to 115 extending from Broad Bridge to Cock Hill" (Lockie), renamed Deancross Street. 2. Off Shadwell High Street (The

Highway), Shadwell, "is the first south parallel to the High Street from numbers 88, Shadwell Park is on the site. 3. Off Upper East Smithfield, East Smithfield, "at 95 about ⅙ of a mile on the right east from Tower Hill leading into Butcher Row" (Lockie).

Dean Swift Public House, 2-6 Deancross Street, Shadwell.

Deanes Court, Griffin Street (Shadwell Park), Shadwell, 1851.

Deborah Place, Wick Road, Hackney, 1862.

Deddington Arms Public House, 37 Castor Street (Birchfield Street), Limehouse.

Dempsey Street, Off Smith Street (Smithy Street), Stepney, 1895, Smith Street to Charles Street.

Dempsey Street, Off Stepney Way, Mile End, east of and parallel with Jubilee Street, Clichy Estate is on the site.

Denbigh Road, Off Fairfield Road, Bromley and Bow, 1891.

Denbigh Terrace, Fairfield Road, Bromley and Bow, 1851.

Denmark Place, Well Street, Hackney, 1841, part of Well Street.

Denmark Street, Off Cable Street, St. George in the East, 1891, renamed Crowder Street.

Deptford & Greenwich Road, Isle of Dogs, 1800, early name for Westferry Road.

Derby Place, Old Ford Road, Bromley and Bow, 1891, renamed Type Street.

Derby Terrace, Harrow Lane, Poplar.

Desart Street, Off St. Leonards Road, Poplar, 1891.

Destitute Sailors Refuge, Well Street (Ensign Street), St. George in the East.

Devon Arms Public House, 1. 63 Green Street (Roman Road), Bethnal Green. 2. 56 Morning lane, Hackney, 1874.

Devon Cottages, Devons Lane (Devons Road), Bromley and Bow, 1851, Devons Lane from Bromley High Street.

Devon Stores Public House, 171-173 Devons Road, Bromley and Bow.

Devonport Passage, Devonport Street, Shadwell, 1950.

Devons Lane, Devons Road, Bromley and Bow, 1851, alternative name for Devons Road.

Devonshire Arms Public House, 1. 10 Burn Street (Carr Street), Stepney, 1874. 2. 49 Devonshire Street (Cephas Street), Mile End, 1874, aka Phoenix Public House. 3. 45 Eastfield Street, Limehouse. 4. 86 New Road, Whitechapel. 5. York Street East (Commercial Road), Limehouse, 1891, Commercial Road East, renamed Flamborough Street.

Devonshire House, 68 East India Dock Road, Limehouse.

Devonshire Place, 1. Cow Lane (Ben Jonson Road), Stepney, "is about ⅛ of a mile on the left from Stepney Old Square and near the same distance from the church by the Worlds End Public House" (Lockie). 2. North Street (Brady Street), Whitechapel, 1851. 3. Old Nichol(s) Street (Boundary Estate), Bethnal Green, 1851. 4. West Street (Westgate Street), Hackney, 1851, London Fields.

Devonshire Road, Hackney, 1891, renamed Brenthouse Road.

Devonshire Street, 1. Off Cambridge Heath Road, Mile End, 1891, from west to east became part of Cephas Street, Colebert Avenue and Bancroft Road. 2. Off Commercial Road, Shadwell, 1891, renamed Winterton Street.

Devonshire Terrace, Westferry Road, Isle of Dogs, 1891, Mast House Terrace is on site.

Diamond Court, Great Pearl Street (Calvin Street), Spitalfields, 1851.

Diamond Point, East India Dock Road, Poplar, 1851.

Diamond Row, Mile End, became part of Redmans Road.

Dibbles Buildings, Upper East Smithfield, East Smithfield.

Dickersons Place, Providence Place (Woolmore Street), Poplar, 1891.

Digby Arms Public House, 46 Digby Street, Bethnal Green.

Digby Walk, Globe Road, Bethnal Green, 1851.

Diggers Arms Public House, 56 Pennyfields, Limehouse, aka Diggers Rest.

Diggon Street, Off Stepney Green, Stepney, 1950, Stepney Green to Aylward Street.

Diners Buildings, Sandys Row, Spitalfields, 1891, east of Sandys Row, and north of Wentworth St.

Diners or Dinahs Buildings, Tripe Yard (Sandys Row), Spitalfields, 1891.

Dingle Court & Lane, Poplar High Street, Poplar, 1891, used to extend south to the Isle of Dogs before construction of West India Docks.

Dispensary for Pregnant Women, Great Ayliffe Street (Alie Street), Whitechapel, 1799.

Dissenters Charity School, Pell Street (Wellclose Square), St. George in the East.

Distillers Arms Public House, 26 Hancock Road, Bromley and Bow, 1874.

Ditchburn House, Ditchburn Street, Poplar.

Dixie Street, Off Brady Street, Whitechapel, 1891, south of Scott Street.

Dixon Street, Off Rhodeswell Road, Limehouse, 1895, parallel with and north of Copenhagen Place.

Dock Cottages, Dolphin Lane, Poplar, 1891.

Dock House Public House, 1. 30 Cuba Street, Isle of Dogs, corner of Alpha Road. 2. 14 Old Gravel Lane (Wapping Lane), Wapping. 3. 293-295 East India Dock Road, Poplar, 1874, Poplar Hospital was built on the site, also known as East India Dock Tavern.

Dock Side, Nightingale Lane (Thomas More Street), Wapping, "at the back of Goodwyn and Skinners brewery extending from Hermitage Bridge towards Nightingale Lane" (Lockie).

Dock Street, 1. Off Cotton Street, Poplar, 1851, Robin Hood Gardens is on the site. 2. Off New Gravel Lane (Garnet Street), Wapping, 1851, east from New Gravel Lane, lost on construction of Shadwell New Basin, aka Shadwell Dock Street.

Dock Tavern Public House, Shadwell Dock Street (Garnet Street), Shadwell, aka Shadwell Dock House.

Dock Yard, Hermitage Dock (Hermitage Basin), Wapping, "is on the east side of it extending from the bridge towards Charlotte Street and Nightingale Lane" (Lockie).

Dockland Settlement, East Ferry Road, Isle of Dogs, community centre established in 1920s, closed and partially

demolished in 21st century, building now houses a school.

Dodds Place, Three Colts Lane, Bethnal Green, 1851.

Dog & Partridge Public House, 249 Bow Road, Bromley and Bow, 1874.

Dog & Truck Public House, 72 Back Church Lane, St. George in the East.

Dog Row, Bethnal Green, "the south continuation of the west side of the green extending to Mile End turnpike about ½ a mile in length" (Lockie), former name for the south section of Cambridge Heath Road from Whitechapel Road to the corner with Cleveland Way.

Dolphin Cottages & House, Dolphin Lane, Poplar, 1891, Poplar High Street.

Dolphin Court, Artillery Place (Artillery Lane), Spitalfields, "Artillery Place, is situated between the south end of Gun Street and Crispin Street three or four doors west from the latter" (Lockie).

Dolphin Lane, 68 Poplar High Street, Poplar, 1891, close to - road extended deep into the Isle of Dogs before the construction of the West India Docks Sometimes named Griggs Gutt or Angel Lane.

Dolphin Public House, 1. 56 Cannon Street Road, St. George in the East, 1874, aka Crown & Dolphin. 2. 85 Church Street

(Bethnal Green Road), Bethnal Green, 1874. 3. 69 Devonshire Street (Bancroft Road), Mile End. 4. 165 Mare Street, Hackney, 1874. 5. 97-99 Whitechapel Road, Whitechapel, 1874.

Donald Street, Off Devas Street, Bromley and Bow, 1891.

Dongola Street, Off Harford Street, Mile End, 1891, west of gasworks.

Dorans Row, Commercial Road, Stepney, "is part of the north side about ¹/₃ of a mile on the left from Cannon Street Road towards Limehouse by the 1½ mile-stone from the Royal Exchange" (Lockie).

Dorian Street, Off Varden Street, Whitechapel, 1950, immediately east of Philpot Street.

Doric Road, Off Type Street, Bethnal Green, Cranbrook Estate is on the site.

Doris House, Philip Street (Ellen Street), St. George in the East.

Dorrins Row, Commercial Road, Stepney, 1862, immediately east of Sidney Street.

Dorset Arms Public House, 1. 377 Manchester Road, Isle of Dogs, aka Bowleys. 2. 1 Perseverance Terrace (Bethnal Green Road), Bethnal Green.

Dorset Place, John Street, Stepney, 1851.

Dorset Street, 1. Off Commercial Road, Ratcliffe, 1851, renamed Pitsea Street. 2. Off Crispin Street, Spitalfields, "the first south parallel to Paternoster Row on the west side the church and the first north parallel to Whites Row extending from Crispin Street to Red Lion Street" (Lockie), parallel with and directly south of Brushfield Street, renamed Duval Street.

Double Cottage, Martha Street (Wadeson Street), Hackney.

Double X Place, Globe Road, Mile End, 1891, alternative spelling of XX Place, Globe Road opposite the Horn of Plenty public house.

Douglas Place, Hackney Road, Bethnal Green, 1851.

Douglas Street, Off Manchester Road, Isle of Dogs, renamed Douglas Place, recognized by nearby Douglas Path.

Douglas Terrace, Manchester Road, Isle of Dogs, 1862, between Stebondale Street and Ship Street.

Douro Street, Off Old Ford Road, Bromley and Bow, 1891.

Dove Court, Dog Row (Cambridge Heath Road), Whitechapel, "Dog Row, the first on the right a few doors from Mile End turnpike towards Bethnal Green" (Lockie).

Dove Street, Off Poplar High Street, Poplar, "is about ¹/₃ of a mile on the left from the

Commercial Road opposite the Black Horse on the west side of Paradise Street and Noble Street" (Lockie).

Dover Castle Public House, 1. 116 Old Bethnal Green Road, Bethnal Green. 2. 30 Red Lion Street (Leman Street), Whitechapel. 3. 55 Sutton Street, Shadwell, 1874.

Dover Wharf, Narrow Street, Ratcliffe, 1895, opposite Shoulder of Mutton Alley.

Doveton Street, Off Cambridge Road (Cambridge Heath Road), Mile End, 1891, formerly Queen Street and Peacock Place.

Dowson Place, Chicksand Street, Whitechapel, 1851.

Drant Street, Off Folgate Street, Spitalfields, 1950.

Drapers Almshouses, 1. Kingsland Road, Hackney, 1868, immediately south of Ironmongers Almshouses. 2. Whitechapel Road, Whitechapel, Whitechapel Road "at 160 forming part of the north side about eight or nine doors west from the turnpike" (Lockie), Albion Brewery was built on the site. 3. Bow Road, Bromley and Bow, just west of Bow Church, 1837.

Dresden House, Wharf Road (Saunders Ness Road), Isle of Dogs, 1871, in later Island Gardens renamed Osborn House.

Drew Street, Off St. Leonards Road, Poplar, 1950, Blackwall

Tunnel entrance road system at East India Dock Road is on the site.

Drews Buildings, Juniper Street, Shadwell, 1891.

Drift Way, Bromley and Bow, became part of Roman Road.

Drill Place, West India Dock Road, Limehouse, "is a few houses on the east side the road by the turnpike at the commencement of Poplar" (Lockie).

Drivers Arms Public House, 1 Lawton Road, Mile End.

Drivers Buildings, Mile End Road, Mile End, immediately west of Mile End Place.

Drum Court, Whitechapel High Street, Whitechapel, "at 50 the third on the left about twenty two doors from the church towards Aldgate" (Lockie).

Drum Yard, Whitechapel High Street, Whitechapel, 1851.

Dry Granary Works, Morris Road, Poplar, 1891.

Dubury Street, renamed Dewberry Street, Poplar, 1862.

Duchess of Kent Public House, 179 Morning Lane, Hackney.

Ducker & Wassersug Cinematograph Theatre, Goldsmiths Row, Bethnal Green, 1921.

Ducket(t)s Canal Cottage or Lock House, Old Ford Road, Bromley and Bow.

Ducking Pond Row, Whitechapel Road (Durward Street), Whitechapel, "the first north parallel to part of it viz from 94 to 154 opposite the London Hospital extending from Bakers Row to North Row" (Lockie), renamed Bucks Row.

Ducks Isle, Poplar High Street, Poplar, 1851.

Dudgeons Wharf, Saunders Ness Road, Isle of Dogs, 1950, Sextant Avenue is on its site.

Dudley Terrace, Beaumont Street (Beaumont Grove), Mile End, 1891, renamed Dudley Grove.

Duffs Fields, Richard Street (Lodore Street), Poplar, 1851, between Lodore Street and St. Leonards Road just north of East India Dock Road.

Duke of Bedfords Head Public House, 9 Old Gravel Lane (Wapping Lane), Wapping, 1874, aka Dukes Head, aka Old Duke William.

Duke of Cambridge Public House, 1. 31 Devons Road, Bromley and Bow. 2. 25 Felix Street, Cambridge Crescent, Bethnal Green, 1874. 3. 26 Loddiges Road, Hackney, 1874. 4. 345 Whitechapel Road, Whitechapel.

Duke of Clarence Public House, 1. 49 Alfred Street, Bromley and Bow. 2. 71 Commercial Road, Stepney. 3. 133-135 Grundy Street, Poplar,

1874. 4. 61 Hackney Road, Bethnal Green, 1874.

Duke of Cornwall Public House, 20 Grenade Street, Limehouse.

Duke of Cumberland Public House, 119 Cable Street, St. George in the East, 1874, aka Dukes Head.

Duke of Devonshire Public House, 72 Darnley Crescent (Darnley Road), Devonshire Road, Hackney, 1874,

Duke of Edinburgh Public House, 1. 73 Devons Road, Bromley and Bow. 2. 114 Fairfoot Road, Bromley and Bow, 1874. 3. 27 Grundy Street, Poplar.

Duke of Gloucester Public House, 1. Gloucester Terrace (Settles Street), Whitechapel, 1874. 2. 81 New Road, Whitechapel. 3. 26 Seabright Street, Bethnal Green, 1874.

Duke of Kent Public House, 36 Martha Street (Wadeson Street), Hackney.

Duke of Lancaster Public House, 21 John Street (Laburnum Street), Bethnal Green.

Duke of Marlborough Public House, 1. 212 Richmond Road, Hackney, 1874. 2. St. Katharines (St. Katharines Way), East Smithfield.

Duke of Norfolk Public House, 30 Norfolk Street (Varden

Street), Whitechapel, address also 30 Massingham Street.

Duke of Richmond Public House, 316 Queensbridge Road, Hackney, 1874.

Duke of Suffolk Public House, 28 Suffolk Street (Bartlett Park), Limehouse, 1874.

Duke of Sussex Public House, 10 Royal Mint Street, East Smithfield, 1874.

Duke of Wellington Public House, 1. 63 Brady Street, Whitechapel, 1874. 2. 22 Brook Street (Cable Street), Ratcliffe, 1874. 3. 30 Brunswick Street (Haggerston Road), Hackney, 1874. 4. 14 Cannon Street Road, St. George in the East, also known as the Wellington. 5. 2 Devas Street, Bromley and Bow. 6. 280 Haggerston Road, Hackney. 7. 22 John Street (Repton Street), Limehouse, 1874, Limehouse Fields, address also 1 Repton Street. 8. 79 Lucas Street (Lukin Street), Shadwell, 1874, Commercial Road. 9. 76 Morning Lane, Hackney, 1874. 10. 26 Shepherd Street (Commercial Street), Spitalfields. 11. 145 St. Leonards Road, Poplar. 12. 29 Three Colts Lane, Bethnal Green, 1874. 13. 12 Wells Street (Cotton Street), Poplar, 1874.

Duke of York Public House, 1. 129 Antill Road, Bromley and Bow, 1874. 2. 36 Berger Road, Hackney, 1891, Wick Road. 3. 674 Commercial Road, Limehouse. 4. 10 Dod Street, Limehouse, 1874, Burdett Road. 5. 3 Grove Street (Ellsworth Street), Bethnal Green, modern Ellsworth Street. 6. 2 Salmon Lane, Limehouse. 7. 29 Shadwell High Street (The Highway), Shadwell, 1874. 8. 15 Turk Street (Brick Lane), Bethnal Green, 1874, address also 241 Brick Lane.

Duke Shore Wharf, Narrow Street, Limehouse, 1950, close to Narrow Street junction with Ropemakers Fields.

Duke Street, 1. Off Bath Street (Darling Row), Whitechapel, heading north parallel with Brady Street, renamed Pereira Street. 2. Off Brushfield Street, Spitalfields, 1891, became part of Fort St. 3. Off Chapman Street (Morris Street), Shadwell, "Chapman Street, New Road" (Langley & Belch), became southern half of Morris Street. 4. Off Gibraltar Row (Gibraltar Walk), Bethnal Green, 1841, "is about the middle of the east side forming the first south parallel to King Street and extending to Gibraltar Row" (Lockie), renamed Ducal Street. 5. Off Orchard Place, Poplar, 1851, renamed Fryatt Street.

Duke(s) Shore, Alley & Stairs, Fore Street (Narrow Street), Limehouse, "the first on the right about five doors from the east end of Narrow Street" (Lockie).

Dukes Court, 1. Elbow Lane (Newlands Quay), Shadwell, 1890. 2. Fore Street (Narrow Street), Limehouse, "the first on the left a few doors from the east end of Narrow Street opposite Dukes shore leading into Ropemakers Fields" (Lockie).

Dukes Head Public House, 1. 119 Cable Street, St. George in the East, 1874, aka Duke of Cumberland. 2. 53 Chamber Street, Whitechapel. 3. 9 Old Gravel Lane (Wapping Lane), Wapping, 1874, aka Old Duke William, aka Duke of Bedfords Head. 4. 181 Whitechapel Road, Whitechapel, 1874.

Dukes Motto Public House, 1. 137 Brick Lane, Whitechapel. 2. 161 Jubilee Street, Stepney.

Dun Horse Public House, 24 Kingsland Road, Hackney, 1874.

Dunbar Cottages, St. Leonards Road, Poplar, 1891.

Dunbar House, Glengall Road (Tiller Rd), Isle of Dogs, later Tiller Road section, built in 1932 and demolished in 1976.

Dunbar Wharf, Limekiln Dock, Narrow Street, Limehouse, 1950.

Dunbridge Buildings & Place, Dunbridge Street, Bethnal Green, 1950.

Duncan Court, Hale Street, Poplar, 1851.

Duncan Place, West Street (Westgate Street), Hackney, 1841.

Duncan Square, Duncan Road, Hackney, 1895, Duncan House is on the site.

Duncan Street, 1. Off Leman Street, Whitechapel, renamed Camperdown Street. 2. Hackney, renamed Welshpool Street.

Dunch Street, Off Watney Street, Shadwell, 1950.

Dundee Arms Public House, 1. 339 Cambridge Road (Cambridge Heath Road), Bethnal Green. 2. 252 Wapping High Street, Wapping.

Dunk Court, King Edward Street (Kingward Street), Whitechapel, 1851.

Dunk Street, Off Hanbury Street (Greatorex Street), Spitalfields, "the first on the left three or four doors from Great Garden Street Whitechapel Road it extends to 86 Church Street being the first east parallel to High Street" (Lockie), Hanbury Street heading south just east of Greatorex Street.

Dunk Street Synagogue, 30 Dunk Street (Hanbury Street), Spitalfields, 1915, also known as Austrian Dzikower Synagogue.

Dunkeld Street, Off Abbott Road, Poplar, close to East India Dock Road.

Dunston House, Dunston Road, Hackney, 1950.

Dupont Street, Off Maroon Street, Limehouse, 1891, Shaw Crescent roughly follows its path.

Durant Arms Public House, 35 Durant Street, Bethnal Green, 1874.

Durham Arms Public House, 406 Hackney Road, Bethnal Green, 1874.

Durham Cottages, Homerton Terrace, Morning Lane, Hackney, 1851.

Durham Grove, Water Lane (Morning Lane), Hackney, 1891.

Durham Place, 1. Dalston Lane, Hackney, 1827, east of Woodland Street. 2. Grange Road (Gayhurst Road), Hackney, 1868, between Mayfield Street and Holly Street. 3. Hackney Road, Bethnal Green, either side of Durham Street.

Durham Street, Off Hackney Road, Bethnal Green, 1841, renamed Teesdale Street.

Durham Terrace, Henry Street (Carr Street), Stepney, 1871.

Dutfields Yard, Upper Berner Street (Henriques Street), St. George in the East.

Duthie Street, Off Prestons Road, Poplar, 1950.

Dutsoms Ways, King Edwards Stairs (Wapping High Street), Wapping, "between King Edwards stairs and New Crane about 1½ mile below London Bridge" (Lockie).

Duval Street, Off Crispin Street, Spitalfields, former Dorset Street, parallel with and directly south of Brushfield Street.

Dye House Lane, Old Ford Road, Bromley and Bow, 1895.

Dyer Street, Off St. Leonards Avenue (St. Leonards Road), Poplar, 1891, between St. Lenoards Avenue and Burcham Street, renamed Mauve Street.

Dyers Almshouses, St. John Street (Grimsby Street), Bethnal Green, "called in the Parliamentary Reports on the City Charities" The Spitalfields Almshouses, " are in St. John Street Brick Lane and contain apartments for ten poor widows of freemen or livery-men of the Company" (Elmes).

Dyers Arms Public House, 44 Brick lane, Spitalfields.

Dyers Court, Whitechapel High Street, Whitechapel, "at 52 the second on the left about twenty doors from Whitechapel Church towards Aldgate" (Lockie).

Dyssel Street, Off Bath Row (Dalston Lane), Hackney, 1891.

E

Eagle Brewery & Tap Public House, 151 Poplar High Street, Poplar.

Eagle Brewery Public House, 52 Wellclose Square, St. George in the East, aka Eagle Distillery.

Eagle Court & Place, King Street (Ming Street), Limehouse.

Eagle Place, 1. Mile End Road, Mile End, "on the north side about ¼ of a mile on the left below the Turnpike opposite 30 Assembly Row it leads to Fullers Almshouses" (Lockie), renamed Eaglet Place, was just to the east of the later ABC cinema. 2. Eagle Place, Princes Street (Princelet Street), Whitechapel, 1851.

Eagle Public House, 1. 106 Coventry Street (Coventry Road), Bethnal Green. 2. 52 Wellclose Square, St. George in the East, 1874. 3. 103 Wick Road, Hackney.

Eagle Sufferance Wharf, Wapping High Street, Wapping, 1895, south east of Dundee Street, became part of Morocco & Eagle Sufferance Wharves.

Eagle (Tavern) Public House, 1. 182 East India Dock Road, Poplar. 2. 95 Mile End Road, Mile End, 1874.

Eagle Wharf, Wapping High Street, Wapping, 1895, south of Sampson Street.

Eagling Road, Off Bruce Road, Bromley and Bow, Regent Square is on site.

Eale or Ely Place, Chicksand Street, Whitechapel, 1851.

Earl Darnley Public House, 1 Elsdale Street, Hackney, 1874.

Earl Derby Public House, 138 King Edwards Road, Hackney.

Earl Grey(s) Castle Public House, 1. 44 Mile End Road, Mile End, 1874. 2. 272 Bethnal Green Road, Bethnal Green. 3. 1 Luke Street (Lukin Street),

Shadwell. 4. 71 Vallance Road, Whitechapel.

Earl of Aberdeen Public House, 1. 181 Grove Road, Bromley and Bow, 1874. 2. 142 Whitechapel Road, Whitechapel.

Earl of Devon Public House, 213 Devons Road, Bromley and Bow, 1874.

Earl of Effingham Public House, 235 Whitechapel Road, Whitechapel, 1874.

Earl of Eglington Public House, 40 St. Stephens Road, Bromley and Bow.

Earl of Ellesmere Public House, 1. 19 Chisenhale Road, Bromley and Bow. 2. 36 Ellesmere Street, Poplar, 1874, aka Ellesmere Tavern.

Earl of Essex Public House, 27 James Street (Cadiz Street), Mile End.

Earl of Warwick Public House, 214 Whitechapel Road, Whitechapel, 1874.

Earl of Zetland Public House, 1. 137 Burdett Road, Bromley and Bow. 2. 50 Lee Street, Hackney, 1874, corner of Lee Street and Stean Street.

Earl Russell Public House, 35 Wick Road, Hackney.

Earl St. Vincent Public House, 41 Philpot Street, Whitechapel.

Earl Street, Off Calvin Street, Whitechapel, renamed Calvin Street.

Earl Terrace, Galbraith Street, Isle of Dogs, 1891, part of Galbraith Street.

Early Bird Public House, 50 Chrisp Street, Poplar.

Easington Buildings, Old Montague Street, Whitechapel, 1851.

East Court, East Street (Bishops Way), Bethnal Green, 1851.

East End Juvenile Mission, Hope Place (Rhodeswell Road), Limehouse, Rhodeswell Road.

East End Maternity Hospital, 384-398 Commercial Road, Shadwell, 1884-1968.

East End Mission to the Jews, 119 Leman Street, Whitechapel, 1921.

East India Almshouses, Poplar High Street, Poplar, "is about 3 of a mile on the in the High Street or Road from the Commercial Road nearly opposite Queen Street and the Spotted dog" ZZZ.

East India Arms Public House, 1. 31 Broad Street (The Highway), Ratcliffe, address also 31 Broad Street, also 110 Cock Hill, also 453 The Highway. 2. 95 East India Dock Road, Limehouse. 3. 5 Naval Row, Poplar. 4. 125 Poplar High Street, Poplar.

East India Coffee House, 225 Poplar High Street, Poplar, 1874.

East India Dock Tavern, 293-295 East India Dock Road, Poplar, 1874, Poplar Hospital was built on the site, also known as Dock House Tavern.

East India Hospital & Chapel, East India Dock Road, Poplar, 1862, site of East India Almshouses and later Poplar Recreation Ground.

East India House Public House, Poplar, renamed India House Tavern in 1824, demolished for construction of Blackwall Tunnel.

East India Road, Poplar, 1891, Occasional (old) spelling of East India Dock Road.

East India Row, Wells Street (Cotton Street), Poplar, "turns off at No18 Well Street near Robin Hood Lane High Street between Cotton Street and Garden Street" (Elmes).

East London Hospital for Children & Dispensary for Women, Glamis Road, Shadwell, 1891, Glamis Road, later Queen Elizabeth Hospital for Children.

East London Mission to the Jews, 87 Commercial Road, Whitechapel, 1892-1898.

East London Place, Martha Street, Shadwell, 1851.

East London Public House, 100 Whitechapel Road, Whitechapel, aka Earl of Effingham.

East London Shoeblack Society, 1. 86 Leman Street, Whitechapel. 2. 4 Mansell Street, Whitechapel.

East London Synagogue, Rectory Square, Mile End, 1877-1993.

East London Theatre, Wellclose Square, St. George in the East, aka Royalty aka Royal Brunswick Theatre.

East Mount Street & Terrace, Oxford Street (Stepney Way), Whitechapel, 1851, Whitechapel Road to Stepney Way, east of the original, main Whitechapel Hospital building.

East Place, Poplar High Street, Poplar, "is about a mile on the right from the Commercial Road and the first east from the Harrow Public House or the Kings Road" (Lockie).

East Row, St. Ann Street, Limehouse, renamed Chusan Place.

East Seabright Place, Hackney Road, Bethnal Green, 1851.

East Street, 1. Off Bancroft Road, Mile End, became part of Bancroft Road, section next to Moody Street. 2. Bromley and Bow, renamed Coborn Street. 3. Off Martha Street (Wadeson Street), Hackney, 1868, renamed Lyte Street. 4. Off North Street (Northiam Street), Hackney, 1891. 5. Off Preston Street (Roman Road), Bethnal Green, 1851. 6. Off Red Lion Street (Commercial Street), Spitalfields, short entrance street on east side of Spitalfields Market, "Spitalfields Market extends from the middle of the east side of it to 35 Red Lion Street" (Lockie). 7. Off Smart Street, Bethnal Green, 1841. 8. Off Usk Street, Bethnal Green, renamed Moss Street.

East Union Street, Off Commercial Street, Spitalfields, 1851.

Eastcot Place, 167-171 East India Dock Road, Poplar, 1851.

Eastern Dispensary, Goodmans Fields (Alie Street), Whitechapel, "Great Ayliffe Street Goodmans Fields at 46 about six doors west from Red Lion Street" (Lockie).

Eastern Empire Music Hall, 156 Bow Road, Bromley and Bow, later Regal Cinema.

Eastern Hotel & Public House, 2 East India Dock Road, Limehouse, 1874, renamed The Londoner.

Eastern Shades Public House, 1 North Street (Portman Place), Bethnal Green.

Eastern Star Public House, 40 Brunswick Street, Poplar.

Eastfield Cottages, Eastfield Street, Limehouse, 1891.

Eastfield Street, Off White Horse Street (White Horse Road), Stepney, 1891, from east of church to Regents Canal.

Eastman Street, Off Brady Street, Whitechapel, 1891, opposite Collingwood Estate.

Eastmans Court, Wentworth Street, Spitalfields, 1891,

Whitechapel "Wentworth Street a few doors on the left from Bell Lane nearly facing Old Castle Street from 120 Whitechapel High Street" (Lockie), rear of premises at north east corner of Wentworth Street and Bell Lane.

Eastward Street, Off Furze Street, Bromley and Bow.

Eaton Place, Ely Terrace (White Horse Lane), Mile End, 1891, close to White Horse Lane renamed, Shiloh Place.

Eaton Place & Terrace, Well Street, Hackney, 1868, at its corner with Cassland Road.

Ebbs Court, Old Castle Street, Whitechapel.

Ebeneza or Ebenezer Place, 1. Chrisp Street, Poplar, 1950. 2. West India Dock Road, Limehouse, 1851.

Ebenezer & William Cottages, Powis Road, Bromley and Bow, 1891.

Ebenezer Chapel, Shadwell High Street (The Highway), Shadwell, "at 240 about ten doors west from Union Street" (Lockie).

Ebenezer Place, 1. Broadway London Fields (Broadway Market), Hackney, 1891. 2. Commercial Road, Limehouse, "is part of the south side about $1/5$ of a mile on the right below Limehouse Church extending from Penson Place to Gun Lane" (Lockie). 3. Halley Street, Limehouse, 1891.

Ebenezer Terrace, 1. Turner Street, Whitechapel, 1851. 2. Westferry Road, Isle of Dogs, 1851, between Byng Street and Strafford Street.

Ebners Wharf, Stewart Street, Isle of Dogs, 1950, north of Samuda Estate.

Eckersley Street, Off Buxton Street, Whitechapel, 1891, Allen Gardens is on the site.

Eden House, Homerton Terrace, Hackney, 1891, Morning Lane.

Edgar Place, James Street (Cadiz Street), Mile End, 1891.

Edinburgh Castle Public House, 1. 91 Lower East Smithfield (St. Katharines Way), East Smithfield. 2. Edinburgh Castle Public House, 37 Rhodeswell Road, Limehouse, 1874.

Edinburgh Road, Off St. Dunstans Road (Mile End Stadium), Mile End, 1891.

Edith Gardens, Bird Cage Walk (Columbia Road), Bethnal Green, 1827, became part of Simpsons Place.

Edith Place, Hackney Road, Bethnal Green, Shoreditch "Hackney Road is the first turning on the left hand in Bird Cage Walk, a few doors from the Nags Head going towards Shoreditch Church" (Elmes).

Edith Street, Off Queens Road (Queensbridge Road), Hackney, Haggerston Park is on the site.

Edna Place, Ann Street (East India Dock Road), Poplar, 1891.

Edward Court, Spital Street, Spitalfields, "is in Spital Street" (Elmes).

Edward Place, Hackney Road, Bethnal Green, "forms part of the south side adjoining Bright on Place a few doors on the right east from Allports nursery, and about ⅓ of a mile from Shoreditch Church" (Lockie).

Edward Street, 1. Off Catherine Street (Maroon Street), Limehouse, 1868, renamed Blount Street. 2. Off Cephas Street, Mile End, 1891, renamed Edwin Street. 3. Off Church Street (Bethnal Green Road), Bethnal Green, renamed Kerbela Street. 4. Off Ernest Street, Mile End, renamed Duckett Street. 5. Edward Street, Off St. Pauls Road (St. Pauls Way), Bromley and Bow, 1891, renamed Leopold Street.

Edwards Cottages, Woolpack Place, Hackney, 1851.

Edwards Place, 1. Hackney Road, Bethnal Green, 1851. 2. Pell Street (Wellclose Square), St. George in the East, 1891.

Edwards Road, Off Solebay Street, Bromley and Bow, immediately east of Burdett Road.

Edwin Place, Salmon Lane, Limehouse, 1851.

Edwins Terrace, Wilman Grove, Hackney, 1868.

Eel Pye House, Robin Hood Lane, Poplar, 1750.

Eele Place & Street, Off King Edward Street (Kingward Street), Whitechapel, 1851.

Effringham Saloon, Whitechapel Road, Whitechapel, 1870, opposite St. Mary Street.

Egleton Road, Off Grace Street, Bromley and Bow, 1891.

Egleton Road, Off Talwin Street, Bromley and Bow.

Eglinton Road, Off Saxon Road, Bromley and Bow, became part of Saxon Road.

Eight Bells Public House, 1. Chrisp Street, Poplar, 1874. 2. Church Street (Mare Street), Hackney, 1874. 3. 1 Elder Street, Spitalfields, 1874. 4. 24 Poplar High Street, Poplar.

Eileen House, Splidts Street (Forbes Street), St. George in the East.

Eileen Mansions, Fairclough Street, St. George in the East, 1950.

Elbow Lane, Shadwell High Street (The Highway), Shadwell, "the first south parallel to part of it say from 23 to 38 extending from New Gravel Lane four doors from High Street to Farmer Street" (Lockie).

Elder Court, Elder Street, Spitalfields, 1891.

Elder Tree Public House, 1. 119 Chrisp Street, Poplar, 1874. 2. 1 Elder Street, Spitalfields.

Eleanor Arms Public House, 458 Old Ford Road, Bromley and Bow.

Eleanor House, Whiston Road, Bethnal Green, 1950, just west of Nicholl Street.

Eleanor Place, Newcastle Street (Sunbury Workshops), Bethnal Green, 1851.

Elephant & Castle Court, Whitechapel High Street, Whitechapel, 1851.

Elephant & Castle Public House, 1. 22-23 Whitechapel High Street, Whitechapel, 1874. 2. 302 Wick Road, Hackney.

Elgin Street, Hackney, renamed Chapman Road.

Eli Street, Off Pearson Street, Bethnal Green, 1895, renamed Shap Street.

Elijah Cottages, Samuel Street (Wicker Street), St. George in the East, 1891.

Elim Chapel, Pekin Street, Limehouse, 1883.

Eliza Cottages, Homerton Terrace, Hackney, 1891, Morning Lane.

Eliza Terrace, Rhodeswell Road, Limehouse, 1871.

Elizabeth Cottage, Bridge Street (Solebay Street), Bromley and Bow, 1891.

Elizabeth(s) Cottages, 1. Castor Street (Birchfield Street), Limehouse, 1891. 2. Avenue Road (Kitcat Terrace), Bromley and Bow, 1851. 3. Cowley Street (Martineau Estate), Shadwell, renamed Cowley Gardens. 4. Pundersons Gardens (Bethnal Green Road), Bethnal Green.

Elizabeth Cottages, Place & Fibre Works, Ingelheim Place (Westferry Road), Isle of Dogs, 1891.

Elizabeth Court, Brook Street (Cable Street), Ratcliffe, 1890, Barnardo Gardens is on the site.

Elizabeth Court or Place, Dorset Street (Pitsea Street), Ratcliffe, 1891, south end of Dorset Street, renamed Horndon Place.

Elizabeth Fry Refuge or Mansion House, 195 Mare Street, Hackney, 1851.

Elizabeth House, Park Road (Parkholme Road), Hackney, 1851.

Elizabeth Place, 1. Burn Street (Carr Street), Stepney, 1891. 2. Fountain Alley (Columbia Road), Bethnal Green, 1841. 3. George Street (Patriot Square), Bethnal Green, "on the north-west side of Patriot Square near the green" (Lockie), renamed Betton Place. 4. Lisbon Street (Cambridge Heath Road), Bethnal Green, 1841. 5. Orchard Place, Poplar, 1851. 6. Ricardo Street, Poplar.

Elizabeth Row, George Street (Patriot Square), Bethnal Green.

Elizabeth Street, 1. Off Brunswick Street, Poplar, 1885, Brunswick Street to St. Leonards Road, close to Grundy Street. 2.

Off Duff Street, Poplar, renamed Rigden Street. 3. Off Hackney Road, Bethnal Green, 1860, became the northern half of Mansford Street. 4. Off Kerbey Street, Poplar, became part of Southill Street. 5. St. George in the East, renamed Stutfield Street.

Elizabeth Terrace, 1. Alpha Road (Alpha Grove), Isle of Dogs, 1891. 2. Hackney Road, Bethnal Green, 1851. 3. Sophia Street (Shirbutt Street), Poplar, 1891.

Elizabeth Villas, Albert Road (Albion Drive), Hackney, 1868, between Queens (now Queensbridge) Road and Malvern Road.

Ellen Cottage, Stockmar Road (Morning Lane), Hackney, 1891.

Ellen Court, Ellen Street, St. George in the East, 1891.

Ellen Mansions, Christian Street, St. George in the East.

Ellen Place, Ellen Street, St. George in the East, 1891.

Ellens Place, Newcastle Street (Sunbury Workshops), Bethnal Green, 1841.

Ellerman Street, Off Latham Street (Bartlett Park), Limehouse, 1860, Latham Street to Upper North Street, Bartlett Park is on the site.

Ellerthorpe Arms Public House, 60 Kerbey Street, Poplar, 1874.

Ellerthorpe Street, Poplar, 1891, Chrisp Street to Kerbey Street, Chrisp Street Market is on the site.

Ellesmere Tavern, 36 Ellesmere Street, Poplar, aka Earl of Ellesmere.

Elliotts Row, Bethnal Green Road, Bethnal Green, "the first south parallel to a part of it about ²/₃ of a mile from 65 Shoreditch extending from White Street to Thomas Street and is behind the Admiral Cornwallis Public House" (Lockie), became part of Voss Street.

Ellison Street, Off Petticoat Lane (Middlesex Street), Spitalfields, "the third on the left from 41 Aldgate High St, a few doors north from Little Middlesex Street" (Lockie).

Elm Cottages, 1. Castor Street (Birchfield Street), Limehouse, 1891. 2. Kerbey Street, Poplar, 1851. 3. Mare Street, Hackney, 1860, Trelawney Estate is on site.

Elm House, Row & Cottage, Love Lane (Brodlove Lane), Shadwell, 1891, Cable Street, renamed Elf Row.

Elm Row, Sun Tavern Fields (The Highway), Shadwell, 1746.

Elm Terrace, Andrews Road, Hackney, 1851.

Elms Cottages, Grundy Street, Poplar, 1851, west of Chrisp Street.

Elsden Mews, Old Ford Road, Bromley and Bow, north of Cyprus Place.

Elsie House, Philip Street (Ellen Street), St. George in the East.

Eltham Place, Charles Street (Aylward Street), Stepney, 1891.

Eltham Place or Terrace, Church Passage (Aylward Street), Stepney, 1895.

Elves & Halford Cinematograph Theatre, 72 Bow Common Lane, Bromley and Bow.

Elvidge Cottages & Terrace, Wick Road, Hackney, 1862.

Ely Place, 1. Chicksand Street, Whitechapel, 1950. 2. Digby Street, Bethnal Green. 3. Globe Road, Bethnal Green, 1891, renamed Lansdell Place. 4. White Horse Lane, Mile End, 1891.

Ely Terrace, White Horse Lane, Mile End, 1950, White Horse Lane to Harford Street, south of and parallel with Mile End Road.

Emery Mission Hall, Augusta Street, Poplar, 1921.

Emerys Place, Butler Street, Spitalfields, 1891.

Emily Cottage, Johns Place (Robin Hood Lane), Poplar, 1891.

Emma Place, 213-215 East India Dock Road, Poplar, 1860.

Emma Terrace, Brook Street (Cable Street), Ratcliffe, 1851.

Emmanuel Mission Church, Devonport Street, Shadwell, 1890, corner of Steels Lane.

Emmanuels or Jews Almshouses, Wellclose Square, St. George in the East, 1891.

Emmett Place, Catherine Street (Anthony Street), St. George in the East, 1851.

Emmett Street, Off Three Colt Street, Limehouse, 1951, Three Colt Street to Westferry Road.

Emmott Street, Off Harford Street, Mile End, 1891, part became part of Essian Street.

Empire Mansions, 293-297 Mare Street, Hackney, 1950.

Empire Wharf, Saunders Ness Road, Isle of Dogs, 1950, Empire Wharf Road is on its site.

Empress of India Public House, 130 Lauriston Road, Hackney.

Endive Street & Place, Rhodeswell Road, Limehouse, parallel with and south of Dora Street.

England Place & Row, Poplar High Street, Poplar, "about 1/3 of a mile on the left below the Commercial Road nearly opposite the Harrow Public House or the Kings Road" (Lockie), approximately 165-177 Poplar High Street.

Englands Queen Public House, 74 Eastfield Street, Limehouse.

Englefield Place, East India Dock Road, Poplar, 1851, corner of Robin Hood Lane.

Enterprise Public House, 1. 67-69 Chicksand Street, Whitechapel, aka Halifax Arms. 2. 69 Grundy Street, Poplar, corner of Kerbey Street. 3. 145 Three Colt Street, Limehouse.

Entick Street, Off Railway Place (Malcolm Place), Bethnal Green, 1891, formerly Albert Street and Colebrook Terrace, renamed Malcolm Place.

Episcopal Jews Chapel, Palestine Place (Cambridge Heath Road), Bethnal Green, 1809.

Epping Place, Mile End Road, Mile End, "on the south side about a mile on the right from Aldgate Pump extending from the turnpike to Mile End Grove and leading towards Stepney Green" (Lockie), became part of Sidney Street.

Era Place, Bow Lane, Poplar, 1851.

Eric Street, Off Bow Common Lane, Bromley and Bow, 1891, takes in Brantridge Street and part of St. Dunstans Road in 1905.

Ernest Place, Russia Lane, Bethnal Green, 1891.

Ernest Street West, Mile End, renamed Eastbury Terrace.

Escott(s) Cottages, Robert Street (Cuba Street), Isle of Dogs, 1851.

Esmond Road, Off Roman Road, Bromley and Bow.

Essex Arms Public House, 110 St. Stephens Road, Bromley and Bow.

Essex Place, 1. Essex Street (Blythe Street), Bethnal Green. 2. Grange Road (Gayhurst Road), Hackney, 1868, between Queens Road and Holly Street. 3. Hackney Road, Bethnal Green, 1868, east of Tuilerie Street. 4. Hertford Place (Haggerston Road), Hackney, 1868. 5. Mare Street, Hackney, 1860, south of Devonshire Road. 6. Old Bethnal Green Road, Bethnal Green, 1841. 7. Orchard Place, Poplar, 1891. 8. Wells Street (Cotton Street), Poplar, 1851.

Essex Street, 1. Off Bethnal Green Road, Bethnal Green, renamed Blythe Street. 2. Hackney, renamed Bocking Street. 3. Off James Street (Chilton Street), Bethnal Green, 1827, Wessex Street follows some of its route. 4. Off Prestons Road, Poplar, 1851. 5. Off Three Colts Lane (Three Colts Lane), Bethnal Green, renamed Buckhurst Street. 6. Off Whitechapel High Street, Whitechapel, "at 105 about ¼ of a mile on the left below Aldgate Church nearly opposite Red Lion Street it leads to Wentworth Street nearly opposite Rose Lane late Catherine Wheel Alley" (Lockie), became the southern end of Commercial Street.

Essex Wharf, Narrow Street,

Ratcliffe, 1895, east of Duke Shore Wharf.

Essex Wharf & School House, Bucks Row (Durward Street), Whitechapel, 1891.

Esther Hawes Almshouses, Bow Lane (Bazely Street), Poplar, "founded in 1686 by a person of that name for six poor widows who have a room and thirty shillings a year each" (Elmes), south end of Bow Lane later Bazely Street.

Eton Place, Well Street, Hackney, 1895, renamed Purcell Place and Priory Place.

Evan Hurndall Mission, 109 Bow Road, Bromley and Bow, 1921.

Evans Street, Off Upper North Street, Poplar, renamed Pekin Street.

Evans Yard, Poplar High Street, Poplar, "near + of a mile on the left from the Commercial Road leading to Paradise Street Noble Street and the East India Dock Road".

Evelyn Villas, Malvern Road, Hackney, 1868, between Grange Road and Shrubland Grove.

Everard Street, Off Back Church Lane, St. George in the East, 1891, south of Boyd Street. Not connected to Everards Place.

Everards Place, Back Church Lane, St. George in the East, 1891, parallel with and west of Back Church Lane, immediately north of the railway. Not connected to Everard Street.

Ewing Street, Off Maidman(s) Street (Burdett Road), Bromley and Bow, 1891.

Ewings Buildings, Mile End Road, Mile End, "is part of the south side about ¼ of a mile on the right east from Bencrofts Almshouses near two miles from Aldgate" (Lockie), immediately east of Regents Canal.

Excelsior Terrace & Baths, Mansford Street, Bethnal Green, 1891, corner of Florida Street.

Exchange Tavern Public House, 241 Poplar High Street, Poplar, 1874, aka Sun & Sawyers, aka Rising Sun.

Execution Dock, Brewhouse Lane, Wapping, on the riverfront south of Brewhouse Lane King Henrys Stairs are on the site.

Exmouth Arms Public House, 9 Exmouth Street, Stepney, 1874, aka Hollands.

Exmouth Place, 1. Catherine Street (Anthony Street), St. George in the East, 1851. 2. Exmouth Street, Stepney, 1862, close to Commercial Road.

Experienced Fowler Public House, 83 Northey Street, Limehouse, 1874.

Express Wharf, Westferry Road, Isle of Dogs, 1950, north of Hutchings Street.

Ezras Chaim Synagogue,

Heneage Street, Whitechapel, 1935.

F

Factory Place, Ferry Street, Isle of Dogs, 1891, ran along side of Ferry House Public House.

Factory Road, Off Commercial Road, Stepney, 1851.

Factory Street, Off Byng Street (Vaughan Way), Wapping, 1790, London Docks, Western Dock was built on the site.

Fair Place, Charles Street (Aylward Street), Stepney, 1862, became part of Charles Street.

Fair Street, Off Oxford Street (Stepney Way), Whitechapel, renamed Dunelm Street.

Fairclough Street, Off Back Church Lane, St. George in the East, 1891.

Fairclough Street School, Fairclough Street, St. George in the East, renamed Harry Gosling School.

Fair Field, Bow Road, Bromley and Bow, 1837, field opposite Drapers Almshouses.

Fairfield Place, Fairfield Road, Bromley and Bow, 1851.

Faith Street, Off Cambridge Heath Road, Mile End, 1950, north of Trinity Almshouses, heading east.

Falcon Buildings, Old Bethnal Green Road, Bethnal Green, 1891, between Mansford Street and Blythe Street.

Falcon Court, Essex Street (Blythe Street), Bethnal Green, 1868.

Falcon Public House, 1. 67 Blythe Street, Bethnal Green. 2. 202 East India Dock Road, Poplar. 3. 1 Green Street (Roman Road), Bethnal Green, 1874, sometimes known as the Old Blind Beggar.

Falcon Wharf, Saunders Ness Road, Isle of Dogs, 1950, Storers Quay is on its site.

Fan Alley, Webb Square (Wheler Street), Spitalfields, "at the north-east corner entering at 47 Shoreditch it leads to Cock hill and to 47 Wheler Street" (Lockie).

Fan Court, Bakers Row (Vallance Road), Whitechapel, 1851.

Faraday Dwellings, Brightlingsea Place, Limehouse, 1950.

Farmer Street, Off Shadwell High Street (The Highway), Shadwell, High Street south to Milk Yard east of New Gravel Lane Shadwell Basin is on the site.

Farmers Arms Public House, 169 Mile End Road, Mile End, aka Black Boy.

Farmers Place or Row, Salmon Lane, Limehouse, "forms a part of the east side about $\frac{1}{8}$ of a mile on the right from the Commercial Road towards Stepney" (Lockie).

Farnfield Street, Off Kerbey Street, Poplar, 1950.

Farrance Terrace, Dora Street, Limehouse, 1891, later part of Spenlow Street.

Farrant Terrace, Mary Street (Bigland Street), St. George in the East, 1871.

Farthing Alley, Upper East Smithfield, East Smithfield, 1851.

Farthing Fields, New Gravel Lane (Garnet Street), Wapping, between King Henry Court and New Gravel Lane.

Farthing Street, Off Phoenix Street (Brick Lane), Spitalfields, "the first on the left about sixteen doors from 39 Wheler Street or the third on the right from 163 Brick Lane" (Lockie).

Fashion Court, Fashion Street, Spitalfields, 1891, south side of Fashion Street.

Fashion Street Sephardic Synagogue, Fashion Street, Spitalfields.

Favonia Street, Off Empson Street, Bromley and Bow, 1891.

Fawcett Road & Square, Hackney, 1868, renamed Fassett Road and Square.

Fawe Street, Off Morris Road, Poplar, 1891.

Feathers Court, (Old) Castle Street (Virginia Road), Bethnal Green, "the first on the right from the back of Shoreditch Church about three or four doors from the north end of Cock Lane" (Lockie). Old Castle Street became westernmost part of Virginia Road...

Feathers Public House, 1, 16 Old Castle Street, Bethnal Green, 1874. 2. Feathers Public House, 33 Virginia Road, Bethnal Green.

Featherstone Buildings, Salmon Lane, Limehouse, "the first east parallel to a part of it the entrance is a few doors on the right from the barge river or from the Commercial Road" (Lockie), now part of Rhodeswell Road.

Felix House, Splidts Street (Forbes Street), St. George in the East.

Felix Street, Off Cambridge Crescent, Bethnal Green, 1851, Hackney Road.

Fellbrigg Street, Whitechapel, east of and parallel with Collingwood Street.

Felstead Wharf, Ferry Street, Isle of Dogs, 1950, Felstead Gardens is on its site.

Fenners Wharf, Westferry Road, Isle of Dogs, 1950, close to Wateridge Close.

Fenton Street, Off Commercial Road, St. George in the East, 1950, Commercial Road to Mariner Street.

Fenton Street Synagogue, 15 Fenton Street, St. George in the East, 1950, Commercial Road.

88

Fergusons Wharf, Westferry Road, Isle of Dogs, 1950, Ferguson Close is on its site.

Ferriers Court, Globe Road, Mile End, 1891.

Field Court, Ducking Pond Row (Durward Street), Whitechapel, "the fourth on the right from Court Street 110 Whitechapel Road or the third on the left from North Street in the opposite direction" (Lockie).

Field Street, Off Poplar High Street, Poplar, "is about ½ a mile on the left from the Commercial Road and the second below the East India Almshouses leading to Fowlers Rents and the East India Dock Road" (Lockie).

Field View, London Terrace (London Fields), Hackney, 1891, London Fields.

Field(s) Cottages, Lamb Lane, Hackney, 1891.

Fieldgate Street Great Synagogue, 41 Fieldgate Street, Whitechapel, 1899-2014.

Fieldwick Cottages, Mead Place, Hackney, 1891, Retreat Place.

Fighting Cocks Public House, 46 St. John Street (Grimsby Street), Bethnal Green.

Finch Street, Off Brick Lane, Whitechapel, 1851, renamed Hopetown Street.

Finch Yard, Poplar High Street, Poplar, "the second on the left below North Street opposite the Town hall" (Lockie).

Finchingfield Terrace, Chrisp Street, Poplar, 1851.

Finicks (or Phoenix) Court, Shorter Street (Wellclose Square), St. George in the East, 1878, Wellclose Square.

Fir Tree Public House, 22 Church Lane (White Church Lane), Whitechapel.

Fish & (the) Ring Public House, 141 White Horse Street (White Horse Road), Stepney, 1874.

Fishers & Griggs Almshouses, Cambridge Road (Cambridge Heath Road), Bethnal Green, 1841.

Fishers Alley, Middlesex Street, Spitalfields, 1891, "the third turning on the right hand in Middlesex Street formerly Petticoat Lane a few doors northward of Wentworth Street" (Elmes), East of Sandys Row and north of Wentworth St.

Fishers Almshouses, Dog Row (Cambridge Heath Road), Whitechapel, "Two or three houses on the left hand from the Turnpike towards Bethnal Green They were erected and endowed by Captain Fisher in 1711, for the widows of six masters of ships under the trusteeship of the Corporation of Trinity House" (Elmes).

Fishing Boat Public House,

Three Mill Lane, Bromley and Bow.

Fishing Smack Public House, 9 Cold Harbour, Poplar, formerly known as Fishermans Arms.

Five Bell Alley or Place, Three Colt Street, Limehouse, "is opposite the east side of the church by the Five Bells Public House" (Lockie).

Five Bell Court, Wheler Street, Spitalfields, "at 43 nearly facing Webb Square from Shoreditch about five doors north from Phoenix Street it extends to Farthing Street" (Lockie).

Five Bells (and Blade Bone) Public House, 27 Three Colt Street, Limehouse, 1874.

Five Constable Row, Mile End Road, Mile End, "part of the north side commencing by Dog Row a few yards on the left east from the Turnpike about a mile from Aldgate Pump" (Lockie), corner of Mile End Road and Cambridge Heath Road.

Five Houses Corner, Tyson Street (Brick Lane), Bethnal Green, "at 10 the first on the left ten doors from 52 Church Street opposite Brick Lane" (Lockie).

Five Ink Horns Public House, 31-32 New Nichol(s) Street (Boundary Estate), Bethnal Green, 1874.

Five Inkhorn Court, Whitechapel High Street, Whitechapel, "at 91 about ¼ of a mile on the left below Aldgate Pump and eighteen or twenty doors west from Osborn Street" (Lockie).

Flank Street, Off Dock Street, St. George in the East, 1950.

Flaschs Synagogue or Congregation, Mansell Street, Whitechapel, 1870.

Fleet Street, Off St. John Street (Grimsby Street), Bethnal Green, "the first south parallel to part of St. John Street Brick Lane, extending from George Street to Fleet Street Hill" (Lockie) renamed Pedley Street.

Fleet Street Hill, Bethnal Green Road, Bethnal Green, "St. John Street Spitalfields or Bethnal Green the fourth on the right about ⅛ of a mile from 105 Brick Lane, it leads to Fleet Street and extends to Weavers Street" (Lockie).

Fleetwood Arms Public House, 85 Pritchards Road, Bethnal Green.

Flemings Court, Wentworth Street, Whitechapel, 1851.

Fletchers Villas, Bridge Road (Westferry Road), Limehouse.

Fletchers Ways, Shadwell High Street (The Highway), Shadwell, "about 1¾ of a mile below London Bridge by the line of the river the first east of Shadwell Dock and nearly opposite the Surrey canal Rotherhithe" (Lockie).

Fleur de Lis Buildings, Fleur de Lis Street, Spitalfields, 1950.

Fleur de Lis Court & Street, Off Wheler Street, Spitalfields, 1851.

Fleur de Lis Public House, 17 Fleur de Lis Street, Spitalfields, 1874.

Flint Avenue, Hobday Street, Poplar, 1891.

Flint Court, King Street (Mace Street), Bromley and Bow, 1841, Old Ford Road.

Flint Street, Off Guildford Road (Upper North Street), Poplar, renamed Hobday Street.

Flint Terrace, Mace Street, Bethnal Green, Cranbrook Estate is on the site.

Florence Cottages, Avenue Road (Kitcat Terrace), Bromley and Bow, 1851.

Florence Terrace, Alpha Road (Alpha Grove), Isle of Dogs, 1891.

Floreston Street, Off Mile End Road, Mile End, 1891, just east of White Horse Lane.

Florfield Arms Public House, 40 Florfield Road, Hackney.

Florida Terrace, Florida Street, Bethnal Green, 1891.

Florist Public House, 255 Globe Road, Bethnal Green.

Flower & Dean Street, Off Brick Lane, Spitalfields, "at 200 Brick Lane the third on the left from 74 Whitechapel High Street it extends to Rose Lane" (Lockie).

Flower de Luce Street, Off Fleur de Lis Street, Spitalfields, "the east continuation of Flower de Luce Court going from Shoreditch" (Elmes), renamed Fleur de Lis Street.

Flower Pot Public House, 1. 120 Bethnal Green Road, Bethnal Green. 2. 43 Old Bethnal Green Road, Bethnal Green.

Flowers Terrace, Stainsby Road, Limehouse, 1851.

Flying Horse Public House, 1. 63 Lambeth Street (Alie Street), Whitechapel, 1874, Little Alie Street. 2. 149 Marc Street, Hackney, 1874. 3. 32 West Street (Usk Street), Bethnal Green.

Flying Horse Yard, 1. Brick Lane, Spitalfields, "Spitalfields at 31 about $^1/_5$ of a mile on the right from 74 Whitechapel and 10 or 12 doors on the left from Church Street Spitalfields" (Lockie). 2. Mare Street, Hackney, 1841.

Flying Scud Public House, 1 Sutton Street, Shadwell.

Folkestone Terrace, 241-243 East India Dock Road, Poplar, 1851.

Folly House (Tavern) Public House, Folly Wall, Isle of Dogs, 1874.

Folly Street, Off Folly Wall, Isle of Dogs, now part Folly Wall, part Stewart Street.

Ford Road, Off Old Ford Road, Bromley and Bow, renamed Ford Street.

Forage Wharf, Broad Street (The Highway), Shadwell, 1895, east of Shadwell Park, became part of Charringtons Wharf.

Fore Street, Off Narrow Street, Limehouse, "the east continuation of Narrow Street and first parallel to the Thames extending from the second Drawbridge to Three colt Street" (Lockie), the section of Narrow Street between Ropemakers Fields and Three Colt Street.

Forest Cottages & House, Forest Row, Hackney, 1851.

Forest Grove, Richmond Road, Hackney, 1851, became part of Woodland Street.

Forest Place, Forest Row, Hackney, 1851, Kingsland Road.

Forest Row, Kingsland Road, Hackney, 1841, renamed Forest Road.

Forester Street, Off Canal Road (Mile End Road), Bromley and Bow, 1891, Canal Road to Burdett Road, immediately north of Solebay Street.

Foresters Arms Public House, 1. 94 Brady Street, Whitechapel, Collingwood Estate is now on the site. 2. 87-89 Myrdle Street, Whitechapel. 3. 121 Salmon Lane, Limehouse, corner of Parnham Street. 4. 253 St. Leonards Road, Poplar, 1874. 5. 19 Woolmore Street, Poplar.

Foresters Musical Hall & Public House, 95 Cambridge Road (Cambridge Heath Road), Whitechapel.

Foresters Public House, 1. 93 Cambridge Road (Cambridge Heath Road), Whitechapel, aka Artichoke. 2. 19 Rhodeswell Road, Limehouse.

Fortunate Place, Victoria Street (Dellow Street), Shadwell, 1851.

Fosseys Court, Robert Street (Cuba Street), Isle of Dogs, 1851.

Fosskett Buildings, Globe Road, Mile End, 1891.

Foster Street, Off Bath Street (Darling Row), Whitechapel, 1841, Collingwood Estate is now on the site.

Foulks Buildings, Wilmot Square, Bethnal Green, "behind the George on the north side of Wilmot Square near ¼ of a mile on the left from 65 Shoreditch" (Lockie).

Foundary Wharf, Wapping High Street, Wapping, 1895, opposite corner with Hilliards Court (Cinnamon Street).

Foundation School, Leman Street, Whitechapel, 1891.

Founders Arms Public House, 213 Brick Lane, Spitalfields, 1874.

Fountain Alley, Court & Place, Crab Tree Row (Columbia Road), Bethnal Green, 1841, Virginia Row.

Fountain Public House, 1. 39 James Street (Chilton Street), Bethnal Green, 1874. 2. 436 Mile

End Road, Mile End, 1874. 3. Stracey Street (Jamaica Street), Stepney, 1874, Stracey Street renamed Jamaica Street, address also 86 Stacey Street. 4. 93 Virginia Road, Bethnal Green, 1874.

Fountain Street, Off Columbia Road, Bethnal Green, 1891, opposite Georgina Gardens.

Four Mills Street, Bromley and Bow, 1851, renamed St. Leonards Street.

Fournier Street Synagogue, 29 Fournier Street, Spitalfields.

Fowlers Rents, Poplar High Street, Poplar, "is about ½ a mile on the left from the Commercial Road the second Row below the East India Almshouses it extends from Field Street to the East India Dock Road" (Lockie).

Fox & Goose Public House, 40 Shakespeare(s) Walk (Shadwell Basin), Shadwell.

Fox & Goose Yard, Coleman Street (Coleman Close), Wapping, 1851.

Fox & Hounds Public House, 57 Hare Street (Cheshire Street), Whitechapel, 1874.

Fox & Yorkshire Grey Public House, 38 Mile End Road, Mile End.

Fox Court, Petticoat Lane (Middlesex Street), Spitalfields, "on the east side about nine doors south from Wentworth Street nearly opposite Stoney Lane ⅛

of a mile on the right from 41 Aldgate High Street" (Lockie).

Fox Lane, Middleton Road, Hackney, 1891, now part of Haggerston Road.

Fox Public House, 1. 65 Bishops Road (Bishops Way), Bethnal Green. 2. 20 Braintree Street, Mile End. 4. 3 Foxs Lane (Shadwell Basin), Shadwell. 4. 44 Russell Street (Halcrow Street), Whitechapel, 1874.

Fox Street, Off Lucas Street (Newcourt House), Bethnal Green, 1841.

Fox(e)s Cottages, Stockmar Road (Morning Lane), Hackney, 1851.

Fox(e)s Lane, 1. Morning Lane, Hackney, 1851, Morning Lane to Paragon Road. 2. Shadwell High Street (The Highway), Shadwell, High Street to Lower Shadwell immediately west of St. Pauls Church renamed Pear Tree Lane in 1862 Shadwell Basin is on the site.

Framework Knitters (or Stocks Weavers) Almshouses, Kingsland Road, Hackney, 1895, immediately north of Ironmongers Almshouses.

Frampton Arms Public House, 65 Well Street, Hackney, 1874.

Francis Gray House, Masters Street, Mile End, 1950.

Francis Place, Princes Row (Old Montague Street), Whitechapel, "the second on the left a few doors west from Bakers Row entering at 94 Whitechapel Road" (Lockie).

Francis Street, 1. Limehouse, renamed Farrance Street. 2. Became part of Weymouth Place (Weymouth Terrace), Bethnal Green.

Frederick Place, 1. Bromley and Bow, renamed Aberavon Road. 2. Devonshire Street (Bancroft Road), Mile End, 1891, opposite Barrows Almshouses. 3. Nelson Street, Whitechapel, 1891, renamed Cameron Place. 4. Tetley Street (Chrisp Street), Poplar, 1851.

Frederick Street, 1. St. George in the East, 1891, became part of Pinchin Street. 2. Off Salmon Lane, Limehouse, renamed Galt Street.

Frederick Villas, Lavender Grove, Hackney, 1868, between Queens Road and Malvern Road.

Fredericks Cottages, 148-152 East India Dock Road, Poplar, 1856.

Fredericks Terrace, Kingsland Crescent (Kingsland Road), Hackney, 1862.

Free Passage Alley, Cock Hill, Shadwell, "The first turning on the right hand on Cock Hill going from High Street Shadwell" (Elmes).

Free Technical School, 5 Rupert Street (Goodman Street), Whitechapel, 1910, Goodmans Fields.

Free Trade Wharf, The Highway, Shadwell, 1950, south of Heckford Street.

Freeman Street, Off Shepherd Street (Commercial Street), Spitalfields, 1891, Brune House was built on the site.

Freemans Cottages, Old Church Road, Stepney, 1891.

Freemans Court, James Street (Chilton Street), Bethnal Green, 1851.

Freemasons Arms Public House, 1. 70 Goulston Street, Whitechapel. 2. 45 Pereira Street (Darling Row), Whitechapel. 3. 96-98 Salmon Lane, Limehouse, 1874, corner with Rhodeswell Road.

French (Protestant) Hospital & Lodge, Victoria Park Road, Hackney, 1718-1949, Mare Street.

French Alley, Dorset Street, Spitalfields, 1746, later Paternoster Row.

French Church or Chapel, Brick Lane, Spitalfields, "on the west side the corner of Church Street about ¼ of a mile on the left from Whitechapel" (Lockie).

French Court or Place, Great Hermitage Street (Hermitage Wall), Wapping, 1891.

French Protestants Almshouse, Black Eagle Street (Brick Lane), Spitalfields, "established in 1733 for the supplying poor French protestants with soup meat and bread" (Elmes).

French Row, Green Street
(Roman Road), Bethnal Green,
"the second north parallel to part
of Green Street about $1/3$ of a
mile east from the green it
extends from Bonner Street to
Cross Street" (Lockie).

Friars Mount Court, Mount
Street (Swanfield Street), Bethnal
Green, 1851.

Friars or Fryers Hill, Great
Hermitage Street (Hermitage
Wall), Wapping, "at 41 about the
middle of the north side it leads
to Redmaid Lane by the London
Dock" (Lockie).

Friendly Buildings, 1. Back
Church Lane, St. George in the
East, 1851, diagonally opposite
North Street. 2. Old Ford Road,
Bromley and Bow, 1851.

Friendly Place, 1. Whitechapel,
renamed Ely Terrace (White
Horse Lane). 2. King David
Lane, Shadwell, "Sun Tavern
Fields on the south side the rope
ground entrance by the first on
the right in King David Lane
from 198 Shadwell High Street"
(Lockie). 3. Tait Street, St.
George in the East, 1895. 4.
Weaver Street, Whitechapel,
1841.

**Friends Wheler Street Meeting
House**, Quaker Street,
Spitalfields.

Frimley Street, Off Alderney
Road, Mile End, 1891.

Frog Island, Nightingale Lane
(Thomas More Street), Wapping,

"is at the north end near the New
Cut on the north side of Pools
rope walk" (Lockie).

Frostic Place, Old Montague
Street, Whitechapel, 1851,
renamed Frostic Walk.

Frosts Alley, Old Montague
Street, Whitechapel, "a few doors
on the left hand east from Osborn
Street" (Elmes).

Fryatt Street, Off Orchard
Place, Poplar.

Frying Pan Public House, 13
Brick Lane, Spitalfields.

Frying Pan Stairs, Cinnamon
Street, Wapping, 1746.

**Frys Alley, Shakespeare(s)
Walk** (Shadwell Basin),
Shadwell, "at No 67
Shakespeares Walk" (Elmes).

Fullchers Buildings, Fordham
Street, Whitechapel, 1891.

Fuller Court, Hare Street
(Cheshire Street), Whitechapel,
1841.

Fuller House, Coventry Cross
Estate, Bromley and Bow, St.
Leonards Street.

Fuller Street, Off Bethnal Green
Road, Bethnal Green, Bethnal
Green Road to Cheshire Street,
west of St. Matthew's Row.

Fullers Almshouses, Mile End
Road, Mile End, "by Eagle Place
founded and endowed in 1592 by
Judge Fuller for twelve ancient
poor men of the parish of
Stepney for whose relief he

endowed it with lands in Lincolnshire" (Elmes).

Fullers Cottages, Westferry Road, Isle of Dogs, 1851, Lion Wharf, Sir John McDougall Gardens are on the site.

Fullers Cottages or Rents, Cotton Street, Poplar, 1851.

Fullers Rents, North Street (Brady Street), Whitechapel, 1851.

G

Gainsborough Cottages, Gainsborough Road (Eastway), Hackney.

Gainsborough Road, 1. Bethnal Green, renamed Alloway Road. 2. Hackney, renamed Eastway. 3. Off Lichfield Road, Bromley and Bow, 1891.

Gainsborough Square, Victoria Road (Wick Road), Hackney, 1891.

Gales Gardens, Bethnal Green Road, Bethnal Green, 1891.

Gallant Hussar Public House, 69 Carr Street, Limehouse.

Galsworthy House, Carr Street, Limehouse, 1950, Limehouse Fields Estate.

Galt Street, Off Rhodeswell Road, Limehouse, ran to Parnham Street close to its corner with Salmon Lane.

Gandy Court, Bow High Street (Bow Road), Bromley and Bow,

1851, next to 226 Bow High Street.

Garden Cottages, 1. Renamed Cruden Place (Kerbey Street), Poplar. 2. Ropemakers Fields, Limehouse, 1891, just west of Barley Mow Brewery.

Garden Court, 1. Glasshouse Street (John Fisher Street), East Smithfield, Royal Mint Street. 2. Petticoat Lane (Middlesex Street), Spitalfields, Whitechapel, "Petticoat Lane, the second on the left about fourteen doors from 41 Aldgate High Street, leading to Gravel Lane and 148 Houndsditch" (Lockie). 3. Risbies Ropewalk (Narrow Street), Limehouse, "about the middle of the north side entering from Narrow Street about three doors on the left below Mr Turners house" (Lockie). 4. Whitechapel High Street, Whitechapel, "the first on the right a few doors from 88 Whitechapel High Street or the first on the left from Wentworth Street in the opposite direction" (Lockie).

Garden House, Shakespeare(s) Walk (Shadwell Basin), Shadwell, 1851.

Garden Place, 1. Bere Street, Ratcliffe, 1851. 2. Chicksand Street, Whitechapel, "the first on the left a few yards from 16 High Street entering by 50 Whitechapel Road" (Lockie). 3. Hertford Place (Haggerston Road), Hackney, 1868, close to canal. 4. Hope Town (Bethnal Green Road), Bethnal Green, 1841. 5. James Street (Chilton Street), Bethnal Green, 1851. 6. Kerbey Street, Poplar, 1851. 7. Montague Street (Hanbury Street), Whitechapel, 1851. 8. Primrose Street (Allenbury Street), Bethnal Green, Primrose Street to Violet Street. 9. Turin Street, Bethnal Green, renamed Rappley Place. 10. White Hart Place (Poplar High Street), Poplar, Poplar High Street.

Garden Row, Brick Lane, Bethnal Green, "St. Lukes at 43 about $1/6$ of a mile on the right from 113 Old Street three or four doors south from St. Johns Road" (Lockie), later Gibraltar Walk.

Garden Street, 1. Off Osborn Street (Kennet Street), Wapping, 1790, Osborn Street to Byng Street London Docks, Western Dock was built on the site. 2. Off Poplar High Street, Poplar, renamed Butt Place.

Gardners Arms Public House, 1. 115 Lefevre Road (Lefevre Walk), Bromley and Bow, 1874. 2. Off Roman Road, Bromley and Bow, 1891, Mile End Park is on site.

Garford House, Garford Street, Limehouse, between Garford Street and Bowley Street.

Garibaldi Public House, 1. 29 Bale Street (Harford Street), Mile End. 2. 59 Turner Street, Whitechapel.

Garnett Place, Old Bethnal Green Road, Bethnal Green, 1851.

Garrick Theatre & Public House, 70 Leman Street, Whitechapel, 1874.

Garricks Buildings, Nightingale Lane (Thomas More Street), Wapping, 1851.

Garth Street, Off Goulds Hill (Shadwell Park), Shadwell, 1891, Shadwell Park is on the site.

Gartners Terrace, Prospect Place (Mile End Road), Mile End, Mile End Road close to Guardian Angels Church.

Gasometer Yard, Emma Street, Bethnal Green, 1891.

Gates Court, Ropemakers Fields, Limehouse, 1851.

Gates Street, Limehouse, renamed Canton Street.

Gateshead or Gates Head Place, Mile End Road, Mile End, opposite Drapers Almshouses.

Gaveric(k) Street, Off Westferry Road, Isle of Dogs, 1891, renamed Gaverick Mews.

Gawthorne Street, Off Morville Street, Bromley and Bow, 1891, Eastside Mews follows part of route.

Gays Buildings, Durham Street (Teesdale Street), Bethnal Green, 1841.

Gemini Villas, Grove Road, Bromley and Bow.

General Blakeney Public House, 143 Poplar High Street, Poplar, sometime name of Blakeneys Head Public House.

General Canrobert Public House, 40 Canrobert Street, Bethnal Green, 1874.

General Gordon Public House, 289 Wick Road, Hackney.

General Havelock Arms Public House, 1. 16 St. Leonards Street, Bromley and Bow. 2. 28 Westgate Street, Hackney, 1874.

George & Catherine Wheel Alley, Duke Street (Fort Street), Spitalfields, 1891, between Duke Street and Bishopsgate, north of Brushfield St.

George & Dragon Public House, 1. 15 Bishops Way, Bethnal Green. 2. 9 Cayley Street (Whitehorse Road Park), Stepney. 3. 3 Church Lane (White Church Lane), Whitechapel. 4. 2-4 Hackney Road, Bethnal Green, 1874. 5. 192 Shadwell High Street (The Highway), Shadwell, 1874, address also 345 The Highway. 6., Stepney Rents (Hackney Road), Bethnal Green.

George (& Dragon) Public House, 14 Whitechapel Road, Whitechapel, 1874, aka Old George.

George & Guy (aka George Guy) Public House, 41 Brick Lane, Spitalfields, 1874.

George & Vulture Public House, 1. 39 St. George Street (The Highway), St. George in the East, 1874. 2. 15 Wapping Wall, Wapping, 1874.

George Alley, 1. Pelham Street (Woodseer Street), Whitechapel, "ten houses from Brick Lane" (Elmes). 2. Shadwell, "on the east side of Shadwell Dock" (Elmes).

George Court, 1. Casson Street, Whitechapel, 1891, renamed Casson Place. 2. Commercial Road, Limehouse, Boulcott Street.

George Garden(s), Old Bethnal Green Road, Bethnal Green, 1841, immediately west of and parallel with Canrobert Street.

George Greens Sailors Home, 133 East India Dock Road, Poplar.

George Inn or Tavern Public House, 74 Brunswick Street, Poplar, 1850.

George IV Public House, 1. 68 Berner Street (Henriques Street), St. George in the East. 2. 9 Cayley Street (Whitehorse Road Park), Stepney. 3. 259 Green Street (Roman Road), Bethnal Green, 1874. 4. 7 Ida Street, Poplar. 5. 5 Richard Street (Whitehorse Road Park), Limehouse, 1856. 6. 41 Royal Mint Street, East Smithfield. 7. 40 West Street (Braintree Street), Mile End.

George Passage, Blythe Street, Bethnal Green, 1891.

George Peabody Public House, 146 Shadwell High Street (The Highway), Shadwell, 1874, address also 401 The Highway.

George Place, 1. Brady Street, Whitechapel, became part of Brady Street. 2. Commercial Road, Limehouse, 1851, renamed Boulcott Street. 3. Essex Street (Blythe Street), Bethnal Green. 4. George Gardens (Bethnal Green Road), Bethnal Green, 1851.

George Public House, 1. 62 Anchor and Hope Alley (Reardon Path), Wapping, 1874. 2. 379 Bethnal Green Road, Bethnal Green, 1874. 3. Blackwall Way, Poplar, 1874. 4. 25 Broad Street (The Highway), Ratcliffe. 5. 145 Cable Street, St. George in the East. 6. 1 Goodmans Yard, Whitechapel. 7. 32 Mansell Street, Whitechapel. 8. 58 Pelham Street (Woodseer Street), Whitechapel, 1874.

George Street, 1. Off Ada Street, Hackney, renamed Antwerp Street. 2. Off Butler Street, Bethnal Green, renamed Bonwell Street. 3. Off Carter Street (Spital Street), Spitalfields, "the first east parallel to part of Brick Lane, say from 67 to 105 it extends from Carter Street opposite Hanburys brewery to St. John Street" (Lockie), mostly absorbed into brewery premises, Code Street follows part of its path. 4. Off Catherine Street (Maroon Street), Limehouse, 1868, renamed Brenton Street. 5.

Off Commercial Road, Ratcliffe, renamed Boulcott Street. 6. Bromley and Bow, renamed Empson Street. 7. Bromley and Bow, 1851, renamed Four Mills Street (St. Leonards Street). 8. Off Lansdowne Road (Lansdowne Drive), Hackney, renamed Hamburg Street and later Croston Street. 9. Off Little George Street (Poyser Street), Bethnal Green, "extends from Little George Street towards Hackney Road" (Lockie), became part of Poyser Street. 10. Off Lolesworth Street, Spitalfields.

George Street, 1. Off Old Montague Street, Whitechapel, renamed Casson Street. 2. Off Salmon Lane, Limehouse, renamed Brenton Street. 3. Off Turin Street, Bethnal Green, 1891, renamed Cymon Street. 4. Off Westferry Road, Isle of Dogs, 1851, renamed Tobago Street.

George Tavern Public House, 13 Tapley Street (St. Leonards Road), Poplar.

George Terrace, 1. Commercial Road, Stepney, 1868, just east of Jubilee Place. 2. East Ferry Road, Isle of Dogs, 1884, north of the George public house.

George Yard, 1. Grove Street (Golding Street), St. George in the East, 1891, immediately north of railway line, renamed Marmaduke Court. 2. Whitechapel High Street,

Whitechapel, 1851, renamed Gunthorpe Street.

George Yard Mission, 19 Deal Street, Spitalfields.

George(s) Terrace, Turville Street, Bethnal Green, 1851.

Georges Court, Brook Street (Cable Street), Ratcliffe, 1851.

Georges Place, Old Ford Road, Bromley and Bow, 1851.

Georgiana Place, Rhodeswell Road, Limehouse, 1891.

Georgina Gardens, Crab Tree Row (Columbia Road), Bethnal Green, 1891, Columbia Road.

German & Dutch Jews Hospital, Mile End Road, Mile End, 1860, east of its corner with White Horse Lane.

German Chapel, 1. Browns Lane (Hanbury Street), Spitalfields, "between numbers 8and 9 three doors east from Wood Street and about eight ditto on the left from opposite 55 Brick Lane" (Lockie). 2. Little Ayliffe Street (Alie Street), Whitechapel, "the second door on the left from Red Lion Street Whitechapel" (Lockie).

German Flag Public House, 167 St. George Street (The Highway), St. George in the East.

German Hospital, Clifton Grove, Hackney, 1950.

German Protestant Reformed Church, Hooper Square, Whitechapel, 1870.

German Sailors Home, 14 West India Dock Road, Limehouse, 1891.

Germans Public House, Devons Lane (Devons Road), Bromley and Bow, 1851, Devons Lane from Bromley High Street, also called Bow Common Lane or Devons Road.

Gertrude House, Great Prescot Street (Prescot Street), Whitechapel, 1891.

Gilbert Wharf, Narrow Street, Ratcliffe, 1895, east of Duke Shore Wharf.

Gibraltar (Tavern) Public House, Gibraltar Walk, Bethnal Green, 1784.

Gibraltar Buildings or Place, Gibraltar Gardens (Gibraltar Walk), Bethnal Green, 1891.

Gibraltar Chapel, Shacklewell Street, Bethnal Green, 1868.

Gibraltar Fields, Bird Cage Walk (Columbia Road), Bethnal Green, "a district now chiefly built upon situated between the middle of Church Street and Birdcage Walk" (Lockie).

Gibraltar Gardens, Bethnal Green Road, Bethnal Green, 1891, immediately east of Gibraltar Walk.

Gibraltar Row Burial Ground, Gibraltar Walk, Bethnal Green, 1793.

Giles (or Gyles) Place, Periwinkle Street (Ratcliffe Cross Street), Ratcliffe, 1891.

Giles Row, Cambridge Road (Cambridge Heath Road), Bethnal Green, 1851.

Gill Place, Gill Street, Limehouse, Gill Street to Jamaica Place.

Gills Alley, Cotton Street, Poplar, 1851.

Gin Alley, Narrow Street, Ratcliffe, 1865, immediately east of The Opening.

Gingels Yard, Bakers Row (Vallance Road), Whitechapel, 1891.

Gingerbread Alley, Queen Street (Horseferry Road), Ratcliffe, "the first turning on the right hand in Queen Street below London Street" (Elmes).

Gladstone Public House, 26 Boundary Street, Bethnal Green.

Gladstone Public House, 1. 37 Dean Street (Deancross Street), Shadwell. 2. 129 St. Leonards Road, Poplar.

Glaskin Road, Off Well Street, Hackney, Frampton Estate is on site.

Glasshouse Buildings, Glasshouse Street (John Fisher Street), East Smithfield, Royal Mint Street.

Glasshouse Street, 1. East Smithfield, renamed John Fisher Street. 2. Off Sampsons Gardens (Sampson Street), Wapping, "the second on the right in Redmaids Lane from Hermitage Yard towards the London Dock" (Lockie).

Glasshouse Yard, Glasshouse Street (John Fisher Street), East Smithfield, 1870.

Glasshouse Wharf, Orchard Place, Poplar, 1950.

Glen Terrace, Manchester Road, Isle of Dogs, 1891, now part of Manchester Road, just south of eastern West India Docks entrance.

Glencoe Street, Off Brunswick Road, Poplar, 1891, Blackwall Tunnel Approach Road and Abbot Road are on the site.

Glendower Public House, 296 Westferry Road, Isle of Dogs.

Glengall Road School, Glengall Road (Glengall Avenue), Isle of Dogs, school buildings taken over by Cubitt Town School c1970.

Glengall Arms Public House, 367 Westferry Road, Isle of Dogs.

Glengall Causeway, Westferry Road, Isle of Dogs, formerly an extension of Glengall Road between Westferry Road and the Thames.

Glengall Place, Westferry Road, Isle of Dogs, 1851, between Mellish Street and Glengall Road.

Glengall Road, Off Westferry Road, Isle of Dogs, 1891, renamed Glengall Grove In 1963 the western half of the road was renamed Tiller Road.

Glengall Wharf, Westferry Road, Isle of Dogs, 1950, Sir John McDougalls Gardens are on its site.

Glenuff & Clyde Houses, Bruce Road, Bromley and Bow, 1891, Devons Road.

Globe & Friends Public House, 13 Morgan Street (Hessel Street), St. George in the East, 1874.

Globe & Three Pigeons Public House, 140 Shadwell High Street (The Highway), Shadwell, 1874, aka Peabody(s) Arms.

Globe Alley, Narrow Street, Limehouse, 1851, parallel with Shoulder of Mutton Alley.

Globe Buildings, Globe Road, Mile End, 1891.

Globe Cottages, Russia Lane, Bethnal Green, 1891, now part of Russia Lane.

Globe Court, 1. Narrow Street, Limehouse, "Limehouse at 54 the second on the left below the Draw bridge it leads to Pleasant Row and the New Cut" (Lockie). 2. Wapping High Street, Wapping, "at 57 is about ⅙ of a mile on the left and fifty seven doors below Hermitage Bridge or two doors west from Globe Street" (Lockie).

Globe Fields, Mile End Road, Mile End, 1851, Bethnal Green.

Globe House, Bethnal Green (Roman Road), Bethnal Green,

"a few doors on the left from Green Street towards Cambridge heath Hackney Road" (Lockie).

Globe Lane, Mile End Road, Mile End, "is the north continuation of Globe Lane from Mile End or is the first on the right about ½ of a mile east from the green" (Lockie), southern section of what is now Globe Road.

Globe Passage, Globe Street (Globe Road), Bethnal Green, "the north continuation of Globe Street on the left leading towards Hackney Road being a part of the west side of Back Lane" (Lockie).

Globe Place or Court, Ellen Street, St. George in the East, 1891.

Globe Public House, 1. 20 Brierly Street (Globe Road), Bethnal Green, 1874, equivalent 274 Globe Road. 2. 109 Columbia Road, Bethnal Green. 3. Elizabeth Street (Ellen Street), St. George in the East, renamed Ellen Street. 4. 44 Ellen Street, St. George in the East. 5. 8 Globe Street (Wapping High Street), Wapping, 1874, corner of Wapping High Street (address also known as 58 Wapping High Street), address also 33 Wapping High Street. 6. 128 Goldsmiths Row, Bethnal Green, 1874. 7. 32 Morning Lane, Hackney.

Globe Road & Devonshire Street Railway Station, Globe Road, Mile End, 1884-1916.

Globe Rope Works, East Ferry Road, Isle of Dogs, 1891, close to corner of Thermopylae Gate.

Globe Row, Chester Place (Burnham Estate), Bethnal Green, 1841.

Globe Street, 1. Off Green Street (Roman Road), Bethnal Green, "is the north continuation of Globe Lane from Mile End or is the first on the right about $^1/_8$ of a mile east from the green" (Lockie), northern section of what is now Globe Road. 2. Off Wapping High Street, Wapping, renamed Sampson Street (part). 2. 33 Brunswick Street, Poplar, 1851.

Globe Terrace & Yard, Brunswick Street, Poplar, 1851.

Globe Wharf, Wapping High Street, Wapping, 1895, east of corner with Hellings Street, absorbed into Colonial Wharves.

Globe Yard Almshouses, Brunswick Street, Poplar, 1851.

Gloster Place, Parmiter Street, Bethnal Green, 1917.

Gloucester Arms, 93-95 Commercial Road, Whitechapel, aka Gloster Arms.

Gloucester Buildings, Back Church Lane, St. George in the East, 1891, north of Boyd Street.

Gloucester Court, 1. Salmon Lane, Limehouse, renamed Notgrove Court, close to 128 Salmon Lane. 2. Gloucester Court, Settles Street,

Whitechapel, renamed Settles Court.

Gloucester Gardens, Little Collingwood Street (Collingwood Street), Whitechapel, 1891, renamed Colling Street.

Gloucester Passage, Bethnal Green, renamed Garner Passage (Teale Street).

Gloucester Place, 1. Cambridge Road (Cambridge Heath Road), Bethnal Green. 2. Hackney Road, Bethnal Green, 1851, renamed Kay Street. 3. Hackney, renamed Harrowgate Road. 4. Prospect Place (Cambridge Heath Road), Bethnal Green, 1841. 5. Russia Lane, Bethnal Green, 1851. 6. Salmon Lane, Limehouse, 1851, close to 128 Salmon Lane.

Gloucester Street, 1. Off Cambridge Road (Cambridge Heath Road), Bethnal Green, renamed Parmiter Street. 2. Off Cannon Street Road, St. George in the East, "the third west parallel to part of Cannon Street Road extending from 59 Charlotte Street to the Commercial Road" (Lockie). 3. Off Commercial Road, Limehouse, renamed Settles Street. 4. Off Kingsland Road, Hackney, western end renamed Mansfield Street. 5. Whitechapel, renamed Settles Street.

Gloucester Street Schoolhouse, Cambridge Road (Cambridge Heath Road), Bethnal Green, 1841.

Gloucester Terrace, 1. Cambridge Road (Cambridge Heath Road), Bethnal Green, 1851. 2. Cannon Street Road, St. George in the East, "forms part of the west side, it extends from the Commercial Road to Charlotte Street Whitechapel" (Lockie). 3. Robin Hood Lane, Poplar, 1851.

Glovers Court, White Horse Street (White Horse Road), Stepney, 1851.

Go(u)lden or Goulding Place, Old Bethnal Green Road, Bethnal Green, 1841, either side of its corner with Hope Street.

Goddard Court, Pennington Street, St. George in the East, 1891.

Godfrey House, Thrawl Street, Spitalfields, 1950.

Godfrey(s) Place & Court, Austin Street, Bethnal Green, 1841.

Gold or Goulds Hill, Shadwell High Street (The Highway), Shadwell, "at 97 about of a mile on the right below Shadwell Church it extends to Lower Shadwell by the side of the Thames" (Lockie), Shadwell Park is on the site.

Gold Street, Off Stepney Green, Stepney, 1891, formerly William Street and Prospect Place.

Golden Anchor Public House, 182 Wapping High Street, Wapping, 1874.

Golden Eagle Public House, 1. 56 Cleveland Street (Cleveland Way), Mile End, aka Peasants Revolt. 2. 56 Cleveland Way, Mile End. 3. 47 Quaker Street, Spitalfields. 4. 234 Shadwell High Street (The Highway), Shadwell, 1874.

Golden Hart (or Harp or Heart) Public House, 110 Commercial Street, Spitalfields, 1874.

Golden Horseshoe Public House, 54 St. George Street (The Highway), St. George in the East.

Golden Lion Public House, 1. 135 Cannon Street Road, St. George in the East, 1874. 2. 3 Goodmans Yard, Whitechapel. 3. 104 Leman Street, Whitechapel, 1874.

Golding Terrace, Commercial Road, St. George in the East.

Goldsmiths & Jewellers Asylum (Workhouse), Well Street, Hackney, 1895, west of Holcroft Road.

Goldsmiths Almshouses, Goldsmiths Row, Bethnal Green, Hackney Road.

Goldsmiths Arms, 81 Goldsmiths Row, Bethnal Green, 1874, Hackney Road.

Goldsmiths Place, Hackney Road, Bethnal Green, "on the north side about ³/₄ of a mile on the left from Shoreditch Church opposite Birdcage walk and leading towards London field"

(Lockie), renamed Goldsmiths Row.

Good Intent Public House, 1. 5 Elizabeth Street (Mansford Road), Bethnal Green. 2. 22 Mowlem Street, Bethnal Green.

Good Samaritan Public House, 87 Turner Street, Whitechapel.

Good Shepherd Mission House, Goldsmiths Row, Bethnal Green.

Goodhart Place, Lower Chapman Street (Bigland Street), St. George in the East, 1891.

Goodliffe Place & Street, Off Giraud Street, Poplar, 1891, Giraud Street to Alton Street.

Goodman Street, Off Alie Street, Whitechapel, 1950, Alie Street to Hooper Street.

Goodmans Buildings & Court, Wentworth Street, Whitechapel.

Goodmans Place, James Street (Chilton Street), Bethnal Green, 1841.

Goodmans Rents, Ropemakers Fields, Limehouse, 1871.

Goodmans Stile, Church Lane (White Church Lane), Whitechapel, "the second on the right a few doors from 72 Whitechapel High Street extending to Lambert Street and Little Ayliffe Street" (Lockie).

Goodwins Buildings, Wentworth Street, Whitechapel, 1851.

Goodwins Place, Ropemakers Fields, Limehouse, 1891.

Gordon Terrace, Launch Street, Isle of Dogs, 1891.

Gore Arms Public House, Approach Road, Bethnal Green, 1874.

Gore Crescent, Hackney, renamed Gore Road.

Gore Place, Morpeth Road, Hackney, 1891, now part of Morpeth Road.

Gore Terrace, Bishops Road (Bishops Way), Bethnal Green.

Goring Arms Public House, 24 Broadway Market, Hackney.

Goring Street, Off Broadway London Fields (Jackman Street), Hackney, 1891, renamed Jackman Street.

Gosset Arms Public House, 111 Gosset Street, Bethnal Green, 1874.

Gotha Street, Off Fremont Street, Hackney, 1891, became part of Warneford Street.

Gough Street, Off Stainsby Road, Limehouse, 1891, renamed Gough Grove and Walk.

Goulden Terrace, Richmond Road, Hackney, 1851, at its corner with Holly Street.

Goulds Hill, see *Golds Hill*.

Goulston Court, Goulston Square, Whitechapel, "on the east side leading to Old Castle Street" (Lockie).

Goulston Square, Whitechapel Road, Whitechapel, "about twelve doors on both the right and the left from 140 Whitechapel along Goulston Street" (Lockie), renamed Goulston Street.

Goulston Street Synagogue, Goulston Street, Whitechapel, 1870.

Goveys Place, Mile End Road, Mile End, "Mile End High Road, is situated between the Three Mackerel and the Mackerel and Bell Public Houses near two miles on the left from Aldgate Pump" (Lockie), east of St. Benets Church Queen Mary College is on the site.

Gowers Place & Row, Mill Yard, Whitechapel, 1891.

Goyer Street, Off Beale Road, Bromley and Bow, renamed Chad Street.

Graces Lane, Devons Lane (Devons Road), Bromley and Bow, 1851.

Grafton Arms Public House, 9 Alderney Road, Mile End, 1874.

Grafton Street, Mile End, renamed Grantley Street.

Graham Cottages, Castalia Street (Castalia Square), Isle of Dogs, 1891, East Ferry Road.

Graham Court, House & Place, Graham Road, Hackney.

Graham Mansions, Graham Road, Hackney, 1950.

Gramophone Public House, 60-62 Commercial Road, Whitechapel.

Granby Terrace, Fuller Street (Bethnal Green Road), Bethnal Green, 1841, renamed Granby Street.

Granby(s) Row, James Street (Chilton Street), Bethnal Green, "about three doors on the left from James Street and near the same distance on the right from Oakleys Row leading into Busby Street" (Lockie), renamed Granby Street.

Grange (Tavern) Public House, 56 Mayfield Road, Hackney, 1874.

Grange Cottages & House, Grange Road (Gayhurst Road), Hackney, 1851.

Grange Place, Grange Road (Gayhurst Road), Hackney, 1868, between Mayfield Street and Holly Street.

Grange Road, Off Queens Road (Queensbridge Road), Hackney, east end renamed Gayhurst Road, west end renamed Lenthall Road.

Grange Terrace & Villas, Grange Road (Gayhurst Road), Hackney, 1868, between Blomfield Street and Mayfield Street.

Granville Mews, Bow Road, Bromley and Bow, 1891.

Grape Vine Public House, 1. 506 Mile End Road, Mile End. 2. 66 White Horse Lane, Mile End.

Grapes Public House, 1. 15 Crispin Street, Spitalfields, 1874. 2. 3 New Gravel Lane (Garnet Street), Wapping, aka Swan and

Lamb. 3. 2 North East Passage (Wellclose Square), St. George in the East, Wellclose Square. 4. 6 Paternoster Row, Spitalfields. 5. 13 Sandys Row (Sandys Road), Spitalfields, aka Bunch of Grapes.

Grasshopper Public House, 72 Vallance Road, Whitechapel.

Grave Maurice Public House, 1. 18 St. Leonards Street, Bromley and Bow, 1874. 2. 269 Whitechapel Road, Whitechapel, 1874.

Gravel Pit Chapel & Field, Morning Lane, Hackney, 1841, just east of Chatham Place.

Gravel Street, Off New Gravel Lane (Garnet Street), Wapping.

Gray Street, Off Bow Lane (Adderley Street), Poplar, 1851, renamed Adderley Street.

Gray Street, Off Nelson Street, Whitechapel, 1891, renamed Dorian Street.

Grays Place, Mile End Road, Mile End, immediately east of Cambridge Heath Road.

Great Alie Street, Off Leman Street, Whitechapel, 1851, combined with Little Alie Street to form Alie Street.

Great Assembly Hall, Mile End Road, Mile End, between Trinity Almshouses and Vintners Almshouses opened in 1886 became a cinema in 1911 burned down during WWII.

Great Bacon Street, Off Church Street (Bethnal Green Road), Bethnal Green, "the first south parallel to Church Street near Shoreditch extending from the middle of Club Row to 140 Brick Lane" (Lockie), renamed Bacon Street.

Great Cambridge Street, Off Hackney Road, Bethnal Green, 1827, became the southernmost section of Queensbridge Road.

Great Eastern Buildings, 1. Dunbridge Street, Bethnal Green, 1950. 2. Fieldgate Street, Whitechapel. 3. Grove Lane (Reading Lane), Hackney, 1891.

Great Eastern Hotel & Public House, 31 Ashwell Road (Roman Road), Bromley and Bow.

Great Eastern Public House, 395 Westferry Road, Isle of Dogs, corner of British Street (Harbinger Road).

Great Garden Street, Off Whitechapel Road, Whitechapel, "at 50 on the north side being the fourth on the left and near $1/8$ of a mile below Whitechapel Church it leads to High Street" (Lockie), renamed Greatorex Street.

Great Garden Street Synagogue, 7/11 Greatorex Street, Whitechapel, 1970.

Great Hermitage Street, Off Wapping High Street, Wapping, "the first north parallel to part of Wapping Street say from number 15 to 72 commencing on the east side Hermitage Bridge and extends to the London Docks" (Lockie), renamed Hermitage Wall.

Great Holloway Street, Off Whitechapel Road, Whitechapel, "the second on the left in Union Street from 281 Whitechapel Road it is a few doors south of Sion chapel and extends to Mulberry Street" (Lockie), now part of Coke Street.

Great Manchester Street, Off Little Manchester Street (Cheshire Street), Whitechapel, combined with Little Manchester Street to form Manchester Street.

Great or New Somerford Street, Off Collingwood Street, Whitechapel, 1851, renamed Somerford Street.

Great Paternoster Row, Spitalfields, alternative name for Paternoster Row.

Great Pearl Street (aka Pearl Street), Fleur de Lis Street, Spitalfields, 1891, "the continuation of Flower de Lis Street" (Elmes), renamed Calvin Street.

Great Prescot Street, Whitechapel, 1890, renamed Prescot Street.

Great Spring Street, Off Lower Turning (Shadwell Basin), Shadwell, "extends from the south side the church yard to lower turning" (Lockie), Shadwell Basin is on the site.

Great Tongue Yard, Whitechapel Road, Whitechapel, Whitechapel Road renamed Tongue Alley, just east of the corner of Fieldgate Street and Whitechapel Road.

Great Yard, Gun Alley (Wapping Gardens), Wapping, "the second turning on the right hand in Gun Alley going from Wapping Street" (Elmes).

Great York Street, Off Bethnal Green Road, Bethnal Green, 1891, renamed Ebor Street.

Grebe Court, Mile End Road, Mile End, Mile End Road to Drivers Buildings, west of Mile End Place.

Green Dragon Alley, 1. Narrow Street, Limehouse, "the second on the left about nine doors from Mr Turners Wharf leading into Risbys rope walk" (Lockie). 2. Wapping High Street, Wapping, "at 194 Wapping Street two doors west from New Gravel Lane nearly opposite New Crane Stairs" (Lockie).

Green Dragon Public House, 1. 179 Poplar High Street, Poplar, 1874, aka Railway Tavern. 2. 4 Shadwell Dock Street (Garnet Street), Shadwell, Shadwell Basin is on the site. 3. 19 Spring Garden Place (Shadwell Park), Shadwell. 4. 123 Well Street, Hackney, 1874.

Green Dragon Yard, Whitechapel Road, Whitechapel,

immediately east of Osborn Street.

Green Gate Public House, 230 Bethnal Green Road, Bethnal Green, 1874.

Green Man Lane, 1. Poplar High Street, Poplar, 1851. 2. 287 Cambridge Heath Road, Bethnal Green, 1874. 3. 24 Jane Street, St. George in the East. 4. 44 Mansell Street, Whitechapel, 1874, aka Hercules. 5. 40 New Castle Street (Tyne Street), Whitechapel. 6. 68 Poplar High Street, Poplar, 1874.

Green Place, Green Street (Roman Road), Bethnal Green, "the first turning on the right hand in Green Street below Globe Street about one third of a mile eastward of the Green" (Elmes).

Green Street, 1. Off Bethnal Green (Roman Road), Bethnal Green, "at the south east corner of [Bethnal] green extending east towards Bow common about of a mile in length" (Lockie), renamed Roman Road. 2. Off Cephas Street, Mile End, renamed Nicholas Street, later Nicholas Road. 3. Off Jubilee Street, Stepney, 1862, Jubilee Street to Stracey Street, became part of Stepney Way. 4. Off New Road, Whitechapel, 1891, renamed Pasteur Street parallel with and immediately south of Mount Terrace. 5. Off White Horse Street (White Horse Road), Stepney, renamed Wakeling Street.

Green Street Licenced Lunatic Asylum, Green Street (Roman Road), Bethnal Green, 1841.

Green Yard, 1. Coopers Row (Upper East Smithfield), East Smithfield, 1851, Upper East Smithfield. 2. Gibraltar Walk, Bethnal Green.

Greenfield Court, Greenfield Street (Greenfield Road), Whitechapel.

Greenfield Road or Street Synagogue, 81 Greenfield Road, Whitechapel, 1940.

Greenfield Street, 1. Off Orchard Street (Orchard Place), Poplar, 1851. 2. Off Whitechapel Road, Whitechapel, "the third on the right from 266 Whitechapel Road along Fieldgate Street extending to the Commercial Road or the sixth on the right in the Commercial Road west from Cannon Street Road" (Lockie), renamed Greenfield Road.

Greenland Fishery Public House, 61 Redmans Road, Mile End, 1874.

Greens Almshouses, Upper North Street, Poplar, 1851.

Greens Place, Princes Street (Princelet Street), Whitechapel, 1851.

Greens Terrace, Upper North Street, Poplar, 1851.

Greens Yard, Brunswick Street, Poplar, 1891.

Greenwich Pensioner Public House, 2 Bow Lane (Bazely Street), Poplar, 1874, later Bazely Street.

Greenwood Court, Harrow Alley (Little Somerset Street), Spitalfields, Petticoat Lane, Rocque 1F7.

Greenwood Street, Off Mile End Road, Mile End, opposite Trinity Almshouses.

Greenwoods Court, Nightingale Lane (Thomas More Street), Wapping, 1792.

Greggs Alley, Essex Street (Commercial Street), Spitalfields, "the third turning on the right hand in Essex Street going from Whitechapel High Street" (Elmes).

Greggs Buildings, Trinity Almshouses (Mile End Road), Mile End, 1891.

Gregory(s) Court, Spitalfields Market (Commercial Street), Spitalfields, 1851.

Gregorys Stables, Bell Lane, Spitalfields.

Grenada Terrace, Commercial Road, Stepney, Immediately east of Jamaica Street.

Gresham Place & Terrace, Queens Road (Queensbridge Road), Hackney, 1851, opposite Laurel Street.

Gretton Place, Old Ford Road, Bromley and Bow, 1851.

Gretton Terrace, Green Street (Roman Road), Bethnal Green, 1851.

Grey Eagle Public House, 52 Grey Eagle Street, Spitalfields, 1874.

Grey Street, Off St. Leonards Road, Poplar, 1891.

Greyhound Court, St. Catherines Lane (St. Katharine Docks), East Smithfield, 1746, St. Katharine Dock is on the site.

Greyhound Lane, Whitechapel Road, Whitechapel, "opposite the London Hospital" (Elmes), became part of Thomas Street.

Greyhound Public House, 32 Old Ford Road, Bromley and Bow.

Griffin Cottages, Chapel House Street, Isle of Dogs, 1891.

Griffin Place, Dog Row (Cambridge Heath Road), Whitechapel, "the first on the right a few doors from Mile End turnpike towards Bethnal Green" (Lockie).

Griffin Street, Off Peal or Pearl Alley (Shadwell Park), Shadwell, "the continuation of Peal Alley from 61 Shadwell High Street or the first east parallel to Foxs Lane extending from Shadwell market to Shadwell Dock" (Lockie), Shadwell Park is on the site.

Griggs Court, 1. Goodmans Yard, Whitechapel, 1891. 2. Swan Street (Cygnet Street), Bethnal Green.

Grimdales Yard, Unanimous Row (Fournier Street), Whitechapel, 1851.

Gripey Alley, Artichoke Lane (Spirit Quay), Wapping, 1746.

Grocer(s) Court, Upper Well Alley (Green Bank), Wapping, "the second on the left a few doors from 110 Wapping Street on the east side the church" (Lockie).

Grog Court, Nightingale Lane (Thomas More Street), Wapping, "The north end of Nightingale Lane by the New Cut" (Elmes).

Grosvenor Arms Public House, 33 Grosvenor Street (Reading Lane), Hackney, 1874, address also 33 Mountmorres Road

Grosvenor Buildings, Robin Hood Lane, Poplar, 1891, Robin Hood Lane to Cotton Street, either side of Manisty Street, Robin Hood Gardens are on the site.

Grosvenor Place, Globe Street (Globe Road), Mile End, 1841.

Grosvenor Street, 1. Off Globe Road, Mile End, 1891. 2. Stepney, 1895, renamed Mountmorres Road, opposite Pitsea Street to Stepney Way. 3. Mentmore Terrace, Hackney.

Grosvenor Wharf, Saunders Ness Road, Isle of Dogs, 1950, Grosvenor Wharf Road is on its site.

Groudens Place, Torrington Street (Kennet Street), Wapping,

1790, London Docks Western Dock was built on the site.

Grove Buildings, South Grove (Southern Grove), Bromley and Bow, south of Mile End Road.

Grove Cottage(s), 1. James Street (Chilton Street), Bethnal Green, 1891. 2. Parkholme Road, Hackney, 1891. 3. Bath Street (Poplar Bath Street), Poplar, East India Dock Road.

Grove Hall Lunatic Asylum, Fairfield Road, Bromley and Bow, 1891.

Grove Hall Lunatic Asylum, Old Ford Road, Bromley and Bow, 1895, north of present-day Grove Hall Park.

Grove House, 1. Cambridge Road (Cambridge Heath Road), Mile End, Cambridge Road "about $1/8$ of a mile on the left below the Plough towards Thompsons nursery and Bow near $2^1/3$ miles from Aldgate" (Lockie). 2. Hare Row, Bethnal Green.

Grove Lane or The Grove, Mare Street, Hackney, 1891, renamed Reading Lane.

Grove Passage, Hackney, 1895, renamed Sylvester Path.

Grove Place, 1. Adelina Grove, Mile End, renamed Adelina Place. 2. Artichoke Hill, St. George in the East, renamed Cuttle Place. 3. Mile End Road, Mile End, "is parallel to part of the south side of it viz from the turnpike to Assembly Row, it extends from Epping Place to Redmans Row leading towards Stepney Green" (Lockie). 4. Mile End Road, Mile End, renamed Lawton Road. 5. Sylvester Road, Hackney, 1862, Church Street.

Grove Row, Hackney Road, Bethnal Green, "behind the Hare Public House by the turnpike, about a mile from Shoreditch Church" (Lockie).

Grove Street, 1. Off Camden Street (Ellsworth Street), Bethnal Green, 1891, Camden Street renamed Shetland Street, later Ellsworth Street. 2. Mile End, renamed Clinton Road. 3. St. George in the East, renamed Golding Street, originally extended to Commercial Road. 4. Off Grove Road, Bromley and Bow, 1841. 5. Off Grundy Street, Poplar, 1891, renamed Bygrove Street. 6. Hackney, connected Three Colts Bridge to Well Street, slightly east of modern Lauriston Road.

Grove Street Great Synagogue, 96 Golding Street, St. George in the East, 1940.

Grove Street Lane, Victoria Park Road, Hackney, Victoria Park Road largely follows route.

Grove Terrace, 1. Balcorne Street, Hackney, became part of Balcorne Street. 2. Grove Lane (Reading Lane), Hackney, 1851.

Grove Terrace & Villas, 144-150 East India Dock Road,

Poplar, 1851, Wade Street to Wades Place.

Grove(s) Court, White Horse Street (Butcher Row), Ratcliffe, "at the east end of Brook Street nearly opposite Butcher Row by Bull or Ball Yard" (Lockie).

Grundy Arms Public House, 83 Grundy Street, Poplar, 1874, corner of Vesey Street.

Guardian Asylum, 21 Old Ford Road, Bromley and Bow.

Guelph Wharf, Westferry Road, Isle of Dogs, 1950, Torres Square is on its site.

Guerin Road, Off Malmesbury Road, Bromley and Bow, 1891.

Guildford Arms Public House, 93 Guildford Road (Upper North Street), Poplar.

Guildford Road, Off Upper North Street, Poplar, 1891, Upper North Street to corner of Chrisp Street and Morris Road.

Gun & Star Public House, 51 Middlesex Street, Spitalfields.

Gun & Tent Public House, 10 Fort Street, Spitalfields.

Gun Alley, Green Bank, Wapping, 1790, Wapping Gardens are on the site.

Gun Dock, Wapping High Street, Wapping, "nearly opposite 104 Wapping Street two or three doors east from the London Docks and about $1\frac{1}{6}$ of a mile below London Bridge by the line of the river" (Lockie).

Gun Lane, Three Colt Street, Limehouse, 1851, renamed Grenade Street.

Gun Public House, 1. 54 Brushfield Street, Spitalfields. 2. 354 Wapping High Street, Wapping, 1874.

Gun Row, Devons Lane (Devons Road), Bromley and Bow, 1851.

Gun Square, Gun Lane (Grenade Street), Limehouse, 1851, renamed Padstow Place.

Gun Street, Off Artillery Lane, Spitalfields, 1891, extended as far north as Lamb St, subsumed by western expansion of Spitalfields Market.

Gun Street Synagogue, 37a Gun Street, Spitalfields.

Gun Tavern (& Hotel) Public House, 75 Wapping High Street, Wapping.

Gun Tavern Public House, 1. Shadwell High Street (The Highway), Shadwell. 2. 235 Well Street, Hackney.

Gun Wharves, Wapping High Street, Wapping, 1950, south of junction with Wapping Lane.

Gunboat Public House, 105 St. George Street (The Highway), St. George in the East, renamed New Gunboat.

Gunmakers Arms Public House, 1. 51 Canal Road (Mile End Road), Bromley and Bow, at its corner with Solebay Street. 2.

438 Old Ford Road, Bromley and Bow.

Gunmakers Company Poor House, Church Lane (White Church Lane), Whitechapel, 1870.

Gunns Terrace, Old Road (Stepney Green), Stepney, 1851.

Gurley Street, Off Manner Street (Devas Street), Bromley and Bow, 1891.

Gut House Public House, Poplar Gut (Westferry Road), Isle of Dogs, close to site of later City Arms public house.

Guy Earl of Warwick Public House, 5 Chrisp Street, Poplar, 1874.

Guys Buildings, Claremont Street (Hackney Road), Bethnal Green, 1891.

Gwynns Place, Hackney Road, Bethnal Green, 1841, opposite Felix Street.

H

Ha(r)rold Street, Off Green Street (Roman Road), Bethnal Green, 1891.

Hack Street, Off Byron Street, Poplar, 1891.

Hackney Free & Parochial School, Paragon Road, Hackney.

Hackney Greyhound Racing Stadium, Waterden Road, Hackney, 1950, Waterden Road since redirected and goes through site of stadium.

Hackney Infant School, Paragon Road, Hackney, 1868.

Hackney Jewish Cemetery, Lauriston Road, Hackney, 1788-1886.

Hackney New Road, Off Mile End Road, Mile End, "commences nearly opposite the Plough, Mile End Road about 2 miles on the left below Aldgate Pump leading to Hackney" (Lockie).

Hackney Parochial Schools, Paradise Place (Elsdale Street), Hackney, 1868.

Hackney Road Crescent, Hackney Road, Bethnal Green, 1860, "forms part of the east side of the road, about, of a mile on the right from Shoreditch Church opposite Middlesex Place" (Lockie), immediately west of King Street.

Hackney Synagogue, Brenthouse Road, Hackney, 1897.

Hackney Terrace, Well Street, Hackney, 1827, renamed Cassland Road.

Hackney Wick School, Brookfield Road, Hackney, 1862.

Hackney Working Mens Institute, The Triangle (Mare Street), Hackney, 1868, Mare Street.

Haggerston Lane, Victoria Place (Laburnum Street), Bethnal Green, 1868, became part of Laburnum Street.

Haggerston Place, Hackney Road, Bethnal Green, 1860, opposite Charles Street.

Hague Buildings, Hague Street, Bethnal Green, 1891.

Hague Place, Sale Street, Bethnal Green, 1841.

Hairbrain Court, Blue Anchor Yard (Royal Mint Street), East Smithfield.

Hales Terrace, 1. Bloomsbury Street (St. Leonards Road), Poplar, 1862. 2. West India Dock Road, Limehouse, 1851.

Half Moon & Crown Public House, 37 Bacon Street, Bethnal Green, 1874.

Half Moon & Punchbowl Public House, 20 Buckle Street, Whitechapel, 1874.

Half Moon & Seven Stars Public House, 119 St. George Street (The Highway), St. George in the East, 1874.

Half Moon Court, Wapping High Street, Wapping, "at 8 the first on the left eight doors east from Hermitage Bridge about 1/3 of a mile below the Tower" (Lockie).

Half Moon Passage or Alley, Whitechapel High Street, Whitechapel, "at 18 on the south side about eighteen doors east from Somerset Street or Aldgate High Street it leads to 35 Great Ayliffe Street" (Lockie).

Half Moon Public House, 1. 233 Bow Road, Bromley and

Bow. 2. 14-15 Lower Shadwell (Shadwell Park), Shadwell, 1874, aka (White) Swan, address also 43a and 62 Lower Shadwell.

Half Nichol(s) Street, Off Cock Lane (Boundary Street), Bethnal Green, "the third on the right in Cock Lane from behind 65 Shoreditch" (Lockie), Boundary Estate is on the site.

Half Walk Court, Great Pearl Street (Calvin Street), Spitalfields, 1891.

Halfway House Public House, 388 Hackney Road, Bethnal Green.

Halifax Arms Public House, 1. 67-69 Chicksand Street, Whitechapel, aka Enterprise. 2. Great Garden Street (Greatorex Street), Whitechapel, 1891. 3. 17 Hawkins Street (Sidney Street), Stepney, 1874.

Halifax Head Public House, 1 Dunk Street (Hanbury Street), Spitalfields, 1874, later Three Crowns.

Halifax Street, Whitechapel, renamed Chicksand Street.

Hall Street, 1. Bromley and Bow, renamed Hedworth Street (St. Pauls Way School). 2. Off Robeson Street, Bromley and Bow, 1891.

Hallets Court, Shakespeare(s) Walk (Shadwell Basin), Shadwell, 1851.

Halley Place, Halley Street, Limehouse.

Halliford Terrace, Grove Road, Bromley and Bow.

Halls Cottages, Old Ford Road, Bromley and Bow, 1851.

Halsey Court, Back Street (Wades Place), Poplar, 1851.

Halsey Place, Bromley High Street, Bromley and Bow, 1851.

Hamburg Street, Off London Fields, Hackney, 1891, renamed Croston Street.

Hamlet Court, Brook Street (Cable Street), Ratcliffe, 1851.

Hammer & Crown Court, Broad Street (The Highway), Ratcliffe, 1891.

Hammond House, Glengall Road (Tiller Rd), Isle of Dogs, later Tiller Road section of Glengall Road.

Hammond(s) Gardens, Old Bethnal Green Road, Bethnal Green, 1851, close to its corner with Teesdale Street.

Hampden Place, Smart Street, Bethnal Green, 1841.

Hampshire Court or Place, Batty Street, St. George in the East, 1891.

Hampshire Place, Whitechapel Road, Whitechapel, close to 100 Whitechapel Road site of St. Marys Tube Station.

Hanbury Buildings, Hanbury Place (Pennyfields), Limehouse, Poplar High Street, demolished in the 1950s, south of Ming Street at its corner with Pennyfields.

Hanbury Place, King Street (Ming Street), Limehouse, 1890, close to corner with Pennyfields.

Hand & Flower Public House, 72 Parnell Road, Bromley and Bow, 1874.

Hangmans Gains Alley, St. Catherines (St. Katharines Dock), East Smithfield, 1746, St. Katharine Dock is on the site.

Hanks Court, Robin Hood Lane, Poplar, "the first on the right a few doors from the East India Dock gate" (Lockie).

Hanley Cottage, Derbyshire Street, Bethnal Green.

Hannah Place, Green Street (Stepney Way), Mile End, 1862, corner with Jubilee Street.

Hannibal Mews, Hannibal Road, Mile End.

Hanover Court, Brick Lane, Whitechapel, "at 10 the third on the right about $\frac{1}{8}$ of a mile from 74 Whitechapel High Street along Osborn Street" (Lockie).

Hanover Place, Brick Lane, Spitalfields, 1891, "the first west parallel to part of Brick Lane say from 200 to 213 or the first on the right in Wentworth Street from Osborn Street Whitechapel, extending to Flower and Dean Street" (Lockie), renamed Lolesworth Street.

Harads Place or Alley, Wellclose Square, St. George in the East, "at the south-west corner leading to Well Street,

Parsons Street and Upper East Smithfield", (Lockie).

Hardy(s) Place, Essex Street (Commercial Street), Spitalfields, 1891.

Hare Public House, 180 Brick Lane, Spitalfields.

Hare Alley, Hare Street (Cheshire Street), Whitechapel, "at 58 a few doors west from the Workhouse or the third on the right from 109 Brick Lane" (Lockie).

Hare Court, Hare Street (Cheshire Street), Whitechapel, "on the north side the first on the left a few doors from 110 Brick Lane" (Lockie).

Hare Passage & Place, Cambridge Heath (Hare Row), Bethnal Green, 1841.

Hare Public House, 1. 180 Brick Lane, Spitalfields, 1874. 2. 505 Cambridge Heath Road, Bethnal Green, 1874.

Hare Street, 1. Off Apsley Street (Wickham Close), Stepney, 1895, renamed Harry Street. 2. Off Brick Lane, Whitechapel, Brick Lane to present-day Hereford Street, became part of Cheshire Street. 3. Off Poplar High Street, Poplar, "the first west from the East India Almshouses and nearly opposite the Queens Head, about $\frac{1}{2}$ a mile on the left from the Commercial Road", (Lockie).

Harford Place, Whitechapel High Street, Whitechapel, the second on the left in it from 16 High Street" (Lockie).

Harlestone Place, Salmon Lane, Limehouse, 1851.

Harley Cottages, Chrisp Street, Poplar, 1851.

Harley Place, Bow Road, Bromley and Bow, 1851, renamed Harley Grove.

Harley Street, Off Bow Road, Bromley and Bow, renamed Harley Grove.

Harlow Place, Mile End Road, Mile End, "the second on the right about fifteen doors below the turnpike extending to Grove Place" (Lockie).

Harlowe House, Clarissa Street, Hackney, 1950.

Harlow Wharf, Narrow Street, Ratcliffe, 1895, east of Duke Shore Wharf.

Harmony Cottages, Wellington Row, Bethnal Green, 1841.

Harold Street, Off Roman Road, Bethnal Green, Cranbrook Estate is on the site.

Harolds Alley, Harads Place (Wellclose Square), St. George in the East, renamed Harads Place, south west corner of Wellclose Square.

Harper Place, Back Road (Cable Street), St. George in the East, 1860, north side of Back Road, west of Charles Street.

Harrap Street, Off Prestage Street (Prestage Way), Poplar, 1891.

Harrels Row, Green Bank, Wapping, "the second on the left from Wapping Church towards Gravel Lane it leads to Knights court and Tench Street" (Lockie), Wapping Gardens are on the site.

Harriett Square, Cremer Street, Bethnal Green, 1950.

Harriett(s) or Harriots Place, Fashion Street, Spitalfields, 1891, "at 56 about eight or nine doors east from Rose Lane or the fourth on the right from 194 Brick Lane" (Lockie), north of Fashion St, heading north.

Harris Albion Brewery, Whitechapel Road, Whitechapel, 1851, later Albion Brewery.

Harris Buildings, 1. Grove Street (Golding Street), St. George in the East, Grove Street and Wicker Street. 2. Whitechapel Road, Whitechapel, "at 132 about $1/3$ of a mile on the left below Whitechapel Church nearly opposite the London Hospital" (Lockie).

Harris Court, Brook Street (Cable Street), Ratcliffe, 1851, Cranford Street is on the site.

Harris Place, 1. Back Church Lane, St. George in the East. 2. White Bear Gardens (Hackney Road), Bethnal Green, "Hackney Road, is a few yards north from Harris Row" (Lockie).

Harris Row, White Bear Gardens (Hackney Road), Bethnal Green, "Hackney Road, the first on the right from the north end of Union Walk, Union Street" (Lockie).

Harris Terrace, The Highway, St. George in the East, south of St. George in the East churchyard.

Harris Yard, Back Church Lane, St. George in the East, 1851.

Harrisons Buildings, North Street (Brady Street), Whitechapel, 1851.

Harrisons Court, Popes Head Court (Quaker Street), Spitalfields.

Harrisons Wharf, St. Katharines Way, East Smithfield, 1950, east of St. Katharine Dock entrance.

Harrow Alley, Little Somerset Street, Whitechapel, 1895, became part of Little Somerset Street.

Harrow House, Harrow Lane, Poplar, Poplar High Street.

Harrow Public House, 210 Poplar High Street, Poplar, aka Resolute (Tavern).

Harry Street, Off Apsley Street (Wickham Close), Stepney, 1950, close to Wickham Close.

Harry Tavern Public House, 131 Brunswick Road, Poplar.

Harts Buildings, Coxs Square (Wentworth Street), Spitalfields.

Harts Lane, Bethnal Green Road, Bethnal Green, "the first on the left a few doors below the turnpike near $^1/_2$ a mile from 65

Shoreditch" (Lockie), renamed Barnet Grove.

Harts Row, Westferry Road, Isle of Dogs, "is near a mile below the entrance to the West India Docks by the side of the river about $^1/_8$ of a mile east of the Kings arms" (Lockie), also known as Paradise Row demolished to make room for Millwall Dock entrance lock.

Harts Yard, 1. Chambord Street, Bethnal Green, 1891. 2. Princes Street (Padbury Court), Bethnal Green, 1851.

Hartwell Cottages & Street, Off Dalston Lane, Hackney, 1851.

Hartwell Street, Off Dalston Lane, Hackney, 1895, close to Dalston Junction.

Harwar Street, Off Kingsland Road, Hackney, renamed Cremer Street.

Hassard Place, Hassard Street, Bethnal Green, 1891.

Hasties Wharf, Wapping High Street, Wapping, 1950, west of corner with Knighten Street.

Hastings Arms Public House, 397 Cable Street, Shadwell.

Hastings Court, Back Road (Cable Street), St. George in the East, 1851.

Hat & Plough Public House, 44 Whitechapel High Street, Whitechapel, 1874.

Hatchet Alley, 1. Church Lane (White Church Lane),

Whitechapel, 1746. 2. Off Nightingale Lane (Thomas More Street), Wapping, 1800, St. Katharine Dock is on its site.

Hatfield Place, Wheler Street, Spitalfields, 1851.

Havelock Cottages, Cranbrook Street, Bethnal Green, 1851.

Havelock Place, Cranbrook Street, Bethnal Green, 1891, renamed Gathorne Street.

Havelock Public House, 1 Winchester Street (Dunbridge Street), Bethnal Green.

Havelock Road, Off Well Street, Hackney, 1895, Frampton Park Estate is on the site.

Havering (Atte) Bower Public House, 21 Ann Street (Devonport Street), Shadwell.

Hawkins Buildings, Risbies Ropewalk (Narrow Street), Limehouse, 1851.

Hawkins Street, Off Sidney Street, Whitechapel, 1895, Sidney Street to Jubilee Street, south of Lindley Street.

Hawthorne Cottage, York Street (Commercial Road), Limehouse, 1891, Commercial Road East renamed Flamborough Street.

Haydon Passage, Goodmans Fields (Mansell Street), Whitechapel, "is about nine houses on the right hand in Mansel Street going from Somerset Street" (Elmes).

Haydon Square, Mansell Street, Whitechapel, 1851.

Hayes Buildings & Cottage, Duncan Square (Duncan Road), Hackney, 1891, Part of Duncan Square.

Hayes Court, Glasshouse Street (John Fisher Street), East Smithfield, 1851, Royal Mint Street.

Hayes Place, Kingsland Road, Hackney, 1868, north of Grange Road.

Hayfield Place, Mile End Road, Mile End, Stepney Way to Beaumont Street.

Hayfield Public House, 158 Mile End Road, Mile End, 1874, aka Pearly Queen, aka Hayfield Tavern, aka Hay Field.

Hearns Court, Glasshouse Street (John Fisher Street), East Smithfield, 1851, Royal Mint Street.

Hearns or Hurns Buildings, Royal Mint Street, East Smithfield, Upper East Smithfield.

Heart Place, Cassland Road, Hackney, 1851.

Hearts of Oak Public House, 1. 36 Dock Street, St. George in the East, address also 2 Dock Street. 2. 36 St. Leonards Road, Poplar.

Heasman Terrace, Sewardstone Road, Bethnal Green, 1895.

Heath Place, 1. Cambridge Road (Cambridge Heath Road), Bethnal Green, 1827, north of its corner with Hackney Road. 2. Commercial Road, Stepney, 1868, at its corner with Heath Street.

Heath Street, Off Commercial Road, Stepney, "about ⅓ of a mile on the left below the Halfway House and opposite Stepney Causeway" (Lockie), renamed Head Street.

Hebrew Boarding School, Cambridge Road (Cambridge Heath Road), Bethnal Green, 1851.

Hebrew Centre Synagogue, 74 Jane Street, St. George in the East, 1940.

Hebrew Place, Petticoat Lane (Middlesex Street), Spitalfields, 1851.

Hedges Place, Gill Street, Limehouse, 1851.

Hedworth Street, Off Rowsell Street (St. Pauls Way School), Bromley and Bow, St. Pauls Way School is on the site.

Helena Mansions, Umberston Street, St. George in the East, 1950.

Helena Terrace, Chicksand Street, Whitechapel, 1891.

Helens Court, Chester Street, Bethnal Green, 1851.

Helmsley Terrace, Exmouth Place, Hackney, 1841.

Henderson House, Wentworth Street, Spitalfields, 1950.

Henrietta Street, Bethnal Green, renamed Allgood Street.

Henry Lance Home for Girls, Grove Road, Bromley and Bow.

Henry Street, 1. Off Back Church Lane, St. George in the East, renamed Boyd Street. 2. Off Jubilee Street, Stepney, renamed Rutland Street. 3. Off Rhodeswell Road, Limehouse, 1891, now part of Clemence Street. 4. Off Salmon Lane, Limehouse, 1851, became part of Carr Street Stepney. 5. Off White Horse Lane, Mile End, renamed Cadiz Street. 6. Off York Square, Limehouse, 1891, renamed Chaseley Street.

Hephzibah Terrace, Grange Road (Gayhurst Road), Hackney, 1851, west of Mayfield Street.

Hepworth Place, Crab Tree Row (Columbia Road), Bethnal Green, 1841.

Her Majestys Hospital for Sick Children, 13-19 Stepney Causeway, Ratcliffe, 1888-1922, later Barnardos.

Herat Street, Off Columbia Road, Bethnal Green, 1891, now part of Brick Lane.

Herbert Street, Off Queens Road (Queensbridge Road), Hackney, 1862, renamed Holms Street Haggerston Park is on the site.

Herbert Terrace, Suffolk Street (Three Colts Lane), Bethnal Green, 1891, now part of Coventry Street.

Hercules Public House, 44

Mansell Street, Whitechapel, 1874, aka Green Man.

Hercules Wharf, Orchard Place, Poplar, 1950.

Hereford Buildings, Cheshire Street, Whitechapel, renamed Cheshire Buildings.

Hereford Place, Commercial Road, Whitechapel, 1860, between Mulberry Street and Turner Street.

Hereford Terrace, Oxford Street (Stepney Way), Whitechapel, 1851.

Hermit (Tavern) Public House, 56 Bedford Street (Cavell Street), Whitechapel, 1874.

Hermitage Bridge, Hermitage Dock (Hermitage Basin), Wapping, about $^1/_3$ below the Tower, and near $^7/_8$ of a mile from London Bridge by the side of the Thames, it leads from St. Catherines Street to Wapping"(Lockie).

Hermitage Dock, St. Catherines Street (St. Katharine Docks), Wapping, "divides St. Catherines Street and the parish of Aldgate from Wapping" (Lockie).

Hermitage Stairs, Little Hermitage Street (Orton Street), Wapping, 1746.

Hermitage Terrace, Fairfield Road, Bromley and Bow, 1851.

Hermitage Wharf, Wapping High Street, Wapping, 1950, south east of corner with Orton Street.

Hermitage Yard, Hermitage Street (Wapping High Street), Wapping, "the continuation of Little Hermitage Street from 14 Wapping Street leading to Redmaids Lane by the side of the London Docks" (Lockie).

Hersee Place, Bonner Street, Bethnal Green, Cranbrook Estate is on the site.

Hertford Place, Devonshire Street (Bancroft Road), Mile End, close to its corner with West Street.

Hertford Place, Haggerston Road, Hackney, 1895, became part of the southern section of Haggerston Road.

Hertford Street, Off Hertford Place (Haggerston Road), Hackney, 1895, south of present-day Lovelace Street.

Hewitts Court, Jubilee Street, Stepney, 1891, close to Mile End Road.

Hickfield Place, Devons Lane (Devons Road), Bromley and Bow, 1851.

High Street, 1. Off Dinmont Street, Bethnal Green, 1860, renamed Hill Street. 2. Off Great Garden Street (Greatorex Street), Whitechapel, 1862, Great Garden Street to Church Street, became northern section of Great Garden Street. 3. Earlier name of Shadwell High Street (The Highway), aka Upper Shadwell, ran from Dellow Street to Love Lane later Brodlove Lane.

High Street Bow, Bromley High Street, Bromley and Bow, see *Bow High Street*.

High Street Bromley, Bromley High Street, Bromley and Bow, see *Bromley High Street*.

Highland Mary Public House, 252-254 Westferry Road, Isle of Dogs.

Highland Street, Off Brunswick Road, Poplar, 1891, Abbot Road and Blackwall Tunnel Approach Road are on the site.

Highlander Public House, 302 Cable Street, Shadwell.

Higley House, Maroon Street, Limehouse, 1950, Limehouse Fields Estate.

Hilcot House, Clarissa Street, Hackney, 1950.

Hilcot Street, Off Lee Street, Hackney, 1895, close to its corner with Haggerston Road.

Hilditch Street, Off St. Leonards Road, Poplar, 1950.

Hill Place, Union Buildings (Long Street), Bethnal Green, 1868.

Hill Place Street, Off Cotall Street, Limehouse, 1890, Cotall Street to Northumberland Street, Bartlett Park is on the site.

Hill Street, 1. Bethnal Green, renamed Coate Street. 2. Hill Street, Off Dinmont Street, Bethnal Green, 1860, became part of Coate Street.

Hill Street, Off Seabright Street, Bethnal Green, 1841.

Hilton Street, Off Stepney Causeway, Ratcliffe, 1891, Stepney Causeway to Dorset Street, immediately south of Commercial Road.

Hilton Street Causeway, Middle and Lower John Street, Ratcliffe, 1891, formerly Middle and Lower John Street.

Hind Arms Public House, 61 Upper North Street, Poplar, 1874.

Hind Street, Off Upper North Street, Poplar, renamed Hind Grove.

Hinks Place, St. Leonards Street, Bromley and Bow, 1891.

Hinks Rents, Bromley High Street, Bromley and Bow, 1851.

Hinton Street, Off Collingwood Street, Whitechapel, 1851.

Hippodrome Theatre, 51-55 East India Dock Road, Limehouse, corner of Stainsby Road renamed Hippodrome Super Cinema.

Hitch(e)s Court, West Street (Birchfield Street), Limehouse, 1851, West Street (later Birchfield Street).

Hobbs Court, Old Castle Street, Whitechapel.

Hobday Street, Off Giraud Street, Poplar, 1950, Godalming Road follows part of route.

Hobsons Cottages & Place, Pelham Street (Woodseer Street), Whitechapel, 1891.

Hobsons Court, Featherstone Buildings (Rhodeswell Road), Limehouse, 1871, renamed Hopsons Court.

Hockley Street, Off Water Lane (Morning Lane), Hackney, 1841.

Hodges Place, Gill Street, Limehouse.

Hodgsons Place, Shakespeare(s) Walk (Shadwell Basin), Shadwell, 1851.

Hog Alley or Yard, Dock Street, St. George in the East, 1870.

Hog Lane, Petticoat Lane (Middlesex Street), Spitalfields, early name for Petticoat Lane, southern part of route followed by later Middlesex Street.

Hogarth Houses, Batty Street, St. George in the East.

Holden Road, Off Botolph Road (Regent Square), Bromley and Bow, 1891, Regent Square is on the site.

Holden Road, Off Bruce Road, Bromley and Bow, Bruce Road to Botolph Road.

Holes Terrace, East India Dock Road, Poplar, 1851.

Holford Street, Off Carlton Road (Portelet Street), Mile End, 1891, renamed Holton Street.

Holidays Court, Blue Anchor Alley (Cable Street), Ratcliffe, 1746.

Hollands Public House, 9 Exmouth Street, Stepney, 1874, aka Exmouth Arms.

Holloway Cottages, Smiths Place (Hackney Road), Bethnal Green.

Holloway Court, Blue Anchor Yard (Royal Mint Street), East Smithfield.

Holloway Street, 1. Off Plumbers Row, Whitechapel, 1891. Off Union Street (Adler Street), Whitechapel, western end of present day Coke Street.

Holly Bush Public House, 56 Woodland Street, Hackney.

Holmes Avenue, Brady Street, Whitechapel, Collingwood Estate is on the site.

Holmes Street, Off Charles Street (Aylward Street), Stepney, Charles Street to Green Street, became part of Exmouth Street.

Holms Street, Off Queensbridge Road, Hackney, 1895, was south of Edith Street.

Holy Child Roman Catholic School, Grundy Street, Poplar, 1926.

Holy Cross House, Old Gravel Lane (Wapping Lane), Wapping, 1891.

Holy Trinity Mission & Institute, Maplin Street, Bromley and Bow.

Homer Terrace, Homer Road, Hackney, 1862, became part of Victoria Park Road.

Homerton Terrace, Retreat Place, Hackney, 1827, Retreat Place to Morning Lane.

Homeward Bound Public House, 536 Commercial Road, Ratcliffe.

Honduras Terrace, Commercial Road, Stepney, "on the right hand side, near Arbour Square" (Elmes).

Honest Lawyer Public House, 66 Oxford Street (Stepney Way), Whitechapel.

Hoods Terrace, Mape Street, Bethnal Green.

Hoop & (Bunch of) Grapes Public House, 112 St. George Street (The Highway), St. George in the East, 1874, aka Hoop & Bunch of Grapes.

Hoop & Grapes Public House, 68 Cable Street, St. George in the East, 1874.

Hoop & Horseshoe Public House, 10 Queen Street (Mansell Street), Whitechapel.

Hooper Square, Leman Street, Whitechapel, 1870, renamed Hooper Street.

Hop Pole Public House, 1. 32 Centre Street, Bethnal Green. 2. 32 Finch Street (Hopetown Street), Whitechapel.

Hop Poles Public House, 68 Sutton Street, Shadwell.

Hopcroft Street, Off Milborne Street, Hackney.

Hope & Anchor Public House, 1. Dock Street (Garnet Street), Shadwell, Shadwell Basin is on the site. 2. 14 Newby Place, Poplar.

Hope Cottage, Pollard Row, Bethnal Green.

Hope Cottages, 1. Douro Street, Bromley and Bow, 1851. 2. Myrtle Street (Mapledene Road), Hackney, 1851.

Hope Court, Denmark Street (Crowder Street), St. George in the East, 1891.

Hope Place, 1. Ben Jonson Road, Mile End, 1891. 2. Rhodeswell Road, Limehouse, 1851. 3. Westferry Road, Isle of Dogs, 1851. 4. Whitechapel Road, Whitechapel, "at 131 nearly opposite the London Hospital, leading to Ducking Pond Row" (Lockie).

Hope Public House, 1. 1 Bere Street, Ratcliffe. 2. 1 Braemar Street (Usk Street), Bethnal Green. 3. 89 Holly Street, Hackney. 4. 101 Old Bethnal Green Road, Bethnal Green, 1874.

Hope Street, 1. Off Brick Lane, Spitalfields, 1891, "the second on the right a few doors from 173 Brick Lane north side Hanburys brewery or the second on the left from 29 Wheeler (sic) Street" (Lockie), Quaker Street later part of Wilkes Street. 2. Off Hackney Road, Bethnal Green, 1851, renamed Treadway Street. 3. Whitechapel, renamed Monthope Road.

Hope Tavern Public House, 2 Pollard Row, Bethnal Green.

Hope Terrace, Four Mills Street (St. Leonards Street), Bromley and Bow, 1851.

Hope Town, Church Street (Bethnal Green Road), Bethnal Green, 1841, later called Union Street and then Turin Street.

Hopes Brewery, 35 Folgate Street (Spitalfields), Spitalfields, aka White Lion Brewery.

Hopsons Court, Rhodeswell Road, Limehouse, 1851.

Horhams Court, Ratcliffe Square (Ratcliffe Cross Street), Ratcliffe, "at the back of the south-east corner of the said square, by Paradise court" (Lockie).

Horn of Plenty Public House, 1. 588 Mile End, aka Horn of Plenty, aka Cornucopia. 2. 5 Crispin Street, Spitalfields. 3. 36 Globe Road, Mile End, 1874. 4. 10 Market Street (Cordelia Street), Poplar, 1899. 5. 41 Poplar High Street, Poplar. 6. Reeves Street (Giraud Street), Poplar, 1874, address also 26 Giraud Street. 7. 111 Rhodeswell Road, Limehouse. 8. 73 Underwood Road, Whitechapel.

Horns & Chequers Public House, Thames Place (Emmett Street), Limehouse, 1874.

Horns & Horseshoe Public House, 10 Cable Street, St. George in the East, 1874.

Horns Public House, 1. 73 Lefevre Road (Lefevre Walk), Bromley and Bow. 2. 53

Middlesex Street, Spitalfields. 3. 16 Whitechapel High Street, Whitechapel, 1874.

Hornsey Place, Westferry Road, Isle of Dogs, 1851, opposite Jane Street.

Horse & Groom Public House, 1. 234 Hackney Road, Bethnal Green. 2. 255 Mare Street, Hackney, 1874. 3. 21 White Church Lane, Whitechapel. 4. 71 White Horse Street (White Horse Road), Stepney, 1874.

Horse & Leaping Bar Public House, 58 Whitechapel High Street, Whitechapel, 1874, aka White Horse & Leaping Bar.

Horse Ride, Fleet Street (Pedley Street), Whitechapel, 1841.

Horse Ride, William Street (Ivimey Street), Bethnal Green, 1851.

Horse Shoe Alley, Petticoat Lane (Middlesex Street), Spitalfields, "the sixth on the right about thirty two doors from 41 Aldgate High Street leading to Goulston Square" (Lockie).

Horseferry (or Horse Ferry) Branch Road, Branch Road, Ratcliffe, 1860, renamed Branch Road.

Horsley Buildings, Adelina Grove, Mile End, 1891, Sidney Street.

Hosford Arms (and Royal Cricketers) Public House, Old Ford Road, Bromley and Bow, 1874, also known as simply Royal Cricketers.

Hospital Tavern Public House, 176 Whitechapel Road, Whitechapel, 1874, aka London Hospital Tavern.

Howard Buildings, Albert Place (Deal Street), Albert Street, Spitalfields, 1891.

Howard Place, Hackney Road, Bethnal Green, "forms part of the north side by the turnpike, about a mile on the left from Shoreditch Church" (Lockie).

Howard Street, Off Grundy Street, Poplar, renamed March Street.

Howards Court, Risbies Ropewalk (Narrow Street), Limehouse, "is about in the middle of the north side of Risbys rope walk" (Elmes).

Howards or Howes Rents, Chigwell Street (Chigwell Hill), Shadwell, "three doors on the right from 51 Ratcliffe Highway towards the London Docks" (Lockie).

Howards Place, Hackney Road, Bethnal Green, 1841.

Howletts Place, Brook Street (Cable Street), Ratcliffe, 1851.

Howrah House, 83 East India Dock Road, Limehouse.

Hoy & Helmet Public House, Lower East Smithfield (St. Katharine Dock), East Smithfield.

Hubbocks Wharf, The Highway, Ratcliffe, 1950, east of Heckford Street.

Huddards Rope Ground, Copenhagen Place, Limehouse, 1851.

Hudson Buildings, Prestons Road, Poplar, 1900.

Hudson(s) Court, 1. Wheler Street, Spitalfields, "is about the sixth of a mile on the left hand in Wheler Street going from Lamb Street" (Elmes). 2. Kingsland Road, Hackney, 1895, became part of Cottons Gardens.

Hughes Buildings, North Street (Portman Place), Bethnal Green, 1841.

Humberston Street, Off Commercial Road, St. George in the East, "the second on the left from Cannon Street Road towards Whitechapel and nearly opposite York Street" (Lockie).

Humphries Buildings, Margaret Street (Whiston Road), Hackney, 1841.

Hungerford Arms Public House, 240 Commercial Road, St. George in the East.

Hungerford Street, Off Commercial Road, St. George in the East, Commercial Road to Mariner Street (1950.

Hunt Court, Hunt Street (Hunton Street), Whitechapel, 1851, renamed Hunton Court.

Hunt Place, Hunt Street (Hunton Street), Whitechapel, 1851, renamed Hunton Place.

Hunt Street, Off Buxton Street,

Whitechapel, Hunton Street follows part of its route.

Huntingdon Buildings, Bethnal Green Road, Bethnal Green, 1891.

Hunts Mews, Juniper Street, Shadwell, 1851.

Hunts Row, Cotton Street, Poplar, 1851.

Huntslet Street, Bethnal Green, renamed Hunslett Street.

Hutchings Wharf, Westferry Road, Isle of Dogs, 1950, at the end of Hutchings Street.

Hutchinsons Arms Public House, 34 Devonport Street, Shadwell, 1874.

I

Imperial Crown Public House, 50 St. Leonards Street, Bromley and Bow.

Imperial Gasworks, Gloucester Street (Mansfield Street), Hackney, Haggerston Park is on the site.

Imrays Court, Butler Street, Spitalfields.

India Arms Public House, 31 Broad Street (The Highway), Ratcliffe, 1874, aka East India Arms.

India House Tavern Public House, Poplar, 1824, Demolished for construction of Blackwall Tunnel.

India Row, Wells Street (Cotton Street), Poplar, 1809, also known as East India Row.

India Terrace, West India Dock Road, Limehouse, 1871.

Infirmary for Asthma, Consumption and other Diseases of the Chest, Brushfield Street, Spitalfields.

Ingelheim (or Ingleheim) Place, Westferry Road, Isle of Dogs, 1891, short road off Westferry Road contained Ingelheim Cottages, junction of Spindrift Avenue and Westferry Avenue is on the site.

Ingelheim Terrace, Westferry Road, Isle of Dogs, row of houses on Westferry Road next to Ingelheim Place.

Ink Horn Court, Half Nichol(s) Street (Boundary Street), Bethnal Green, 1891.

Ink Horn Yard, Whitechapel High Street, Whitechapel, 1851.

Inner Court, Quaker Street, Spitalfields, 1851.

Inverness Arms, 8 Lower East Smithfield (St. Katharines Way), East Smithfield.

Invicta Wharf, Saunders Ness Road, Isle of Dogs, 1950, just west of Glenaffric Avenue.

Ion Arms Public House, 34 Andrews Road, Hackney.

Ipswich Road, Off Pownall Road, Hackney, 1950.

Ireland Row, Mile End Road, Mile End, "part of the left side near the Eagle Public House about ¼ of a mile east from the turnpike" (Lockie).

Irene House, Flower and Dean Street, Spitalfields, 1950.

Irish Court, Whitechapel High Street, Whitechapel, "two or three doors east from Somerset Street about ⅕ of a mile on the right from Aldgate (Lockie).

Iron Bridge Tavern Public House, 447 East India Dock Road, Poplar, 1874.

Iron Bridge Wharf Cottages, East India Dock Road, Poplar, 1891, close to Lanrick Road.

Iron Foundry Court, Old Nichol(s) Street (Boundary Estate), Bethnal Green.

Irongate Wharf, St. Katharines Way, East Smithfield, 1950, east of Tower Bridge.

Ironmonger Court, Old Nichol(s) Street (Boundary Estate), Bethnal Green, 1891.

Ironmongers Almshouses, Kingsland Road, Hackney, 1895, later Geffrye Museum.

Ironmongers Arms Public House, 210 Westferry Road, Isle of Dogs, 1874.

Island Lead Mills, Commercial Road, Limehouse, 1891.

Island Row, 1. Commercial Road, Limehouse, "on the south side about ¼ of a mile west from the church it leads to Richardsons timber yard and Risbys rope walk" (Lockie). 2.

Westferry Road, Isle of Dogs, 1851, short terrace behind south side of Westferry Road half way between Harbinger Road and Chapel House Street.

Islanders Public House, 3-5 Tooke Street (Westferry Road), Isle of Dogs.

Isle of Dogs Police Station, 126 Manchester Road, Isle of Dogs, 1908.

Isle of Dogs School, Glengall Road (Tiller Rd), Isle of Dogs, west half of Glengall Road, former Millwall School.

Ivan House, Kingsland Road, Hackney, 1950, south of Pearson Street.

Ives or Jeves Terrace, Manor Street (Plimsoll Close), Poplar, 1851.

Ivy Cottage & School House, Mowlem Street, Bethnal Green, 1891.

Ivy Cottages, Bath Place/Street (Poplar Bath Street), Poplar, 1891.

Ivy House Public House, Brunswick Street, Poplar, 1891, corner of Prestage Street.

Ivy House Salvation Army Maternity Hospital, 271 Mare Street, Hackney, 1890-1913.

Ivy Place, Wells Street (Cotton Street), Poplar, 1851, Robin Hood Gardens are on the site.

J

Jackson(s) Buildings, Morning Lane, Hackney, 1841, close to Mare Street.

Jacobin Street, Off Talavera Place (Whiston Estate), Bethnal Green, 1827.

Jacobs House, Carr Street, Limehouse, 1950, Limehouse Fields Estate.

Jacobs Well Public House, 127 Hanbury Street, Spitalfields.

Jamaica Hotel, West India Dock Road, Limehouse, at entrance to West India Docks.

Jamaica House, Limehouse Causeway, Limehouse, St. Vincent Estate, demolished in 1994.

Jamaica Passage, Jamaica Place (Beccles Street), Limehouse, Jamaica Place to Rich Street.

Jamaica Place, West India Dock Road, Limehouse, West India Dock Road to Gun Lane, later Grenade Street Beccles Street follows part of route.

Jamaica Tavern Public House, 118 West India Dock Road, Limehouse, 1874.

Jamaica Terrace, West India Dock Road, Limehouse, 1871.

James Place, 1. Devonport Street, Shadwell, 1890, Devonport Street to Stepney Causeway, Barnardo Gardens is on the site. 2. Hackney Road, Bethnal Green, 1860, west of Elizabeth Street. 3. James Street (Burslem Street), St. George in the East. 4. Silver Street (Prusom Street), Wapping, "the second on the right a few doors from King Street and nearly opposite Raines hospital" (Lockie).

James Place or Row, North Street (Saltwell Street), Poplar, later part of Saltwell Street.

James Street, 1. Off Cadiz Street (Masters Street), Mile End, 1891, Cadiz Street to Masters Street, renamed Knott Street. 2. Off Catherine Street (Maroon Street), Limehouse, 1868, renamed Conder Street. 3. Off Church Street (Bethnal Green Road), Bethnal Green, "at 124 the first east of Brick Lane and about $^1/_3$ of a mile on the right from 65 Shoreditch" (Lockie), renamed Chilton Street. 4. Off Columbia Road, Bethnal Green, 1891, renamed Ezra Street. 5. Off Devonport Street, Shadwell, Devonport Street to Hardinge Street, immediately north of railway. 6. Off East India Dock Road, Poplar, opposite Poplar Baths renamed Vesey Street. 7. Off Fleet Street Hill (Pedley Street), Whitechapel, renamed Weaver Street. 8. Off Green Street (Roman Road), Bethnal Green, 1895, renamed Sceptre Road. 9. Off Grove Street (Golding Street), St. George in the East, 1891, renamed Burslem Street. 10. Off Red Lion Street (Reardon Street), Wapping, 1790, close to Worcester Street,

London Docks Western Dock was built on the site. 11. Off Salmon Lane, Limehouse, renamed Conder Street. 12. Bethnal Green, renamed Sceptre Street. 13. Off St. Leonards Street, Bromley and Bow, 1891, renamed Shenfield Place.

James Villas, Albert Road (Albion Drive), Hackney, 1868, between Queens (now Queensbridge) Road and Malvern Road.

James Yard, Whitechapel, renamed Brady Place (Brady Street).

Jane Street, Isle of Dogs, renamed Janet Street.

Janes Street, Bethnal Green, renamed Venice Street (Somerford Street).

Jarrett Place, Old Bethnal Green Road, Bethnal Green, 1851.

Jealous Row, 1. New Road, Whitechapel, "a part of the north side nearly opposite Betts Street from 164 Ratcliffe Highway" (Lockie). 2. Pinchin Street, St. George in the East, 1860, became part of Pinchin Street.

Jechau Place, Martha Street (Wadeson Street), Hackney, 1841.

Jeffer Terrace, Bridge Street (Solebay Street), Bromley and Bow, 1891, immediately east of Canal Road.

Jefferson Street, Off St. Leonards Street, Bromley and Bow, 1891, A12 is on part of its route.

Jeffery(s) Court, Grey Eagle Street, Spitalfields, 1851.

Jenkins Court, Ropemakers Fields, Limehouse, "at 49 the first on the left a few doors from the east end of Narrow Street" (Lockie).

Jerome House, Blount Street, Poplar, 1950.

Jersey Court, Glasshouse Street (John Fisher Street), East Smithfield, 1851, Royal Mint Street.

Jerusalem Gardens, Jerusalem Passage (Valette Street), Hackney, 1841, east of Jerusalem Passage, Church Street.

Jerusalem Passage, Church Street (Mare Street), Hackney, 1851, renamed Valette Street.

Jerusalem Square, Church Street (Mare Street), Hackney, 1851, Church Street to Jerusalem Passage.

Jewel Street, Off Mile End Road, Mile End, 1895, immediately west of 322 Mile End Road.

Jewish & East London Model Lodgings, 45-55 Commercial Street, Spitalfields.

Jewish Association Home for the Protection of Girls & Women, 45 Great Prescot Street (Prescot Street), Whitechapel.

Jewish Centre Synagogue, 25 Lower Chapman Street (Bigland

Street), St. George in the East, 1950, later 22 Sidney Square then 86 Ashfield Street.

Jewish Converts Home, Palestine Place (Cambridge Heath Road), Bethnal Green.

Jewish Free School, Bell Lane, Spitalfields, 1891.

Jewish Infants School, Buckle Street, Whitechapel, 1891.

Jewish Maternity Hospital, 24-26 Underwood Road, Whitechapel, 1911-1939, Vallance Road.

Jewish School, Palestine Place (Cambridge Heath Road), Bethnal Green.

Jewish Working Mens Club, 31-37 Great Alie Street (Alie Street), Whitechapel, 1950.

Jews Cemetery, Lauriston Road, Hackney, 1891.

Jews Free School, Commercial Street, Spitalfields, 1891, west side of Commercial Street, just north of Wentworth St.

Jews Hospital, Mile End Road, Mile End, 1891, west of Bancrofts Almshouses.

Jews or Emanuel Almshouses, Wellclose Square, St. George in the East, 1895.

Jews Orphanage & Asylum, Leman Street, Whitechapel, 1860.

Jews Temporary Shelter, 82 Leman Street, Whitechapel.

Jews Walk, Bethnal Green (Old Ford Road), Bethnal Green, "the north side of the green about $1/8$ of a mile north from the Salmon and Ball Public House" (Lockie), became westernmost section of Old Ford Road.

Jobs Castle Public House, 40 White Lion Street (Folgate Street), Spitalfields, 1874.

Jodrell Road, Off Wick Lane, Bromley and Bow, 1891.

Jodrell Terrace, Wick Lane, Bromley and Bow, 1891.

John Benn Hostel & Milner Hall, 1 Bower Street, Shadwell.

John Bull Public House, 1. 2 Bath Street (Poplar Bath Street), Poplar. 2. 34 Bruce Road, Bromley and Bow. 3. 202 Roman Road, Bethnal Green, 1874. 4. 27 Turk Street (Brick Lane), Bethnal Green.

John Bussey Cinematograph Theatre, 127-129 Bow Road, Bromley and Bow, 1921.

John Court, John Street (Vyner Street), Bethnal Green, 1841, Cambridge Road.

John Knox Presbyterian Church, Stepney Way, Mile End, 1900-1939, east of Dempsey Street.

John Street, 1. Off Ben Jonson Road, Mile End, renamed Halley Place. 2. Off Bonner Street, Bethnal Green, renamed Tagg Street. 3. Off Browns Lane (Hanbury Street), Spitalfields, Middle section of present day

Wilkes Street. 4. Off Cambridge Road (Cambridge Heath Road), Bethnal Green, 1841, Cambridge Heath renamed Vyner Street. 5. Off Cannon Street Road, St. George in the East, 1891, renamed Crellin Street. 6. Off Church Lane (White Church Lane), Whitechapel, renamed Assam Street. 7. Off Commercial Road, Shadwell, renamed Johnson Street. 8. Off Dove Row, Bethnal Green, 1862. 9. Off Ducking Pond Row (Durward Street), Whitechapel, "on the west side of Liptraps distillery and nearly opposite Court Street from 110 Whitechapel Road" (Lockie). 10. Off Ford Square, Stepney, renamed Clark Street. 11. Off George Street (Broadway Market), Hackney, 1841, London Fields, renamed Bremen Street, then Dericote Street. 12. Off Hackney Road, Bethnal Green, renamed Gorsuch Place. 13. Off James Street (Conder Street), Limehouse, 1868, renamed Repton Street. 14. Off Kingsland Road, Hackney, renamed Laburnum Street. 15. Off Rhodeswell Road, Limehouse, renamed Endive Street. 16. Off Samuel Street (Camdenhurst Street), Limehouse, renamed Repton Street. 17. Bromley and Bow, renamed South Grove. 18. Whitechapel, now Spelman Street. 19. Off Upper North Street, Poplar, now the westernmost part of Grundy Street. 20. Off Walter Street, Bethnal Green, 1851. 21. Off Watney Street, Shadwell, renamed Sheridan Street. 22. Off White Horse Lane, Mile End, renamed Skidmore Street.

John Street Almshouses, Church Lane (White Church Lane), Whitechapel, 1891.

John Terrace, Hackney Road, Bethnal Green, 1860, opposite Coleharbour Street.

Johns Cottages, Charles Street (Vallance Road), Whitechapel.

Johns Court, 1. Heneage Street, Whitechapel. Johns Hill (The Highway), St. George in the East, 1891.

Johns Court or Place, 1. Hunt Street (Hunton Street), Whitechapel, 1851. 2. Princes Street (Princelet Street), Whitechapel, 1851.

Johns Hill, St. George Street (The Highway), St. George in the East, 1891, St. George Street to Pennington Street.

Johns Place, 1. Back Road (Cable Street), St. George in the East, 1851. 2. Mayfield Road, Hackney, 1851. 3. Nelson Street, Whitechapel, 1891. 4. Robin Hood Lane, Poplar, 1891, East India Dock Road.

Johns Rents, Old Gravel Lane (Wapping Lane), Wapping, "at the north end of Silver Street behind Raines Hospital" (Elmes).

Johns Row, Old Ford Road, Bromley and Bow, 1851.

Johns Square, Church Lane (Back Church Lane), St. George in the East, "about the middle of the east side, viz between the Commercial Road and Cable Street" (Lockie).

Johns Street or Hill, Ratcliffe Highway (The Highway), St. George in the East, "at 34 about 1/8 of a mile east from Wellclose Square extending to 110 Pennington Street" (Lockie).

Johns Terrace, 233–239 East India Dock Road, Poplar, 1880, opposite Cotton Street.

Johnson Street Synagogue, 2a Johnson Street, Wapping, 1955, Cable Street.

Johnson(s) Street, 1. Off Manchester Road, Isle of Dogs, 1891, ran between Johnsons Draw Dock and Manchester Road Now part of Ferry Street. 2. Off Old Gravel Lane (Wapping Lane), Wapping.

Johnsons Buildings, 1. Church Court (Wapping High Street), Wapping, 1891. 2. Kerbey Street, Poplar, 1891, East India Dock Road.

Johnsons Change, Royal Mint Street, East Smithfield, 1870, rear of Royal Mint Street, opposite Cartwright Street.

Johnsons Court, 1. Goodmans Fields (Leman Street), Whitechapel, 1890, "about the middle of the east side leading to 76 Lambert Street" (Lockie), Leman Street to Lambeth Street

renamed Leman Passage. 2. Shakespeare(s) Walk (Shadwell Basin), Shadwell, "at 62 the third on the left from 48 High Street near the west side of the church" (Lockie).

Johnsons Street, 1. Off Bridge Street (Solebay Street), Mile End, Bridge Street to Commodore Terrace, became part of Harford Street. 2. Off King Edward Street (Kingward Street), Whitechapel, 1851. 3. Spitalfields, now Meggs Places.

Joiners Arms Public House, 1. 118 Hackney Road, Bethnal Green. 2. 154 Tredegar Road, Bromley and Bow.

Jolly Brewer(s) Public House, 1 Fellbrigg Street (Collingwood Street), Whitechapel, original address 15 Norfolk Street.

Jolly Butchers, 157 Brick Lane, Whitechapel, 1874, aka Turkish Slave, aka Turk and Slave, aka Turkish Head.

Jolly Gardeners Public House, 10 Margaret Street (Whiston Road), Hackney.

Jolly Gun Maker Public House, 9 Ranwell Street (Alice Street), Bromley and Bow.

Jolly Sailor Public House, 1. 314 Cable Street, Shadwell, 1874, aka Jolly Sailors & Little Billet. 2. 85 Grove Street (Golding Street), St. George in the East. 3. 63 Jamaica Place (Beccles Street), Limehouse. 4. 8 New Gravel Lane (Garnet

Street), Wapping. 5. 272 Oxford Street (Stepney Way), Whitechapel. 6. 182-183 St. George Street (The Highway), St. George in the East, 1874. 7. 52 West Street (Braintree Street), Mile End, part renamed Braintree Street part renamed Malcolm Road.

Jolly Sailors & Little Billet Public House, 314 Cable Street, Shadwell, 1874, aka Jolly Sailor.

Jolly Tar Public House, 3 Dock Street, St. George in the East.

Jolly Weavers Public House, 60 Wheler Street, Spitalfields.

Jones Buildings, Lambeth Street (Alie Street), Whitechapel, 1851.

Jones Court, Mile End Road, Mile End, "about a mile on the left below Whitechapel Church and a few doors west of the Old Globe Public House on the right from London Bridge" (Lockie).

Joseph Street, 1. Off Cable Street, Shadwell, 1891, renamed Martineau Street. 2. Off Cannon Street Road, St. George in the East, 1891, renamed Sly Street.

Josephine House, Thrawl Street, Spitalfields, 1950.

Joyds Court, Batty Street, St. George in the East, 1891.

Jubilee Chapel, Manchester Road, Isle of Dogs, 1869, alternative naming of Cubitt Town Primitive Methodist Church.

Jubilee Cottages, London Place, Hackney, 1891.

Jubilee Place, 1. Commercial Road, Stepney, "near ¼ of a mile on the left from Whitechapel Church and on the west side the Halfway House" (Lockie), became southern end of Jubilee Street. 2. Parliament Street (Witan Street), Bethnal Green, 1841.

Jubilee Street Zionist Synagogue, 165 Jubilee Street, Stepney, 1960.

Jubilee Wharf, 1. Orchard Place, Poplar, 1950. 2. Wapping Wall, Wapping, 1950, west of Monza Street.

Judkin(s) Street, Off East Ferry Road, Isle of Dogs, 1891.

June Buildings, Devonshire Street (Bancroft Road), Mile End, close to Red Lion Public House.

Juniper Court, Chigwell Street (Chigwell Hill), Shadwell, "three doors on the right from 51 Ratcliffe Highway" (Lockie).

Juniper Row, King David Lane, Shadwell, "Sun Tavern Fields, on the south side the Rope ground entrance by the first on the right in King David Lane from 198 Shadwell High Street" (Lockie), renamed Juniper Street.

Juniper Street, Off Glamis Road, Shadwell, 1950, Glamis Road to King David Lane.

Jupps Road, Off Whitman

Road, Bromley and Bow, Mile End Park is on the site.

Jupps Terrace, Commercial Road, Limehouse, 1851.

K

Katharine Buildings, Cartwright Street (Royal Mint Street), East Smithfield, 1891.

Katharine Wheel Public House, 50 St. Peters Road (Cephas Avenue), Mile End, aka Catherine Wheel, address also 50 Cephas Avenue.

Katherine Place, Garden Place (Robin Hood Gardens), Poplar, 1830, south of Wells Street, Robin Hood Gardens are on the site.

Keat(e) Court, Keat(e) Street (Thrawl Street), Spitalfields, 1792.

Keat(e) Street, Spitalfields, renamed Thrawl Street.

Keates House, Lolesworth Street (Lolesworth Close), Spitalfields, 1950.

Kedgeree Place, 168-170 East India Dock Road, Poplar, 1851.

Keepier Wharf, Broad Street (The Highway), Ratcliffe, 1895, corner with Narrow Street.

Kehal Chasidim Synagogue, 85/87 Fieldgate Street, Whitechapel, 1920.

Kehillath Israel Synagogue, 14-16 Vallance Road, Whitechapel, 1940.

Kehillath Moshe Anshe Belz Synagogue, 69 Cavell Street, Whitechapel, also 63 Cavell Street.

Kehol Chasidim Synagogue, 5 Old Montague Street, Whitechapel, 1905.

Kelday Road, Off Wansbeck Road, Bromley and Bow, 1891.

Kendalls Place, Great Pearl Street (Calvin Street), Spitalfields, 1851.

Kenilworth Road, Off Roman Road, Bromley and Bow, 1891.

Kent & Essex Tavern, 114 Whitechapel High Street, Whitechapel.

Kent & Essex Wharf, Lower Shadwell (Shadwell Park), Shadwell, 1895.

Kent & Essex Yard, Whitechapel High Street, Whitechapel, 1851.

Kent Villas, Grange Road (Gayhurst Road), Hackney, 1868, between Malvern Road and Lansdowne Road.

Kenton Arms Public House, 38 Kenton Road, Hackney, 1874.

Keppel Street, Off Old Gravel Lane (Wapping Lane), Wapping, "is the second turning on the left hand going from Ratcliffe Highway" (Elmes), the Eastern London Dock was built on the site.

Kerrs Buildings, Mansford Street, Bethnal Green, 1891.

Kettleby Court, Blue Anchor Yard (Royal Mint Street), East Smithfield, 1851.

Kettledrum Public House, 153 St. George Street (The Highway), St. George in the East, 1874.

Key Street, Off Cambridge Heath Road, Mile End, 1950, heading east north of Trinity Almshouses.

Kidney Stairs, Narrow Street, Limehouse, "a few houses westward of the drawbridge in Narrow Street about two miles below London Bridge" (Elmes).

Kimberley Arms Public House, 79 Swinnerton Street, Hackney.

Kinder Arms Public House, 19 Little Turner Street (Commercial Road), St. George in the East, 1874.

King & Queen Public House, 1. Cold Harbour, Poplar, 1722, an early name of the Gun public house. 2. 89 Hare Street (Cheshire Street), Whitechapel, 1874. 3. 30 Norton Folgate, Spitalfields. 4. 51 Tait Street, St. George in the East, 1874. 5. 34 Three Colt Street, Limehouse, 1874.

King Albert Public House, 126 Harford Street, Mile End, aka Prince of Prussia, west of gasworks.

King Charles II Public House, 11 Lamb Street, Spitalfields.

King Edward Industrial School for Girls / Refuge, Andrews Road, Hackney, 1891, The Broadway.

King Edward Institute, 17 Three Colts Lane, Bethnal Green, 1950.

King Edward Institution, 1. Brady Street, Whitechapel, 1921, corner of Tent Street. 2. 19 Deal Street, Spitalfields.

King Edward Ragged School & Mission, King Edward Street (Kingward Street), Spitalfields.

King Edward Street, 1. Off Church Street (White Church Lane), Whitechapel, 1851, renamed Kingward Street. 2. Off Wapping High Street, Wapping, "at 172 Wapping Street opposite King Edward Stairs, it extends to Cinnamon Street" (Lockie), renamed Clave Street.

King Edward(s) Stairs, Wapping High Street, Wapping, on river, opposite corner of King Edward Street and Wapping High Street.

King George Public House, 25 Burr Street (St. Katharine Dock), East Smithfield, 1874, Lower East Smithfield.

King Georges Hall, East India Dock Road, Poplar, former United Methodist Free Church corner of Poplar Bath Street.

King Harry (VIII) Public House, 279 Mile End Road, Mile End, Also known as Old King Harry, King Henry VIII, King Harrys Head.

King Harry(s) Public House, 1. 253 Cambridge Road (Cambridge Heath Road), Bethnal Green. 2. 33 Red Lion Street (Leman Street), Whitechapel. 3. 279 Mile End Road, Mile End, Also known as Old King Harry, King Harry (VIII), King Henry VIII.

King Henry Court, Prusom Street, Wapping, Prusom Street to Pearl Street.

King Henry VIII Public House, 279 Mile End Road, Mile End, Also known as Old King Harry, King Harry (VIII), King Harrys Head.

King Henry Yard, Off Nightingale Lane (Thomas More Street), East Smithfield, 1800, St. Katharine Dock is on its site.

King Henrys Wharf, Wapping High Street, Wapping, 1950, south of corner with Brewhouse Lane.

King James Stairs, Wapping Wall, Wapping, "at 70 opposite Star Street, nearly opposite the Kings Mills Rotherhithe" (Lockie).

King John Public House, 110 Mile End Road, Mile End.

King Johns Court, Limehouse Causeway, Limehouse, "is facing the Lime Kilns Dock at the east end of Fore Street" (Lockie).

King of Denmark Public House, 24 Wapping High Street, Wapping, 1874.

King of Prussia on Horseback Public House, 93 Middlesex Street, Spitalfields, 1874, aka King of Prussia.

King of Prussia Public House, 1. 39 Cartwright Street (Royal Mint Street), East Smithfield, 1874. 2. 5-6 Dean Street (Shadwell Park), Shadwell, 1874, address also Garth Street. 3. 26 Gowers Walk, Whitechapel. 4. 93 Middlesex Street, Spitalfields, 1874, aka King of Prussia on Horseback.

King of Sardinia Public House, 391 Mile End Road, Mile End.

King Stables, Viaduct Street, Bethnal Green.

King Street, 1. King Street, Off Brick Lane, Bethnal Green, "Spitalfields, at 158 the fourth on the right from 155 Church St, it extends to Farthing Street" (Lockie), became western end of Gossett Street. 2. Off Doveton Street, Mile End, renamed Wickford Street. 3. Off Hackney Road, Bethnal Green, 1841, renamed Diss Street. 4. Off Hanbury Street, Spitalfields, 1950, south of Queen Street, with which it combined, the resulting road was later renamed Rowland Street. 5. Stepney, became part of Jamaica Street. 6. Limehouse, renamed Ming Street. 7. Off Old Ford Road, Bromley and Bow, 1841, renamed Mace Street. 8. King Street, Off Old Gravel Lane (Wapping Lane), Wapping, renamed Prusom Street. 9. Off

Old Montague Street, Whitechapel, became part of Queen Street. 10. Off Turk Street (Brick Lane), Bethnal Green, "the first on the left a few doors from Virginia Row behind Shoreditch Church" (Lockie). 11. Bethnal Green, 1891, renamed Viaduct Place.

King William (IV) Public House, 100 New Gravel Lane (Garnet Street), Wapping.

Kings Arms Gardens, King David Lane, Shadwell, "Sun Tavern Fields a few houses eastward of King Davids Lane" (Elmes).

Kings Arms Place, Commercial Road, Ratcliffe, 1865, Caroline Street to Ratcliffe Street.

Kings Arms Public House, 1. 11 Abbey Street (Buckfast Street), Bethnal Green, 1874. 2. 10 Annes Place (Pritchard Road), Bethnal Green, 1874. 3. Blackwall (Raleana Road), Poplar, Old Blackwall riverside, aka Old Kings Arms. 4. 167 Bow Road, Bromley and Bow, 1874. 5. 83 Brook Street (Cable Street), Ratcliffe, 1874, address also 513 Cable Street, 83 Stepney Causeway, 39 Broad Street. 6. 357 Cable Street, Shadwell, 1874. 7. 12 Carr Street, Limehouse, 1874. 8. 514 Commercial Road, Ratcliffe, aka Mariners. 9. 32 Fieldgate Street, Whitechapel, 1874. 10. 17 Green Bank, Wapping, aka Cherry Tree. 11. 2 John Street (Repton Street), Limehouse, 1874, Limehouse Fields. 12. 214 Jubilee Street, Stepney. 13. Kings Arms Stairs (Westferry Road), Isle of Dogs, Westferry Road. 14. 16 Market Hill (Shadwell Park), Shadwell. 15. 230 Mile End Road, Mile End, 1874. 16. 43 Narrow Street, Limehouse. 17. Neptune Street (Wellclose Square), Wapping, 1874. 18. 81 New Gravel Lane (Garnet Street), Wapping. 19. 67 Old Bethnal Green Road, Bethnal Green. 20. 19 Pritchards Road, Bethnal Green. 21. 83 Sclater Street, Whitechapel, 1874. 22. 211 St. George Street (The Highway), St. George in the East. 23. 109 Three Colt Street, Limehouse, 1874. 24. 53-55 Whitechapel Road, Whitechapel, 1874. 25. 20 Wilkes Street, Spitalfields, 1874. 21. 20 Wilkes Street, Spitalfields.

Kings Arms Stairs, Westferry Road, Isle of Dogs, "about ¾ of a mile below the entrance to the West India Docks nearly opposite Greenland dock" (Lockie), just north of Millwall Dock entrance lock.

Kings Arms Yard, 1. Bow Road, Bromley and Bow, 1921. 2. Old Ford Road, Bromley and Bow.

Kings Cottage, 1. Bonner Street, Bethnal Green, 1891. 2. Mace Street, Bethnal Green, 1891, Old Ford Road. 3. Salmon Lane, Limehouse.

Kings Court, 1. King Street (Brick Lane), Spitalfields, "about the middle of the north side viz between 158 Brick Lane and Farthing Street" (Lockie). 2. King Street (Brick Lane), Whitechapel.

Kings Head Alley, Virginia Street, St. George in the East, "Parsons Street, Upper East Smithfield about ten doors on the right from 47 Parsons Street and is opposite Pennington Street" (Lockie).

Kings Head Court, Red Lion Street (Commercial Street), Spitalfields, "a few doors on the left from the west side of the church or from Paternoster Row" (Lockie).

Kings Head Public House, 1. 50 Bishops Road (Bishops Way), Bethnal Green. 2. Bow Road, Bromley and Bow. 3. British Street (Harbinger Road), Isle of Dogs, 1874. 4. 131 Brook Street (Cable Street), Ratcliffe, 1874, address also 555 Cable Street. 5. 128 Commercial Road, St. George in the East, 1874. 6. 24 Mare Street, Hackney. 7. 67 Old Bethnal Green Road, Bethnal Green, 1874. 8. 20 ½ Prospect Place (Cambridge Heath Road), Bethnal Green, 1874, Cambridge Heath Road. 9. 80 Three Colt Street, Limehouse, 1874. 10. 31 Vallance Road, Whitechapel.

Kings Head Yard, Bow High Street (Bow Road), Bromley and Bow, 1851, next to 202 Bow High Street.

Kings Place, 1. Chapel Street, Bethnal Green, 1841. 2. Commercial Road, St. George in the East, 1860, Back Church Lane to Grove Street. 3. Diss Street, Bethnal Green, 1891. 4. King Street (Hackney Road), Bethnal Green, 1851, Hackney Road. 5. Bethnal Green, renamed Stamp Place.

Kings Road, Off Poplar High Street, Poplar, sometime name of Harrow Lane.

Kings Row, Dog Row (Cambridge Heath Road), Whitechapel, "Bethnal Green forms part of the west side nearly opposite Red Cow Lane, about ¼ of a mile on the left from Mile End turnpike" (Lockie).

Kings Square, Brick Lane, Spitalfields, "at 162 two doors north from Phoenix Street" (Lockie).

Kings Street, Off Lee Street, Hackney, 1868, renamed Loanda Street, parallel to and in between Stean Street and Clarissa Street.

Kings Terrace, 1. Commercial Road, Ratcliffe, 1861, White Horse Street to London Street. 2. Digby Road, Hackney. 3. John Street (Grundy Street), Poplar, 1851, renamed Grundy Street.

Kingsbridge Arms Public House, 156 Westferry Road, Isle of Dogs.

Kingsbridge Place, Westferry Road, Isle of Dogs, 1868, terrace from just north of Gaverick Street to south of Claude Street.

Kingsland Crescent, Kingsland Road, Hackney, 1841.

Kingsland Place, Kingsland Road, Hackney, 1851, close to corner with Dalston Lane.

Kingsland Row, 1. Dalston Green (Dalston Junction), Hackney, Dalston Junction. 2. Old Gravel Lane (Wapping Lane), Wapping, "at 114 about ten doors on the right from 65 Ratcliffe Highway" (Lockie).

Kingward Street, Off Old Montague Street, Whitechapel, 1950, Old Montague Street to Hanbury Street, at the eastern end of Chicksand Street.

Kinnear Dwellings, Bakers Alley (Bow Road), Bromley and Bow, 1891.

Kirks Place & Row, Rhodeswell Road, Limehouse, 1891.

Kirvan Cottages, Northey Street, Limehouse, 1871.

Kite Place, Warner Place, Bethnal Green, 1950, Warner Place to Old Bethnal Green Road.

Kittisford or Kidsford Place & Terrace, Hackney Road, Bethnal Green, 1851, immediately west of Charles Street.

Knave of Clubs Public House, 25 Club Row, Bethnal Green, 1874.

Knightly Court, St. John Street (Grimsby Street), Bethnal Green, 1841.

Knights Buildings, Tagg Street (Cranbrook Estate), Bromley and Bow, 1891.

Knights Court, Tench Street (Wapping Gardens), Wapping, "the continuation of Harrels Court bearing to the right it leads to Tench Street Labour in Vain Street Market at the south east corner being a few doors south from 66 Shadwell High Street" (Lockie), Wapping Gardens are on the site.

Knights Terrace, Rhodeswell Road, Limehouse, 1851.

Knott Street, Off Cadiz Street (Masters Street), Mile End, 1891.

Konin Synagogue, 48 Hanbury Street, Spitalfields.

L

La Patente French Church, Paternoster Row, Spitalfields.

Labour In Vain Street, Off Shadwell High Street (The Highway), Shadwell, "a few houses southward of Shadwell High Street" (Elmes), Shadwell Park is on the site.

Laburnam or Laburnum Cottage(s), Seabright Street, Bethnal Green, 1851.

Laburnham Terrace, 1. Old Ford Road, Bromley and Bow, 1851. 2. John Street (Laburnum

Street), Bethnal Green, renamed Laburnum Street.

Lacey Street, Off Mostyn Grove, Bromley and Bow, Mostyn Grove to Morville Street, north of the present-day Matilda Gardens.

Ladies Charity School, 67 Cotton Street, Poplar, 1813.

Lady Ashburtons Home for Girls, Globe Road Place (Globe Road), Mile End, 1891.

Lady Coborn Public House, 740 Old Ford Road, Bromley and Bow.

Lady Franklin Public House, 381 Old Ford Road, Bromley and Bow, 1874.

Lady Holles School for Girls, 182 Mare Street, Hackney, 1910.

Lady Lakes Grove, Sidney Street, Whitechapel, 1891, renamed Adelina Grove.

Lagston Street, Limehouse, Bartlett Park is on the site.

Lake Street, Off Hardinge Street, Shadwell, 1950, Hardinge Street to Devonport Street, just north of railway line.

Lamb (Tavern) Public House, 1. 24 Dorset Street (Pitsea Street), Ratcliffe. 2. 512 Kingsland Road, Hackney, 1874.

Lamb (Tavern) Public House, 64 New Road, Whitechapel.

Lamb Cottages, Red Lion Court (Commercial Street), Spitalfields, 1792.

Lamb Court, Lamb Street, Spitalfields, 1851.

Lamb Farm, Grange Road (Gayhurst Road), Hackney, 1841, in the area of the later Grange Road and Mayfield Road.

Lamb Gardens & Street, Off Three Colts Lane, Bethnal Green, 1841, later part of Three Colts Lane.

Lamb Place, Kingsland Road, Hackney, 1868, north of Grange Road.

Lamb Public House, 1. 212 Wick Road, Hackney. 2. 36 Wilmot Street, Bethnal Green.

Lamb Row & Street, Off Wilmot Street, Bethnal Green, "at the south end on the left by the Lamb public house leading towards Dog Row" (Lockie), later part of Three Colts Lane.

Lamb Terrace North, Lamb Lane, Hackney, 1860.

Lambert Street, Whitechapel, 1810, renamed Lambeth Street (Alie Street).

Lamberts Court, Ashton Street, Poplar, 1851.

Lamberts Terrace, Brunswick Street, Poplar, 1825.

Lambeth Street, Off Alie Street, Whitechapel, 1891, Alie Street to Hooper Street, parallel with the railway line.

Lambs Court, Old Montague Street, Whitechapel, 1851, south side just east of Osborn Street.

Lambs Place, Primrose Street (Allenbury Street), Bethnal Green, 1851.

Lammas House & Road, Off Penshurst Road, Hackney, 1891.

Lance Street, Off Gill Street, Limehouse, 1891.

Lanark Wharf, Narrow Street, Ratcliffe, 1895, east of Duke Shore Wharf.

Landers Buildings, Petticoat Lane (Middlesex Street), Spitalfields, 1851.

Landowne Terrace, Grove Road, Bromley and Bow.

Landseer Road, Off Addington Road, Bromley and Bow, 1891, Lawrence Close is on the site.

Landseer Terrace, Brunswick Street, Poplar, 1891.

Lane Cottages, Ropemakers Fields, Limehouse, 1871.

Langbourne Wharf, Westferry Road, Isle of Dogs, 1950, Langbourne Place is on its site.

Langdale Court, Langdale Street, St. George in the East, 1891.

Langdale Mansions, Langdale Street, St. George in the East, 1950, Langdale Street and Wicker Street.

Langley House & Place aka Langley House Home for Orphans, 54 East India Dock Road, Limehouse, 1825.

Langley Place, 1. Cold Harbour, Poplar, 1851. 2. Commercial Road, Whitechapel, "Mile End Old Town, forms part of the north side between Greenfield Street and Gloucester Street near ¼ of a mile on the left from Whitechapel Church" (Lockie).

Langley Villas, 60-66 East India Dock Road, Limehouse, 1825.

Langton Street, Off Upper North Street, Poplar, 1890, renamed Langstone Street, Upper North Street to Sabbarton Street, Bartlett Park is on the site.

Lansdell Place, Globe Road, Bethnal Green, 1891.

Lansdown Cottages, 1. Tenter Ground, Spitalfields, 1851. 2. Durham Street (Teesdale Street), Bethnal Green, 1841. 3. London Fields, Hackney, 1841. 4. Richmond Road, Hackney, 1851.

Lansdowne Place, renamed Lansdowne Grove (Lansdowne Drive).

Lansdowne Road, Hackney, renamed Lansdowne Drive.

Lansdowne Terrace, Richmond Road, Hackney, 1851.

Lansmere Terrace, Old Ford Road, Bromley and Bow.

Lanyard Street, Off Cayley Street (Whitehorse Road Park), Stepney.

Lardners Buildings, Sandys Row, Spitalfields, 1891, east of Sandys Row, and north of Wentworth St.

Largo & Folly Cottages, East India Dock Road, Poplar, 1851.

Latham Street, Off Stainsby Road, Limehouse, 1860, parallel with Stainsby, Bartlett Park is on the site.

Latham Street, Off Sussex Street (Lindfield Street), Limehouse, 1891.

Lathams Buildings, Little Bacon Street (Bacon Street), Bethnal Green.

Latimer Chapel, Bridge Street (Solebay Street), Mile End, close to its corner with Harford Street.

Latimer Street, Off Oxford Street (Stepney Way), Whitechapel, 1891.

Laughtons Rents, Cinnamon Street, Wapping, 1746.

Laura Cottages, Ingelheim Place (Westferry Road), Isle of Dogs, 1891.

Laura Place, 1. Rhodeswell Road, Limehouse, 1851. 2. Queens Road (Queensbridge Road), Hackney, 1851, north of Laurel Street.

Laurel Tree Public House, 69 Brick Lane, Spitalfields, 1874.

Lavender Place, Pennington Street, St. George in the East, 1891.

Lavers Cottages, Canton Street, Limehouse, 1891.

Lawes Street, Off Bow Common Lane, Bromley and Bow, north of St. Pauls Way.

Lawfranc Road, Off Gernon Road, Bromley and Bow, 1891.

Lawless Street, Off Bath Street (Poplar Bath Street), Poplar, 1950, East India Dock Road.

Lawn House, 1. Glen Terrace, Isle of Dogs, 1891, rear of Glen Terrace, Manchester Road. 2. Stepney Green, Stepney, 1891.

Lawrence Road, Off Malmesbury Road, Bromley and Bow, 1891, east of Alfred Street.

Lax Street, Off Cotall Street, Limehouse, 1950.

Layfield Place or Street, Off Byron Street, Poplar, 1950.

Le (or Leigh) Hoy Public House, 163 Hanbury Street, Spitalfields, 1874.

Lea Conservancy House, Ammiel Terrace (Bromley High Street), Bromley and Bow, 1891, just south of Bow Bridge.

Lea Cottage or Place, East India Dock Road, Poplar, 1891.

Lea Passage, Orchard Place, Poplar, 1891, renamed Leamouth Passage.

Lea Tavern Public House, 90 White Post Lane, Hackney.

Lea Wall, Orchard Place, Poplar, 1851.

Lead Street, Off Westferry Road, Isle of Dogs, 1891, close to corner with East Ferry Road.

Lead Yard, Whitechapel High Street, Whitechapel, "is in Goodmans Fields the second turning on the left hand from Whitechapel High Street" (Elmes).

Leading Street, Off Foxes Lane (Shadwell Basin), Shadwell, "is the first turning on the left hand in Foxs Lane near Shadwell High Street and on the east side of the church" (Elmes), Shadwell Park is on the site.

League of Helpers Meeting Room, 1A London Fields, Hackney, 1921.

Leamouth Passage, Orchard Street (Orchard Place), Poplar, 1950.

Leamouth Place, Orchard Place, Poplar, 1851.

Lear Street, Off South Grove (Southern Grove), Bromley and Bow, south of Mile End Road.

Lebecks Head Public House, 75 Shadwell High Street (The Highway), Shadwell.

Lee Place, Old Ford Road, Bromley and Bow, 1851.

Lee Street, 1. Off Burgess Street, Limehouse, 1891. 2. Off Kilner Street, Poplar.

Lefevre Grove, Lefevre Road (Lefevre Walk), Bromley and Bow, Hadrian Close is partially on the site.

Lefevre Road, Off Old Ford Road, Bromley and Bow, 1891, part renamed Lefevre Walk, part renamed Legion Terrace.

Lefevre Terrace, Lefevre Road (Lefevre Walk), Bromley and Bow, 1891.

Leggs Buildings or Court, Bow Common Lane, Bromley and Bow, 1891.

Leicester Place, Augusta Street, Poplar, 1851.

Leicester Street, Off Prestons Road, Poplar, 1851, renamed Duthie Street.

Leigh (or Le) Hoy Public House, 163 Hanbury Street, Spitalfields, 1874.

Leigh Place, Bow Common Lane, Bromley and Bow, 1851.

Leman Passage, Leman Street, Whitechapel, 1890, Leman Street to Lambeth Street.

Leman Row, Leman Street, Whitechapel, 1851.

Leman Street Railway Station, Leman Street, Whitechapel, 1877-1941.

Lemon Court, Old Nichol(s) Street (Boundary Estate), Bethnal Green, 1841.

Lemon Street, Off Leman Street, Whitechapel, early alternative spelling of Leman Street.

Lemons Terrace, Stepney Way, Mile End, eastern corner of Stepney Way with Mile End Road.

Lenham(s) Buildings, Mount Street (Swanfield Street), Bethnal Green, "Are a few houses on the right hand side of Mount Street going from Church Street" (Elmes).

Lenthall House, 13-18 Lenthall Road, Hackney, 1950.

Leopold Buildings, Columbia Road, Bethnal Green, 1891.

Leopold House Barnardos, 199 Burdett Road, Bromley and Bow.

Leslie or Lislie Street, Off Mile End Road, Mile End, 1891, opposite Vintners Almshouses.

Lessada Street, Off Roman Road, Bromley and Bow, 1891, Mile End Park is on site.

Letchfords Factory Lodges, Three Colts Lane, Bethnal Green.

Lewington Buildings, Adelina Grove, Mile End, 1891, Sidney Street.

Lewis Cottages, James Street (Chilton Street), Bethnal Green, 1841, Ravenscroft Street.

Library Place, 232 Cable Street, St. George in the East, next to 232 Cable Street.

Lidgett Street, Off Woolmore Street, Poplar, Robin Hood Gardens are on the site.

Life Boat Public House, 1. 283 East India Dock Road, Poplar. 2. 232 Rhodeswell Road, Limehouse.

Lilian House, Philip Street (Ellen Street), St. George in the East.

Lime Cottages, Albert Road (Albion Drive), Hackney, 1868, between Queens (now Queensbridge) Road and Malvern Road.

Lime Grove, Lyme Grove, Hackney, 1851, Burford Lane.

Lime Kiln Yard, Emma Street, Bethnal Green.

Lime Kilns Court, Fore Street (Narrow Street), Limehouse, "a few yards on the right from the east end of Fore Street by the Ship and Lamb public house" (Lockie).

Lime Kilns Dock, Fore Street (Narrow Street), Limehouse, "at the east end of Fore Street on the right by the side of the Thames or the south end of Three Colt Street" (Lockie).

Limehouse Hole, Three Colt Street, Limehouse, "the continuation of Three Colt Street Extending from the lime kilns towards Millwall on the bank of the Thames" (Lockie).

Limehouse Hole Stairs, Three Colt Street, Limehouse, "a few yards on the right below the Lime Kilns Dock by Mitchells rope walk, nearly opposite Cuckolds Point Rotherhithe" (Lockie).

Limehouse Railway Station, Three Colt Street, Limehouse, 1840-1926.

Limehouse Synagogue, 22b Baythorne Street, Limehouse, 1940, Burdett Road.

Limehouse Town Hall, Commercial Road, Limehouse, 1891, at corner of Newell Street.

Limehouse Wharf, Narrow

Street, Ratcliffe, 1895, west of corner with Three Colt Street.

Limekiln Wharf, Limekiln Dock, Narrow Street, Limehouse, 1950.

Lincoln Street, renamed Brokesley Street, Bromley and Bow.

Lindale Street, Off Grundy Street, Poplar, 1950.

Linden Buildings, Shacklewell Street, Bethnal Green, 1891.

Lindon Street, Off Towcester Road, Bromley and Bow.

Lingen Street, Off St. Leonards Street, Bromley and Bow, 1891.

Lintons Place, Nightingale Lane (Thomas More Street), Wapping, 1851, renamed Lockside.

Lion & Lamb Public House, 1. 10 Dalgleish Street, Limehouse. 2. 45 Skidmore Street (Harford Street), Stepney, 1874.

Lion (Arms) Public House, 18 Holford Street (Holton Street), Mile End, 1874.

Lion Place, Rhodeswell Road, Limehouse, 1851.

Lion Public House, 1. 83 Carlton Road (Portelet Street), Mile End. 2. 1 Lion Street (Kerbey Street), Poplar. 3. 8 Tapp Street, Whitechapel.

Lion Street, Off Kerbey Street, Poplar, 1851, renamed Farnfield Street.

Lion Wharf, Westferry Road, Isle of Dogs, 1950, Sir John

McDougalls Gardens are on its site.

Lisbon Buildings, Lisbon Street (Cambridge Heath Road), Bethnal Green, 1891.

Lisbon Street, Off Bath Street (Darling Row), Whitechapel, 1950, Bath Street to Cambridge Heath Road.

Liscombes Villas, Shrubland Grove (Mapledene Road), Hackney, 1868, between Queens Road and Malvern Road.

Little Alie Street, Off Leman Street, Whitechapel, 1851, combined with Great Alie Street to form Alie Street.

Little Alie Street Synagogue, Little Alie Street (Alie Street), Whitechapel, 1920.

Little Anchor Street, Off Anchor Street (Boundary Street), Bethnal Green, "parallel to and between Anchor Street and Church Street" (Elmes), renamed Chance Street.

Little Ann(s) Street, 1. St. George in the East, renamed Pace Place. 2. Off Cannon Street Road, St. George in the East, "is the fourth on the left from Cannon Street New Road, a few doors east of Catherine Street" (Lockie).

Little Bacon Street, Off Great Bacon Street (Bacon Street), Bethnal Green, "is north parallel to Great Bacon Street extending from 141 Brick Lane to Swan Street" (Lockie).

Little Bridge Street, Off Bridge Street (Solebay Street), Mile End, 1891, renamed Solebay Place.

Little Burr Street, Off Burr Street (St. Katharine Dock), East Smithfield, "at 41 Burr Street leading to King Henry Yard Maudlins Rents and 41 Lower East Smithfield" (Lockie).

Little Cambridge Street, became the eastern half of Dunloe Street, Bethnal Green, 1895.

Little Church Row, East India Dock Road, Limehouse, renamed Amoy Place.

Little Clarkson Street, renamed Clarkson Street, Bethnal Green.

Little Collingwood Street, Off Thomas(s) Passage (Collingwood Estate), Whitechapel, renamed Colling Street.

Little Crown Public House, 16 William Street (Ponler Street), St. George in the East.

Little Driver Public House, 125 Bow Road, Bromley and Bow, 1874.

Little Field, Bromley High Street, Bromley and Bow, 1851.

Little George Public House, 273 Poplar High Street, Poplar.

Little George Street, 1. Off Bethnal Green (Poyser Street), Bethnal Green, "at the northwest corner of the green near Patriot Square" (Lockie), became part of Poyser Street. 2. Off Fleet Street

Hill (Pedley Street), Whitechapel, renamed Pedley Street.

Little Gun Alley, Green Bank, Wapping, 1746.

Little Halifax Street, Off Chicksand Street, Whitechapel, 1891, renamed Tailworth Street.

Little Hermitage Street, Off Wapping High Street, Wapping, renamed Orton Street.

Little Holloway Street, Off Plumbers Row, Whitechapel, middle section of present day Coke Street.

Little James Street, renamed Vesey Street (East India Dock Road), Poplar.

Little John Street, 1. Off Caroline Street, Ratcliffe, 1891, now part of Pitsea Place. 2. Off Spelman Street, Whitechapel, 1891.

Little Labour In Vain Street, Off Shadwell High Street (The Highway), Shadwell, "on the south side of Shadwell Waterworks and about three houses from Lower Shadwell" (Elmes), Shadwell Park is on the site.

Little Love Court, Petticoat Lane (Middlesex Street), Spitalfields, 1851.

Little Manchester Street, Off Selby Street, Whitechapel, combined with Great Manchester Street to form Manchester Street.

Little Middlesex Street, Off Petticoat Lane (Middlesex Street), Spitalfields, "is about twenty doors on the right in the last described from 41 Aldgate High Street" (Lockie).

Little North Street, Off Brady Street, Whitechapel, 1891, renamed Winthrop Street.

Little Paternoster Row, Dorset Street, Spitalfields, 1891, Dorset Street to Brushfield St, London Fruit Exchange was built on the site.

Little Patience Street, Off Wheler Street, Spitalfields, 1841.

Little Pearl Street, 1. Off Great Pearl Street (Calvin Street), Spitalfields, 1851. 2. Off Vine Street (Brick Lane), Spitalfields, 1891, "the continuation of Vine Street from 24 Lamb Street" (Lockie), renamed Grey Eagle St.

Little Popes Head Court, Quaker Street, Spitalfields, 1851.

Little Prescot(t) Street, Off Great Prescot Street (Prescot Street), Whitechapel, 1851, Great Prescot Street to Royal Mint Street.

Little Russell Street, renamed Russell Street (Halcrow Street), Whitechapel.

Little Rutland Street, became part of Newark Street, Whitechapel.

Little Shadwell, Shadwell High Street (The Highway), Shadwell, "the east continuation of Lower Shadwell to Bell wharf"

(Lockie), Shadwell Park is on the site.

Little Spring Street, 1. Off Foxes Lane (Shadwell Basin), Shadwell, "four houses on the right hand side from the east end of the church yard" (Elmes), Shadwell Basin is on the site. 2. Off Victoria Street (Dellow Street), Shadwell, 1851.

Little Star Public House, 154 White Horse Street (White Horse Road), Stepney, address also 164 White Horse Road.

Little Tap Street, Off Somerford Street, Whitechapel, 1851.

Little Thames Street, East Smithfield, from St. Katharine Dock Entrance to Tower Bridge, renamed St. Katharines Way.

Little Tongue Yard, Renamed Tongue Court, Whitechapel, 1851, just east of the corner of Fieldgate Street and Whitechapel Road.

Little Tower Hill, Little Thames Street (Katharines Way), East Smithfield, Little Thames Street to Upper East Smithfield, renamed St. Katharines Way.

Little Turner Street, Off Commercial Road, St. George in the East, 1891, renamed Rampart Street.

Little Turner Street Synagogue, Little Turner Street (Commercial Road), St. George in the East, 1920.

Little Union Place, Union Place (Cressy Place), Mile End, renamed Cressy Place.

Little York Street, Off Club Row, Bethnal Green, 1841, renamed Whitby Street.

Livingstone Wharf, Ferry Street, Isle of Dogs, 1950, close to present-day street, Felstead Wharf.

Loats Buildings, Upper East Smithfield, East Smithfield, 1870.

Lock House, Old Ford Road, Bromley and Bow.

Lockdale Place, Old Ford Road, Bromley and Bow, 1851.

Lockes Wharf, St. Davids Square, Isle of Dogs, 1950.

Locomotive Public House, 45 Bow Common Lane, Bromley and Bow.

Locton Street, 1. Off Locton Green, Bromley and Bow, Locton Green is on the site. 2. Off Parnell Road, Bromley and Bow, 1891.

Loddiges Buildings or Terrace, Church Street (Mare Street), Hackney, 1851.

Log Hall, Old Ford Road, Bromley and Bow, 1851.

Logan Terrace, Bromley and Bow, renamed Benworth Street.

Loggerheads Public House, 57 Virginia Road, Bethnal Green, 1861, aka Three Loggerheads Arms, Two Loggerheads (1722).

Lolesworth Buildings, Lolesworth Street (Lolesworth Close), Thrawl Street, Spitalfields, 1950.

Lolesworth Lane, Spitalfields, renamed Browns Lane (Hanbury Street).

Lollar Wharf, Westferry Road, Isle of Dogs, 1950, Sir John McDougalls Gardens are on its site.

Lomas Buildings, 21 Ben Jonson Road, Mile End.

Lombard Street, Off Brick Lane, Spitalfields, "the third on the left from 55 Brick Lane along Montague Street and Well Street" (Lockie), now Daplyn Street.

London & Burton Brewery, 112 Medland Street (The Highway), Ratcliffe.

London & Continental Wharf, St. Katharines Way, East Smithfield, 1950, south of corner with Thomas More Street.

London & General Omnibus Yard, Bell Lane, Spitalfields.

London & St. Katharines Dock Hotel & Tavern, 20 Upper East Smithfield, East Smithfield, 1874.

London Brewery Bar/Tap Public House, 1 Cambridge Circus, Bethnal Green.

London City Mission, 1. 77 Augusta Street, Poplar, 1885. 2. 26 King Edwards Road,

Hackney, 1920. 3. 46 Stebondale Street, Isle of Dogs, 1881.

London Court, Whites Alley (Royal Mint Street), East Smithfield, Rosemary Lane, Rocque.

London Dispensary, 27 Fournier Street, Spitalfields.

London Hospital Tavern Public House, 176 Whitechapel Road, Whitechapel, 1874, aka Hospital Tavern.

London Hospital Training Home for Pupil Probationers, 97-99 Bow Road, Bromley and Bow, 1921.

London House Asylum, London Lane, Hackney, 1841.

London Jewish Hospital, Stepney Green, Stepney, 1915-1979.

London Place, 1. Martha Street (Wadeson Street), Hackney. 2. West Street (Westgate Street), Hackney, 1851, renamed London Fields east side of London Fields Park covers the site of the road.

London Stores Public House, 28 Chrisp Street, Poplar, corner of Grundy Street.

London Street, 1. Off Brady Street (Dunbridge Street), Bethnal Green, renamed Dunbridge Street. 2. Off Hackney Road, Bethnal Green, renamed Ropley Street. 3. Off Rose Lane (Ratcliffe Lane), Ratcliffe, 1895, Rose Lane to Medland Street, Bekesbourne

Street and Spert Street follow its path.

London Tavern Public House, 393 Manchester Road, Isle of Dogs, 1874.

London Terrace, 1. Commercial Road, St. George in the East, Commercial Road to James Street, parallel with Morgan Street. 2. Hackney Road, Bethnal Green, 1841, west of London Street. 3. London Fields, Hackney, 1891, renamed London Fields West Side.

London Wharf, 1. Westferry Road, Isle of Dogs, 1950, on the riverfront close to Strafford Street. 2. Narrow Street, Ratcliffe, 1950, south of Spert Street.

Long Alley, New Street (Shadwell Park), Shadwell, "on the east side of New Street nearly opposite Shadwell Dock Stairs leading to the Orchard" (Lockie).

Long Street, 1. Off Cremer Street, Bethnal Green, 1950, south of Cremer Street, route passed under railway line. 2. Whitechapel, renamed Princes Street (Princelet Street).

Longfellow Road, Off Whitman Road, Bromley and Bow, Mile End Park is on the site.

Longman Street, Off Roman Road, Bethnal Green, Cranbrook Estate is on the site.

Lord Campbell Public House, 142 Campbell Road, Bromley and Bow, 1874.

Lord Clyde Public House, 40 Tagg Street (Cranbrook Estate), Bromley and Bow.

Lord Collingwood Public House, 1. 40 Chicksand Street, Whitechapel, 1874. 2. 1 Collingwood Street, Whitechapel, 1874.

Lord Combermere Public House, 2 Conyer Street, Bromley and Bow.

Lord Duncan Public House, 36 Duncan Street (Welshpool Street), Hackney, 1874, London Fields.

Lord Exmouth Public House, 1. 86 Maroon Street, Limehouse, 1874. 2. Lord Exmouth Public House, 8 Star Street (Planet Street), Shadwell.

Lord Hood Public House, 1. 1 London Street (Dunbridge Street), Bethnal Green. 2. 14 Rich Street, Limehouse, 1874.

Lord John Russell Public House, 223 Green Street (Roman Road), Bethnal Green.

Lord Liverpool Public House, 78 Clark Street, Stepney, 1874.

Lord Lovat Public House, 245 Shadwell High Street (The Highway), Shadwell.

Lord Morpeth Public House, 402 Old Ford Road, Bromley and Bow.

Lord Napier Public House, 1. 39 Collingwood Street, Whitechapel, aka Victory. 2. 25 White Post Lane, Hackney. 3.

235 Whitechapel Road, Whitechapel.

Lord Nelson (Tavern) Public House, Robin Hood Lane, Poplar, 1874.

Lord Nelson Public House, 1. 230 Commercial Road, St. George in the East, 1874. 2. 37 Cranbrook Street, Bethnal Green, 1874. 3. 42 Devas Street, Bromley and Bow. 4. 29 Gill Street, Limehouse, 1874. 5. 163 Globe Road, Bethnal Green. 6. 49 Half Nichol(s) Street (Boundary Street), Bethnal Green. 7. 143 Morning Lane, Hackney. 8. 65 Watney Street, Shadwell. 9. 56 West India Dock Road, Limehouse. 10. 299 Whitechapel Road, Whitechapel, 1874.

Lord Palmerston Public House, 45 Hewlett Road, Bromley and Bow, 1874.

Lord Raglan Public House, 1. 100 Chrisp Street, Poplar, 1874. 2. 19 St. Anns Road (Mile End Stadium), Mile End, 1874.

Lord Roberts Public House, 22 Blair Street, Poplar.

Lord Stanley Public House, 1. 56 Carmen Street, Poplar, aka Stanley Arms. 2. 40 Paragon Road, Hackney.

Lotus Court, Hanbury Street, Spitalfields, 1891, just east of Corbets Court.

Louise Cottages, The Grove (Reading Lane), Hackney, 1891, Mare Street.

Louvain Street, Off Cologne Street (Harford Street), Mile End, 1891.

Lovat Arms Public House, 301 Burdett Road, Bromley and Bow.

Love Court or Place, 1. Shadwell, renamed Brodlove Court (Brodlove Lane). 2. Petticoat Lane (Middlesex Street), Spitalfields, "is behind 121 about twenty five doors on the right from 41 Aldgate High Street, it leads to Goulston Square" (Lockie).

Love Lane, 1. Devons Road, Bromley and Bow, 1895, renamed Talwin Street. 2. Old Gravel Lane (Wapping Lane), Wapping, 1895, Old Gravel Lane to Raymond Street, immediately south of Lowder Street. 3. Shadwell High Street (The Highway), Shadwell, "at 117 the first on the left about ⅕ of a mile east from the church it extends to Brook Street" (Lockie), renamed Brodlove Street.

Love Lane Court, Love Lane (Brodlove Lane), Shadwell, 1851.

Lovelace House, Haggerston Road, Hackney, 1950.

Lovers Court, White Horse Street (Butcher Row), Ratcliffe, "White Horse Street, at 9, a few doors on the left from Butcher Row towards the Commercial Road" (Lockie).

Loves Place, Coborn New Road (St. Stephens Road), Bromley and Bow, 1851.

Lowder Street, Off Old Gravel Lane (Wapping Lane), Wapping, 1891, Fowey Close is on the site.

Lower Berner Street, Off Ellen Street, St. George in the East, joined with Upper Berner Street to form Berner Street, southern section later renamed Boyd Street.

Lower Chapman Street, Off Cannon Street Road, St. George in the East, 1899, "is the first turning on the left hand going from the Commercial Road towards Back Lane and extending to Duke Street" (Elmes), renamed Bigland Street.

Lower Cornwall Street, Upper Cornwall Street (Cornwall Street), St. George in the East, combined with Upper Cornwall Street in the west to form Cornwall Street.

Lower East Smithfield, Little Tower Hill (St. Katharines Way), East Smithfield, combined with Little Tower Hill to form St. Katharines Way.

Lower Felix Street, Off Cambridge Crescent, Bethnal Green, 1841.

Lower Fenton Street, Off Anthony Street, St. George in the East, 1891, renamed Mariner Street.

Lower George Street, Bromley

and Bow, renamed Empson Street.

Lower Grove Street, Off Grove Street (Golding Street), St. George in the East, southern section of what would become, along with Middle Grove Street and Upper Grove Street.

Lower Gun Alley, Green Bank, Wapping, "about seven doors on the left east from the London Docks nearly opposite Wapping Church" (Lockie).

Lower John Street, 1. Off Stepney Causeway, Ratcliffe, 1851. 2. Off Upper John Street, Shadwell, combined with Upper John Street and renamed Blakesley Street.

Lower Keate Street, Off Flower and Dean Street, Spitalfields, 1851.

Lower King Street, Off Christian Street, St. George in the East, combined with Upper King Street to form Christian Street.

Lower North Street, Poplar, also known as North Street, renamed Saltwell Street.

Lower Olivers Wharf, Wapping Wall, Wapping, 1950, west of Monza Street.

Lower Oxford Street, Renamed Oxford Street (Stepney Way), Whitechapel.

Lower Rich Street, Off Gun Lane (Grenade Street), Limehouse, 1851.

Lower Shadwell Street, Off Wapping Wall (Shadwell Park), Shadwell, "the continuation of Wapping Wall by the side of the Thames extending from Shadwell Dock (Lockie) ", Shadwell Basin and Park are on the site.

Lower Turning, Great Spring Street (Shadwell Basin), Shadwell, southernmost road connecting Shakespeares Walk and Great Spring Street below Middle Turning and Upper Turning, Shadwell Basin is on the site.

Lower Well Alley, Green Bank, Wapping, 1790, Wapping Gardens are on the site.

Lowther House, Clarissa Street, Hackney, 1950, corner with Lee Street.

Lubner & Lomzer Synagogue, 3 Lawrence Buildings (Cannon Street Road), St. George in the East, 1934, Cannon Street Road.

Lucas Arms Public House, 348 Commercial Road, Stepney, corner of Lukin Street.

Lucas Street, 1. Shadwell, 1891, renamed Lukin Street. 2. Off Pott Street (Newcourt House), Bethnal Green, 1851, perpendicular with the southern end of Pott Street.

Lucas Terrace, Bromley and Bow, renamed Alfred Street.

Ludens Place, Pell Street (Wellclose Square), St. George in the East, 1891, rear of east side of Pell Street.

Lukach Wharf, Wharf Road (Saunders Ness Road), Isle of Dogs, 1895, opposite Brig Street (George Green's School service road).

Luke Street, Off Charles Street (Vallance Road), Whitechapel, 1851, became the easternmost end of Buxton Street.

Lumsden Street, Off Prestons Road, Poplar, 1891.

Luntley Place, Chicksand Street, Whitechapel, 1851.

Lusbys Music Hall, 93-95 Mile End Road, Mile End, later Paragon Theatre and ABC cinema.

Luxor House, Commercial Street, Spitalfields, 1950, corner of Commercial Street and Quaker Street.

Lycett Central Hall, White Horse Lane, Mile End, 1950, at its west corner with Mile End Road.

Lydbrook Street, Off Copenhagen Place, Limehouse.

Lydia Street, Off White Horse Lane, Mile End, 1891, north of and parallel with Shandy Street.

Lyme & Victoria Cottages, Lyme Grove, Hackney, 1891, Mare Street.

Lynn Cottages, Forest Row, Hackney, 1851, Kingsland Road.

Lynton Road, Whitechapel, Ashdown Estate is on the site.

Lynton Terrace, Grove Road, Bromley and Bow.

Lyte Street, Off Bishops Road (Bishops Way), Bethnal Green, 1891.

Lytton House, Woodseer Street, Whitechapel, 1950.

M

Mace Street, Off Tagg Street (Cranbrook Estate), Bromley and Bow, Cranbrook Estate is on the site.

Machzikei Hadath Shomrei Shabbat Synagogue, Fournier Street, Spitalfields, corner of Fournier Street and Brick Lane Former Spitalfields Great Synagogue, now the Brick Lane Mosque.

Mackrow Street, Off Cotton Street, Poplar, 1950, renamed Mackrow Walk.

Mackworth Arms Public House, 158 Commercial Road, St. George in the East, 1874.

Maconochies Wharf, Westferry Road, Isle of Dogs, 1950, Pointers Close is on its site.

Macords Rents, Old Gravel Lane (Wapping Lane), Wapping, "is the first turning on the right hand in Choppins Court a few houses from behind Old Gravel Lane" (Elmes).

Magdalen House, 21 Prescot Street, Whitechapel.

Magnet & Dewdrop Public

House, 194 Westferry Road, Isle of Dogs.

Magpie & Stag Public House, 12 Virginia Row (Virginia Road), Bethnal Green.

Magpie & Stump Public House, 98 Cable Street, St. George in the East, 1874.

Magpye Alley, Wentworth Street, Spitalfields, "two or three doors east of Rose Lane and nearly opposite Essex Street from 115 Whitechapel High Street" (Lockie).

Maharish Beth Hamedrash Synagogue, 62 Fieldgate Street, Whitechapel.

Maid & Magpie Public House, 237-239 Oxford Street (Stepney Way), Whitechapel, 1874.

Maidenhead Court, 1. Farmer Street (Shadwell Basin), Wapping, "Wapping at Shadwell at 61 the fourth left from 38 Shadwell High Street" (Lockie). 2. Wheler Street, Spitalfields, "five houses northward of Fleur de Lis Street entering by Shoreditch High Street" (Elmes).

Maidens Place, Pell Street (Wellclose Square), St. George in the East, 1868.

Maidmans Row, Canal Road (Mile End Road), Bromley and Bow.

Maidmans Street, Off Canal Road (Mile End Road), Bromley and Bow, 1891, Canal Road to Burdett Road, immediately south of Mile End Road.

Maidstone Court & Place, Old Nichol(s) Street (Boundary Estate), Bethnal Green, "a few doors on the right in it from Cock Lane" (Lockie).

Maidstone Place, Rhodeswell Road, Limehouse, 1851.

Maidstone Street, Off Dove Row, Bethnal Green, 1895.

Malaga Court, Nightingale Lane (Thomas More Street), Wapping, "at 36 a few doors on the left below the entrance to the London Docks" (Lockie).

Malay Street, Off Prusom Street, Wapping.

Mallard Arms Public House, 96 Grove Street (Golding Street), St. George in the East, 1874.

Mallard Street, Off Victoria Road (Wick Road), Hackney, 1891.

Mallon House, Carr Street, Limehouse, 1950, Limehouse Fields Estate.

Malmesbury Road Central School, Coborn Street, Bromley and Bow, 1921.

Maltsters Arms Public House, 52 New Road, Whitechapel.

Malvern Cottages, Malvern Road, Hackney, 1868, between Albion Road and Albert Road.

Man in Compass Public House, 21 Chicksand Street, Whitechapel.

Man in the Moon Public House, 27 Plough Street,

Whitechapel, address also 27 Colchester Street.

Managers Road, Off New Road (Prestons Road), Isle of Dogs, 1891, renamed Managers Street.

Manchester Arms Public House, 1. 155 Hackney Road, Bethnal Green. 2. 308 Manchester Road, Isle of Dogs, 1874.

Manchester Buildings, Manchester Street (Winchester Street), Bethnal Green, 1841, renamed Menotti Buildings.

Manchester Place, Derbyshire Street, Bethnal Green, 1841.

Manchester Street, Off Winchester Street (Dunbridge Street), Bethnal Green, 1841, Cheshire Street to Selby Street, west of and parallel with Vallance Road.

Manchester Terrace, Westferry Road, Isle of Dogs, 1851, opposite British Street.

Mandarin Street, Off West India Dock Road, Limehouse, opposite Limehouse Police Station.

Manisty Street, Off Robin Hood Lane, Poplar, 1891.

Manning Place, Limehouse, Limehouse Fields Estate is on the site, renamed Manning Street (Carr Street).

Manning Street, Off Carr Street, Limehouse, 1851.

Manor Arms Public House, 150 East India Dock Road, Poplar.

Manor Cottage, 155 East India Dock Road, Poplar, next to 155 East India Dock Road.

Manor Cottage Ladies Association, 4 Kerbey Street, Poplar.

Manor Cottages, Kerbey Street, Poplar, 1891, East India Dock Road.

Manor Court, Periwinkle Street (Ratcliffe Cross Street), Ratcliffe, 1851.

Manor House, Stepney Green, Stepney, 1891.

Manor Place, Cuba Street, Isle of Dogs, 1891.

Manor Place, Shirbutt Street, Poplar, 1891.

Manor Street, Poplar, renamed Plimsoll Street (Plimsoll Close).

Manor Terrace, Bromley Hall Road, Poplar, 1851.

Mans Buildings, Grace Street, Bromley and Bow, 1851.

Mansell Passage, Mansell Street, Whitechapel, 1851, renamed Haydon Walk.

Mansell Street Synagogue, 26 Buckle Street, Whitechapel, 1885, later address, also known as Buckle Street Synagogue and Peace and Tranquillity Synagogue.

Mansfield Cottages or Terrace, Folly Wall, Isle of Dogs, 1891.

Mansfield Street, Off Kingsland Road, Hackney, 1868, became part of Whiston Road.

Mansford Buildings, Mansford Street, Bethnal Green, 1950, west side north of Florida Street.

Manton Cottages or Place, Fairfield Road, Bromley and Bow.

Mapes Street, Off Bethnal Green Road, Bethnal Green, 1826, renamed Mape Street.

March Street, Off Grundy Street, Poplar, 1950.

Marchant Row, St. Anne Street, Limehouse, 1891.

Margaret Place, 1. Forest Road (Mayfield Road), Hackney, 1868, either side of Mayfield Street. 2. Gascoigne Place, Bethnal Green, 1891. 3. Margaret Street (Salmon Lane), Limehouse, 1851.

Margaret Street, 1. Off Commercial Road, Limehouse, 1860, Commercial Road to Salmon Lane, immediately east of Limehouse Cut. 2. Off Gloucester Street (Mansfield Street), Hackney, 1827, eastern extension of Gloucester Street, became part of Whiston Road. 3. Renamed Lowell Street, Poplar. 4. Off Swale Street (Upper North Street), Limehouse, renamed Swale Street. 5. Off Well Street, Hackney, renamed Collent Street.

Margaret Terrace, Goldsmiths Row, Bethnal Green, 1895, south of Dove Row.

Margate Villas, Brougham Road, Hackney, 1868, corner with Shrubland Road.

Maria Court, Bakers Row (Vallance Road), Whitechapel, 1851.

Maria Place, Bakers Row (Vallance Road), Whitechapel, "the first on the left a few doors from 94 in the said road" (Lockie).

Maria Street, 1. Off Pearson Street, Bethnal Green, 1868, renamed Geffrye Street. 2. Off Westferry Road, Isle of Dogs, 1891.

Maria Street Methodist Chapel & School, Maria Street (Janet Street), Isle of Dogs, 1917, north of.

Marian Arms Public House, 33 Emma Street, Bethnal Green.

Marian Place & Square, Pritchards Road, Bethnal Green, 1895.

Marias Place, Shard Street (Johnson Street), Wapping, 1790, north of Tench Street.

Marine Brewery, Broad Street (The Highway), Ratcliffe, 1895, south of Ratcliffe Orchard.

Mariner Place, Grundy Street, Poplar.

Mariner Street, Off Anthony Street, St. George in the East, 1950.

Mariners Arms Public House, 1. 47 Grundy Street, Poplar. 2. 152 Shadwell High Street (The Highway), Shadwell, address also 395 The Highway.

Mariners Public House, 514 Commercial Road, Ratcliffe, aka Kings Arms.

Marion Arms Public House, 46 Lansdowne Road (Lansdowne Drive), Hackney.

Marion Villas, Lansdowne Road (Lansdowne Drive), Hackney, 1868, either side of Shrubland Grove.

Maritime Hall, West India Dock Road, Limehouse, former Jamaica Hotel at entrance to West India Docks.

Mark(s) Place, Stonebridge Lane (Haggerston Road), Hackney, 1827, just north of the canal.

Market Hill, Shadwell High Street (The Highway), Shadwell, "at 65 the second on the right east of the church it extends to Shadwell Market" (Lockie) immediately east of Glamis Road Shadwell Park is on the site.

Market House (Tavern) Public House, 7 Ricardo Street, Poplar, 1874.

Market House Public House, 30 Broadway Market, Hackney.

Market Inn Public House, 14 Columbia Market (Columbia Road), Bethnal Green, 1874, Baroness Road.

Market Row, Hartwell Street, Hackney, 1851, Dalston Lane.

Market Street, 1. Off Ben Jonson Road, Mile End, 1891, renamed Trader Street. 2. Off Shadwell High Street (The Highway), Shadwell, "at the south-east corner of Shadwell Market leading to Shadwell Dock" (Lockie).

Market Street, Off Upper North Street (Cordelia Street), Poplar, 1891, Upper North Street to Kerbey Street, renamed Cordelia Street.

Market Tavern Public House, 65 Brushfield Street, Spitalfields.

Markhams Yard, Green Street (Roman Road), Bethnal Green, 1891.

Marksman Public House, 254 Hackney Road, Bethnal Green.

Marlborough Cottage, London Terrace (London Fields), Hackney, 1891, London Fields.

Marlborough Court, Petticoat Lane (Middlesex Street), Spitalfields, 1851.

Marlborough Head Public House, 23 Foxs Lane (Shadwell Basin), Shadwell.

Marlborough Road, Off Shrubland Grove (Mapledene Road), Hackney, 1868, renamed Marlborough Avenue.

Marlborough(s) Head Public House, 5 Pelham Street (Woodseer Street), Whitechapel, 1874.

Marlow Road, Off Berger Road, Hackney, 1891.

Marmaduke Court, Grove Street (Golding Street), St. George in the East, 1891, immediately north of railway line.

Marmaduke Place, Langdale Street, St. George in the East, 1891.

Marman Street, Off James Street (Burslem Street), St. George in the East, 1860, later part of Umberston Street.

Marner Street, Off St. Leonards Street, Bromley and Bow, 1891, north of Empson Street.

Marquis (of) Cornwallis Public House, 1. 304 Bethnal Green Road, Bethnal Green, 1874. 2. 337 Old Ford Road, Bromley and Bow, 1874.

Marquis of Granby Public House, St. Katharines (St. Katharines Way), East Smithfield, 1874, London Docks.

Marquis of Lorne Public House, 81 Bancroft Road, Mile End.

Marquis of Wellington Public House, 48 Cornwall Street, St. George in the East, 1874.

Marsh Row, Westferry Road, Isle of Dogs, 1851, close to Moiety Road.

Marsh Street, Off Westferry Road, Isle of Dogs, 1851, renamed Tobago Street.

Marshal(l) Keate Public House, 29 Prestons Road, Poplar, 1874.

Martha Street, 1. Off Cambridge Road (Cambridge Heath Road), Bethnal Green, 1868, renamed Wadeson Street.

2. Off Sutton Street, Shadwell, 1891.

Martins Buildings, Milk Street (or Yard) (Milk Yard), Shadwell, "is opposite the south end of Farmer Street entering by 39 High Street" (Lockie).

Martins Row, Bow Common Lane, Bromley and Bow, 1851.

Mary Ann Place, 1. Chrisp Street, Poplar, 1851. 2. Foxes Lane (Shadwell Basin), Shadwell, 1851.

Mary Ann Street, Off Stutfield Street, St. George in the East, 1891.

Mary Ann Terrace, 1. Fuller Street (Bethnal Green Road), Bethnal Green, 1851. 2. Hereford Street, Bethnal Green.

Mary Place, 1. Bow Lane, Poplar, 1851. 2. Chrisp Street, Poplar, 1851. 3. Mary Street (Bigland Street), St. George in the East, 1891. 4. Redmead Lane, Wapping, 1890.

Mary Street, 1. Renamed Bigland Place (Bigland Street), St. George in the East. 2. Off Davenant Street, Whitechapel, aka St. Marys Street "Whitechapel Road at 76 west side the workhouse about ¼ of a mile on the left below the church" (Lockie). 3. Off Duckett Street, Mile End, renamed Waley Street. 4. Off Fairfield Road, Bromley and Bow, renamed Blondin Street. 5. Off Harley Street (Harley Grove), Bromley and Bow, renamed Benworth Street. 6. Off Ocean Street, Mile End, "the first on the right in Ocean Street from opposite the Walnut Tree public house, Cow Lane - extending to Sommers or Summers Place" (Lockie). 7. Off Poplar High Street, Poplar, 1870, Poplar High Street to Shirbutt Street, renamed Rook Street. 8. Off Rhodeswell Road, Limehouse, 1851, renamed Dora Street. 9. Off St. Leonards Street, Bromley and Bow, renamed Marner Street.

Mary(s) Place, Anglesea Street (Fakruddin Street), Whitechapel, 1891, just west of Vallance Road, Fakruddin Street is partially on the site.

Marys Cottages, Eastfield Street, Limehouse, 1871.

Marys Row, 1. Bethnal Green Road, Bethnal Green, "on the east side of Wilmot Square being the continuation of Ann Street" (Lockie). 2. Bow Common Lane, Bromley and Bow, 1851.

Marys Villas, Lavender Grove, Hackney, 1868, between Queens Road and Malvern Road.

Masons Arms Public House, 1. 121-123 Bow Common Lane, Bromley and Bow. 2. 23 Ida Street, Poplar. 3. 7 Watney Street, Shadwell, 1874.

Masons Cottage & Place, Dalston Lane, Hackney, 1841, close to corner with Park Street.

Masons Court, 1. Brick Lane, Whitechapel, "about eight doors on the right from the north end of Osborn Street" (Lockie), now part of Chicksand Street. 2. Whitechapel High Street, Whitechapel, 1891, "the first on the left three or four doors from the north end of Great Garden Street" (Lockie).

Masons Place, Little Prescot Street (Prescot Street), Whitechapel, 1851.

Mast House & Cottages, Westferry Road, Isle of Dogs, 1851, Mast House Terrace is close to site.

Matilda Place, North East Passage (or Alley) (Wellclose Square), St. George in the East, "Wellclose Square, at 6, the first on the left from 35 Cable Street" (Lockie).

Matilda Street, St. George in the East, 1891, renamed Christian Place.

Matilda Street & Place, Old Bethnal Green Road, Bethnal Green, 1841.

Matthews Buildings, King Street (Gossett Street), Bethnal Green, "three or four houses on the left hand in King Street, going from Brick Lane" (Elmes).

Matthews Court, King Street, Whitechapel, 1851.

Matthews Place, Hackney Road, Bethnal Green, "forms part of the left side between Durham Place and Cambridge Heath turnpike about ⁷/₈ of a mile from Shoreditch Church" (Lockie), opposite Hope Street.

Matthias Place & Street, Off Abbot Street, Hackney, 1851.

Maudlins Rents, Off Nightingale Lane (Thomas More Street), East Smithfield, 1800, St. Katharine Dock is on its site.

Maughflints Court, New Gravel Lane (Garnet Street), Wapping, 1891.

Maunday House Lane, Bethnal Green Road, Bethnal Green, "the last on the left about a mile from 65 Shoreditch" (Lockie).

Mauve Street, Off Burcham Street, Poplar, 1950.

Maxwell House, Narrow Street, Limehouse, close to corner with Three Colt Street, 1950.

May Terrace, Alpha Road (Alpha Grove), Isle of Dogs, 1891.

Mayfield Place, Terrace & Villas, Mayfield Road, Hackney, 1841.

Mayfield Road, Off Dalston Lane, Hackney, part renamed Beachwood Road, part renamed Mayfield Close, part renamed Buxted Road.

Mayfield Street, Off Dalston Lane, Hackney, 1851, renamed Mayfield Road.

Mayfield Terrace, Mayfield Street (Mayfield Road), Hackney, 1868, south of Forest Road.

Mayfields Buildings, Princes Square (Swedenborg Square), St. George in the East, 1891.

Mayflower Court, New Gravel Lane (Garnet Street), Wapping, 1891.

Mayland Street, Off Bromehead Street, Stepney, 1950, Bromehead Street to Bromehead Road, Sidney Street Estate is on the site.

Maypole Court, 1. Sun Court, Whitechapel. 2. Maypole Court, Upper East Smithfield, East Smithfield, 1851.

Mays Buildings, Devonshire Street (Bancroft Road), Mile End, 1891, renamed June Buildings, close to Red Lion Public House.

Mays Cottages, Eastfield Street, Limehouse, 1851.

Mays Cottages & Row, Oak Lane, Limehouse, 1891, close to north end of Nightingale Lane.

Mays or Maize Row, Northey Street, Limehouse, 1851, Followed Limehouse Cut from Church Row to Northey Street.

McDermot Place, Denmark Street (Crowder Street), St. George in the East, 1868.

Mead Street, Off Turville Street, Bethnal Green, "the fourth on the left in Turville Street from 37 Church Street leading into Vincent Street" (Lockie), Boundary Estate is on the site.

Meadow Dwellings, Mansford Street, Bethnal Green, 1950.

Meads Place, West Street (Elsdale Street), Hackney, 1841, Well Street.

Mechanics Arms Public House, 1. 3 Hardinge Street, Shadwell, aka Crown & Anchor. 2. 18 Westferry Road, Isle of Dogs.

Medcalf Cottages, Gales Gardens, Bethnal Green.

Medhurst Road, 1. Off Grove Road, Bromley and Bow, 1891. 2. Bromley and Bow, renamed Medhurst Close.

Medland Congregational Hall Mission & Free Shelter, Queen Street (Horseferry Road), Ratcliffe, 1895, opposite Horse Ferry Branch Road.

Medland Street, Off Butcher Row (Horseferry Road), Ratcliffe, Butcher Row to Regents Canal Dock, became part of The Highway but is now part of Horseferry Road.

Meeting House Alley, Green Bank, Wapping, 1746.

Meeting House Lane, Poplar High Street, Poplar, "about ⅓ of a mile on the left from the Commercial Road and nearly opposite the Harrow public house" (Lockie).

Meeting House Yard, Three Colt Street, Limehouse, "the first on the right from the church towards the Thames" (Lockie).

Meggs Almshouses, Whitechapel Road, Whitechapel, "On the south side of the road about a quarter of a mile eastward of the church They were founded in 1558 for the support of twelve poor widows" (Elmes), opposite the present-day Davenant Street.

Meggs Place, Kingward Street (Old Montague Street), Whitechapel, 1950, Old Montague Street.

Melbourne Arms Public House, 25 Well Street (Ensign Street), St. George in the East.

Melbourne Buildings, Ann Street (East India Dock Road), Poplar.

Melbourne Cottage Asylum, Lamb Lane, Hackney, 1841, Mare Street.

Melbourne Place, Cambridge Road (Cambridge Heath Road), Bethnal Green, 1851.

Melbourne Wharf, Wapping High Street, Wapping, 1895, west of Sampson Street.

Melina Place, 1. Cassland Road, Hackney, 1851. 2. Sheep Lane, Hackney.

Mellishs Wharf, Westferry Road, Isle of Dogs, 1950, south of Arnhem Place.

Mercer Street, Off Cable Street, Shadwell, 1891, Cable Street to The Highway, renamed Shadwell Street.

Mercers Arms Public House, 1. 34 Belgrave Street, Stepney. 2. 320 Cable Street, Shadwell. 3. 116 Jubilee Street, Stepney.

Mercers Micos or Lady Micas Almshouses, White Horse Street (White Horse Road), Stepney, south of churchyard.

Mercers Place, Back Road (Cable Street), St. George in the East, 1851.

Mercers Row, Shadwell High Street (The Highway), Shadwell, "at 209 about ¼ of a mile on the left from St. Georges Church or the second on the right west from Shadwell Church" (Lockie), renamed Mercer Street.

Mercers Terrace, 1. Commercial Road, Stepney, 1865, Arbour Street East to Heath Street. 2. Salmon Lane, Limehouse, 1851.

Merchant Seamens Orphan Asylum, 3 Clarkes Terrace (Cannon Street Road), St. George in the East, Cannon Street Road.

Merchants Buildings, 1. Poplar High Street, Poplar, "on the west side the East India Almshouses about ¹/₃ of a mile on the right down the East India Dock Road from Limehouse" (Lockie). 2. Grove Street (Golding Street), St. George in the East, 1891, east of Ellen Street.

Mermaid Court, Coleman Street (Coleman Close), Wapping, 1851.

Mertons Court, St. George Street (The Highway), St. George in the East, 1878, immediately east of Ship Alley, Wellclose Square.

Metcalf Court, Essex Street (Commercial Street), Spitalfields, "four doors on the left from 197 Wentworth St or from the Star public house" (Lockie).

Metilda Place, North East Passage (Wellclose Square), St. George in the East, 1878, Wellclose Square.

Metropolitan Associations Model Lodging House, Deal Street, Spitalfields, renamed Howard Buildings.

Metropolitan Buildings, Albert Place (Deal Street), Spitalfields, 1891, Albert Street.

Metropolitan Wharf, Wapping Wall, Wapping, 1950, south of Monza Street.

Middle George Street, Bromley and Bow, renamed Empson Street.

Middle Grove Street, Off Grove Street (Golding Street), St. George in the East, middle section of what would become Grove Street, along with Lower Grove Street and Upper Grove Street.

Middle John Street, Off Stepney Causeway, Ratcliffe, 1891, renamed Hilton Street.

Middle Row, Green Street (Roman Road), Bethnal Green, 1851.

Middle Shadwell, Shadwell High Street (The Highway), Shadwell, "the first south parallel to part of High Street say from76 to 87, it extends from Popes hill to Broad Bridge" (Lockie), Shadwell Park is on the site.

Middle Turning, Great Spring Street (Shadwell Basin), Shadwell, the middle of three roads connecting Shakespeares Walk and Great Spring Street between Upper Turning and Lower Turning, Shadwell Basin is on the site.

Middle Walk, George Gardens (Bethnal Green Road), Bethnal Green, 1841, parallel with and west of George Gardens.

Middlesex Place, Hackney Road, Bethnal Green, 1860, north of St. Leonards Almshouses.

Middlesex School, 92 Cannon Street Road, St. George in the East, building taken over by Raines Girls School in 1875.

Middlesex Terrace, Hackney Road, Bethnal Green, "forms part of the right side by Middlesex chapel about ¼ of a mile from Shoreditch Church" (Lockie).

Middleton Arms Public House, 1. 14 Mansfield Street (Whiston Road), Hackney, 1874, Kingsland Road. 2. 80 Middleton Road, Hackney, 1950. 3. 38 Norton Folgate, Spitalfields, 1874. 4. 123 Queens Road (Queensbridge Road), Hackney,

1895. 5. 114 St. Anns Road (Mile End Stadium), Mile End.

Middleton Cottages & Place, Queens Road (Queensbridge Road), Hackney, 1841.

Middletons & St Brides Wharves, Wapping High Street, Wapping, 1950, close to corner with Clave Street.

Midland Wharf, Ferry Street, Isle of Dogs, 1950, west of Poplar, Blackwall and District Rowing Club.

Mildmay Mission, 37-41 Turville Street, Bethnal Green, 1891.

Mildmay Mission Hospital, Austin Street, Bethnal Green, 1950.

Mile End & Bow District Synagogue, Harley Grove, Bromley and Bow, 1927-1977, became a Sikh temple.

Mile End Charity School, Mile End Road, Mile End, "about one third of a mile on the right hand side going from Mile End Road towards Stepney Church" (Elmes).

Mile End Corner, Dog Row (Cambridge Heath Road), Whitechapel, "a few doors on the left from the Mile End turnpike, towards Bethnal Green" (Lockie).

Mile End Distillery, Assembly Passage, Mile End, 1895, just west of Assembly Passage.

Mile End Gate Public House, 174 Whitechapel Road, Whitechapel.

Mile End New Town, former administrative district bounded by Spitalfields Bethnal Green and Whitechapel.

Mile End Old Town, Mile End Old Town (Mile End Road), Whitechapel, former administrative district covering very roughly the area on either side of Mile End Road from Commercial Road in the south to close to Bethnal Green Road in the north.

Mile End Railway Station, Cambridge Heath Road, Whitechapel.

Mile End Workhouse, Bancrofts Place (Bancroft Road), Mile End, "A few yards on the right hand going from opposite Bancrofts Almshouses" (Elmes), site of later Mile End Hospital.

Miles Place, 1. Martha Street (Wadeson Street), Hackney. 2. Park Road (Parkholme Road), Hackney, 1841.

Milk Street, Shadwell, alternative name for Milk Yard (aka Milk Alley).

Mill Cottages, Bowen Street (Chrisp Street), Poplar, 1891.

Mill Hill & Yard, Old Ford Road, Bromley and Bow, 1851.

Mill Place, Kerbey Street, Poplar, 1851, became part of Bowen Street.

Mill Street, Off Old Ford Road, Bromley and Bow.

Mill Terrace, Kerbey Street, Poplar, 1851, corner of Bowen Street.

Mill Yard & Malt Yard, Four Mills Street (St. Leonards Street), Bromley and Bow, 1851.

Mill Yard & Passage, Leman Street, Whitechapel, 1891.

Miller Place, Park Road (Parkholme Road), Hackney, 1841.

Millers Cottages or Grove, Barnet Grove, Bethnal Green, 1851.

Millers Court, Dorset Street, Spitalfields, opposite the south west corner of Spitalfields Churchyard.

Millers Rents, Dorset Street, Spitalfields, 1851, opposite the south west corner of Spitalfields Churchyard.

Millers Yard, Redmans Road, Mile End, 1891.

Millicent Cottages, Forest Row, Hackney, 1841, Kingsland Road.

Mills Court, Petticoat Lane (Middlesex Street), Spitalfields, 1851.

Millwall Brewery, Westferry Road, Isle of Dogs, 1851.

Millwall Central School, Janet Street, Isle of Dogs.

Millwall Dock Club, Westferry Road, Isle of Dogs, 1874-1892, behind St. Pauls Church.

Millwall Dock Railway Station, East Ferry Road, Isle of Dogs, 1871-1926, Crossharbour DLR is on the site.

Millwall Dock Tavern & Hotel, 233 Westferry Road, Isle of Dogs, 1874, next to Millwall Dock entrance.

Millwall Independent or Congregational Chapel, 127A Westferry Road, Isle of Dogs, 1900.

Millwall Junction Railway Station, Harrow Lane, Poplar, 1871-1926.

Millwall Recreation Ground, Stebondale Street, Isle of Dogs, renamed Millwall Park.

Millwall School, Glengall Road (Tiller Rd), Isle of Dogs, 1897, west half of Glengall Road, renamed Isle of Dogs School in 1928.

Millwall Seamens Rest, Westferry Road, Isle of Dogs, see Seamens Institute and Rest.

Millwall Tap Public House & Brewery, 112 Westferry Road, Isle of Dogs.

Millwall United Reform Church, Westferry Road, Isle of Dogs, 1972, former St. Pauls Church.

Millwall Wharf, Manchester Road, Isle of Dogs, 1950, Schooner Close is on its site.

Millwall Working Mens Club & Institute, Cuba Street, Isle of Dogs, 1910.

Milman Cottages, Lansdowne Road (Lansdowne Drive), Hackney, 1851.

Milton Arms Public House, 38 Wrights Road, Bromley and Bow.

Milton Cottages, Bloomfield Street (Freshfield Avenue), Hackney, 1851.

Milton Place, Chrisp Street, Poplar, 1891, opposite Bowen Street, renamed Milton Road.

Milton Road, 1. Off Old Ford Road, Bromley and Bow, 1891, now contains Milton Place and Homer Cottages. 2. Off Wrights Road, Bethnal Green, McCullum Road roughly follows its route.

Minerva Terrace, Hackney Road, Bethnal Green, 1841, between Hope Street and Minerva Street.

Minor Court, Anchor and Hope Alley (Reardon Path), Wapping, "at 13 about six doors on the right from the London Docks wall" (Lockie).

Minting Row, Thomas Street, East Smithfield, 1950, opposite Thomas More Street.

Minto Place, Canrobert Street, Bethnal Green, 1891, south of corner with Clarkson Street.

Miss Macphersons Home of Industry, 60 Commercial Street (Commercial Street), Spitalfields.

Mission Hall Court, Brick Lane, Spitalfields, 1891, Bounded by

Lolesworth St, Brick Lane, Wentworth Street and Thrawl St.

Missions to Seamen Institute, 1. 6 Cable Street, St. George in the East, 1921. 2. 154 East India Dock Road, Poplar, renamed Pope John House.

Mitchell Street, Off Brick Lane, Bethnal Green, Brick Lane, "Old Street, St. Lukes, at 64 the first on the right from 113 Old Street it leads by the north side of the church to Old Street Square" (Lockie).

Mitford Castle Public House, 129 Cadogan Terrace, Hackney, 1874.

Mitford Terrace, Wick Lane, Bromley and Bow, 1891.

Mitre Buildings, Three Colt Street, Limehouse, "is about the middle of the west side of Three Colt Street and leads to Church Row" (Elmes).

Mitre Public House, 5 White Horse Lane, Mile End.

Mitre Refuge & Shoeblack Home, Three Colt Street, Limehouse, 1891.

Mo(u)ntague Place, Ord Street (Westferry Road), Isle of Dogs, 1846, site of later extended City Arms.

Mockford Buildings, Three Colts Lane, Bethnal Green, 1851.

Moffats Court, Gascoigne Place, Bethnal Green, "is about the middle of the west side [of the green]" (Lockie).

Moiety Street, Off Westferry Road, Isle of Dogs, part renamed Moiety Road, part renamed Hutchings Street.

Molly(s) Alley, Fleet Street (Pedley Street), Whitechapel, 1841.

Monastery House, East India Dock Road, Poplar, 1834, former George Greens School is on part of the site.

Monastery, The, Underwood Road, Whitechapel, 1891.

Moness Street, Off Abbott Road, Poplar, 1891.

Money Bag Alley, Blue Anchor Yard (Royal Mint Street), East Smithfield, 1746.

Money Lane, Hackney, renamed Morning Lane.

Mongers Almshouses, Church Crescent, Hackney, 1851.

Monier Tap Public House, 115 Monier Road, Bromley and Bow.

Monkford Court, Three Colts Lane, Bethnal Green.

Monmouth Street, 1, Off Brick Lane, Spitalfields, now covered by Hanbury's Brewery. 2. Off Shadwell High Street (The Highway), Shadwell, "the first south parallel to part of Shadwell High Street, say from 57 to 75, it extends from Shadwell market to Popes hill" (Lockie), Shadwell Park is on the site.

Monsey Street, Off Harford Street, Mile End, 1891,

immediately east of East London Cemetery.

Montague Buildings, Victoria Road (Wick Road), Hackney, 1891.

Montague Court, Spital Yard, Spitalfields, 1891, renamed Stothard Place.

Montague Place, 1. Montague Road (Trowbridge Road), Hackney, renamed Trowbridge Place. 2. Old Montague Street, Whitechapel, south side of, just west of Monthope Road.

Montague Road, Off Prince Edward Road, Hackney, renamed Trowbridge Road.

Montague Street, 1. Off Brick Lane, Whitechapel, 1891, "at 55 on the east side opposite Browns Lane leading into Well Street" (Lockie), short Street to Bell Lane, became part of Hanbury Street. 2. Off Gosset Street, Bethnal Green, 1851, became part of Turin Street.

Monteagle Street, Off Harford Street, Mile End, 1891, opposite gasworks.

Montefiore House, Cannon Street Road, St. George in the East, opposite Rampart Street.

Monteith Road, Off Old Ford Road, Bromley and Bow, 1891, renamed Hawthorn Avenue.

Montreal Buildings, Cotton Street, Poplar, 1900.

Montrose Villas, Pownall Road, Hackney, 1868.

Moores Court, Essex Street (Commercial Street), Spitalfields, "the third on the left from 105 Whitechapel High Street" (Lockie).

Moores Yard, Fashion Street, Spitalfields, "Fashion Street, the third on the right from 196 Brick Lane" (Lockie).

Moors Arms Public House, 78 Bow Common Lane, Bromley and Bow, 1874.

Moors Cottages, Bow Common Lane, Bromley and Bow, 1851.

Moors Gardens, Norton Folgate, Spitalfields.

Morden Court, Upper Turning (Shadwell Basin), Shadwell, "between 55 Shakespeares walk and 20 Great Spring Street" (Lockie).

Morgan Arms Public House, 43 Morgan Street, Bromley and Bow, 1874.

Morgan Cottages, Mill Place (Bowen Street), Limehouse, 1851.

Morgan Square, Mile End Road, Mile End, "a new square on the north side of Mile End Road lately built on the estate of Sir Charles Morgan Bart" (Elmes), probably Tredegar Square.

Morgan Street, Off Commercial Road, St. George in the East, 1891, renamed Hessel Street.

Morgan Terrace, Coborn Road, Bromley and Bow.

Morley House, Bruce Road, Bromley and Bow, 1891, Devons Road.

Morning Lane Court, Morning Lane, Hackney, 1868, close to Mare Street.

Morning Place, Mount Street (Swanfield Street), Bethnal Green.

Mornington Road, Bromley and Bow, renamed Mornington Grove.

Morocco & Eagle Sufferance Wharves, Wapping High Street, Wapping, 1950, south of Dundee Street.

Morpeth Castle Public House, 1. 69 Cadogan Terrace, Hackney. 2. 109 Devonshire Street (Bancroft Road), Mile End.

Morpeth Place, John Street, Hackney, 1851.

Morpeth Terrace, Grove Street (Lauriston Road), Hackney, 1851.

Morris Terrace, East India Dock Road, Poplar, 1851.

Moses Almshouses, Devonshire Street (Colebert Avenue), Mile End, 1891, close to present-day Fox Close.

Moses Moores Synagogue, 66 Mansell Street, Whitechapel.

Mosley Place, Brick Lane, Spitalfields, "at 204 the third on the left about $^1/_7$ of a mile from opposite the church Whitechapel" (Lockie).

Moss Buildings, St. Mary Street (Davenant Street), Whitechapel, 1851.

Moss Street, 1. Off Smart Street, Bethnal Green, 1891. 2. Off Usk Street, Bethnal Green, south of Roman Road.

Mossford Court, Three Colts Lane, Bethnal Green, 1851.

Moulders Arms Public House, 50-52 Bromley High Street, Bromley and Bow.

Mount Court, Mount Street (Swanfield Street), Bethnal Green, 1851.

Mount Place, Mount Street (Stepney Way), Whitechapel, "Whitechapel Road at 206 on the east side the London Hospital being the first on the right east from the last described" (Lockie).

Mount Pleasant, 1. Stainsby Road, Limehouse, 1851. 2. York Place (Mile End Road), Stepney, "a few houses on the left in York Place from the Worlds End public house towards Mile End" (Lockie).

Mount Square, Mount Street (Swanfield Street), Bethnal Green, 1841.

Mount Street, 1. Off Cannon Street Road, St. George in the East, renamed Mount Terrace. 2. Off Rose Street (Swanfield Street), Bethnal Green, "the continuation of Rose Street entering by 45 Church Street nearly opposite Brick Lane, it leads to Virginia Street or Row behind Shoreditch Church" (Lockie), renamed Swanfield Street.

Mountmorres Road, Off Commercial Road, Stepney, 1950, opposite Pitsea Street to Stepney Way.

Moye Street, Off Dove Row, Bethnal Green, 1895, Moye Close is close to route.

Mud(d)s Court, Cock Hill, Shadwell, immediately east of Schoolhouse Lane.

Mulberry Court, Three Colt Street, Limehouse, "between the south side of the church and Mitre court or Buildings" (Lockie).

Mulberry Gardens, Nightingale Lane (Thomas More Street), Wapping, 1790.

Mulberry Place, Princes Square (Swedenborg Square), St. George in the East, 1891.

Mulberry Tree Public House, 1. 1 Mulberry Street, Mile End, 1874. 2. 161 St. Leonards Street, Bromley and Bow, 1874. 3. 133 Stepney Green, Stepney, 1874.

Mulberry Tree Row, Four Mills Street (St. Leonards Street), **Bromley and Bow, 1851.**

Mulberrys Court, Off Nightingale Lane (Thomas More Street), Wapping, 1800, London Docks were built on the site.

Mundys Place, Back Church Lane, St. George in the East,

north end and west side of Back Church Lane.

Murdens Place, Batty Street, St. George in the East, 1891.

Murdock Cottages, Grove Road, Bromley and Bow, 1891.

Muriel House, Philip Street (Ellen Street), St. George in the East.

Museum Buildings, Chester Street, Bethnal Green, 1891.

Museum Public House, Globe Street (Globe Road), Bethnal Green.

Mutton Lane, 1. Mile End Road, Mile End, "the third on the right below the turnpike, extending from Assembly Row to Redmans Row" (Lockie). 2. Hackney, became part of Westgate Street.

Myddleton Street, Off Canrobert Street, Bethnal Green, 1860, early spelling of Middleton Street.

Myrtle Cottages, 1. Bath Street (Poplar Bath Street), Poplar, 1891, East India Dock Road. 2. Holly Street, Hackney, 1851.

Myrtle Place, Mayfield Road, Hackney, 1851.

Myrtle Street, Off Queensbridge Road, Hackney, 1895, became the western half of Mapledene Road.

Myrtle Villas, Roswell Street (Ackroyd Drive), Mile End, 1891, Ackroyd Drive approximately on route of Roswell Street.

Myrtleberry Street, Off Queensbridge Road, Hackney, 1895, north of Forest Road.

N

Nags Head Court, Wentworth Street, Spitalfields, 1746, close to corner with Wentworth Street.

Nags Head Public House, 1. 25 Bow Common Lane, Bromley and Bow. 2. 70 Cotton Street, Poplar, 1874. 3. 324 Hackney Road, Bethnal Green, 1841. 4. 229 Mare Street, Hackney, 1874. 5. 17-19 Whitechapel Road, Whitechapel, 1874.

Nags Head Yard, 1. Mare Street, Hackney, 1851. 2.

Nags Head Yard, Whitechapel Road, Whitechapel, 1851.

Nailsea or Nailsey Place, Salmon Lane, Limehouse, "about ¹/₈ of a mile on the left from the Commercial Road towards Stepney Church" (Lockie).

Nankin Street, Off Pekin Street, Limehouse, 1860.

Napier Cottages, House and Yard, Westferry Road, Isle of Dogs, 1851, close to Napier Avenue.

Napoleon III Public House, 88 St. Leonards Street, Bromley and Bow.

Nassau Place, Commercial Road, St. George in the East, 1860, Cannon Street Road to Catherine Street.

Nathaniel Dwellings, Flower and Dean Street, Spitalfields, 1950.

Naval Volunteer Public House, 17 Well Street (Ensign Street), St. George in the East, aka Royal Naval Volunteer.

Navarino Cottages, Grove & Terrace, Dalston Lane, Hackney, 1851.

Navarino Place, Dalston Lane, Hackney, 1851, renamed Navarino Grove.

Navarino Public House, 47 Navarino Road, Hackney.

Neat Boys Court, Fashion Street, Spitalfields, "the third on the right from 191 Brick Lane" (Lockie).

Neat(s) Cottages, Church Passage (Aylward Street), Stepney, 1895.

Neath Place, Brady Street, Whitechapel, 1891, Collingwood Estate is now on the site.

Neatsby Court, Fashion Street, Spitalfields, 1851.

Needle Gun Public House, 215 Roman Road, Bethnal Green.

Needlemakers Arms Public House, 22 Dalgleish Street, Limehouse, 1874.

Nelson Alley, Little North Street (Brady Street), Whitechapel, 1851.

Nelson Beer House Public House, 46 Berner Street (Henriques Street), St. George in the East.

Nelson Court, 1. Fashion Street, Spitalfields, 1851. 2. Little North Street (Brady Street), Whitechapel.

Nelson Court(s) & Street, Off Empson Street, Bromley and Bow, 1891, renamed Favonia Street.

Nelson Place, 1. Bath Street (Cranbrook Street), Bethnal Green, renamed Cranbrook Street. 2. Hackney Road, Bethnal Green, renamed Nelson Street. 3. Whitechapel, renamed Winthrop Place.

Nelson Public House, 1. 46 Berner Street (Henriques Street), St. George in the East. 2. 65 Watney Street, Shadwell, also known as Lord Nelson.

Nelson Street, 1. Off Boundary Street, Bethnal Green, 1841, Boundary Estate is on the site. 2. Off Hackney Road, Bethnal Green, renamed Horatio Street. 3. Bethnal Green, renamed Nelson Gardens. 4. Off St. Peter Street (St. Peter Square), Bethnal Green, 1891.

Nelson Wharf, Westferry Road, Isle of Dogs, 1950, Langbourne Place is on its site.

Nelsons Court, 1. Fashion Street, Spitalfields, 1891, south of Fashion Street, east of Fashion Court. 2. Rear of 197 Poplar High Street, Poplar, 1870. 3. Salmon Lane, Limehouse, 1851.

Nelsons Head Public House, 32 Horatio Street, Bethnal Green, 1874.

Neptune Street, St. George in the East, renamed Wellclose Street.

Nesbitts Court & Rents, Three Colt Street, Limehouse, "at 26 a few doors on the right from Ropemakers Fields towards Gun Lane" (Lockie), renamed Padstow Place corner of Northey Street.

Nethaniel Heckford aka Cable Street School, Cable Street, St. George in the East, 1898.

Nevill House, Ellingfort Road, Hackney, 1891, Mare Street.

Neville Court, Pearl Street, Wapping, 1851.

Nevills Turkish Baths, 7 Commercial Road, Whitechapel, 1921.

Nevis House, Limehouse Causeway, Limehouse, St. Vincent Estate, demolished in 1997.

New Albion Theatre, Poplar High Street, Poplar, renamed Queens Theatre.

New Alley Square, Three Colt Street, Limehouse, "at 63 the first on the left from Ropemakers Fields towards the church" (Lockie).

New Blomfield Street, Off Roseberry Place, Hackney.

New Buildings, Tenter Street, Whitechapel, 1891.

New Castle Place, New Castle Street (Tyne Street), Whitechapel, renamed Tyne Place.

New Castle Street, Off Whitechapel High Street, Whitechapel, "at 120 nearly opposite Red Lion Street, it is continued by New Castle Place and Old Castle Street to Wentworth Street" (Lockie), renamed Tyne Street.

New Charles Street, Off Charles Street (Vallance Road), Whitechapel, renamed Vallance Road (section south of railway line).

New Charles Street, Bethnal Green, renamed Hassard Street.

New Church Road, Hackney, became part of Balcorne Street.

New Church Street, Off Fleet Street (Pedley Street), Whitechapel, 1851, Shuttle Street follows part of its route.

New Clay Hall Place, Old Ford Road, Bromley and Bow, 1851.

New Cottages, West Street (Usk Street), Bethnal Green.

New Court, 1. Austin Street, Bethnal Green, 1841. 2. Bethnal Green (Patriot Square), Bethnal Green, "a few doors on the left from the north west corner of the green and nearly opposite Patriot Square" (Lockie). 3. Blue Anchor Alley (Cable Street), Ratcliffe, 1746. 4. Blue Anchor Yard (Royal Mint Street), East Smithfield, 1851. 5. Browns Lane (Hanbury Street), Spitalfields, 1851. 6. Dorset Street, Spitalfields, 1891, London Fruit Exchange was built on the site. 7. Fashion Street, Spitalfields, 1891, south of Fashion Street, west of Fashion Court. 8. Fieldgate Street, Whitechapel, "Mile End Old Town, the first on the right from Fieldgate Street Whitechapel Road" (Lockie). 9. George Yard (Gunthorpe Street), Whitechapel, "the second on the left from 88 Whitechapel High Street" (Lockie). 10. Great Pearl Street (Calvin Street), Spitalfields, 1851. 11. Nightingale Lane (Thomas More Street), Wapping, "at 43 being the first on the left from the entrance to the London Docks" (Lockie). 12. Quaker Street, Spitalfields, "the second on the right about twelve doors from 29 Wheler Street" (Lockie), renamed New Square. 13. Sandys Row, Spitalfields, 1851. 14. Three Colt Street, Limehouse, "at 14 about the middle of the east side, it is also called Three Colt Court" (Lockie). 15. Upper Chapman Street (Chapman Street), St. George in the East, "the second on the left a few doors from Cannon Street Road" (Lockie).

New Crane Wharf, Wapping Wall, Wapping, 1950, south of junction with Garnet Street.

New Cut, Church Lane (Ropemakers Fields), Limehouse, "a few doors on the left from 70 Ropemakers Fields leading to the barge river and the Drawbridge in Narrow Street" (Lockie), alternative name for Limehouse Cut.

New Derbyshire Street, Bethnal Green, 1891, renamed Hereford Street.

New Dundee Wharf, Wapping High Street, Wapping, 1895, south of Dundee Street, became part of Morocco & Eagle Sufferance Wharves.

New England Lighthouse Public House, 3 Stone Stairs, Broad Street (The Highway), Ratcliffe.

New Ford Road, Off Old Ford Road, Bromley and Bow.

New Globe Public House, 359 Mile End Road, Mile End, 1874.

New Gravel Lane, Wapping, 1891, renamed Garnet Street.

New Grove, Mile End Road, Mile End, "between the Plough and Thompsons nursery about 2¼ miles on the right from Aldgate" (Lockie).

New Gun Public House, Wapping High Street, Wapping, 1874.

New Gunboat Public House, The Highway, St. George in the East, 1950, formerly Gunboat public house.

New Hambro Synagogue, Adler Street, Whitechapel.

New James Street, Off Pedley Street, Whitechapel, 1851.

New King Street, Off James Street (Chilton Street), Bethnal Green, became part of Busby Street.

New Market Street, Wapping, 1851, southern end of Old Gravel Lane (Wapping Lane).

New Martin or Martan Street, Off John Fisher Street, East Smithfield, 1851, Royal Mint Street.

New Montague Street, Off Brick Lane, Spitalfields, became part of Hanbury Street.

New Naval Row, Brunswick Street, Poplar, 1851.

New Nichol(s) or Nichol(s) Street, Off Boundary Street, Bethnal Green, " the first north parallel to the last described or the second on the right in Cock Lane" (Lockie), the Boundary Estate is on the site.

New or Great Somerford Street, Off Collingwood Street, Whitechapel, 1851, renamed Somerford Street.

New Pavilion Music Hall, Mile End Road, Mile End.

New Princes Theatre, 51-55 East India Dock Road, Limehouse, corner of Stainsby Road renamed the Hippodrome.

New River Head Cottages, Stainsby Road, Limehouse, 1851.

New River Head Public House, 124 Stainsby Road, Limehouse.

New Road, Off Preston New Road (Prestons Road), Poplar,

1862, combined with Preston New Road to form Prestons Road.

New Road Synagogue, 115 New Road, Whitechapel, 1900.

New Spanish & Portuguese Jewish Cemetery, Mile End Road, Mile End, 1733, Queen Marys College.

New Square, 1. North Street (Brady Street), Whitechapel, 1851, Collingwood Estate is now on the site. 2. Quaker Street, Spitalfields, 1891, renamed Quaker Square, Wheler House was built on the site.

New Street, 1. Off Blanchard Road (Aldington Court), Hackney, 1891. 2. Off Fieldgate Street, Whitechapel, "at 24 about ten doors on the right from 266 Whitechapel Road" (Lockie) renamed Yalford Street. 3. Off Gosset Street, Bethnal Green, 1891, part renamed Newling Street. 4. Off New Road, Whitechapel, renamed Newark Street. 5. Off Shadwell High Street (The Highway), Shadwell, "at the south east corner entering by 67 Shadwell High Street and extending to Shadwell Dock" (Lockie), Shadwell Park is on the site. 6. Off Three Colt Street, Limehouse, 1851, renamed Phoebe Street.

New Suffolk Street, Whitechapel, renamed Walden Street.

New Sun Wharves, Narrow Street, Ratcliffe, 1950, west of Regent's Canal entrance.

New Tyssen (or Tysson) Street, Off Orange Street (Satchwell Road), Bethnal Green, 1841.

New Union Wharf, Stewart Street, Isle of Dogs, 1950, New Union Close is close to its site.

New York Street, 1. Off Bethnal Green Road, Bethnal Green, 1841, renamed Jersey Street. 2. Off Varden Street, Whitechapel, became part of Varden Street.

Newbold Street, Off Bromehead Street, Stepney, 1950, Bromehead Street to Bromehead Road.

Newcastle (or New Castle) Street, Off Mount Street (Swanfield Street), Bethnal Green, Sunbury Workshops approximately follows its route.

Newcastle Arms Public House, 1 Newcastle Street (Glenaffric Avenue), Isle of Dogs, 1874, renamed Watermans Arms.

Newcastle Place, Mile End Road, Mile End, 1891, renamed Gateshead Place.

Newcastle Street, Off Manchester Road, Isle of Dogs, renamed Glengarnock Avenue (west of Manchester Road) and Glenaffric Avenue (east of Manchester Road).

Newcourt, Wentworth Street, Spitalfields, renamed Corea Place.

Newling Street, Off Gosset Street, Bethnal Green, 1891.

Newlys Court, Pleasant Row (Coverley Close), Spitalfields, "the fourth on the right from Pelham Street entering by 60 Brick Lane" (Lockie).

Newmans Buildings, 1. Coxs Square (Wentworth Street), Spitalfields, 1891. 2. Pelham Street (Woodseer Street), Whitechapel, 1891.

Newmarket Terrace, Hackney Road, Bethnal Green, "Cambridge Heath forms part of the east side opposite Heath Place, being the first row on the right from the turnpike towards Hackney" (Lockie), south of present-day Wadeson Street.

Newnham Street, Off Tenter Street West (West Tenter Street), Whitechapel, 1891, St. Marks Street to Tenter Street West.

Newport Street, Off Essex Street (Blythe Street), Bethnal Green, 1891, renamed Cudworth Street.

Newports Gardens, Canton Place (East India Dock Road), Limehouse, 1851, East India Dock Road.

Newtons Rent, Twine Court, Shadwell, 1891.

Nezach Israel Beth Hamedrash Synagogue, 31b Vallance Road, Whitechapel, 1945.

Nichol(s) Row, Half Nichol(s) Street (Boundary Street), Bethnal Green, 1841, south to Church Street, Boundary Estate is now on the site.

Nicholas Street, 1. Off Cephas Street, Mile End, 1895, renamed Nicholas Road. 2. Off Globe Street (Globe Road), Bethnal Green, 1891, now includes Green Street and Alma Cottages.

Nichols Square, Hackney Road, Bethnal Green, 1891.

Night Lane, Brick Lane, Bethnal Green, St. Lukes "the continuation of Brick Lane entering by 113 Old Street" (Lockie).

Nightingale Buildings, Ropemakers Fields, Limehouse, 1851.

Nightingale Lane, Wapping, renamed Thomas More Street.

Nightingale Public House, 321 Hackney Road, Bethnal Green.

Noahs Ark Alley, Medland Street (Horseferry Road), Ratcliffe, 1895, Medland Street to Narrow Street.

Noahs Ark Public House, 1. 59 Narrow Street, Ratcliffe, 1874. 2. 30 Teesdale Street, Bethnal Green.

Noble Street, Off Hale Street, Poplar, 1810, between Wades Place and Hale Street.

Norah Street, Off Florida Street, Bethnal Green, 1891.

Norfolk Arms Public House, 1. 460 Hackney Road, Bethnal Green. 2. 15 Ivimey Street, Bethnal Green.

Norfolk Hero Public House, 92 Canton Street, Limehouse.

Norfolk Street, 1. Off Brunswick Street, Poplar, 1851, renamed St. Lawrence Street. 2. Whitechapel, 1841, renamed Fellbrigg Street (Collingwood Street). 3. Mile End, renamed Massingham Street. 4. Whitechapel, became part of Varden Street.

Norfolk Terrace, 1. Grange Road (Gayhurst Road), Hackney, 1868, between Queens Road and Holly Street. 2. Manchester Road, Isle of Dogs, 1860, northern part (east side), between Samuda Street and Davis Street.

Norman Road, Off Saxon Road, Bromley and Bow, renamed Norman Grove.

Normans Buildings, 1. Garden Place (Haggerston Road), Hackney, 1868, Haggerston Road. 2. Salter Street, St. George in the East, 1891, opposite Salter Street, renamed Norman Court.

Norris Almshouses, Victoria Park Road, Hackney, 1950.

Norris Court, Off Nightingale Lane (Thomas More Street), Wapping, 1800, London Docks were built on the site.

Norris Road, Off Devons Road, Bromley and Bow, 1891, opposite Talwin Street.

North Bow & Victoria Park Synagogue, Argyle House (Parnell Road), Bromley and Bow, 1900.

North Briton Public House, 83 Bedford Street (Prestons Road), Poplar.

North Conduit Street, Off Canrobert Street, Bethnal Green, became part of Canrobert Street.

North Country Cat Public House, Wapping High Street, Wapping, 1874.

North Country Pink Public House, Shoulder of Mutton Alley, Limehouse.

North Country Sailor Public House, 109 Wapping High Street, Wapping.

North East Passage, 1. St. Thomas Square, Hackney, 1841. 2. Wellclose Square, St. George in the East, 1950.

North Greenwich Railway Station, Wharf Road (Saunders Ness Road), Isle of Dogs, 1872-1926, Poplar, Blackwall & District Rowing Club is on its site.

North Holly Street, Off Dalston Lane, Hackney, 1851.

North Passage, 1. Green Street (Roman Road), Bethnal Green. 2. North Place (Globe Road), Bethnal Green, 1891. 3. Bethnal Green, renamed Peary Place.

North Pavement, Preston Street (Roman Road), Bethnal Green, 1851.

North Place, 1. Buxton Street, Whitechapel, parallel with and north of a short section of Buxton Street 1851, north of Allen

Gardens. 2. Globe Street (Globe Road), Bethnal Green, 1851, near North Street. 3. Green Street (Roman Road), Bethnal Green, "the first north parallel to part of Green Street about $1/8$ of a mile on the left from the green, extending from Back Lane towards Bonner Street" (Lockie), renamed Kirkwall Place. 4. Kingsland Road, Hackney, 1860, either side of Mansfield Street. 5. Talavera Place (Whiston Estate), Bethnal Green, 1827, became part of Whiston Estate.

North Pole Public House, 1. 82 Elsa Street, Limehouse. 2. 74 Manilla Street, Isle of Dogs. 3. 58 Sutton Street, Shadwell, 1874.

North Square, Portman Place, Bethnal Green, 1891, Off Globe Road.

North Star Public House, 58 North Street (Northiam Street), Hackney.

North Street, 1. Stepney, renamed Elsa Street. 2. Off Back Church Lane, St. George in the East, renamed Fairclough Street. 3. Off James Street (Cadiz Street), Mile End, 1891. 4. Off Lamb Street, Spitalfields, 1891, Short entrance street on north side of Spitalfields Market. 5. Off Mare Street, Hackney, 1891, renamed Northiam Street. 6. Off Poplar High Street, Poplar, Poplar High Street to East India Dock Road, renamed Saltwell Street. 7. Bethnal Green, became part of Portman Place. 8. Off

Sidney Street, Whitechapel, renamed Lindley Street. 9. Off West Street (Usk Street), Bethnal Green, "the first on the left in West Street entering by Green Street nearly opposite Bonner Street" (Lockie). 10. Off Wilmot Street, Bethnal Green, "near the south end of it leading to Ducking Pond Row" (Lockie), renamed Brady Street.

North Wharf Receiving Station, Managers Street, Poplar, 1884-1930, Cold Harbour.

Northampton Arms Public House, 11 Headlam Street, Bethnal Green, address also 11 Northampton Street.

Northampton Place, Hackney Road, Bethnal Green, 1860, between Warner Place and St. Peter Street.

Northampton Street, Off Cambridge Road (Cambridge Heath Road), Whitechapel, 1841, renamed Headlam Street.

Northey Arms Public House, 1 Northey Street, Limehouse.

Northumberland Arms Public House, 1. 44-45 Fashion Street, Spitalfields, 1874. 2. 78 Well Street, Hackney, 1874.

Northumberland Head Public House, 8 Fort Street, Spitalfields, 1874.

Northumberland Place, Commercial Road, Whitechapel, 1860, Turner Street to Philpot Street.

Northumberland Street,
Limehouse, 1860, renamed
Northumbria Street, Bartlett Park
is on the site.

Northumberland Wharf, off
Releana Road, Prestons Road,
Poplar, 1950.

Norton Folgate Almshouses,
Puma Court, Spitalfields.

Norton Folgate Court House, 1
Folgate Street (Spitalfields),
Spitalfields.

**Norton Folgate Girls Charity
School,** Blossom Street,
Spitalfields.

Norton Gardens, Gibraltar
Walk, Bethnal Green, 1841.

Norton Street, Off Green Street
(Roman Road), Bethnal Green,
Cranbrook Estate is on the site.

Nortons Buildings, New Gravel
Lane (Garnet Street), Wapping,
1851.

Norway Place, Hackney Road,
Bethnal Green, 1841,
immediately west of Henrietta
Street.

Norwell Place, Church Street
(Bethnal Green Road), Bethnal
Green, Church Street forms part
of the north side by the turnpike
about ½ a mile on the left from
65 Shoreditch" (Lockie),
immediately west of Harts Lane.

Norwich Court, Upper East
Smithfield, East Smithfield,
1851.

Norwich Road, Off Pownall
Road, Hackney, 1895.

Nottingham Place, Fordham
Street, Whitechapel, renamed
Parfett Street.

Nottingham Street, Off
Winchester Street (Dunbridge
Street), Bethnal Green, became
part of Vallance Road.

Nova Scotia Gardens, Barnet
Street (Barnet Grove), Bethnal
Green, 1841.

Nye Street, Off Grundy Street,
Poplar, 1950, renamed Susannah
Street.

O

Oak Brewery Public House,
Charles Street (Vallance Road),
Whitechapel.

Oak Place, Grove Lane
(Reading Lane), Hackney, 1851.

Oak Wharf, Spratleys Row
(Westferry Road), Isle of Dogs,
1895, later Torrington Wharf.

Oakhill Public House, 202 Mile
End Road, Mile End.

Oakley Row & Street, Off
Thomas Street (Granby Street),
Bethnal Green, became part of
Granby Street.

Oakley Street, Off Chilton
Street, Bethnal Green, renamed
Granby Street.

Ocean Row, Cow Lane (Ben
Jonson Road), Stepney, "forms
that part of Cow Lane which is
nearly opposite the Walnut Tree
public house" (Lockie).

Ocean Street, Off Cow Lane (Ben Jonson Road), Stepney, "the first on the left a few doors from Stepney Old Square, it leads to Trafalgar Square" (Lockie), Ben Jonson Road to Cadiz Street

Ocean Wharf, Westferry Road, Isle of Dogs, 1950, the present-day street named Ocean Wharf is on its site.

Oceana Close, East India Dock Road, Poplar, Blackwall Tunnel entrance road system at East India Dock Road is on the site.

Octagon Place, Collingwood Street, Whitechapel, 1851, renamed Somerford Street.

Octagon Street, Off Coventry Road, Bethnal Green, 1891.

Ohavei Emeth Synagogue, 44b Philpot Street, Whitechapel, 1945.

Ohrens Court, Periwinkle Street (Ratcliffe Cross Street), Ratcliffe, 1891.

Old Aberdeen Wharf, Wapping High Street, Wapping, 1950, east of corner with Reardon Path.

Old Axe Public House, 69 Hackney Road, Bethnal Green, 1874.

Old Bell & Mackerel Public House, 1. 333 Mile End Road, Mile End, aka Old Bell and (Three) Mackerel. 2. Shadwell High Street (The Highway), Shadwell, also known as the Bell and Mackerel.

Old Blind Beggar, 1 Green Street (Roman Road), Bethnal Green, 1874, sometimes known as the Falcon.

Old Britannia Public House, 232 Cable Street, St. George in the East, aka Britannia.

Old Carpenters Arms, 79 Ben Jonson Road, Mile End, aka (New) Carpenters Arms.

Old Castle Court, Old Castle Street, Bethnal Green, 1891, became part of Virginia Road.

Old Castle Street Synagogue, 42 Old Castle Street, Whitechapel, 1870-1966, renamed the Agudath Achim Synagogue.

Old Clay Hall Place, Old Ford Road, Bromley and Bow, 1851.

Old Cock Lane, Bethnal Green, 1841, also known as Cock Lane, renamed Boundary Street.

Old Commodore Public House, 1. 52 Old Montague Street, Whitechapel, aka Commodore. 2. 209 Poplar High Street, Poplar, aka Red Lion.

Old Crown Public House, 182 Brick Lane, Spitalfields, 1874, aka Crown.

Old Dock House Public House, 36 Wapping Wall, Wapping.

Old Duke of Cambridge Public House, 158 Devons Road, Bromley and Bow.

Old Duke William Public House, 9 Old Gravel Lane (Wapping Lane), Wapping, 1874,

end of what is now Chicksand Street.

Osborn Street, Off Torrington Street (Kennet Street), Wapping, 1790, London Docks Western Dock was built on the site.

Osborn Street Dwellings, Osborn Street, Whitechapel, 1891.

Osborne Place, Union Street (Bullivant Street), Poplar, 1891.

Ostler Public House, 151 Well Street, Hackney.

Otis Street, Off Hancock Road, Bromley and Bow, 1891.

Ottawa Buildings, Prestons Road, Poplar, 1900.

Our Lady & St. Catherine's Church, Bow Road, Bromley and Bow.

Ovex Wharf, Stewart Street, Isle of Dogs, 1950, Ovex Close is on its site.

Oval Cottages, Hackney Road, Bethnal Green, 1841.

Oxford Arms Public House, 1. 62 Brushfield Street, Spitalfields. 2. 137 Cambridge Road (Cambridge Heath Road), Whitechapel. 3. 43 Oxford Street (Stepney Way), Whitechapel. 4. 77 St. Peter Street (St. Peter Square), Bethnal Green.

Oxford House (Club), 87 Derbyshire Street, Bethnal Green, 1950.

Oxford House University Settlement, Mape Street, Bethnal Green.

Oxford Place, 1. Hackney Road, Bethnal Green, 1860, opposite Goldsmiths Row. 2. Oxford Street (Stepney Way), Whitechapel, 1862, Richardson Street to Jubilee Street.

Oxford Public House, 286 Oxford Street (Stepney Way), Whitechapel.

Oxford Street, 1. Off Cambridge Road (Cambridge Heath Road), Bethnal Green, 1851, renamed Wingham Street. 2. Off Stepney Way, Whitechapel, subsumed by Stepney Way.

Oxford Terrace, 1. Manchester Road, Isle of Dogs, 1860, opposite Queens Terrace. 2. Middleton Road, Hackney, 1851. 3. Oxford Street (Stepney Way), Whitechapel, 1851.

P

Pacificos Almshouses & Terrace, London Place, Hackney, 1895.

Padstow Place, Grenade Street, Limehouse.

Paget Villas, Shrubland Grove (Mapledene Road), Hackney, 1868, west of Lansdowne Road.

Pagets Court & Place, Ratcliffe Highway (The Highway), St. George in the East, "The third on the right a few doors from 95 Ratcliffe Highway" (Lockie).

Paines Gardens, Elizabeth Street (Mansford Road), Bethnal Green, 1851.

Painters Rents, Broad Street (The Highway), Ratcliffe, parallel with Butcher Row.

Palace Road, Off Well Street, Hackney, 1895, renamed Cole Road.

Palaseum Cinema, 226 Commercial Road, St. George in the East.

Palatine Place, Commercial Road, Whitechapel, "forms part of the north side between Plumbers Row and Greenfield Street near ¼ of a mile on the left from Whitechapel Church" (Lockie).

Palestine Place, Cambridge Road (Cambridge Heath Road), Bethnal Green, 1841, Bethnal Green Hospital was built on the site.

Palestine Place Jewish School, Palestine Place (Cambridge Heath Road), Bethnal Green, 1841.

Palm Cottage, 153 East India Dock Road, Poplar, 1851.

Palm Street, Off Grove Road, Bromley and Bow, 1891, Mile End Park is on site.

Palm Tree Public House, 24 Palm Street (Grove Road), Bromley and Bow, 1874, Mile End park is on the site.

Palmer Street, 1. Off Shepherd Street (Commercial Street), Spitalfields, 1891, Brune House was built on the site. 2. Off White Horse Street (White Horse Road), Stepney, 1891, renamed Troon Street.

Palmers Folly, Perseverance Place (The Highway), St. George in the East, St. George Street.

Palmers Roadway, Green Street (Roman Road), Bethnal Green.

Palmerston Arms Public House, 184 Well Street, Hackney.

Pamela House, Haggerston Road, Hackney, 1950.

Panther Public House, 15 Turin Street, Bethnal Green, 1874.

Paper Makers Arms Public House, 17 St. Leonards Street, Bromley and Bow.

Paradise Cottages, Gray Street (Adderley Street), Poplar, 1851.

Paradise Fields, Burford Lane (Lyme Grove), Hackney, 1851.

Paradise Passage or Place, West Street (Elsdale Street), Hackney, 1851, became part of Chatham Place.

Paradise Place, 1, Bell Lane, Spitalfields, 1851, Petticoat Lane. 2. Cambridge Road (Cambridge Heath Road), Bethnal Green, 1891, renamed Nant Street. 3. Coxs Square (Wentworth Street), Spitalfields, 1891, Petticoat Lane.

Paradise Row, 1. Cambridge Road (Cambridge Heath Road), Bethnal Green, 1827, north of its corner with Bethnal Green Road. 2. Charles Street (Wapping Lane), Wapping, "the east continuation of it entering by 44 Gravel Lane" (Lockie). 3. Old Ford Road, Bromley and Bow, 1851. 4. Ratcliffe Square (Ratcliffe Cross Street), Ratcliffe, "entrance by the south east corner near Butcher Row" (Lockie). 5. Westferry Road, Isle of Dogs, 1851, also known as Harts Row demolished to make room for Millwall Dock entrance lock.

Paradise Street, Off Poplar High Street, Poplar, "is nearly opposite the Black Horse about ⅓ of a mile on the left from the Commercial Road leading into Noble Street" (Lockie).

Paragon, Paragon Road, Hackney, 1841, at corner with Chatham Place.

Paragon Theatre, 93-95 Mile End Road, Mile End, aka Lusbys Music Hall later ABC cinema.

Parian Street, Off East India Dock Road, Poplar, East India Dock Road to Lanrick Road.

Paris Row, Old Ford Road, Bromley and Bow.

Paris Terrace, Hind Street (Hind Grove), Limehouse, Hind Street to Gough Street, Saracen Street is on the site.

Parish Almshouses, Kingsland Road, Hackney, 1868, north of Union Street.

Park Grove Cottages, Park Road (Parkholme Road), Hackney, 1851.

Park Hotel & Public House, 105 Approach Road, Bethnal Green.

Park House, Grove Road, Bromley and Bow.

Park Lane, 1. Bonner Lane (Bonner Street), Bethnal Green. 2. Grove Road, Bromley and Bow. 3. Old Ford Road, Bromley and Bow. 4. Sale Street, Bethnal Green.

Park Place, 1. Bethnal Green, renamed Bonner Street. 2. Chatham Place, Hackney, 1891, renamed Ram Place. 3. Grove Street (Lauriston Road), Hackney, 1851. 4. Mile End Road, Mile End, immediately west of Cleveland Street later Way. 5. Park Road (Parkholme Road), Hackney, 1868, north of Forest Road. 6. Sale Street, Bethnal Green, 1851. 7. Talavera Place (Whiston Estate), Bethnal Green, 1827, became part of Whiston Estate. 8. Bethnal Green, renamed Yerwood Place.

Park Place Row & Street, Off Milligan Street, Limehouse, "is by Mitchells Rope walk being a few doors on the left from the lime kilns" (Lockie), the original Milligan Street followed its route.

Park Road, 1. Off Dalston Lane, Hackney, 1841, renamed Parkholme Road. 2. Bromley and Bow, renamed Leith Road. 3. Bromley and Bow, renamed Parnell Road. 4. Off St. Dunstans Road (Mile End Stadium), Mile

End, 1891. 5. Off Brookfield Road, Hackney, 1862, became part of Wick Road. 6. Mile End, renamed Cephas Street. 7. Bethnal Green, renamed Welwyn Street. 8. Off Wick Lane, Bromley and Bow, 1851.

Park Terrace, 1. Grove Street (Lauriston Road), Hackney, 1851. 2. Old Ford Road, Bromley and Bow, 1851. 3. Three Colt Street, Limehouse, 1851.

Park Villas, Park Road (Parkholme Road), Hackney, 1868, north of Forest Road.

Parker Street, Off Dunloe Street, Bethnal Green, 1890, renamed Ormsby Street.

Parkhurst Buildings, Samuel Street (Camdenhurst Street), Limehouse, Salmon Lane.

Parks or Parkers Court, Whitechapel High Street, Whitechapel, "at 48 about sixteen doors east of Red Lion Street" (Lockie).

Parliament Alley, Artillery Lane, Spitalfields, 1746.

Parliament Court, Parliament Street (Witan Street), Bethnal Green, 1851.

Parliament Street, Off Cambridge Road (Cambridge Heath Road), Bethnal Green, 1851, renamed Witan Street.

Parmiters Charity Almshouses, Gloucester Street (Parminter Street), Bethnal Green, 1841.

Parmiters School, Approach Road, Bethnal Green.

Parnham Place & Terrace, Back Road (Cable Street), St. George in the East, 1851, later part of Cable Street.

Parochial Infant School, Paragon Road, Hackney, 1921.

Parseys Gardens, Little North Street (Brady Street), Whitechapel, 1851.

Parsons Court, Blue Anchor Yard (Royal Mint Street), East Smithfield.

Parsons Street, Off St. George Street (The Highway), St. George in the East, 1851, became the west end St. George Street.

Parrys Wharf, south of Factory Place, Ferry Street, Isle of Dogs, 1950.

Pascoe Street, Hackney, renamed Bayford Street.

Passmore Edwards Sailors Palace, West India Dock Road, Limehouse, 1901, also known as the British Sailors Society Hostel.

Paternoster Row, Union Street (Brushfield Street), Spitalfields, 1792, "the east continuation of Union Street entering by 69 Bishopsgate Street Without" (Lockie), present eastern end of Brushfield Street, also known as Great Paternoster Row.

Patience Street, Off Wheler Street, Spitalfields, "at the north end of it three or four doors south from Anchor Street near Webb Square entering by 47 Shoreditch High Street" (Lockie).

Patientia Place, Westferry Road, Isle of Dogs, 1851, close to Moiety Road.

Patriot Row, Bethnal Green (Patriot Square), Bethnal Green, "adjoining Patriot Square and extending towards the green" (Lockie).

Patriot Street, St. George in the East, later the south half of Morgan Street (Hessel Street).

Pattison or Patterson Street, Off Jamaica Street, Stepney, 1891, connecting corner of Jamaica Street and Oxford Street with West Arbour Street.

Pauline Terrace, Old Montague Street, Whitechapel, 1891, Brick Lane.

Pauls Head Public House, 1 Crispin Street, Spitalfields.

Pavilion Public House, 187 Whitechapel Road, Whitechapel.

Pavilion Theatre, Whitechapel Road, Whitechapel, just west of Vallance Road.

Pavilion Yard, Whitechapel Road, Whitechapel, 1851.

Payne Road, Off Bow Road, Bromley and Bow, 1891.

Paynes Place, Old Ford Road, Bromley and Bow, 1851.

Paynton Street, Limehouse, renamed Hind Street (Hind Grove).

Paynton Terrace, East India Dock Road, Limehouse, 1851.

Peabody Arms Public House, 140 Shadwell High Street (The Highway), Shadwell, 1874, aka Globe & Three Pigeons.

Peabody Buildings, 1. Glasshouse Street (John Fisher Street), East Smithfield, 1891. 2. New Gravel Lane (Garnet Street), Wapping, 1891.

Peabody Place, Lion Street (Kerbey Street), Poplar, 1891, Kerbey Street.

Peace & Tranquillity Synagogue, 26 Buckle Street, Whitechapel, 1885, also known as Buckle Street Synagogue.

Peace Street, Off Hemming Street, Whitechapel, Fakruddin Street is on the site.

Peacock Alley, Court & Place, Bethnal Green, Bethnal Green, "near the north west corner of [Bethnal] green" (Lockie).

Peacock Public House, 1. 145-147 Aylward Street, Stepney. 2. 325 Cambridge Heath Road, Bethnal Green, 1874.

Peal or Peel Alley, Shadwell High Street (The Highway), Shadwell, "at 61 about six doors on the right east from or below the church" (Lockie), road to Shadwell Market Shadwell Park is on the site.

Pear Tree Alley, Cinnamon Street, Wapping, 1746.

Pearl Court, Little Pearl Street (Calvin Street), Spitalfields, 1746.

Pearl Place, Redmans Road, Mile End, 1895.

Pearl Street (aka Great Pearl Street), Fleur de Lis Street, Spitalfields, 1891, "the continuation of Flower de Lis Street" (Elmes), renamed Calvin Street.

Pearl Yard, Pollard Street, Bethnal Green, 1891.

Peartree Alley, Cinnamon Street, Wapping, "is nearly opposite King Edward Street entering by 272 Wapping Street" (Lockie).

Peasants Revolt Public House, 56 Cleveland Street (Cleveland Way), Mile End, aka Golden Eagle.

Pecks Yard or Place, Browns Lane (Hanbury Street), Spitalfields, 1851.

Peculiar People Mission Hall, Grundy Street, Poplar, close to corner of Augusta Street.

Pedlars Orchard, Rhodeswell Road, Limehouse, 1860, north side, south of East London Cemetery.

Peel Court, Peel Alley (Shadwell Park), Shadwell, 1851.

Peel Terrace, Old Ford Road, Bromley and Bow.

Peirces Place, Virginia Row (Virginia Road), Bethnal Green, 1841.

Pekin Place, 174-178 East India Dock Road, Poplar, 1810.

Pelham House, Pelham Street (Woodseer Street), Whitechapel, 1891.

Pelham Street, Off Brick Lane, Whitechapel, 1860, renamed Woodseer Street.

Pelham Street Synagogue, Pelham Street (Woodseer Street), Whitechapel, 1915.

Pelican Public House, 33 Clive Street (Stepney Way), Mile End.

Pelican Stairs, Wapping Wall, Wapping, "at 57 near Foxes Lane from Shadwell Church about 1¼ mile below London Bridge and opposite the Kings Mills Rotherhithe" (Lockie).

Pelican Wharf, Wapping Wall, Wapping, 1950, west of The Prospect of Whitby.

Pell Place, Pell Street (Wellclose Square), St. George in the East.

Pell Street, Off St. George Street (The Highway), St. George in the East, 1895, St. George Street to Cable Street, immediately east of Wellclose Square.

Pelton Place, Bow Lane, Poplar, 1851.

Pemberton Arms Public House, 99 Clinton Road, Mile End, 1874.

Pembroke House Asylum, Mare Street, Hackney, 1841.

Pembroke Terrace, Lamb Lane, Hackney, 1891.

Pembroke Villas, Albert Road (Albion Drive), Hackney, 1868, between Queens (now Queensbridge) Road and Malvern Road.

Pendennis Castle Public House, 7 Lamb Street, Spitalfields, 1874.

Pendergast Arms Public House, 305 St. Leonards Road, Poplar.

Pennington Buildings & Place, Pennington Street, St. George in the East, 1891.

Peoples Arcade, Back Church Lane, St. George in the East, 1915.

Peoples Palace, Mile End Road, Mile End, Queen Marys College is built on the site.

Percival Buildings, Whitechapel, 1851, East Mount Street and Terrace, Oxford Street (Stepney Way).

Percy Street or Road, Hackney, renamed Kingshold Road.

Pereira Street, Off Bath Street (Darling Row), Whitechapel, 1891. Collingwood Estate and large supermarket are now on its route.

Periwinkle Street, Off Brook Street (Cable Street), Ratcliffe, "is nearly opposite Butcher Row from Ratcliffe Cross, it leads to Ratcliffe Square" (Lockie), became part of Ratcliffe Cross Street.

Perring Street, Off Devons Road, Bromley and Bow.

Perrys Close, East India Dock Road, Limehouse, 1891.

Perrys Dock, Blackwall Causeway (Blackwall Way), Poplar, "on the east side of Blackwall causeway and the south side of the East India Dock" (Lockie).

Perrys Place, Hackney Road, Bethnal Green, 1895, opposite Baroness Road.

Perrys Rents, 1. Hackney Road, Bethnal Green, Shoreditch Hackney Road "about ¹/₅ of a mile on the left from Shoreditch Church near the Axe public house" (Lockie). 2. Old Gravel Lane (Wapping Lane), Wapping, "is the continuation of Johns Rents in Old Gravel Lane" (Elmes).

Perseverance House, Billson Street, Isle of Dogs, 1891.

Perseverance Place, 1. St. George Street (The Highway), St. George in the East, just east of the church. 2. Green Street (Roman Road), Bethnal Green, 1851.

Perseverance Public House, 1. 125 Gosset Street, Bethnal Green. 2. 112 Pritchards Road, Bethnal Green. 3. 57 Tarling Street, Shadwell. 4. 7 Wallis Road, Hackney. 5. 20 York Road, Limehouse.

Perseverance Terrace, 113-117 Church Street (Bethnal Green Road), Bethnal Green, 1851.

Perth Street, 1. Off Aylward Street, Stepney, 1950, Aylward Street to Bermuda Street. 2. Off Church Street (Bethnal Green Road), Bethnal Green, "the first on the right from 45 Church Street along Rose Street" (Lockie).

Peter Street, 1. Off Four Mills Street (St. Leonards Street), Bromley and Bow, 1851. 2. Off Mount Street (Swanfield Street), Bethnal Green, 1891, Mount Street to Brick Lane, renamed Rhoda Street. 3. Off St. Leonards Street, Bromley and Bow, 1891, close to and opposite Devas Street.

Peters Court, Royal Mint Street, East Smithfield, 1851.

Peters Road, Off Mayfield Road, Hackney, 1851.

Petits Walk, Wilmot Street, Bethnal Green, 1841, between Camden Gardens and Wilmot Street.

Petticoat Lane, Originally named Hog Lane, and now Middlesex Street (Whitechapel High Street).

Petticoat Square, Petticoat Lane (Middlesex Street), Spitalfields, "about $^1/_6$ of a mile on the left from 41 Aldgate High Street and nearly opposite Wentworth Street" (Lockie).

Pewter Platter Public House, 1. 12 Broad Street (The Highway), Ratcliffe, 1874. 2. 11 White Lion Street (Folgate Street), Spitalfields, 1874.

Philadelphia Place, Hackney Road, Bethnal Green, 1851, between Temple Street and Hope Street.

Philip Street, 1. Off Ellen Street, St. George in the East, 1891, renamed Philchurch Street, Philchurch Place is close to the site. 2. Shadwell, renamed Shadwell Place.

Philip Street & Shadwell Synagogue, 25 Philchurch Place, St. George in the East, 1955.

Phillips Buildings, Crellin Street (Cannon Street Road), St. George in the East.

Phillips House, Coventry Cross Estate, Bromley and Bow, St. Leonards Street.

Philpot Place, Philpot Street, Whitechapel, 1891.

Philpot Street Great Synagogue, 44 Philpot Street, Whitechapel, 1950.

Philpot Street Sephardic Synagogue, 39 Philpot Street, Whitechapel, 1911.

Phoebe Street, Off Three Colt Street, Limehouse, 1890, Three Colt Street to Park Place/Street.

Phoenix Court, 1. Shorter Street (Wellclose Square), St. George in the East, 1891, sometimes spelled Finicks. 2. Butcher Row (St. Katharine Dock), East Smithfield, 1746.

Phoenix Distillery, Cephas Street, Mile End, 1895, west end of Cephas Street.

Phoenix Place, 1. Phoenix Street (Brick Lane), Spitalfields, 1851. 2. Queen Street (Horseferry Road), Ratcliffe, 1860, north side and west end of Queen Street.

Phoenix Public House, 1. 159 Brick Lane, Spitalfields, address also 79, 126 and 180 Brick Lane. 2. 49 Devonshire Street (Cephas Street), Mile End, 1874, aka Devonshire Arms Public House. 3. 104 East India Dock Road, Poplar. 4. 24 Norton Folgate (Folgate Street), Spitalfields. 5. 3 Queen Street (Horseferry Road), Ratcliffe, 1874. 6. 24 Upper East Smithfield, East Smithfield, 1874.

Phoenix Street, Off Wheler Street, Spitalfields, "at 40 the third on the right from Lamb Street, it extends to 159 Brick Lane" (Lockie), north of Quaker Street, the railway line is on its site.

Phoenix Wharf, 1. Narrow Street (The Highway), Ratcliffe, 1895, east of Ratcliffe Cross Stairs. 2. Wapping High Street, Wapping, 1895, south west of Brewhouse Lane, absorbed into St. Johns Wharf. 3. Westferry Road, Isle of Dogs, 1895, south of Millwall Dock entrance.

Phoenix Works, Weston Street (Watts Grove), Bromley and Bow, 1891, Devons Road.

Pier Head, Wapping High Street, Wapping, 1891, south of Wapping Basin.

Pier Head Cottages, Westferry Road, Isle of Dogs, 1891, on north quay of Millwall Dock entrance lock.

Pier Tavern Public House, 283 Manchester Road, Isle of Dogs, 1874.

Pig Alley, Wheler Street, Spitalfields, "the first on the right fifteen doors from 32 Lamb Street, Spital Square" (Lockie).

Pigott(s) Arms Public House, 1 East India Dock Road, Limehouse, 1874, corner of Pigott Street and Burdett Road.

Pigwell Path, The Grove (Reading Lane), Hackney, 1895, renamed Wilton Way.

Pikes Buildings, Barnet Street (Barnet Grove), Bethnal Green, 1841.

Pilgrims Lodge, Lyme Grove, Hackney, 1891, Mare Street.

Pillory Lane, Nightingale Lane (Thomas More Street), Wapping, 1746, St. Catherines (or Katharines) Street to Red Cross Street, St. Katherine Dock is on its site.

Pipemakers Alley, 1. Narrow Street, Limehouse, "the third on the left a few doors below Mr Turners Wharf" (Lockie). 2. Old Montague Street, Whitechapel, "the first on the left a few yards from Osborn Street" (Lockie). 3. White Horse Street (White Horse

Road), Stepney, "the first on the left a few yards from the Commercial Road towards Stepney" (Lockie).

Pitt Street, Off Green Street (Roman Road), Bethnal Green, 1841, renamed Coventry Street.

Pitts Court, Crispin Street, Spitalfields, "three doors south from 25 Union Street, Bishopsgate" (Lockie).

Pitts Head Public House, 1. 57 Broad Street (The Highway), Ratcliffe, 1874. 2. 6 Lucas Street (Newcourt House), Bethnal Green. 3. 230 Tyssen Street, Bethnal Green, 1874.

Planet Street, Off Watney Passage, Shadwell, 1950, between Commercial Road and Watney Passage.

Plantation Place, Commercial Road, Stepney, "a few yards on the right from White Horse Street towards Whitechapel" (Lockie).

Pleasant Cottages, Paragon Road, Hackney.

Pleasant Court or Place, Redmans Road, Mile End, 1891.

Pleasant Passage, Off Mile End Road, Mile End, "the first on the left east a few doors from the Old Globe, about 1½ mile on the left from Aldgate" (Lockie).

Pleasant Place, 1. Bonner Lane (Bonner Street), Bethnal Green, renamed Hersee Place. 2. Brady Street, Whitechapel, 1891, renamed Dagnall Place. 3. Cambridge Road (Cambridge

Heath Road), Bethnal Green, 1851.

Pleasant Place & Row, 1. Church Street (Mare Street), Hackney, 1841, became part of Paragon Road. 2. North Street (Brady Street), Whitechapel, 1841, Collingwood Estate is now on the site.

Pleasant Row, 1. Ashley Place (Pitsea Street), Ratcliffe, 1891. 2. Globe Alley (Narrow Street), Limehouse, "the second on the right from 54 Narrow Street on the east side the draw bridge" (Lockie). 3. Green Street (Roman Road), Bethnal Green, "the first on the right in Bonner Street from Green Street about $1/3$ of a mile east from the green" (Lockie). 4. Nightingale Lane (Thomas More Street), Wapping, 1851. 5. Pelham Street (Woodseer Street), Whitechapel, 1820, Pelham Street to Charles Street, Coverley Close is close to the route. 6. Stepney Green, Stepney, 1862, west of Wellington Street.

Plimsoll Street, Off Grundy Street, Poplar, 1891, Grundy Street to East India Dock Road, part renamed Plimsoll Close.

Plotsker Synagogue, 45 Commercial Road, Whitechapel, 1930.

Plough (or Plow) Alley, Wapping High Street, Wapping, "at 48 about that number of houses on the left below Hermitage Bridge" (Lockie).

Plough (Tavern) Public House, Cold Harbour, Poplar.

Plough Court, Whitechapel High Street, Whitechapel, 1851.

Plough Inn Public House, 606 Mile End Road, Mile End, 1874.

Plough Public House, 1. 193 Cassland Road, Hackney. 2. 36 Fuller Street (Bethnal Green Road), Bethnal Green. 3. 5 Narrow Street, Limehouse. 4. 557 Old Ford Road, Bromley and Bow. 5. 13 Repton Street, Limehouse. 6. 141 Sidney Street, Whitechapel. 7. 144 White Horse Street (White Horse Road), Stepney, address also 154 White Horse Road.

Plough Street, Off Buckle Street, Whitechapel, 1950, Whitechapel High Street.

Plough Wharf, Olliffe Street, Isle of Dogs, 1895, became part of Millwall Wharf.

Plover Street, Off Gainsborough Road (Eastway), Hackney, 1891.

Plumbers Arms Public House, 55 Columbia Road, Bethnal Green.

Plumbers or Plummers Buildings, Wilmot Street, Bethnal Green, "at the south end of it behind the Lamb public house" (Lockie).

Plumbers Row Synagogue, Plumbers Row, Whitechapel, 1945.

Plume of Feathers Public House, 24 Lower Shadwell (Shadwell Park), Shadwell, 1874.

Plymm Cottage, Lefevre Terrace (Lefevre Walk), Bromley and Bow, 1891, Lefevre Road.

Plymouth Wharf, Saunders Ness Road, Isle of Dogs, 1950, present-day street, named Pyrimont Wharf, is on its site.

Pole Street, Off Redmans Road, Mile End, 1950, Redmans Road to Stepney Way.

Pollards Place, Bethnal Green Road, Bethnal Green, 1827, renamed Pollard Row.

Poltava Synagogue, 10 Spital Street, Spitalfields.

Pond Cottage(s), Hackney Road, Bethnal Green, 1841.

Pool(e)s Square & Place, Quaker Street, Spitalfields, 1891, Wheler House was built on the site.

Poole Villa, The Grove (Reading Lane), Hackney, 1891, Mare Street.

Poonah Street, Shadwell, 1891, Hardinge Street to Johnson Street, immediately north of railway line.

Popes Head Alley, Broad Street (The Highway), Ratcliffe, 1746.

Popes Head Court, Quaker Street, Spitalfields, 1891, "about four doors on right from 29 Wheler Street" (Lockie), Wheler House was built on the site.

Popes Hill, Shadwell High Street (The Highway), Shadwell, "at the fourth on right east from the church leading to Shadwell Water Works" (Lockie) Shadwell Park is on the site.

Poplar & Blackwall Free British School, Poplar, 1870, renamed Woolmore Street School.

Poplar & Blackwall National School, Poplar High Street, Poplar, built on part of site of Poplar Workhouse.

Poplar & Blackwall School of Trade & Navigation, 135-151 East India Dock Road, Poplar.

Poplar & Stepney Sick Asylum, Devons Road, Bromley and Bow, 1891.

Poplar Board of Works, 117 Poplar High Street, Poplar, 1891.

Poplar Brewery, 151 Poplar High Street, Poplar.

Poplar Charity School, Poplar High Street, Poplar, "by the Town hall about 1/3 of a mile on the right from the Commercial Road" (Lockie).

Poplar Dispensary for the Prevention of Consumption, 135 Bow Road, Bromley and Bow, 1921.

Poplar Gas Works, Leven Road, Poplar.

Poplar Gut, Isle of Dogs, a large inland stretch of water in the north west of the Isle of Dogs, caused by a breach of the river wall in 1660. The City Canal and later West India Docks were constructed at its location.

Poplar Hospital for Accidents, 303-315 East India Dock Road, Poplar, 1855-1975.

Poplar House Academy, 119-123 Poplar High Street, Poplar, 1820.

Poplar Institution, 100 Poplar High Street, Poplar, alternative name for Poplar Workhouse.

Poplar Manor House, 152 East India Dock Road, Poplar, 1750, Demolished in 1935.

Poplar Marine Hospital, Poplar High Street, Poplar, 1858, in part of former East India Companys Almshouses.

Poplar Methodist Mission, East India Dock Road, Poplar, 1975, corner of Woodstock Road, former Wesleyan Church.

Poplar Pavilion Cinema, 192-200 East India Dock Road, Poplar, 1920, site of later Ladbroke Social Club.

Poplar Presbyterian Church, Plimsoll Street (Plimsoll Close), Poplar, 1901-1913, East India Dock Road.

Poplar Public Baths & Laundry, East India Dock Road, Poplar, 1890.

Poplar Public Health Department, 157 Bow Road, Bromley and Bow, 1921.

Poplar Railway Station,

Brunswick Street (Aspen Way), Poplar, 1840-1926.

Poplar Railway Station, East India Dock Road, Poplar, Poplar All Saints DLR station is on the site.

Poplar Sailors Home, Manchester Road, Isle of Dogs, 1854, behind houses in Glen Terrace.

Poplar Synagogue, East India Dock Road, Poplar, 1923-1948, First at 239 East India Dock Road, then Bow Lane in the former Bow Lane School, later Bazely Street.

Poplar Terrace, 126 Poplar High Street, Poplar, 1851, near to 126 Poplar High Street.

Poplar Town Hall, Newby Place, Poplar, 1824, Poplar High Street.

Poplar Union Infirmary, Upper North Street, Poplar, 1891, East India Dock Road.

Poplar Union Receiving Home, 54 East India Dock Road, Limehouse.

Poplar Union Workhouse, 100 Poplar High Street, Poplar.

Poplar Workhouse, 100 Poplar High Street, Poplar.

Portabella Public House, 52 Turville Street, Bethnal Green.

Porters Court, Old Montague Street, Whitechapel, "the second on the left a few doors from Osborn Street" (Lockie).

Portia Road, Off Eric Street, Bromley and Bow, Eric Street to Wager Street.

Portland Place, 1. Cambridge Road (Cambridge Heath Road), Bethnal Green, 1851. 2. Commercial Road, Stepney, 1868, Grosvenor Street to Portland Street. 3. White Street (Vallance Road), Bethnal Green, 1851.

Portland Street, Off Commercial Road, Stepney, 1891, renamed Westport Street.

Portland Terrace, Victoria Road (Brougham Road), Hackney, 1862, close to its corner with Shrubland Road.

Portman Terrace, Allas Road (Portman Place), Bethnal Green, became part of Allas Road, north of Portman Place.

Portswood Place, Dunbridge Street, Bethnal Green, Weavers Fields is on the site.

Portugal Place, Cambridge Road (Cambridge Heath Road), Bethnal Green, 1851.

Potters Dwellings, Limehouse Causeway, Limehouse, 1950, between Three Colt Street and Gill Street.

Potters Row, 1. Prospect Place (Cambridge Heath Road), Bethnal Green, 1841. 2. Russia Lane, Bethnal Green, 1827, renamed Mowlem Street.

Powder House Fields, Brunton Place, Stepney, 1851.

Powells or Powers Place, Hackney Road, Bethnal Green, 1851.

Powis Road, Off Westferry Road, Isle of Dogs, 1891, was south of Claude Street, renamed Cyclops Place.

Pownall Terrace, Pownall Road, Hackney, 1862.

Pratts Alley, Little North Street (Brady Street), Whitechapel.

Pratts Buildings, New Gravel Lane (Garnet Street), Wapping, "at 76 a few doors on the right from 22 High Street Shadwell" (Lockie).

Premierland Cinematograph Theatre, Back Church Lane, St. George in the East.

Prescot Place, Little Prescot Street (Prescot Street), Whitechapel, 1851.

Prescot Street Synagogue, Prescot Street, Whitechapel, 1870.

Prestage Street, Off Brunswick Street, Poplar, 1891, Prestage Way is on the site.

Preston New Road, Off New Road (Prestons Road), Poplar, 1862, combined with New Road to form Prestons Road.

Preston Street, Off Spital Street, Spitalfields, became part of Hanbury Street, the section between Spital Street and Greatorex Street.

Preston Street & Terrace, Green Street (Roman Road),

Bethnal Green, 1851, Roman Road to Meath Gardens.

Prevots Row, Old Ford Road, Bromley and Bow, 1851.

Pride of Stepney Public House, 269 Stepney Way, Mile End, aka Clare Hall.

Pride of the Isle Public House, 20 Havannah Street, Isle of Dogs, 1874.

Pride Road, Off Greenwood Road, Hackney, 1868, renamed Fassett Road.

Primrose Cottages, Green Street (Roman Road), Bethnal Green, 1851.

Primrose Street, Off Three Colts Lane, Bethnal Green, 1841, renamed Allenbury Street.

Prince Albert Public House, 1. 21 Brushfield Street, Spitalfields, 1874. 2. 83 Clark Street, Stepney. 3. 6 Lincoln Street (Brokesley Street), Bromley and Bow, 1874, now Brokesley St. 4. 2 Mape Street, Bethnal Green, 1874. 5. 61 Old Ford Road, Bromley and Bow. 6. 58 Orchard Place, Poplar. 7. 221 Queens Road (Queensbridge Road), Hackney.

Prince Alfred Public House, 1. 86 Cotton Street, Poplar, 1874, address also 86 Locksley Street. 2. 46 Eleanor Road, Hackney, 1874. 3. 86 Locksley Street, Limehouse. 4. 7 Poplar High Street, Poplar. 5. 22 Tobago Street, Isle of Dogs.

Prince Arthur Avenue, St. Stephens Road, Bromley and Bow, 1891.

Prince Arthur Public House, 1. 55 Brunswick Road, Poplar, 1874. 2. 150 Turners Road, Bromley and Bow, 1874.

Prince Earnest Public House, Clarissa Street, Hackney, 1950.

Prince Edward Public House, 97 Wick Road, Hackney.

Prince Edward Road, Off Victoria Road (Wick Road), Hackney, 1891.

Prince George Public House, 40 Parkholme Road, Hackney.

Prince Leopold Public House, 39 Ford Street, Bromley and Bow.

Prince of Denmark Public House, 1 Graces Alley, St. George in the East, 1874, Wellclose Square.

Prince of Hesse Public House, 30 Fieldgate Street, Whitechapel, 1874, aka Prince of Wales.

Prince of Orange Court, Philip Street (Ellen Street), St. George in the East, 1891.

Prince of Orange Public House, 16 Fieldgate Street, Whitechapel.

Prince of Orange Public House, 1. 25 Philip Street (Ellen Street), St. George in the East, 1874. 2. 4 Bruges Terrace (Harford Street), Mile End, 1874, aka King Albert, address also 126 Harford Street.

Prince of Prussia Public House, 1. Gowers Walk, Whitechapel,

1874, address also 93 Middlesex Street. 2. 2 Grove Road, Bromley and Bow, aka Prince of Wales. 3. 93 Middlesex Street, Spitalfields, 1874, address also Gowers Walk. 4. 24 Arbour Street, Stepney. 5. 64 Back Church Lane, St. George in the East. 6. 59 Barnet Grove, Bethnal Green. 7. 76 Bishops Road (Bishops Way), Bethnal Green. 8. 66 Buxton Street, Whitechapel, address also 35 Buxton Street. 9. 6 Chrisp Street, Poplar. 10. 36 Church Lane (Commercial Road), St. George in the East, Church Lane now part of Commercial Road. 11. Church Street (Mare Street), Hackney, 1874. 12. 108 Duckett Street, Mile End, aka British Flag, address also 14 Waley Street. 13. 30 Fieldgate Street, Whitechapel, 1874, aka Prince of Hesse. 14. 2 Folly Wall, Isle of Dogs, 1874. 15. 124 Globe Road, Whitechapel. 16. 24 Gloucester Place (Cambridge Heath Road), Bethnal Green. 17. 102 Grafton Street (Grantley Street), Mile End, 1874, address also Grantley Street. 18. Grange Road (Gayhurst Road), Hackney, 1851, Kingsland Road. 19. 61 Great Hermitage Street (Hermitage Wall), Wapping, address also 71 Great Hermitage Street. 20. 29 Great Pearl Street (Calvin Street), Spitalfields. 21. 2 Grove Road, Bromley and Bow, aka Prince of Prussia. 22. 447 Kingsland Road, Hackney. 23. 57 Lenthall Road, Hackney. 24.

85 Maroon Street, Limehouse. 25. 28 Naval Row, Poplar, 1874. 26. 49 New Road, Whitechapel. 27. 52 Old Nichol(s) Street (Boundary Estate), Bethnal Green. 28. 26 Preston Street (Roman Road), Bethnal Green. 29. Princes Street (Raine Street), Wapping, 1874, address also 61 Great Hermitage Street. 30. Regent Street (Maplin Street), Mile End, 1874. 31. 28 Sheep Lane, Hackney. 32. 137 Solebay Street, Bromley and Bow. 33. 163 St. Leonards Road, Poplar. 34. 26 St. Thomas Road, Mile End. 35. 10 Turville Street, Bethnal Green. 36. 155 Upper North Street, Poplar. 37. 37 Wickford Street, Mile End.

Prince Patrick Place, Westferry Road, Isle of Dogs, 1851, opposite Maria Street.

Prince Regent Public House, 1. 105 Globe Road, Whitechapel, 1874. 2. 81 Salmon Lane, Limehouse, 1874. 3. 8 St. George Street (The Highway), St. George in the East, 1874.

Princes (or Princess) Street, Off Tyson Street (Brick Lane), Bethnal Green, "the second on the right about sixteen doors from opposite Brick Lane" (Lockie).

Princes Court, 1. Brick Lane, Bethnal Green, 1891. 2. Princes Street (Padbury Court), Bethnal Green, "the first on the right a few yards from Virginia Street behind Shoreditch Church"

(Lockie), renamed Padbury Court. 3. Princes Street (Raine Street), Wapping, became part of Choppins Court. 4. Tyssen Street, Bethnal Green, 1851.

Princes Place, 1. Commercial Road, St. George in the East, 1860, from Amberston Street to Cannon Street Road. 2. Gosset Street, Bethnal Green, 1891, renamed Fountain Street. 3. New Road, Whitechapel, "a few doors on the left from Cable Street and nearly opposite the entrance to Princes Square" (Lockie). 4. Nightingale Lane (Thomas More Street), Wapping, 1891.

Princes Row, Whitechapel, 1830, renamed Princes Street (Old Montague Street).

Princes Schools, Princes Place (Columbia Road), Bethnal Green, 1868.

Princes Square, Cable Street, St. George in the East, 1891, renamed Swedenborg Square.

Princes Square British School, Princes Square (Swedenborg Square), St. George in the East.

Princes Street, 1. Off Brick Lane, Spitalfields, 1916, "Brick Lane, opposite Booth Street or 50 in the said lane it extends to Wood Street" (Lockie), renamed Princelet Street. 2. Off Lee Street, Hackney, 1868, renamed Clarissa Street. 3. Off Old Gravel Lane (Wapping Lane), Wapping, 1891, renamed Raine Street. 4. Off Oxford Street (Stepney

Way), Whitechapel, renamed Silver Street. 5. Bethnal Green, renamed Padbury Court. 6. Off Princes Square (Swedenborg Square), St. George in the East, renamed Swedenborg Street. 7. Off Stepney Green, Stepney, 1891, Tinsely Road crosses its route. 8. Off Virginia Street, Bethnal Green, "the first on the left a few doors from the Birdcage towards Shoreditch Church" (Lockie), renamed Chambord Street. 9. Off Wapping High Street, Wapping, became part of Redmead Lane.

Princes Street Synagogue, 18 Princes Street (Princelet Street), Whitechapel.

Princes Terrace, Bethnal Green, renamed Bonner Road.

Princess (or Princes) Street, Off Tyson Street (Brick Lane), Bethnal Green, "the second on the right about sixteen doors from opposite Brick Lane" (Lockie).

Princess Alexandra Public House, 69 Salmon Lane, Limehouse.

Princess Alice Public House, 1. 9 Allas Road (Portman Place), Bethnal Green, Portman Place. 2. 40 Commercial Street, Whitechapel, 1874. 3. 129 St. Stephens Road, Bromley and Bow.

Princess Mary Public House, 67 Kerbey Street, Poplar.

Princess of Prussia Public House, 15 Great Prescot Street (Prescot Street), Whitechapel.

Princess of Wales Public House, 1. 110 Brady Street, Whitechapel, Collingwood Estate is now on the site. 2. 17 Copley Street, Stepney. 3. 144-146 Grundy Street, Poplar. 4. 84 Manchester Road, Isle of Dogs, 1874, corner of Barque Street. 5. 1 Well Street (Ensign Street), St. George in the East.

Princess Royal Public House, 1. 365 Cable Street, Shadwell, address also 58 Lucas (now Lukin) Street. 2. 30 Johnson Street, Wapping, 1874. 3. 33 Sidney Square, Whitechapel, 1874. 4. 30 Treadway Street, Bethnal Green.

Princess Street, Off Old Montague Street, Whitechapel, became the easternmost end of Old Montague Street, Greatorex Street to Vallance Road.

Priory Place, Well Street, Hackney, 1895, Frampton Park Estate is on the site.

Priory Tavern Public House, 37 St. Leonards Street, Bromley and Bow, 1874.

Priory Terrace, Victoria Road (Brougham Road), Hackney, 1862, close to its corner with Shrubland Road.

Priscilla Road, Off Bow Road, Bromley and Bow, 1891, east of Bow Church tube station.

Pritchards Arms Public House, 439 Hackney Road, Bethnal Green.

Prospect Cottages & Terrace, West Street (Usk Street), Bethnal Green.

Prospect Place, 1. Bishops Road (Bishops Way), Bethnal Green, 1851. 2. Bow Common Lane, Bromley and Bow, 1851. 3. Cable Street, St. George in the East, renamed Library Place St. George in the East directly north of the church. 4. Cambridge Road (Cambridge Heath Road), Bethnal Green. 5. Devons Lane (Devons Road), Bromley and Bow, 1851. 6. Eastfield Street, Limehouse, renamed Eastfield Cottages. 7. King Street (Ming Street), Limehouse, 1851. 8. Morpeth Street, Bethnal Green, 1851. 9. Queens Road (Queensbridge Road), Hackney, 1851, opposite Brownlow Road. 10. Salmon Lane, Limehouse, 1851. 11. Tooke Street (Westferry Road), Isle of Dogs.

Prospect Place or Row, Kingsland Road, Hackney, 1827, north of its corner with Middleton Road.

Prospect Place or Terrace, 116-126 East India Dock Road, Poplar, 1851.

Prospect Row, 1. Cambridge Road (Cambridge Heath Road), Bethnal Green, corner of Cambridge Road and Russia Lane. 2. Prospect Row or Place, Mile End Road, Mile End,

"forms part of the north side opposite Ewings Buildings near two miles from Aldgate" (Lockie), close to Guardian Angels Church.

Prospect Terrace, Usk Street, Bethnal Green, renamed Prospect Walk was north of Meath Gardens.

Prospect Walk, Usk Street, Bethnal Green, 1950.

Protestant Dissenters (or Dissenting) Charity School, Wood Street (Wilkes Street), Spitalfields.

Providence (Row) Night Refuge, 50 Crispin Street, Spitalfields.

Providence Chapel, Paragon Road, Hackney, 1868.

Providence Cottages, Bridge Road (Westferry Road), Limehouse, later Westferry Road, site of later Providence House.

Providence Court or Place, Back Church Lane, St. George in the East, 1851, north end and west side of Back Church Lane.

Providence House, Emmett Street, Limehouse, Westferry Road.

Providence Place, 1. Austin Street, Bethnal Green, 1851. 2. Bath Street (Darling Row), Whitechapel. 3. Blue Anchor Lane (Cable Street), Ratcliffe, 1841. 4. Burdett Road, Bromley and Bow, Burdett Road to Regents Canal, just south of Mile

End Road. 5. Cotton Street, Poplar, parallel with and east of northernmost part of Cotton Street. 6. Duke Street (Ducal Street), Bethnal Green, 1851. 7. Halley Street, Limehouse. 8. Limehouse Causeway, Limehouse, 1851, renamed Holker Place. 9. Morning Lane, Hackney, 1841, renamed Meeting Field Path. 10. Petticoat Lane (Middlesex Street), Spitalfields, "opposite Horse shoe Alley, about $1/8$ of a mile on the left from Aldgate High Street" (Lockie). 11. Bethnal Green, renamed Poulton Street (Russia Lane). 12. Ravenscroft Street, Bethnal Green, 1851. 13. Russia Lane, Bethnal Green, 1891. 14. Shipton Street, Bethnal Green, renamed Ezra Street. 15. Stepney Causeway, Ratcliffe, 1851. 16. Westferry Road, Isle of Dogs, 1868, between Robert Street and George Street.

Providence Row, 1. Cambridge Heath Road, Bethnal Green. 2. Duke Street (Ducal Street), Bethnal Green, "the second on the right a few doors from the middle of Gibraltar Row towards Turk Street" (Lockie). 3. Grove Street (Ellsworth Street), Bethnal Green, 1841. 4. Grove Street (Lauriston Road), Hackney, 1841, close to present-day Victoria Park Road. 5. Old Ford Road, Bromley and Bow, 1851.

Providence Street, 1. Off Bishops Road (Bishops Way), Bethnal Green, 1851. 2. Off Ellen Street, St. George in the East, 1891.

Providence Terrace, Wick Road, Hackney, 1862.

Prusoms Island, Wapping, 1851, (Hilliards Court follows some of its path.

Prussian Eagle Tavern Public House, 19 Ship Alley (Wellclose Square), St. George in the East.

Pughs Place & Row, Heneage Street, Whitechapel, 1851, easternmost end of Heneage Street.

Pullens Buildings or Court, Patience Street (Wheler Street), Spitalfields, 1851.

Pullens Passage, Collingwood Street, Whitechapel, 1841.

Pump Yard, Queen Street (Horseferry Road), Ratcliffe, 1850, part of west end of Queen Street.

Pundersons Place, Bethnal Green Road, Bethnal Green, "Bethnal Green Road, forms part of the north side near the green" (Lockie).

Purcell Place, Well Street, Hackney, 1895, Frampton Park Estate is on the site.

Purcers Court, Booth Street (Princelet Street), Whitechapel, 1851.

Purim Place, Dog Row (Cambridge Heath Road), Whitechapel, "part of the right side a few doors from Mile End turnpike towards the said green" (Lockie).

Pykes Buildings, Bird Cage Walk (Columbia Road), Bethnal Green, 1851.

Pyrimont Wharf, Saunders Ness Road, Isle of Dogs, 1950, present-day street, also named Pyrimont Wharf, is on its site.

Q

Quaker Street National School, 41a Quaker Street, Spitalfields.

Quakers or Friends Burial Ground, Charles Street (Vallance Road), Whitechapel, 1820, Vallance Gardens are on the site.

Quay (or Quag) Lane, East India Dock Road, Poplar, renamed Brunswick Road.

Quebec Buildings, Prestons Road, Poplar, 1900.

Queen Adelaide Public House, 1. 481-483 Hackney Road, Bethnal Green, 1874. 2. 27 King Edward Street (Kingward Street), Whitechapel, address also 16 King Edward Street.

Queen Adelaides Dispensary, 41-45 Pollard Row, Bethnal Green, 1950.

Queen Ann Street, Off Ducking Pond Row (Durward Street), Whitechapel, "is opposite Court Street entering by 110 Whitechapel Road nearly facing the London Hospital" (Lockie).

Queen Anne Street, Whitechapel, renamed Wodeham Street (Wodeham Gardens).

Queen Caroline Gardens, Seabright Street, Bethnal Green, 1891.

Queen Caroline Place, Pritchards Road, Bethnal Green, 1851.

Queen Catherine Court, Brook Street (Cable Street), Ratcliffe, "at 23 a few doors on the right from Butcher Row towards Stepney Causeway" (Lockie), east of Pitsea Street.

Queen Catherine Public House, 119 Brook Street (Cable Street), Ratcliffe, 1874.

Queen Eleanor Public House, 19 Tower Street (Martello Street), Hackney.

Queen Elizabeth Hospital for Children, 1. Glamis Road, Shadwell, 1868-1963, Glamis Road. 2. 321-335 Hackney Road, Bethnal Green.

Queen Elizabeth Public House, 9 Graham Road, Hackney, 1874.

Queen of England Public House, 87 Well Street, Hackney.

Queen Place, Whitechapel High Street, Whitechapel.

Queen Public House, 1. 571 Manchester Road, Isle of Dogs, 1874, aka Queen of the Isle. 2. 128 Rhodeswell Road, Limehouse.

Queen Stairs, Ratcliffe Cross (Narrow Street), Ratcliffe, 1746.

Queen Street, 1. Off Broad Street (The Highway), Ratcliffe, "the east continuation of Broad Street extending from Ratcliffe Cross towards Limehouse" (Lockie), renamed Medland Street. 2. Off Cambridge Road (Cambridge Heath Road), Mile End, 1891, renamed Doveton Street. 3. Off Chrisp Street, Poplar, renamed Cording Street. 4. Off Green Street (Stepney Way), Mile End, 1862, Green Street to Smith Street, became part of Exmouth Street. 5. Off Hanbury Street, Spitalfields, 1950, north of King Street, with which it combined, the resulting road was later renamed Rowland Street. 6. Off Hassard Street, Bethnal Green, 1891, renamed Arline Street. 7. Off Poplar High Street, Poplar, renamed Bickmore Street. 8. Off Prusom Street, Wapping, 1891, renamed Clegg Street. 9. Off Quaker Street, Spitalfields, "the first on the right a few yards from 173 Brick Lane extending to Phoenix Street" (Lockie), renamed Sheba Street. 10. Off Rowland Street (Hanbury Street), Spitalfields, renamed Rowland Street. 11. Off Royal Mint Street, East Smithfield, 1870, Royal Mint Street to Little Tower Hill, 40 Tower Hill is on the site. 12. Off Seabright Street, Bethnal Green, 1851, renamed Weldon Street.

Queen Street Independent Church, Queen Street (Horseferry Road), Ratcliffe, 1868, later Medland Congregation Hall and Mission (and free shelter).

Queen Terrace, Old Ford Road, Bromley and Bow.

Queen Victoria Public House, 1. 1 Barnet Grove, Bethnal Green. 2. 184 Devons Road, Bromley and Bow. 3. 96 Exmouth Street, Stepney. 4. 151 Globe Road, Bethnal Green. 5. 31 Medland Street (Horseferry Road), Ratcliffe, 1874, address also 31 Queen Street. 6. 3 Old Gravel Lane (Wapping Lane), Wapping. 7. 179 St. Leonards Street, Bromley and Bow, 1874.

Queens Arms Public House, 1. 73 Belgrave Street, Stepney. 2. 288 Hackney Road, Bethnal Green. 3. 202 Mile End Road, Mile End. 4. 275-279 Poplar High Street, Poplar, 1874, aka Angel. 5. 161 Shadwell High Street (The Highway), Shadwell. 6. 32 Wapping High Street, Wapping, aka Crown & Queens Arms. 7. Wentworth Street, Spitalfields.

Queens Buildings, 1. Chambord Street, Bethnal Green, 1891. 2. Princes Place (Columbia Road), Bethnal Green, 1891.

Queens Cottages, Cleveland Street (Cleveland Way), Mile End, 1891.

Queens Court, 1. King Street (Christian Street), St. George in the East, 1851, "Commercial Road, at 12 a few doors from the said road extending to 13 Batty Street" (Lockie). 2. Well Street, Hackney, 1851, opposite Balcorne Street.

Queens Head Alley, Green Bank, Wapping, "at 122 near $1/8$ of a mile on the left below the church extending to Green bank" (Lockie).

Queens Head Court, Charlotte Street (Fieldgate Street), Whitechapel, 1851.

Queens Head Public House, 1. 113 Broad Street (The Highway), Ratcliffe. 2. 98 Cambridge Heath Road, Mile End, 1874. 3. 74 Commercial Street, Spitalfields. 4. Fashion Street, Spitalfields, 1874. 5. 83 Fieldgate Street, Whitechapel. 6. 57 Greatorex Street, Whitechapel. 7. King Street (Gossett Street), Bethnal Green, 1874, 18 Gossett Street. 8. 14 Medland Street (Horseferry Road), Ratcliffe, address also 491 The Highway. 15. 10 Pedley Street, Whitechapel. 16. 95 Poplar High Street, Poplar. 17. Pump Yard (Horseferry Road), Ratcliffe, 1874. 18. 24 Queen Street (Dorset Estate), Bethnal Green. 19. Rhodeswell Road, Limehouse, 1851. 20. Wapping High Street, Wapping, 1874. 21. 317 Whitechapel Road, Whitechapel, 1874. 22. 8 York Street (Commercial Road), Limehouse.

Queens Hotel & Public House, 274 Victoria Park Road, Hackney.

Queens Landing Public House, 5 Wapping Wall, Wapping.

Queens Place, 1. King Street (Hackney Road), Bethnal Green, 1841, Hackney Road, immediately north of St. Thomas Church. 2. Silver Lion Court (Pennyfields), Poplar, 1851. 3. St. George in the East, renamed Stutfield Place (Stutfield Street).

Queens Place & Terrace, Manchester Road, Isle of Dogs, 1862, south of the Queen Public House.

Queens Road, Hackney, renamed Queensbridge Road.

Queens Row, 1. Cambridge Road (Cambridge Heath Road), Mile End, between railway line and Queen Street. 2. Queens Road (Queensbridge Road), Hackney, 1862, south of Forest Row.

Queens Street, Off London Street (Bekesbourne Street), Ratcliffe, 1851.

Queens Terrace, 1. Commercial Road, Limehouse, 1871. 2. Old Ford Road, Bromley and Bow.

Queens Theatre, 275-279 Poplar High Street, Poplar.

Queens Wharf, Wapping Wall, Wapping, 1859, absorbed into Metropolitan Wharf.

Queensbridge Road Baptist Chapel, Queensbridge Road, Hackney, 1895, north of Pownall Road, building later occupied by the Essence Distillery.

Quickett(s) Street, Off Arnold Road, Bromley and Bow, 1891.

Quinn Square, Russia Lane, Bethnal Green, 1950, part became Quinn Close.

Quinns Buildings, Russia Lane, Bethnal Green, 1891.

R

Raccoon Beer House Public House, 392 Kingsland Road, Hackney.

Rachels or Rachaels Court, Whitechapel, renamed Seven Stars Court (Royal Mint Street).

Radish Row, Red Maid Lane (Redmead Lane), Wapping, 1790, Red Maid Lane to Artichoke Lane.

Radnor Terrace, Brownlow Road, Hackney, 1862.

Rahns Court & Place, Back Church Lane, St. George in the East, 1891, east side of Back Church Lane, halfway between Ellen Street and railway.

Railway Arms Public House, 1. 95 Anthony Street, St. George in the East. 2. 421 Old Ford Road, Bromley and Bow. 3. 60 Sutton Street, Shadwell.

Railway Buildings, Poplar, renamed Stocks Place.

Railway Crescent, Hackney, renamed Chapman Road.

Railway Hotel & Public House, 30 Grove Road, Bromley and Bow, 1874.

Railway Place, 1. Bethnal Green, renamed Malcolm Place. 2. Wilkes Street, Spitalfields. 3, York Road, Limehouse, 1891, close to Chasely Street. 4. Limehouse, renamed Yorkshire Place.

Railway Street, 1. Limehouse, 1891, renamed Hay Currie Street. 2. Off Willis Street, Poplar, 1891.

Railway Tap Public House, 1. 95 Anthony Street, St. George in the East, aka Railway Arms. 2. 150 Cambridge Road (Cambridge Heath Road), Bethnal Green.

Railway Tavern Public House, 1. 154 Wapping High Street, Wapping, aka Royal Oak. 2. Brunswick Wharf (Jamestown Way), Poplar. 3. 50 Cadogan Terrace, Hackney. 4. 576-578 Commercial Road, Ratcliffe, 1874. 5. 11 Dalston Lane, Hackney. 6. 131 Globe Road, Bethnal Green. 7. 393 Old Ford Road, Bromley and Bow. 8. 179 Poplar High Street, Poplar, 1874, aka Green Dragon. 9. 6 Three Colt Street, Limehouse. 10. West India Dock Road, Limehouse, corner of Garford Street more commonly known as Charlie Browns. 11. 7 Willis Street, Poplar.

Rainbow Public House, 18 Medland Street (Horseferry Road), Ratcliffe, 1874, address also 404 The Highway.

Raines Charity School, Charles Street (Wapping Lane), Wapping, Old Gravel Lane.

Raines Girls School, 92 Cannon Street Road, St. George in the East, 1895.

Raines Hospital, Charles Street (Wapping Lane), Wapping, "facing the east end of Charles Street from 46 Old Gravel Lane" (Lockie).

Ram & Magpie Public House, 17 Pedley Street, Whitechapel, 1874.

Ram Alley, Spicer Street (Buxton Street), Whitechapel, "the third on the left from 83 Brick Lane and nearly opposite Spital Street" (Lockie).

Ram Place, Chatham Place, Hackney, 1891, renamed Ram Place.

Rama Ramar or Ramah Place, Heneage Street, Whitechapel, 1851.

Rams Episcopal Chapel Boys School, Retreat Place, Hackney, 1868.

Ramsgate Pink Public House, Cold Harbour, Poplar, 1722, an early name of the Gun public house.

Rances Court, Shakespeare(s) Walk (Shadwell Basin), Shadwell, "is at Lower Turning behind Shakespeares Walk" (Elmes).

Randall Street, Off Upper North Street, Poplar, Upper North Street to East India Dock Road, named after its developer Onesiphorus Randall, renamed Augusta Street.

Randall Terrace, East India Dock Road, Poplar, 1851.

Randalls Buildings, Canton Street, Limehouse, 1890, Canton Street to Pekin Street.

Randalls Market, Grundy Street, Poplar, 1891, Grundy Street to Market Street, named after its developer Onesiphorus Randall.

Ranelagh Arms Public House, 279 Roman Road, Bethnal Green, 1874.

Ranwell Street, Off Old Ford Road, Bromley and Bow, 1891, Ranwell Close is on the site.

Rap(p)ley Place, New Tyssen Street (Satchwell Road), Bethnal Green, 1950, North of New Tyssen Street.

Ratcliffe Baths, Betts Street, St. George in the East, 1895, St. Georges Baths are on the site.

Ratcliffe Street, Off St. George Street (The Highway), St. George in the East, 1890, south of the church.

Ratcliffe Cross, Narrow Street, Ratcliffe, at the westernmost end, Ratcliffe Cross Stairs are on the site.

Ratcliffe Cross Wharf, The Highway, Ratcliffe, 1950, west of Ratcliffe Cross Stairs.

Ratcliffe Dock, Ratcliffe Cross Stairs (Narrow Street), Ratcliffe, "on the west side of Ratcliffe Cross stairs and on the east side of Mr Whitings Wharf" (Lockie).

Ratcliffe Highway, The Highway, St. George in the East, "the east continuation of Parsons Street and Upper East Smithfield commencing near the south east corner of Wellclose Square, where the numbers begin and end, viz 1 and 198 it extends to Shadwell High Street about ⅓ of a mile in length" (Lockie), later part of westmost section of The Highway - Ratcliff Highway had different names for each of its sections. From west to east these ran: St. George Street, High Street (Shadwell), Cock (or Cook) Hill, and Broad Street.

Ratcliffe Highway Refuge, Betts Street, St. George in the East, 1895.

Ratcliffe or Radcliffe Court, Bethnal Green, "Johns Row, St. Lukes, the first on the left from the north end of Brick Lane, entering by 113 Old Street" (Lockie).

Ratcliffe Square, Commercial Road, Stepney, 1917, "between White Horse Street and Stepney Causeway, about 1¼ mile from Whitechapel Church" (Lockie) renamed Ratcliffe Cross Street.

Ratcliffe Street (West), Commercial Road, Ratcliffe, 1862, Commercial Road to Periwinkle Street, renamed Ratcliffe Square then Ratcliffe Cross Street.

Raven Row, Artillery Lane, Spitalfields, 1950, became part of Artillery Lane.

Raven Street, Off Oxford Street (Stepney Way), Whitechapel, 1891, renamed Bedford Street.

Raverley Street, Off Devons Road, Bromley and Bow, 1891.

Rawalpindi House, Mellish Street, Isle of Dogs, Westferry Road.

Rawsell Street, Off Bow Common Lane, Bromley and Bow.

Raymond Place or Street, Off Green Bank, Wapping, 1891, Green Bank to Watts Street.

Rayner Street, Off Loddiges Road, Hackney, 1950, Loddiges Road to Brenthouse Road.

Recreation Tavern Public House, 155 East India Dock Road, Poplar, corner of Kerbey Street.

Rectory Cottages, Bloomfield Street (Freshfield Avenue), Hackney, 1851.

Rectory House & Place, Bow Road, Bromley and Bow, 1851.

Rectory Road, Off Stepney Green, Stepney, 1891.

Red Cow Lane, Mile End Road, Mile End, Cleveland Way is on the site, "Mile End Road the first coach turning on the left ⅕ of a mile east of the turnpike leading to Dog Row" (Lockie).

Red Cow Public House, 1. 67 Mile End Road, Mile End, 1874, also known as the Old Red Cow. 2. 13 Old Castle Street, Bethnal Green, 1874.

Red Cross Public House, 1. 21 Hare Street (Cheshire Street), Whitechapel, 1874. 2. 10 Upper East Smithfield, East Smithfield.

Red Cross Street, Off Nightingale Lane (Thomas More Street), Wapping, 1746, south west to Pillory Lane, St. Katherine Dock is on its site.

Red Deer Public House, 393 Cambridge Road (Cambridge Heath Road), Bethnal Green, 1874.

Red Lion & Spread Eagle Court, Whitechapel High Street, Whitechapel.

Red Lion & Spread Eagle Public House, 94 Whitechapel High Street, Whitechapel, 1874.

Red Lion & Spread Eagle Yard, Whitechapel High Street, Whitechapel, 1851.

Red Lion Brewery, Lower East Smithfield (St. Katharines Way), East Smithfield, 1890.

Red Lion Court, 1. Commercial Street, Spitalfields, 1891. 2. George Street (Code Street), Whitechapel, "or Spitalfields nearly opposite Fleet Street about ten doors on the left north from Spicer Street" (Lockie). 3. George Street (Pedley Street), Whitechapel, "nearly opposite Fleet Street about ten doors on the left north from Spicer Street" (Lockie). 4. Poplar High Street, Poplar, also known as Old Commodore Court.

Red Lion Court, 1. Spitalfields, 1792, renamed Puma Court. 2. Red Lion Street (Reardon Street), Wapping, "the first on the left from 120 Wapping Street leading to Upper Well Alley" (Lockie).

Red Lion Court Almshouse, Commercial Street, Spitalfields.

Red Lion Inn, Whitechapel High Street, Whitechapel, "at 30, the corner of Red Lion Street" (Lockie).

Red Lion latterly the Old Red Lion Public House, 217 Whitechapel Road, Whitechapel, 1874.

Red Lion Place, Red Lion Street (Reardon Street), Wapping, 1851.

Red Lion Public House, 1. 24 Batty Street, St. George in the East, 1874. 2. 2 Black Lion Yard (Old Montague Street), Whitechapel, 1874, address also 7 or 8 Black Lion Yard. 3. 1 Breezers Hill, St. George in the East. 4. 488-490 Cable Street, Shadwell, 1874. 5. 31 Chamber Street, Whitechapel. 6. 92 Commercial Street, Spitalfields. 7. 228 Devonshire Street (Bancroft Road), Mile End. 8. 272 Globe Road, Bethnal Green. 9. Hunt Street (Hunton Street), Whitechapel, 1874. 10. 81 Kerbey Street, Poplar, aka Old

Red Lion. 11. Leman Street, Whitechapel, 1874, Leman Street previously named Red Lion Street. 12. 34 Old Gravel Lane (Wapping Lane), Wapping, 1874. 13. Pennington Street, St. George in the East, 1874, corner with St. George in the East, address also 60 St. George in the East. 14. 209 Poplar High Street, Poplar, aka Old Commodore. 15. 34 Spicer Street (Buxton Street), Whitechapel. 16. 196-197 St. George Street (The Highway), St. George in the East, 1874. 17. 79 Warner Place, Bethnal Green. 18. 30 Whitechapel High Street, Whitechapel, aka Old Red Lion. 19. 217 Whitechapel Road, Whitechapel, aka Old Red Lion.

Red Lion Street, 1. Off Anchor and Hope Alley (Reardon Path), Wapping, "at 120 the fourth on the left near $1/8$ of a mile below the church leading into Anchor and Hope Alley" (Lockie), that part of Red Lion (now Reardon) Street north of Green Bank. 2. Off Fashion Street, Spitalfields, "on the west side of the church being the fifth on both the right and the left from 69 Bishopsgate along Union Street and Paternoster Row" (Lockie), now that part of Commercial Street near Spitalfields Church. 3. Off Whitechapel High Street, Whitechapel, 1820, Whitechapel High Street to Great and Little Ayliffe Street, later part of Leman Street.

Red Lion Tavern Public House, 196 St. George Street (The Highway), St. George in the East.

Red Lion Yard, Leman Street, Whitechapel, 1851.

Red White & Blue Public House, 75 Northey Street, Limehouse.

Redmans Gardens, Redmans Road, Mile End, 1891, south of Mile End Distillery.

Redmans Row, Mile End Road, Mile End, "the continuation of Grove Place entering by the turnpike Mile End Road" (Lockie), renamed Redmans Road.

Redmead or Red Maid Lane, Great Hermitage Street (Hermitage Wall), Wapping, "on the north side of Great Hermitage Street by the wall of the London Docks" (Elmes), part of route is followed by Spirit Quay.

Reeves Place, Wheler Street, Spitalfields, 1851.

Reeves Street, Off Giraud Street, Poplar, became southern part of Giraud Street.

Refiners Arms Public House, 53 Buross Street, St. George in the East, 1874, Commercial Road.

Reform Place, Eastfield Street, Limehouse, 1851.

Reform Place & Square, Mount Street (Swanfield Street), Bethnal Green, 1891.

Regal Place, Old Montague Street, Whitechapel, 1891.

Regent Cottages Court & Place, Parnham Street, Limehouse, 1891.

Regent Dock Road, Off Westferry Road, Isle of Dogs, 1851, close to Byng Street.

Regent Place, 1. Henry Street (Carr Street), Stepney, 1851. 2. Maplin Street, Bromley and Bow, 1891, renamed Maplin Place.

Regent Street, 1. Off Blackwall (Gaselee Street), Poplar, 1885, renamed Gaselee Street. 2. Off Limehouse Causeway, Limehouse, 1851.

Regent Street East, Ratcliffe, 1891, renamed London Street (Bekesbourne Street).

Regent Street North, Leicester Street (Duthie Street), Poplar, Leicester Street to Ditchburn Street.

Regent Street South, Bromley and Bow, renamed Maplin Street.

Regent Tavern Public House, 1. 79 Coutts Road (Mile End Park), Bromley and Bow. 2. 29 Regent Street, Limehouse, 1874, address later 79 Coutts Road.

Regents Court, 1. Blossom Street, Spitalfields. 2. Lower East Smithfield (St. Katharines Way), East Smithfield, 1851.

Regents Court or Place, Shadwell, 1929, renamed Parnham Place (Cable Street).

Regents Road North & South, Coutts Road (Mile End Park), Bromley and Bow, combined to form Coutts Road.

Regents Terrace, Commercial Road, Limehouse, 1860, between York Road and Bruntons Place.

Reidy House, Carr Street, Limehouse, 1950, Limehouse Fields Estate.

Reindeer Public House, 1. 50 Old Gravel Lane (Wapping Lane), Wapping. 2. 59 Richard Street, St. George in the East, 1874.

Remus Passage, Bromley and Bow, renamed Remus Road.

Remus Road, Off Monier Road, Bromley and Bow, 1891.

Reno Street, Off Galt Street (Salmon Lane), Limehouse.

Rescue Home for Working Girls, 31 Mile End Road, Mile End, site of later Great Assembly Hall.

Resolute (Tavern) Public House, 210 Poplar High Street, Poplar, aka Harrow.

Retreat Almshouses Retreat Place, Hackney, 1841, aka Widows Retreat aka Robinsons Retreat.

Retreat Cottages, Retreat Place, Hackney, 1851, Water Lane.

Retreat Terrace, Arthur Street (Brooksbank Street), Hackney, 1851.

Reuben Street, Off Brady Street,

Whitechapel, 1891, Collingwood Estate is now on the site.

Rev W Stainers Home for Deaf & Dumb Children, 6 Victoria Park Square, Hackney.

Reverley Street, Off Devons Road, Bromley and Bow, south of Bruce Road.

Revival Refuge, Commercial Street, Whitechapel.

Reynolds Place, North Street (Saltwell Street), Poplar, 1891, later Saltwell Street accessed via Speedings Gardens.

Rhoda Villa, Gore Road, Hackney.

Rhodes Terrace, Queens Road (Queensbridge Road), Hackney, 1862, north of Richmond Road.

Rhodes Wells, Limehouse, "about ⅓ of a mile east from Stepney Church and near the same distance from Limehouse Church" (Lockie).

Rich Street Court, Gun Lane (Grenade Street), Limehouse, 1851.

Richard Cobden Public House, 34 Repton Street, Limehouse.

Richard Court, Richard Street, St. George in the East, 1891.

Richard Street, 1. Stepney, renamed Cayley Street (Whitehorse Road Park). 2. Off Grundy Street, Poplar, renamed Lodore Street. 3. Off Randalls Market (Ricardo Street), Poplar, renamed Ricardo Street. 4. Off Rippoth Road (Wyke Road),

Bromley and Bow, 1891, Wyke Road. 5. Off St. Leonards Road, Poplar, opposite Jollys Green.

Richard Villa, Wick Lane, Bromley and Bow, 1851, Wick Lane to Grove Street.

Richards Villas, Lavender Grove, Hackney, 1868, between Queens Road and Malvern Road.

Richardson Cottages, Green Street (Roman Road), Bethnal Green, 1851.

Richardson House, Clarissa Street, Hackney, 1950.

Richardson Street, 1. Off Lindley Street, Stepney, 1895, Lindley Street to Wolsey Street. 2. Off Oxford Street (Stepney Way), Whitechapel, 1891, renamed Winwood Street.

Richmond Place, Richmond Road, Hackney, 1851, renamed Forest Grove.

Richmond Terrace, Queens Road (Queensbridge Road), Hackney, 1841, south of Richmond Road.

Richmond Villas, 1. London Terrace (London Fields), Hackney, 1891. 2. Malvern Road, Hackney, 1868, between Lavender Grove and Albert Road.

Rickmans Rents, Ropemakers Fields, Limehouse, 1871.

Ride or Ryde, The, King David Lane, Shadwell, 1891.

Riders Buildings, Busby Square

(Busby Street), Bethnal Green, 1891.

Ridges Place, John Street, Bethnal Green, 1841.

Rippoth Road, Off Wyke Road, Bromley and Bow, was between Wyke Road and the canal.

Risbies Ropewalk, Narrow Street, Limehouse, "the first north parallel to part of Narrow Street entering by Tites Alley a few doors on the left below Mr Turners Wharf" (Lockie), also spelled Risbys Ropewalk, Northey Street follows much its route.

Riseholme Street, Off Cadogan Terrace, Hackney, 1891.

Rising Sun & Sword Public House, 31 Cable Street, St. George in the East, 1874, aka Sun & Sword.

Rising Sun Public House, 1. 1 Alma Road (Burdett Road), Bromley and Bow, corner of Eric Street, Burdett Road and Alma Road. 2. 248 Globe Road, Bethnal Green. 3. 152 Hackney Road, Bethnal Green, 1874. 4. 204 Morning Lane, Hackney. 5. 241 Poplar High Street, Poplar, 1874, address also 270 Poplar High Street, aka Exchange Tavern, aka Sun & Sawyers. 6. 12 Royal Mint Street, East Smithfield, address also Sharp(e)s Buildings. 7. 27 Sale Street, Bethnal Green, 1874. 8. 87 Sidney Street, Whitechapel,

1874. 9. 213 St. Leonards Street, Bromley and Bow.

River Street, Off Devons Road, Bromley and Bow, 1891, renamed Maddams Street.

Rix Court, Ellen Street, St. George in the East, 1891, close to corner with Back Church Lane.

Roan Horse Public House, 1 Pollard Street, Bethnal Green.

Roan Horse Yard, Pollard Street, Bethnal Green, 1921.

Robarts Arms Public House, 1 Devonport Street, Shadwell, 1874.

Robert Burns Public House, 248-250 Westferry Road, Isle of Dogs.

Robert Street, 1. Off King Street (Roberta Street), Bethnal Green, 1841, renamed Roberta Street. 2. Off Mandarin Street (West India Dock Road), Limehouse, renamed Mandarin Street. 3. Off Sidney Street, Whitechapel, renamed Wolsey Street. 4. Off St. Pauls Road (St. Pauls Way), Bromley and Bow, renamed Robeson Street. 5. Off Westferry Road, Isle of Dogs, renamed Cuba Street. 6. Commercial Road, Whitechapel, "Mile End Old Town, the third on the right a few doors from Cannon Street Road towards Whitechapel" (Lockie).

Roberts Place, 1. Wades Place, Poplar, "the second on the right from op the green man public house near ⅓ of a mile from the

Commercial Road" (Lockie). 2. Commercial Road, St. George in the East, "the third on the right, a few doors from Cannon Street Road towards Whitechapel" (Lockie).

Robin Hood Public House, 1. 55 Cheshire Street, Whitechapel. 2. 1 Boreham Street (Brooksbank Street), Hackney.

Robinsons Place, Shadwell High Street (The Highway), Shadwell, "the last turning on the left hand side of Farmer Street going from the High Street" (Elmes).

Robinsons Retreat Almshouses, Retreat Place, Hackney, 1841, aka Widows Retreat

Rochester Castle Public House, 76 New Gravel Lane (Garnet Street), Wapping.

Rockmead Road, Off Wetherell Road, Hackney, 1891.

Rodneys Head Public House, 1. 25 Narrow Street, Ratcliffe, 1874. 2. 285 Whitechapel Road, Whitechapel, 1874.

Rodneys Row, Cow Lane (Ben Jonson Road), Stepney, 1851.

Roebuck Public House, 1. 27 Brady Street, Whitechapel. 2. 109 Cannon Street Road, St. George in the East, 1874. 3. 200 Hackney Road, Bethnal Green, 1874.

Roffey House, Roffey Street, Isle of Dogs, East Ferry Road, demolished in 1980s.

Rogers Court, 1. Denmark Street (Crowder Street), St. George in the East, 1891. 2. Lower East Smithfield (St. Katharines Way), East Smithfield, "three doors west of Hermitage Bridge" (Lockie).

Roman Arms Public House, 260 Roman Road, Bethnal Green, 1874.

Romford Arms, 3 Heneage Street, Whitechapel, now named Pride of Spitalfields.

Rook Street, Off Poplar High Street, Poplar, 1891, parallel with and west of Hale Street.

Rooks Yard, 1. Duke Street (Ducal Street), Bethnal Green, 1851. 2. Gibraltar Walk, Bethnal Green.

Rope Ground, Castor Street (Birchfield Street), Limehouse, 1851.

Ropemakers Arms Public House, 135 Ernest Street, Mile End.

Ropner Place, Dixon Street (Rhodeswell Road), Limehouse, 1894, running to Copenhagen Place.

Rosalind Place, West Street (Braintree Street), Mile End, 1851, part renamed Braintree Street part renamed Malcolm Road.

Rose & Crown Court, 1. 6 Booth Street (Princelet Street), Whitechapel, 1851. 2. Essex Street (Commercial Street), Spitalfields, "the first on the left a few doors from 115 Whitechapel High Street" (Lockie). 3. 25 Back Church Lane, St. George in the East, 1874. 4. 21 Bridge Street (Solebay Street), Bromley and Bow. 5. Bromley High Street, Bromley and Bow, 1874. 6. 37 Buxton Street, Whitechapel. 7. 51 Charles Street (Aylward Street), Stepney, 1874. 8. 2 Devons Road, Bromley and Bow. 9. Essex Street (Commercial Street), Spitalfields. 10. 24 Fort Street, Spitalfields, 1874. 11. 65 Globe Road, Whitechapel. 12. 13 Mare Street, Hackney, 1874. 13. 15-17 Pennyfields, Limehouse. 14. 17-18 Queen Street (Mansell Road), Whitechapel. 15. 79 Salmon Lane, Limehouse. 16. 1 Star Street (Planet Street), Shadwell. 17. 51 The Highway, St. George in the East, 1874. 18. 118 Wapping High Street, Wapping, 1874, address also 81 Wapping High Street. 19. 78 Wentworth Street, Whitechapel.

Rose Alley, Flower and Dean Street, Spitalfields, "Flower and Dean Street, the first on the right about seven doors from 200 Brick Lane leading to Fashion Street" (Lockie).

Rose Cottages, 1. Burford Lane (Lyme Grove), Hackney, 1851, Mare Street. 2. Castor Street (Birchfield Street), Limehouse, 1891.

Rose Court, West Street (Braintree Street), Mile End,

1851, part renamed Braintree Street part renamed Malcolm Road.

Rose Court & Place, Turk Street (Brick Lane), Bethnal Green, 1841.

Rose Court or Alley, Upper East Smithfield, East Smithfield, 1870.

Rose Lane, 1. Island Row, Poplar, 1891. 2. Wentworth Street, Spitalfields, Wentworth Street to Fashion Street, became part of Commercial Street. 3. White Horse Street (Butcher Row), Ratcliffe, 1891, White Horse Street to Branch Road, renamed Ratcliffe Lane.

Rose of Denmark Public House, 1. 322 Roman Road, Bromley and Bow. 2. 42 St. George Street (The Highway), St. George in the East. 3. 36 White Horse Lane, Mile End.

Rose Place, Globe Road, Mile End, 1891.

Rose Public House, 1. 7 Dock Street, St. George in the East. 2. Grove Lane (Reading Lane), Hackney. 3. 50 St. George Street (The Highway), St. George in the East, 1874, aka Old Rose, address also 128 The Highway. 4. West Street (Usk Street), Bethnal Green, 1874, address also Twigg Folly, 35 Usk Street.

Rose Street, 1. Off Bethnal Green Road, Bethnal Green, "at 44 the fifth on the left from 65 Shoreditch" (Lockie), became part of Swanfield Street. 2. Off Brick Lane, Bethnal Green, "St. Lukes at 50, the second on the right from 113 Old St, leading to Normans Buildings" (Lockie).

Rose Tavern Public House, 35 Usk Street, Bethnal Green.

Rose Villas & Cottages, Tetley Street (Chrisp Street), Poplar, 1851.

Roses Wharf, Westferry Road, Isle of Dogs, 1950, Ferguson Close is on its site.

Rosebank Road, Off St. Stephens Road, Bromley and Bow, 1891, part renamed Rosebank Grove.

Roseberry Street, Off Dalston Lane, Hackney, 1828, renamed Roseberry Place.

Roselane or Rose Lane, Limehouse, renamed Mill Place (Bowen Street).

Rosemary Branch Alley, Rosemary Lane (Royal Mint Street), East Smithfield, 1746.

Rosemary Court, Fashion Street, Spitalfields, 1891.

Rosemary Lane, Wellclose Square, St. George in the East, "near the north-east corner of Tower Hill Square end extending from the bottom of the Minories to Wellclose Square" (Elmes), later Royal Mint Street.

Rosemary Lane Court, Royal Mint Street, East Smithfield, 1851.

Rosetta Place, Sandys Row, Spitalfields, 1851.

Rosetta Street, Off Catherine Street (Maroon Street), Limehouse, 1868, became part of Aston Street.

Rothbury Terrace, Rothbury Road, Hackney, 1891.

Rothschilds Buildings, Thrawl Street, Spitalfields, 1891.

Rowland Street, Off Hanbury Street, Spitalfields, Coverley Fields to Old Montague Street, crossing Hanbury Street.

Rowlands Row, Assembly Row (Stepney Way), Mile End, "part of the west side, a few doors on the right from Assembly Row" (Lockie), west side, north end of Stepney Way.

Rowlett Street, Off St. Leonards Road, Poplar, 1891, St. Leonards Road to Brunswick Road, Blackwall Tunnel entrance road system at East India Dock Road is on the site.

Rowsell Street, Off Robeson Street, Bromley and Bow, 1891, St. Pauls Way School is on the site.

Royal Albert Dwellings, Cartwright Street (Royal Mint Street), East Smithfield, 1891, Royal Mint Street.

Royal Albert Public House, 116 St. Leonards Street, Bromley and Bow.

Royal Cambridge Music Hall & Tavern, 136 Commercial

Street, Spitalfields, 1874, Jerome Street was built on the site.

Royal Cricketers Public House, 211 Old Ford Road, Bromley and Bow, 1874, also known as Hosford Arms and Royal Cricketers.

Royal Crown Public House, 131 St. George Street (The Highway), St. George in the East, 1874.

Royal Duke Public House, 474 Commercial Road, Ratcliffe, 1874.

Royal Edward Public House, 74 Mare Street, Hackney, 1874.

Royal George Public House, 110 Vallance Road, Whitechapel, address also 7 Selby Street.

Royal Hotel & Public House, 1. Grove Street (Lauriston Road), Hackney. 2. 560 Mile End Road, Mile End. 3. Saville Place (Burdett Road), Bromley and Bow, 1874, Burdett Road.

Royal Jubilee Buildings, Hellings Street, Wapping, 1950, Wapping High Street.

Royal Mason Public House, 17 Shirbutt Street, Poplar.

Royal Mint Square, Cartwright Street (Royal Mint Street), East Smithfield, 1891, Royal Mint Street.

Royal Naval Volunteer Public House, 17 Well Street (Ensign Street), St. George in the East, aka Naval Volunteer.

Royal Navy Public House, 52 Salmon Lane, Limehouse.

Royal Oak Court, Broad Street (The Highway), Ratcliffe, "near Cock Hill" (Elmes).

Royal Oak Public House, 1. 19 Barnet Street (Barnet Grove), Bethnal Green, 1874. 2. 75 Charles Street (Aylward Street), Stepney, 1874. 3. 73 Columbia Road, Bethnal Green. 4. 18 Emmett Street, Limehouse, 1874. 5. 16 Limehouse Causeway, Limehouse. 6. 18 Plumbers Row, Whitechapel. 7. 57 St. Stephens Road, Bromley and Bow. 8. 108 Stepney Green, Stepney, 1874. 9. 40 Turville Street, Bethnal Green. 10. 5 Type Street, Bethnal Green. 11. 154 Wapping High Street, Wapping, 1874. 12. 120 Whitechapel Road, Whitechapel, 1874. 13. 83 Wilton Road (Wilton Way), Hackney.

Royal Sovereign Public House, 1. 109 Gill Street, Limehouse. 2. 11 Victoria Street (Dellow Street), Shadwell.

Royal Standard Public House, 1. 26 Hemming Street, Whitechapel. 2. 62 Maplin Street, Bromley and Bow. 3. 28 Plumbers Row, Whitechapel. 4. Sewardstone Road, Bethnal Green, also known as Royal Cricketers Tavern. 5. 77 St. Leonards Street, Bromley and Bow. 6. St. Thomas Road, Bromley and Bow, 1874, Bow Common Lane. 7. 84 Victoria Park Road, Hackney, 1874. 8. 9

Well Street (Ensign Street), St. George in the East, 1874.

Royal Victor Place, Grove Road Bridge (Grove Road), Bromley and Bow, 1874.

Royal Victor Public House, 234 Old Ford Road, Bromley and Bow, 1874.

Rumanian Synagogue, Christian Street, St. George in the East, 1945.

Rumberts Cottage, North Street (Saltwell Street), Poplar, 1851.

Rumbold House Public House, 114 Redmans Road, Mile End.

Rumsey Place, Emmett Street, Limehouse, 1851.

Rupert Court or Place, Rupert Street (Goodman Street), Whitechapel, 1851.

Rupert Street, Off Alie Street, Whitechapel, 1850, Alie Street to Hooper Street, renamed Goodman Street.

Rural Place, Mile End Road, Mile End, "three or four doors on the left east of the Old Globe about 1½ miles from Aldgate" (Lockie).

Rushbrook Street, Off East Ferry Road, Isle of Dogs, north end of East Ferry Road, combined with Bradfield Street to form Chipka Street.

Rushmead Street, Off Mansford Street, Bethnal Green.

Russel Villas, Lavender Grove, Hackney, 1868, between Malvern Road and Lansdowne Road.

Russell Court, 1. Blue Anchor Yard (Royal Mint Street), East Smithfield, 1851. 2. St. George Street (The Highway), St. George in the East, 1895, south of churchyard.

Russell Place, New Preston Road (Prestons Road), Poplar, 1862.

Russell Street, 1. Off Brunswick Street, Poplar, 1891, renamed Yabsley Street. 2. Off Chrisp Street, Poplar, renamed Carmen Street. 3. Off Oxford Street (Stepney Way), Whitechapel, 1891, renamed Halcrow Street.

Russells Buildings, Great Hermitage Street (Hermitage Wall), Wapping, 1891, renamed Knighten Street.

Russian Flag Public House, 19 Ship Alley (Wellclose Square), St. George in the East, aka Prussian Flag.

Rustic Cottages, Homerton Terrace, Hackney, 1891, Morning Lane.

Ruth House, Flower and Dean Street, Spitalfields, 1950.

Ruth Mansion, Philip Street (Ellen Street), St. George in the East.

Rutland Arms Public House, 57 Pearson Street, Bethnal Green, 1874, Kingsland Road.

Rutland House, 60 Christian

Street, St. George in the East, 1950.

Rutland Street, Whitechapel, 1895, renamed Ashfield Street.

Rutland Street Board School, Rutland Street (Ashfield Street), Whitechapel, 1895, Rutland Street, later Rutland Primary School.

Rycroft Court, Old Gravel Lane (Wapping Lane), Wapping, 1891.

Ryders Buildings, New King Street (Busby Street), Bethnal Green.

Rye Loaf Court, Cock Hill, Shadwell, "turns off at No 119 Cock Hill" (Elmes).

Rygate Street, Off Prusom Street, Wapping, 1891.

S

Sabbages Place, Wick Road, Hackney, 1862.

Sabbarton Arms Public House, 99 Upper North Street, Poplar.

Sabbarton Street, Off Latham Street (Bartlett Park), Limehouse, 1890, Latham Street to Upper North Street, Bartlett Park is on the site.

Safe Harbour Public House, 7 West Arbour Street, Mile End, 1874.

Sailors Asylum or Home, Well Street (Ensign Street), St. George in the East, 1851.

Sailors Church, Wellclose Square, St. George in the East, 1868.

Sailors Female Orphan School, 66 Great Prescot Street (Prescot Street), Whitechapel.

Sailors Orphan School, 14 Wellclose Square, St. George in the East.

Sailors Return Public House, 29 White Horse Street (Butcher Row), Ratcliffe.

Salem Chapel, Mile End Road, Mile End, north side close to Regents Canal later Guardian Angels Church.

Saling Place & Cottage, Three Colt Street, Limehouse, 1851.

Salisbury Arms Public House, 1. 111 Burdett Road, Bromley and Bow, 1874. 2. 135 Eastfield Street, Limehouse, 1874.

Salisbury Place, 1. Morpeth Road, Hackney. 2. Bethnal Green, renamed Walter Street.

Salisbury Place, Street & Terrace, Rhodeswell Road, Limehouse, 1851.

Salisbury Road, Off Wilton Road (Wilton Way), Hackney, 1891, renamed Elrington Road.

Salisbury Street, 1. Off Burdett Road, Bromley and Bow, Burdett Road to Wager Street, renamed Sarum Road. 2. Off Halley Street, Limehouse, 1860, became part of Aston Street. 3. Off Walter Street, Bethnal Green.

Sally Alley, London Street (Bekesbourne Street), Ratcliffe, 1851.

Salmen Street, Off South Grove (Southern Grove), Bromley and Bow.

Salmon & Ball (Tavern) Public House, 502 Bethnal Green Road, Bethnal Green, 1874.

Salmon & Ball Public House, 32 Lamb Street, Spitalfields, 1874.

Salmon Buildings, Sandys Row, Spitalfields, 1851.

Salmon Street & Place, Salmon Lane, Limehouse, next to No 110.

Salmons Row, Salmon Lane, Limehouse, "at the back of Salmons Place" (Lockie).

Saltash Street, Off Derbyshire Street, Bethnal Green, 1950, west of Vallance Road.

Salter Street, Poplar, renamed Kinder Street.

Salters Alley, Green Bank, Wapping, 1820.

Salters Buildings, Orchard Place, Poplar, 1851.

Salters Court, Glasshouse Street (John Fisher Street), East Smithfield, 1870, Royal Mint Street.

Salvation Army Boys Home, 32-34 Bow Road, Bromley and Bow.

Salvation Army Maternity Home, 17-19 Devonshire Road (Brenthouse Road), Hackney.

Salvation Army Maternity Hospital, 271 Mare Street, Hackney.

Salvation Army Receiving Home, 259 Mare Street, Hackney.

Sampson Terrace, Marlborough Avenue, Hackney, 1862, at its corner with Pownall Road.

Sampsons Gardens, Wapping, renamed Sampson Street.

Sampsons Place, Mile End Road, Mile End, "nearly opposite the Old Globe and about 1½ miles on the right from Aldgate" (Lockie).

Samuda Street, Off Manchester Road, Isle of Dogs, part renamed Stewart Street.

Samudas Wharf, Manchester Road, Isle of Dogs, 1950, Samuda Estate is on its site.

Samuel Court, Samuel Street (Spelman Street), Whitechapel, 1891.

Samuel House, Clarissa Street, Hackney, 1950.

Samuel Street, 1. Off Burslem Street, St. George in the East, renamed Wicker Street. 2. Off Church Street (Bethnal Green Road), Bethnal Green, "at 74 about ⅓ of a mile on the left from 65 Shoreditch leading into Gibraltar walk" (Lockie). 3. Off Salmon Lane, Limehouse, 1895, renamed Camdenhurst Street. 4. Off Well Street, Whitechapel, 1851, became the southern section of Spelman Street.

Sander Street, Off Back Church Lane, St. George in the East, 1891.

Sander Street Synagogue, 2 Sander Street (Back Church Lane), St. George in the East, 1945.

Sanders Buildings, Fishers Alley (Middlesex Street), Spitalfields.

Sandown Place, Morgan Street (Hessel Street), St. George in the East, 1891.

Sandpit Road, Off West Street (Birchfield Street), Limehouse, renamed to, and later renamed Birchfield Street.

Sandys Row Synagogue, 4a Sandys Row, Spitalfields.

Sara Pyke House Industrial School, 45 Great Prescot Street (Prescot Street), Whitechapel.

Sarah Court or Street, Off New Gravel Lane (Garnet Street), Wapping, "at 145 about twelve doors on the right from Wapping Wall" (Lockie), Prospect Place is partially on the route.

Sarah Galley Tavern Public House, 143-149 Poplar High Street, Poplar, later Blakeneys Head.

Sarah Place, Hunt Street (Hunton Street), Whitechapel.

Sarah Street, 1, Off New Gravel Lane (Garnet Street), Wapping, 1851. 2. Off Nichols Row (Boundary Estate), Bethnal Green, "the continuation of Nichols Row entering by 30 Church Street" (Lockie). 3. Poplar, renamed Sturry Street. 4. Poplar, renamed Wallwood Street.

Sarahs Cottages, Lindale Street (Grundy Street), Poplar, 1851, Grundy Street.

Sarum Road, Off Burdett Road, Bromley and Bow, Burdett Road to Wager Street.

Satchwell Street, Off Turin Street, Bethnal Green, 1891, Satchwell Rents to Turin Street.

Satchwell(s) Rents, Church Street (Bethnal Green Road), Bethnal Green, 1841, became part of Satchwell Road.

Saul Street, Off Spital Street, Spitalfields, Brick Lane to Spital Street, south of Hanbury's Brewery.

Saunders Terrace, Old Ford Road, Bromley and Bow.

Saville Buildings, Pleasant Row (Redmans Road), Stepney, "the continuation of Pleasant Row and Redmans Road to the Green" (Elmes).

Saville Buildings, Stepney Green, Stepney, 1862, north end of Wellington Street.

Saville Place, Mile End Road, Mile End, "forms part of the south side near the Plough about

24 miles on the right from Aldgate" (Lockie).

Saville Row, Mile End Road, Mile End, "forms part of the south side opposite the Bell and Mackerel public house" (Lockie), immediately west of Regents Canal bridge.

Sawyers Cottages, Old Ford Road, Bromley and Bow, 1851.

Sawyers or Sayers Buildings, Phoenix Street (Brick Lane), Spitalfields, "is between Hope Street and Grey Eagle Street being a few doors on the left from 160 Brick Lane" (Lockie).

Sawyers Yard, Wentworth Street, Whitechapel, 1851.

Saxony Cottages, 182 Mare Street, Hackney, 1841, close to Mare Street.

Sayers Buildings, Park Street (Milligan Street), Limehouse, "the first on the right from Limehouse hole towards Limehouse causeway" (Lockie).

Scales Cottages, Old Ford Road, Bromley and Bow, 1851.

Scandinavian Reading Room, 33 Pennyfields, Limehouse, 1900-1930.

Scandinavian Sailors Temperance Home, Garford Street, Limehouse, 1890, between Garford Street and West India Docks close to West India Dock Road, later became a Salvation Army hostel.

Scarborough Arms Public House, 1. 11 Betts Street, St. George in the East, 1874. 2. 35 St. Mark Street, Whitechapel.

Scarborough Street, Off Tenter Street, Whitechapel, 1860.

Sceptre Street, 1. Bethnal Green, renamed Sceptre Road. 2, Off School Place, Bethnal Green, 1891. 3. Off West Street (Braintree Street), Mile End, 1891, goes further on north side of railway line.

School House Court, Nightingale Lane (Thomas More Street), Wapping.

School Place, St. Bartholomews Church and Recreation Ground, Bethnal Green, south of St. Bartholomews Church and Recreation Ground.

Schoolhouse Court, Off Nightingale Lane (Thomas More Street), Wapping, 1800, London Docks were built on the site.

Schoolhouse Yard, 1. Bow Road, Bromley and Bow, 1891. 2. Great Garden Street (Greatorex Street), Whitechapel, 1851.

Schooner Street, Off Ship Street (Manchester Road), Isle of Dogs, see Ship Street.

Scones Alley, Wapping Wall, Wapping, 1891.

Scooners Alley, Star Street (Planet Street), Shadwell, "at 28 two or three doors east of Star Street" (Lockie).

Scotch Arms Public House, 1 Wapping High Street, Wapping, 1899, aka Scots Arms.

Scouler Street, Off Quixley Street, Poplar, 1890.

Scurr Street, Off Kerbey Street, Poplar, 1950, Kerbey Street to Chrisp Street, opposite Royal Charlie public house.

Sea-Borne Coal Wharf, Broad Street (The Highway), Shadwell, 1895, east of Shadwell Park, became part of Charringtons Wharf.

Seabright Gardens, Dinmont Street, Bethnal Green, 1891.

Seabright Place, Hackney Road, Bethnal Green, 1827, opposite Durham Street.

Seabright Street East, Seabright Place (Seabright Street), Bethnal Green, 1827, immediately east of Seabright Place.

Seabright Terrace, Hackney Road, Bethnal Green, 1827, opposite Elizabeth Street.

Seamens Chapel, St. George Street (The Highway), St. George in the East, 1868, south of Wellclose Square.

Seamens Christian Friendly Society, 255 Burdett Road, Limehouse.

Seamens Institute & Rest, Westferry Road, Isle of Dogs, opposite Millwall Docks entrance, demolished before WWII.

Searles Place, Cambridge Heath Road, Bethnal Green, 1860, at its corner with Victoria Park Road.

Seabright Arms Public House, 31 Coate Street, Bethnal Green.

Seles Place, Ann Street (East India Dock Road), Poplar, 1891.

Self Place, Ann Street (East India Dock Road), Poplar, 1851.

Selina Cottage, Bath Street (Poplar Bath Street), Poplar, 1891, East India Dock Road.

Selles Terrace, William Street (Ponler Street), St. George in the East, 1851.

Selsey Road, Poplar, renamed Selsey Street.

Sermon Lane, Limehouse, renamed Salmon Lane.

Servants Free Registry & Home, 1. 32 Bow Road, Bromley and Bow. 2. 212 Burdett Road, Limehouse.

Session or Court House, Wellclose Square, St. George in the East, 1868.

Settle Cottages, Sage Street, Shadwell, 1891, Cable Street.

Settles Street Synagogue, 34 Settles Street, Whitechapel, 1945.

Seven Star Alley, St. George Street (The Highway), St. George in the East.

Seven Star Cottage, Bromley High Street, Bromley and Bow, 1891.

Seven Stars Court, Royal Mint Street, East Smithfield, 1851.

Seven Stars Public House, 1. 49 Brick Lane, Spitalfields, 1874. 2. Bromley High Street, Bromley and Bow, 1851. 3. 3 Fleet Street (Pedley Street), Whitechapel, 1874. 4. 111 Whitechapel High Street, Whitechapel, 1874. 5. 94 Bromley High Street, Bromley and Bow, aka Seven Star Inn,

Severn House, Pier Street, Isle of Dogs, 1888.

Severn Place, Abingdon Street (Herald Street), Bethnal Green, 1851, renamed Glass Street.

Severne Street, Off Stutfield Street, St. George in the East, 1891.

Shadwell & St. Georges Synagogue, 191 The Highway, St. George in the East, 1951, previously 59 St. George Street.

Shadwell Dock House Public House, Shadwell Dock Street (Garnet Street), Shadwell, aka Dock Tavern.

Shadwell Dock Stairs, Wapping Wall, Shadwell, "near the east end of Wapping Wall and opposite Griffin Street from Shadwell market" (Lockie), Shadwell Park is on the site.

Shadwell Dock Street, Off New Gravel Lane (Garnet Street), Wapping, 1851, east from New Gravel Lane, lost on construction of Shadwell New Basin, aka Dock Street.

Shadwell Fish Market, Bell Wharf Stairs (The Highway), Shadwell, immediately west of Bell Wharf Stairs, Shadwell Park is on the site.

Shadwell Green, Broad Bridge (The Highway), Shadwell, 1891, Shadwell Park is on the site.

Shadwell High Street, Off Shadwell High Street (The Highway), Shadwell, became part of The Highway.

Shadwell Mansions, 357 The Highway, St. George in the East, next to The Highway.

Shadwell Market, Shadwell High Street (The Highway), Shadwell, just south of High Street at the present-day Glamis Road, Shadwell Park is on the site.

Shadwell Market Public House, Shadwell Market (The Highway), Shadwell, 1891.

Shadwell New Basin, Shadwell High Street (The Highway), Shadwell, 1891, now Shadwell Basin.

Shadwell Railway Station, Sutton Street, Shadwell, 1840-1941, Shadwell DLR is on its site.

Shadwell Street, Off Cable Street, Shadwell, 1891, parallel with and west of King David Lane.

Shadwell Water Works, Popes Hill (Shadwell Park), Shadwell, "at the south end of Popes hill on the left entering by 75 Shadwell

High Street" (Lockie), Shadwell Park is on the site.

Shadwell Workhouse, Union Street (The Highway), Shadwell, "about the middle of the west side of Union Street entering by 227 Shadwell High Street" (Lockie).

Shaftesbury Hall, Kerbey Street, Poplar, 1950, close to Grundy Street.

Shaftesbury Terrace, Grove Road, Bromley and Bow.

Shakespeare Arms Public House, 1. 16 Bakers Row (Vallance Road), Whitechapel. 2. 460 Bethnal Green Road, Bethnal Green. 3. 18 Boreham Street (Brooksbank Street), Hackney.

Shakespeares Head Public House, 1. 28 Barnsley Street, Whitechapel. 2. 182 Jubilee Street, Stepney, 1874. 3. 38 Shakespeare(s) Walk (Shadwell Basin), Shadwell.

Shakespeares Walk, Shadwell High Street (The Highway), Shadwell, High Street to Milk Yard immediately west of St. Pauls Church, Shadwell Basin is on the site.

Shakespeares Walk Female School, York Place, Old Gravel Lane, Shadwell.

Shannon Terrace, Broke Road (Broke Walk), Hackney, 1862.

Shard Street, Off Johnson Street, Wapping, 1790, Johnson Street to Tench Street.

Sharman Street, Off Broomfield Street, Limehouse, 1950.

Sharps Buildings, Royal Mint Street, East Smithfield, 1851.

Sharps Wharf, Wapping High Street, Wapping, 1895, south west of Wapping Lane.

Shaw House, Blount Street, Poplar, 1950.

Shell Wharf, Wapping Wall, Wapping, 1895, west of Monza Street, became Lower Olivers Wharf.

Shepherd & Shepherdess Public House, 8 Worcester Street (Reardon Street), Wapping, 1874.

Shepherd or Shepards Terrace, 1. Commercial Road, Stepney, 1851. 2. West India Dock Road, Limehouse, 1851.

Shepherd Street, Off Commercial Street, Spitalfields, 1891, renamed Toynbee St.

Shepherd Street & Buildings, Commercial Street, Spitalfields, 1891.

Shepherd Street & Terrace, Devons Lane (Devons Road), Bromley and Bow, 1851.

Shepherd(s) Place, 1. Tenter Street, Whitechapel, 1851. 2. Whites Row, Whitechapel.

Shepherds Row, Bethnal Green Road, Bethnal Green, "Bethnal Green Road forms part of the south side opposite Wilmot Square about $^2/_3$ of a mile on the

right from 65 Shoreditch"
(Lockie).

Shepperd Street, Off Devons
Road, Bromley and Bow, east of
Violet Road.

Sheridan Street, Off Sutton
Street, Shadwell, 1891.

Sherman Street, Off Hancock
Road, Bromley and Bow, 1891,
north of Otis Street.

Shervills Buildings, George
Street (Pedley Street),
Whitechapel, 1851.

Sherwood Arms Public House,
118 Bow Common Lane,
Bromley and Bow.

Sherwood Buildings, Turville
Street, Bethnal Green.

Sherwood Place, Turville Street,
Bethnal Green, "the second
turning on the right hand side of
Turvill Street going from Church
Street" (Elmes).

Sherwood Street, Off Bow
Common Lane, Bromley and
Bow, 1891, renamed Lawes
Street.

Sheurers Cottages, Westferry
Road, Isle of Dogs, 1840, close
to Moeity Road.

Shiloh Place, White Horse Lane,
Mile End, 1950, close to Mile
End Road Ocean Estate is on the
site.

Ship & Bell Public House, 74
Prusom Street, Wapping.

**Ship & Black Horse Public
House**, 95 Shadwell High Street
(The Highway), Shadwell.

**Ship & Bladebone Public
House**, 8 New Gravel Lane
(Garnet Street), Wapping.

Ship & Blue Ball Public House,
13 Boundary Street, Bethnal
Green, 1874.

**Ship & Chequers Public
House**, 21 Love Lane (Brodlove
Lane), Shadwell.

Ship & Dolphin Public House,
34 New Gravel Lane (Garnet
Street), Wapping, 1874.

**Ship & Green Dragon Public
House**, 17 King Street (Prusom
Street), Wapping.

Ship & Lion Public House, 70
Ropemakers Fields, Limehouse,
1874, address also 20 & 65
Ropemakers Fields.

**Ship & Notchblock Public
House**, 134 St. George Street
(The Highway), St. George in the
East.

Ship & Pilot Public House, 27
Wapping High Street, Wapping,
1874.

**Ship & Punchbowl Public
House**, 55 Wapping High Street,
Wapping, 1874.

**Ship & Rising Sun Public
House**, 134 Shadwell High Street
(The Highway), Shadwell, 1874.

Ship & Shears Public House, 1.
16 Lower Shadwell (Shadwell
Park), Shadwell, 1874. 2. 211-
212 Shadwell High Street (The
Highway), Shadwell, aka Albion

Ship & Star Public House, 1. 41
Lower Shadwell (Shadwell

Park), Shadwell, address also 113 Shadwell Street. 2. 29 Wapping High Street, Wapping.

Ship & Unicorn Public House, 109 New Gravel Lane (Garnet Street), Wapping.

Ship & Whale Public House, 19 Wapping Wall, Wapping, aka Sunderland Bridge.

Ship (Tavern) Public House, 90 Three Colt Street, Limehouse, 1874.

Ship Aground Public House, 56 Broad Street (The Highway), Ratcliffe, 1874.

Ship Alley, 1. Broad Street (The Highway), Ratcliffe, 1746. 2. Fore Street (Narrow Street), Limehouse, 2H6.

Ship Court, Crab Tree Row (Columbia Road), Bethnal Green, 1841.

Ship Passage, Mare Street, Hackney, 1895, opposite Morning Lane.

Ship Public House, 1. 84 Anthony Street, St. George in the East. 2. 6-7 Bacon Street, Bethnal Green, 1874, address also 14 Bacon Street. 3. Bell Wharf (The Highway), Shadwell, 1874, address also 41 Lower Shadwell. 4. 473 Bethnal Green Road, Bethnal Green. 5. Brick lane, Spitalfields, 1874. 6. 57 Brunswick Street, Poplar, 1874. 7. 387 Cable Street, Shadwell, address also 1 Hardinge Street, Sun Tavern Fields, 280 Cable Street. 8. Chapel Street, St.

George in the East, 1874. 8. 21 Charles Street (Aylward Street), Stepney. 9. 109 Green Street (Roman Road), Bethnal Green. 10. Grove Passage (Reading Lane), Hackney, 1895. 11. 140 Hanbury Street, Spitalfields. 12. 10 Hunt Street (Hunton Street), Whitechapel, 1874, address also 14 Hunt Street. 13. 11 Little Hermitage Street (Orton Street), Wapping. 14. 12 Lower Shadwell (Shadwell Park), Shadwell. 15. 10 Narrow Street, Ratcliffe, 1874. 16. 86 New Gravel Lane (Garnet Street), Wapping, aka Barley Mow Public House. 17. 39 Old Gravel Lane (Wapping Lane), Wapping. 18. 314 Poplar High Street, Poplar, 1874. 19. 30 Somerset Street (Mansell Street), Whitechapel. 20. 64 Stepney Green, Stepney, 1874. 21. 243 Wapping High Street, Wapping. 22. Wellclose Square, St. George in the East, 1874, Cable Street. 23. 24 Wheler Street, Spitalfields, 1874. 24. 9 York Street West, Limehouse.

Ship Street, 1. Off Manchester Road, Isle of Dogs, renamed Schooner Street, George Greens School and Schooner Estate were built on the site. 2. Off Prussian Island (Prusom Street), Wapping, "the second on the right from 188 Wapping Street near New Crane" (Lockie).

Ship Tavern Public House, 90 Three Colt Street, Limehouse.

Ship Terrace, 104-108 Manchester Road, Isle of Dogs, 1865.

Ships Alley, Wellclose Square, St. George in the East, 1895, south east corner of Wellclose Square to St. George Street.

Ships Place, Anthony Street, St. George in the East, 1878, just north of Upper Chapman Street.

Shipwrights Arms Public House, 1. 136 East India Dock Road, Poplar. 2. 45 Emmett Street, Limehouse, 1874.

Shipwrights Terrace, Brunswick Street, Poplar, 1851.

Shirleys Court or Yard, Old Montague Street, Whitechapel, "the second on the right from Osborn Street" (Lockie).

Shoeblack Refuge, 86 Leman Street, Whitechapel, 1891.

Shore Place, Well Street, Hackney, 1827, renamed Shore Road.

Shoreditch Methodist Mission Church, 162 Hackney Road, Bethnal Green, 1950, next to 162 Hackney Road.

Shoreditch New Almshouses, Brunswick Street (Haggerston Road), Hackney, 1891.

Shoreditch Tabernacle, Hackney Road, Bethnal Green, 1895, north of Austin Street.

Short Street, Off Bell Lane, Spitalfields, 1851.

Short Street, 1. Off Hardinge Street, Shadwell, 1891, renamed

Poonah Street. 2. Off Mercer Street (Cable Street), Shadwell, became the western end of Juniper Street. 3. Off New Nichol(s) Street (Boundary Estate), Bethnal Green, 1841. 4. Off Sandys Row, Spitalfields, 1891, east of Sandys Row, and north of Wentworth St, became the southern end of Leyden St.

Shorter Street, Off Wellclose Square, St. George in the East, renamed Fletcher Street.

Shorters Rents, 1. East Smithfield, 1870, renamed Flank Street. 2. Lamb Street, Spitalfields.

Shorts Court, Wentworth Street, Spitalfields, Wentworth Street a few doors on the left from Petticoat Lane leading into Coxs Square" (Lockie).

Shoulder of Mutton (and Pig) Public House, 55 Brunswick Street, Poplar.

Shovel Alley, Great Gardens (St. Katharine Dock), East Smithfield, "St. Catherines Lane" Rocque 2F5.

Shovel Public House, 142 Cable Street, St. George in the East, 1874.

Shrubland Cottages, Shrubland Grove (Mapledene Road), Hackney, 1868, between Queens Road and Holly Street.

Shrubland Grove, Queensbridge Road, Hackney, 1895, renamed Mapledene Road.

Sidney Arms Public House, 1. 90 Charles Street (Aylward Street), Stepney. 2. 131 Sidney Street, Whitechapel.

Sidney Place, Commercial Road, Stepney, 1868, immediately east and west of Exmouth Street.

Sidney Street, 1. Hackney, renamed Kenworthy Road. 2. Bethnal Green, renamed Longman Street (Cranbrook Estate).

Sidney Street Synagogue, 101 Sidney Street, Whitechapel, 1950.

Sidney Terrace, 1. Grove Road, Bromley and Bow. 2. Sidney Street (Kenworthy Road), Hackney, 1891.

Silas Street, Off Canal Road (Mile End Road), Bromley and Bow, 1891, north end west to canal.

Silk Mill Row, Cassland Road, Hackney, 1851, became easternmost end of Cassland Road.

Silurian Terrace, Broke Road (Broke Walk), Hackney, 1862.

Silver Court, Silver Street, "about the middle of the west side, viz between Pleasant Row and Well Street" (Lockie).

Silver Lion Court, Pennyfields, Limehouse.

Silver Lion Public House, 65 Pennyfields, Limehouse, 1874.

Silver Street, 1. Off Apsley Street (Wickham Close), Stepney, became part of Apsley Street. 2. Off Devonshire Street (Cephas Street), Mile End, became part of Cephas Street. 3. Off Dod Street, Limehouse, renamed Calcutta Street. 4. Off King Street (Prusom Street), Wapping, "the first on the left from 18 near Wapping" (Lockie). 5. Off Prusom Street, Wapping, renamed Penang Street. 6. Off Redmans Road, Stepney, Redmans Road to Oxford Street, parallel with and east of Jamaica Street. 7. Off Spelman Street, Whitechapel, aka White Cross Street, now the northern end of Spelman Street.

Silver Tavern Public House, 315 Burdett Road, Limehouse, 1874, corner of Dod Street.

Silver Terrace, Westferry Road, Isle of Dogs, 1891, left of the fire station.

Silver Trumpet Public House, 1. 69 Cheshire Street, Whitechapel. 2. 7 Upton Terrace, Shadwell, address also 472 Commercial Road.

Simpsons Buildings & Place, Bird Cage Walk (Columbia Road), Bethnal Green, 1851, Guinness Trust Buildings were built on the site.

Single Place, Single Street (Bow Common Lane), Mile End, Mile End Road to Bridge Street.

Single Street, Off Bow Common Lane, Bromley and Bow, 1891,

Bow Common Lane to Bridge Street.

Single Terrace, Burdett Road, Bromley and Bow, 1891.

Sion Square, Union Street (Adler Street), Whitechapel, 1860, east of St. Marys Church.

Sir Charles Napier Public House, 697 Commercial Road, Limehouse, corner of Lowell Street.

Sir Francis Burdett Public House, Columbia Square (Columbia Road), Bethnal Green.

Sir George Osbornes Head Public House, 131 Old Montague Street, Wapping, 1874.

Sir George Whelers Chapel & St. Marys, Spital Square, Spitalfields.

Sir John Barleycorn Public House, 1. 48 Brick lane, Spitalfields. 2. 32 Fulbourne Street, Whitechapel. 3. 39 Upper North Street, Poplar.

Sir John Cass Public House, 52 Victoria Park Road, Hackney.

Sir John Falstaff Public House, 7 William Street (Ponler Street), St. George in the East, address also 111 Cannon Street Road.

Sir John Franklin Public House, 1. 269 East India Dock Road, Poplar. 2. 48 Narrow Street, Limehouse, next to bridge.

Sir John Russell Public House, 163 Morning Lane, Hackney.

Sir Sidney Smith Public House, 22 Dock Street, St. George in the East, 1874.

Sir Walter Raleigh Public House, 20 New Street (Shadwell Park), Shadwell.

Sir Walter Scott Public House, 2 Broadway Market, Hackney.

Sir William Warrens Square, Wapping High Street, Wapping, 1851, just north of King Edwards Stairs.

Sistern Place, Preston New Road (Prestons Road), Poplar, 1862.

Size Yard, Whitechapel Road, Whitechapel, "at 22 nearly opposite the church" (Lockie).

Skidmore Street, Off Harford Street, Mile End, 1950, south of Solebay Street.

Skinners Almshouses, Mile End Road, Mile End, "A few houses on the north side of the road below the turnpike and adjoining those of the Trinity House They were founded by Lewis Newbury in 1698 for twelve poor widows" (Elmes), immediately west of Trinity Almshouses and sold in 1895 to Vintners Almshouses.

Slade Court, St. John Street (Grimsby Street), Bethnal Green, 1841.

Slater or Slaughter Street, Off Sclater Street, Whitechapel, alternative name for Sclater Street.

Slaters Burial Ground, Mill Yard, Whitechapel, 1851.

Slaughters Court, Blue Anchor Alley (Cable Street), Ratcliffe, 1746.

Sly Street, Off Cannon Street Road, St. George in the East, 1891.

Smallcoal Alley, Fashion Street, Spitalfields, 1746.

Smarts Gardens, Wilmot Street, Bethnal Green, "a group of small houses at the south end of Wilmot Street extending towards Dog Row" (Lockie).

Smeed Road, Off Monier Road, Bromley and Bow, 1891.

Smith Cottage, Warner Place, Bethnal Green.

Smith Street, Off Jubilee Street, Stepney, 1891, renamed Smithy Street.

Smith(s) Buildings, 1. Clarence Place, Bethnal Green, 1841. 2. Diss Street, Bethnal Green, 1891. 3. Essex Street (Blythe Street), Bethnal Green.

Smith(s) Place, King Street (Hackney Road), Bethnal Green, 1841, Hackney Road.

Smiths Alley, Ropemakers Fields, Limehouse, 1851.

Smiths Arms Public House, 32 St. Leonards Street, Bromley and Bow, aka Swiss Arms.

Smiths Buildings, Whitechapel High Street, Whitechapel, 1851.

Smiths Court, 1. Fashion Street, Spitalfields, 1746. 2. Lower Chapman Street (Bigland Street), St. George in the East, "the fifth on the left from Cannon Street Road near Mary St, and Ann Street" (Lockie). 3. Whitechapel Road, Whitechapel, "at 65 about $1/6$ of a mile on the left east of the church" (Lockie).

Smiths Nursery & Nursery Place, Dalston Lane, Hackney, 1841, site of later German Hospital.

Smiths Place, 1. Lower Chapman Street (Bigland Street), St. George in the East, 1891, renamed Agra Place. 2. Salmon Lane, Limehouse, "about $1/8$ of a mile on the left from the Commercial Road and nearly opposite Farmers Row" (Lockie).

Smiths Place or Ways, Wapping High Street, Wapping, "on the east side the Dundee wharf about $1/8$ of a mile below Hermitage Bridge" (Lockie), renamed Wainwright Place.

Smiths Terrace, Ashwell Road (Roman Road), Bromley and Bow.

Smock Alley, Artillery Place (Artillery Lane), Spitalfields, now eastern section of Artillery Lane.

Snelgrove Yard, Old Nichol(s) Street (Boundary Estate), Bethnal Green, 1851.

Snowdon Place, Bromley High Street, Bromley and Bow, Bow Bridge Estate built over street.

Solander Street, Off Cable Street, Shadwell, between Cable Street and Highway, part renamed Solander Gardens.

Solebay Place, Solebay Street, Mile End.

Solomons Buildings, North Street (Brady Street), Whitechapel.

Somerset Arms Public House, 20 New Road, Whitechapel, address also 9 Gloucester Terrace.

Somerset Buildings, 1. Hackney Road, Bethnal Green, "at the first turning on the left hand side of Crabtree Row, going from the High Road(Elmes). 2. Virginia Row (Virginia Road), Bethnal Green, 1841.

Somerset Court, Little Somerset Street, Whitechapel.

Somerset Place, 1. Forest Row, Hackney, 1851. 2. New Road, Whitechapel, 1851.

Sons of Britchan Synagogue, 22 Bromehead Street, Stepney, 1950, Commercial Road.

Sophia Cottage, Chisenhale Road, Bromley and Bow.

Sophia Street, Off Poplar High Street, Poplar, 1851, Poplar High Street to Shirbutt Street.

South African Tavern Public House, Grundy Street, Poplar, Grundy Street corner of Duff

Street, early name of the Africa Tavern.

South Conduit Street, Off Old Bethnal Green Road, Bethnal Green, 1851, also known as Conduit Street, renamed Viaduct Street.

South Devon Wharf, Lower East Smithfield (St. Katharines Way), East Smithfield, 1895, west of corner with Burr Close.

South Dock Railway Station, Blackwall Basin (Wood Wharf), Isle of Dogs, 1872-1926, south of Blackwall Basin.

South Dock Terrace, Cold Harbour, Poplar, 1891, Blackwall.

South East Row, Upper North Street, Poplar, 1851.

South Fair Street, Stepney, renamed Fair Street (Dunelm Street).

South Grove, Bromley and Bow, renamed Southern Grove.

South Hackney Church, Well Street, Hackney, 1895, corner of Glaskin Road, later St. Andrews Mission Church.

South Holly Street, Off Middleton Road, Hackney, 1851.

South Pavement, West Street (Usk Street), Bethnal Green, 1841.

South Street, 1. Off Brushfield Street, Spitalfields, 1891, Short entrance street on south side of Spitalfields Market. 2. Off Harts Lane (Barnet Grove), Bethnal

Green, 1841, renamed Florida Street. 3. Off Rich Street, Limehouse, renamed Trinidad Street. 4. Off Whitechapel Road, Whitechapel, renamed Bedford Street.

Southampton Cottages, Hackney Road, Bethnal Green, 1841, Hadrian Estate is on the site.

Southampton Place & Terrace, Southampton Street, Bethnal Green.

Southampton Street, Off London Street (Dunbridge Street), Bethnal Green, 1841, renamed Portswood Place.

Southboro Place, Temple Street, Bethnal Green.

Southill Street, Off Kerbey Street, Poplar, Kerbey Street to Reeves Street, now Giraud Street.

Southview Cottages, Homerton Terrace, Hackney, 1851, Morning Lane.

Sovereign Public House, 2 Mile End Road, Mile End.

Sowden Place, Bromley High Street, Bromley and Bow, 1891.

Spaniel Dog Public House, New Tyssen Street (Satchwell Road), Bethnal Green.

Sparrow Corner, Royal Mint Street, East Smithfield, 1890, corner of Royal Mint Street and Tower Hill.

Specks Buildings Fields & Yard, John Street (Spelman Street), Whitechapel, 1851, renamed Spelman Street.

Spectacle Alley, Church Lane (White Church Lane), Whitechapel, 1870, renamed White Church Passage.

Speedings Gardens, North Street (Saltwell Street), Poplar, "about the middle of the east side between Poplar High Street and the East India Dock Road" (Lockie).

Speedwell Club, 4 The Terrace (Old Ford Road), Bromley and Bow, Old Ford Road.

Spencer Arms Public House, Spencer Street (Brinsley Street), Shadwell.

Spencer House, Lolesworth Street (Lolesworth Close), Spitalfields, 1950.

Spencer Passage, Dinmont Street, Bethnal Green, 1950.

Spencer Street, 1. Off Endive Street (Rhodeswell Road), Limehouse, 1891. 2. Off Sutton Street, Shadwell, 1891, renamed Brinsley Street.

Spencers Arms Public House, 42 Dean Street (Deancross Street), Shadwell.

Spencers Cab Yard, Fleet Street (Pedley Street), Whitechapel.

Spert House, Carr Street, Limehouse, 1950, Limehouse Fields Estate.

Spey Street, Off St. Leonards Road, Poplar, 1891, St. Leonards Road to Zetland Street.

Spicer Court, Spicer Street (Buxton Street), Whitechapel, "Spicer Street, the first on the right a few yards from 82 Brick Lane" (Lockie).

Spicer Street, Off Brick Lane, Spitalfields, north of Black Eagle brewery, now part of Buxton Street.

Spital Court, Spital Street, Spitalfields, "the first on the right north from Pelham Street" (Lockie).

Spital House, 34-35 Spital Square, Spitalfields.

Spital Square Synagogue, Spital Square, Spitalfields.

Spital Street Synagogue, 12 and 44-46 Spital Street, Spitalfields.

Spitalfields Great Synagogue, Fournier Street, Spitalfields, corner of Fournier Street and Brick Lane, renamed Machzikei Hadath Shomrei Shabbat Synagogue.

Spitalfields School of Design, 37 Crispin Street, Spitalfields.

Spitalfields Work House, Charles Street (Vallance Road), Whitechapel, "On the east side of Charles Street Mile End New Town near the north end of Bakers Row from 94 Whitechapel Road" (Lockie).

Spitalfields Workhouse, Fulbourne Street, Whitechapel, 1930-1944, aka St. Peters Hospital aka Whitechapel Union Workhouse.

Splidts Street, Off Ellen Street, St. George in the East, 1891, renamed Forbes Street.

Sportsman Public House, 1. 8 Calcutta Place (East India Dock Road), Poplar, East India Dock Road. 2. 35 Richard Street, St. George in the East.

Spotted Dog Public House, 108 Poplar High Street, Poplar.

Spratleys Row, Westferry Road, Isle of Dogs, 1851, south diagonally opposite Byng Street.

Spread Eagle Court, Limehouse Causeway, Limehouse, "the first on the left a few yards from Fore Street or from Three Colt Street" (Lockie).

Spread Eagle Public House, 1. 1 Kingsland Road, Hackney, 1874. 2. 66 Limehouse Causeway, Limehouse, 1874.

Spread Eagle Street, Off Gun Lane (Grenade Street), Limehouse, 1851, renamed Gill Street.

Spread Eagle Yard, Whitechapel High Street, Whitechapel, 1891.

Spring Garden Place or Street, Off Oxford Street (Stepney Way), Whitechapel, 1895, Oxford Street to Stepney High Street, became the easternmost end of Stepney Way.

Spring Gardens, King Edward Street (Kingward Street), Whitechapel, 1851, renamed Spring Walk.

Spring Gardens Place, 1. Janet Street, Isle of Dogs, 1891, Westferry Road. 2. Goulds Hill (Shadwell Park), Shadwell, 1891, Shadwell Park is on the site.

Spring Place, Bow Common Lane, Bromley and Bow, 1851.

Spring Street, Off Old Ford Road, Bromley and Bow, 1895, opposite Blondin Street A12 is on the site.

Springfield Terrace, Gascoyne Road, Hackney, 1891, now part Bradstock Road.

Spurstowes Almshouses, Pigwell Path (Wilton Way), Hackney, 1895.

Square & Compasses Public House, 237 Cambridge Road (Cambridge Heath Road), Bethnal Green.

St. Agnes Terrace, Victoria Park Road, Hackney, 1891.

St. Albans Church, 59-61 Giraud Street, Poplar, 1928.

St. Andrew Public House, 93 Lower East Smithfield (St. Katharines Way), East Smithfield.

St. Andrews Church & Schoolhouse, St. Andrews Walk (Weavers Fields), Bethnal Green, Weavers Fields are on the site.

St. Andrews Head Public House, 86 Rhodeswell Road, Limehouse, 1874.

St. Andrews Hospital, Devons Road, Bromley and Bow, 1871-2006.

St. Andrews Mission Church, Well Street, Hackney, 1895, corner of Glaskin Road.

St. Andrews Place & Terrace, Rhodeswell Road, Limehouse.

St. Andrews Scotch Church, Philpot Street, Whitechapel, 1860.

St. Andrews Street, Bethnal Green, renamed St. Andrews Walk (Weavers Fields).

St. Andrews Walk, Cheshire Street, Whitechapel, 1950, Weavers Fields are on the site.

St. Andrews Wharf, Westferry Road, Isle of Dogs, 1950, Mast House Terrace is on its site.

St. Annes Orphanage for Girls, Albert Place (Deal Street), Spitalfields, Spicer Street.

St. Annes School, Underwood Road, Whitechapel, 1891.

St. Anns Church Monastery & School, Albert Street (Deal Street), Spitalfields, 1891.

St. Anns Court, Green Bank, Wapping, "five doors on the right from Green bank near Wapping Church" (Lockie).

St. Anns Orphanage, Albert Place (Deal Street), Spitalfields, 1891, Albert Street.

St. Anns Place, Commercial Road, Limehouse, "is part of the north side commencing at the Britannia by the bridge and extending to opposite the church" (Lockie).

St. Anns Road, 1. Off Burdett Road, Bromley and Bow, 1891, renamed Midlothian Road. 2, Off Midlothian Road, Bromley and Bow, renamed Midlothian Road, Mile End Stadium is on the site.

St. Anns Road or Row, St. Anns Street (St. Anne Street), Limehouse, "the first on the right in St. Anns Street facing the church" (Lockie).

St. Anthonys Institute, Braintree Street, Mile End, 1921.

St. Augustines Church, Settles Street, Whitechapel, 1879-1948.

St. Augustines Church & School, Victoria Park Road, Hackney, 1891.

St. Bartholomews Church, Dalston Lane, Hackney, 1897-1952.

St. Bartholomews School, Essex Street (Blythe Street), Bethnal Green.

St. Benets Church, Mile End Road, Mile End, 1929-1951, now St. Benets Chaplaincy.

St. Catherines Court, St. Katharines Way, East Smithfield, 1746, Tower Hotel is on the site.

St. Catherines Lane, St. Katharines Way, East Smithfield, 1790, St. Katharine Dock is on the site.

St. Christopher House, Limehouse Causeway, Limehouse, St. Vincent Estate, demolished in 1998.

St. Clements Hospital, 2a Bow Road, Bromley and Bow, 1874-2005.

St. Cuthberts Church, Westferry Road, Isle of Dogs, on corner of Cahir Street.

St. Cuthberts Lodge, 1 Ingelheim Place (Westferry Road), Isle of Dogs.

St. Domingo Cottages, Stainsby Road, Limehouse, 1851.

St. Dunstans Arms Public House, 48 St. Dunstans Road (Mile End Stadium), Mile End.

St. Dunstans Place, Stepney Way, Stepney, "is facing the west side of the Churchyard by the Ship public house" (Lockie).

St. Dunstans Road, 1. Off Burdett Road, Bromley and Bow, Mile End Stadium is now on the site. 2. Bromley and Bow, renamed Eric Street. 3. Stepney, renamed Timothy Road.

St. Dunstans School, Stepney Green, Stepney, 1891.

St. Edwards Roman Catholic Chapel, Moiety Road, Isle of Dogs, Westferry Road.

St. Enoder House, Sun Tavern Place (Juniper Street), Shadwell, 1891.

St. Faiths Church, Shandy Street, Mile End, 1890-1945.

St. Francis Home, 157 Richmond Road, Hackney, 1950.

St. Frideswides Church, Follett Street, Poplar, 1895.

St. Gabriels Church & Terrace, Chrisp Street, Poplar, 1891.

St. George Court, 1. John Street (Cannon Street Road), Stepney, renamed Challis Court, John Street was immediately north west of railway line. 2. St. George Street (The Highway), St. George in the East, 1891.

St. George in the East (or Stepney) Workhouse, Princes Street (Raine Street), Wapping, "on the east side at the back of the Iron foundry near 27 Old Gravel Lane" (Lockie), became St. George in the East Hospital.

St. George in the East Hospital, Raine Street, Wapping, 1871-1956.

St. George Street, Off Ratcliffe Highway (The Highway), St. George in the East, 1851, Original name for that part of The Highway from Upper East Smithfield to east of St. George in the East Church.

St. Georges Brewery Tap Public House, 23 Church Lane (Commercial Road), St. George in the East, address also 33 Commercial Road.

St. Georges German & English School, 53 Little Alie Street (Alie Street), Whitechapel, 1910.

St. Georges House & Residence for Girls, George Yard (Gunthorpe Street), Whitechapel, 1891.

St. Georges Mission, Wellclose Square, St. George in the East, 1868.

St. Georges Place, 1. Back Road (Cable Street), St. George in the East, 1860, Cannon Street Road to Anthony Street. 2. Old Ford Road, Bromley and Bow.

St. Georges Tavern Public House, 50 The Highway, St. George in the East, aka Caxton, aka Artichoke.

St. Georges Terrace, 1. Commercial Road, St. George in the East, immediately east of Grove Street. 2. Commercial Road, St. George in the East, renamed Golding Terrace. 3. Commercial Road, Stepney, "the first west from Humberston Street" (Lockie). 4. Mornington Road (Mornington Grove), Bromley and Bow, 1891, Bow Road. 5. Willis Street, Poplar, 1862.

St. Georges Wharf, Wapping Wall, Wapping, 1895, absorbed into New Crane Wharf.

St. Helena House, Grove Road, Bromley and Bow.

St. Helens Wharf, Wapping High Street, Wapping, 1950, west of corner with Knighten Street.

St. James Chambers, 203-207 Poplar High Street, Poplar, 1891.

St. James Church, 1. Butcher Row, Ratcliffe, opposite Cable Street. 2. Old Ford Road, Bromley and Bow, 1851.

St. James Place, 1. Old Ford Road, Bromley and Bow. 2. St. James Place, Silver Street, St. George in the East, 1891, renamed Agatha Street.

St. James Road, Off Old Ford Road, Bromley and Bow, 1891.

St. James Sunday School, White Horse Street (White Horse Road), Stepney, 1862, opposite Green Street.

St. James Terrace, Back Road (Cable Street), St. George in the East, 1851.

St. John Street, Off Brick Lane, Whitechapel, "Spitalfields or at 106 the third on the left $\frac{1}{8}$ of a mile from 145 Church Street it extends to Bethnal Green workhouse" (Lockie), renamed Grimsby Street.

St. John the Evangelist Church, Golding Street, St. George in the East, 1869-1948.

St. John the Evangelist in the East Church, Grove Street (Golding Street), St. George in the East, 1950, next to 83 Grove Street.

St. Johns Chapel, St. John Street (Grimsby Street), Bethnal Green, "about eighteen doors on the left from 105 Brick Lane" (Lockie).

St. Johns Church & School, Roserton Street, Isle of Dogs, 1895.

St. Johns Cottage, Alfred Street, Bromley and Bow, 1891, Bow Road.

St. Johns Parsonage, Cambridge Road (Cambridge Heath Road), Bethnal Green.

St. Johns Place, Well Street, Hackney, 1891, renamed Priory Place.

St. Johns Row, Brick Lane, Bethnal Green, "St. Lukes at 42 the north end of Brick Lane being the third on the right about $\frac{1}{5}$ of a mile from 113 Old Street" (Lockie).

St. Johns Terrace, 1. Grove Street (Lauriston Road), Hackney, 1851. 2. Harwar Street (Cremer Street), Hackney.

St. Johns Wharf, Wapping High Street, Wapping, 1950, west of corner with Brewhouse Lane.

St. Josephs Home, Rose Lane (Ratcliffe Lane), Ratcliffe, Rose (now Ratcliffe) Lane.

St. Judes Church, Commercial Street, Whitechapel, 1870.

St. Judes Church & School, Old Bethnal Green Road, Bethnal Green, 1862, west of St. Judes Road.

St. Judes Place, St. Jude Street, Bethnal Green, 1851.

St. Katharine Wharf, St. Katharines Way, East Smithfield, 1950, west of St. Katharine Dock entrance.

St. Katharines Convent, 181 Bow Road, Bromley and Bow, 1921.

St. Katharines Dock Hotel, 20

Upper East Smithfield, East Smithfield.

St. Lawrence Cottages & Street, Off Prestons Road, Poplar, 1950.

St. Leonards Almshouses, Hackney Road, Bethnal Green, 1860, immediately north west of corner with later Baroness Road.

St. Leonards Arms Public House, 162 St. Leonards Road, Poplar, 1874.

St. Leonards Avenue, St. Leonards Road, Poplar, 1891.

St. Leonards Cottages, Follett Street, Poplar, 1891.

St. Leonards Terrace, Mornington Road (Mornington Grove), Bromley and Bow, 1891.

St. Lucia House, Limehouse Causeway, Limehouse, St. Vincent Estate, demolished in 1995.

St. Lukes Church, 1. Burdett Road, Bromley and Bow, close to Baggally Street. 2. Homerton Terrace, Hackney, 1950, at its corner with Woodbine Terrace. 3. Strafford Street, Isle of Dogs.

St. Lukes School, Westferry Road, Isle of Dogs, close to Strafford Street) moved to Saunders Ness Road in 1970.

St. Lukes Square, Strafford Street, Isle of Dogs, Nos. 1-17 also known as Strafford Villas.

St. Marks Mission, Back Church Lane, St. George in the East.

St. Marks Road, Off Betts Street, St. George in the East, renamed St. Marks Gate.

St. Marks School, Royal Mint Street, East Smithfield.

St. Mary & Street Dominic Roman Catholic Church, Balance Road, Hackney, 1939, corner of Balance Road and Kenworthy Road.

St. Marys Church, 1. Church Passage (Nantes Passage), Spitalfields, 1891, Spitalfields Flower Market was built on site. 2. Haggerston Road, Hackney, 1827-1985, south of Mansfield Street. 3. Whitechapel High Street, Whitechapel, "stands at the eastern end of Whitechapel High Street This church is of some antiquity as appears from Hugh de Fulbourn being its rector in 1329 The old chuch being very ruinous it was taken down in 1673 and rebuilt as at present" (Elmes).

St. Marys Church of England School, Spital Square, Spitalfields.

St. Marys Hall, Hows Street, Bethnal Green, 1950, corner with Weymouth Terrace.

St. Marys Industrial Home for Girls, 31 Stepney Green, Stepney.

St. Marys Mission, Garford Street, Limehouse, 1885.

St. Mary(s) Street, Off Whitechapel Road, Whitechapel, renamed Davenant Street.

St. Marys Street Synagogue, 3 St. Mary Street (Davenant Street), Whitechapel, 1907, now known as Davenant Street.

St. Marys Tube Station, Whitechapel Road, Whitechapel, 1884-1938, close to 100 Whitechapel Road opposite St. Marys Street.

St. Marys Whitechapel Tube Station, Whitechapel Road, Whitechapel, 1884-1938, District Line, west of Whitechapel tube station.

St. Matthews Church, Pell Street (Wellclose Square), St. George in the East, 1868.

St. Matthews Parochial School, Church Row (Bethnal Green Road), Bethnal Green.

St. Matthews Place, Hackney Road, Bethnal Green, 1841.

St. Matthias Church, Woodstock Terrace, Poplar, 1842-1969.

St. Matthias School, Bow Lane (Bazely Street), Poplar, 1871, former Bow Lane School.

St. Michael & All Angels Church, Lamb Lane, Hackney, 1895, at its corner with Helmsley Terrace.

St. Mildreds House, Westferry Road, Isle of Dogs, behind St. Pauls Church.

St. Nicholas & All Hallows Church, Aberfeldy Street, Poplar, 1955-1990.

St. Nicholas Church, Yabsley Street, Poplar, 1900, united with St. Nicholas and All Hallows in 1955.

St. Olaves Church, Commercial Street, Spitalfields.

St. Pauls Church, Broke Road (Broke Walk), Hackney, 1895, corner with Marlborough Road.

St. Pauls Church for Seamen, Dock Street, St. George in the East, 1847-1971.

St. Pauls Industrial School for Boys, 199 Burdett Road, Bromley and Bow.

St. Pauls Presbyterian Church, Westferry Road, Isle of Dogs, briefly named Millwall United Reform Church in the 1970s, now "The Space" arts centre.

St. Pauls Schoolhouse, 1. Blomfield Road (Burdett Road), Bromley and Bow, 1891. 2. St. Pauls Road (St. Pauls Way), Bromley and Bow, 1891.

St. Pelagias Home, 2 Church Row (Newell Street), Limehouse, renamed Magdalen Home or House.

St. Peter Street, Off St. Peters Avenue (St. Peter Square), Bethnal Green, Hackney Road to Gossett Street, immediately west of St. Peter's Church.

St. Peters Church, 1. Cephas Street, Mile End, 1839-1957. 2. Garford Street, Limehouse, close to West India Dock Road.

St. Peters Hospital, Fulbourne Street, Whitechapel, 1930-1944, aka Spitalfields Workhouse aka Whitechapel Union Workhouse.

St. Peters Mission, Gill Street, Limehouse, 1890.

St. Peters Road, Mile End, renamed Cephas Avenue.

St. Peters Street, Off Globe Road, Mile End, 1891, renamed Cephas Street.

St. Philips Church, 1. New Road, Whitechapel, corner of Stepney Way. 2. Turner Street, Whitechapel, 1870, Oxford Street.

St. Philips District Church, Richmond Road, Hackney, 1868, corner of Park Road.

St. Philips National School, New Road, Whitechapel, 1870, south of St. Philips Church.

St. Saviour & the Cross Church & School, Wellclose Square, St. George in the East, 1857-1868, former Danish Church.

St. Saviours Church, Northumbria Street, Limehouse, 1860-1977.

St. Saviours School, Northumberland Street (Northumbria Street), Limehouse, 1865.

St. Stephens Church, 1. East India Dock Road, Limehouse, 1867-1949, corner of Upper North Street. 2. Pritchards Road, Bethnal Green, 1950, south of

the canal. 3. Quaker Street, Spitalfields, 1890, corner of Quaker Street and Commercial Street.

St. Stephens Home for Homeless Boys, 81 East India Dock Road, Limehouse, between St. Stephens Vicarage and Howrah House.

St. Thomas Church, Arbour Street West (West Arbour Street), Stepney, 1840-1940.

St. Thomas Cottages, Lyme Grove, Hackney, 1891, Shakespeare House is on the site.

St. Thomas Road, 1. Hackney, renamed Ainsworth Road. 2. Bromley and Bow, renamed Apostle Road, Mile End Stadium is on the site.

St. Thomas School, William Street (Ivimey Street), Bethnal Green.

St. Vincent House, Limehouse Causeway, Limehouse, St. Vincent Estate, demolished in 1999.

St. Vincent Street, Off Charles Street (Aylward Street), Stepney, 1862, renamed Perth Street.

Stainborough Street, Bethnal Green, renamed Stainsbury Street.

Stainsby Tavern Public House, 49 East India Dock Road, Limehouse, 1874, corner of Stainsby Road.

Stamford or Stanford Place,

Acton Street (Arbutus Street), Hackney, 1841.

Standard Public House, Wetherell Road, Hackney.

Stanfield Road, Off Medway Road, Bromley and Bow, part renamed Viking Close.

Stanley Arms Public House, 1. 56 Carmen Street, Poplar, aka Lord Stanley. 2. 134 Kerbey Street, Poplar.

Stanley Road, Hackney, renamed Mead Place.

Star & Garter Public House, 1. 41 Arbour Square (Wickham Close), Mile End, 1874. 2. 123 Green Street (Roman Road), Bethnal Green. 3. 539 Kingsland Road, Hackney, 1874. 4. 233 Whitechapel Road, Whitechapel, 1874.

Star & Garter Yard, 1. Old Gravel Lane (Wapping Lane), Stepney, renamed Garter Yard. 2. St. George Street (The Highway), St. George in the East, 1891.

Star Court, Off Nightingale Lane (Thomas More Street), East Smithfield, 1800, St. Katharine Dock is on its site.

Star Hotel, 10 Dock Street, St. George in the East.

Star of Devon Public House, 49 Glaucus Street, Bromley and Bow.

Star of the East Public House, 36-38 Tetley Street (Chrisp Street), Poplar.

Star or Starch Yard, Old Gravel Lane (Wapping Lane), Wapping, "at 103 three doors on the left from 65 Ratcliffe Highway" (Lockie).

Star Place, 1. Lower Chapman Street (Bigland Street), St. George in the East, "the last on the left from Cannon Street Road and opposite Albion Place" (Lockie). 2. Star Street (Planet Street), Shadwell, 1891. 3. Stepney, renamed Whites Gardens.

Star Public House, 1. 11 Calvert Street (Watts Street), Wapping, 1874. 2. 21 Charles Street (Aylward Street), Stepney. 3. 21 Duke Street (Morris Street), Shadwell, 1874. 4. 116 Heath Street (Head Street), Stepney. 5. Limehouse Hole (Three Colt Street), Limehouse. 6. 2 Morris Street, Shadwell. 7. 26 Star Street (Planet Street), Shadwell, 1874, Wapping Wall, address also 26 Monza Street. 8. 188 Wapping High Street, Wapping. 9. 108 Wentworth Street, Whitechapel. 10. 40 Wilkes Street, Spitalfields.

Star Street, 1. Off Commercial Road, Shadwell, renamed Planet Street. 2. Off 24 Half Nichol(s) Street (Boundary Street), Bethnal Green.

Star Tavern Public House, 647 Commercial Road, Limehouse, aka York (Tap).

Starvation Farm, Fairfield Road, Bromley and Bow, 1851.

Statchells or Statchwells Court, Church Lane (White Church Lane), Whitechapel, "opposite Union Street" (Lockie).

Station Place, Watney Street, Shadwell, in front of Shadwell railway station, renamed Shadwell Place.

Stationers Arms Public House, 15 Berger Road, Hackney.

Stave Yard, Wapping High Street, Wapping, "at 332 about ¹/₈ of a mile on the right below Hermitage Bridge" (Lockie).

Steam Ferry Tavern Public House, 157 Wapping High Street, Wapping, aka Bell, address also 123 Wapping High Street.

Steam Packet Public House, 1. 17 Halley Street, Limehouse, aka Old Steam Packet. 2. 1 Orchard Place, Poplar.

Steam Ship or Steamship Public House, 24 Naval Row, Poplar, 1874.

Stean House, Stean Street, Hackney, 1950.

Stebbing Place, Cassland Road, Hackney, 1868.

Stebonheath Terrace, Salmon Lane, Limehouse, 1851.

Steelhouse Lane, Stepney Causeway, Ratcliffe, "is opposite the Causeway extending from Brook Street across the fields towards Stepney Church" (Lockie).

Stenhouse Street, Off Dunbridge Street, Bethnal Green.

Stephen Cottages, James Street, Stepney, 1871.

Stephen House, St. Anthonys Close, East Smithfield.

Stephens Buildings, Pedley Street, Whitechapel, 1841.

Stephens or Stephensons Cottage(s), Conder Street, Limehouse.

Stephensons Wharf, Wapping Wall, Wapping, 1859, absorbed into Metropolitan Wharf.

Stepney (Union) Workhouse, St. Leonards Street, Bromley and Bow, 1895, between Talwin Street and the railway line, later Bromley House Institution.

Stepney Ever Open Door Shelter, Stepney Causeway, Ratcliffe.

Stepney Gap, Stepney Causeway, Ratcliffe, "the first on the left from the Commercial Road towards Brook Street" (Lockie).

Stepney Green Terrace, Mile End Road, Mile End, "forms part of the right side of Stepney Green, entering by Mile End Road, it extends from Prospect Place to Cross Row (Lockie).

Stepney Homes Refuge, 6 and 18-26 Stepney Causeway, Ratcliffe.

Stepney Jewish School, Stepney Green, Stepney.

Stepney Junction Railway Station, Commercial Road, Ratcliffe, 1895, renamed Stepney East now Limehouse Docklands Light Railway station.

Stepney Meeting Almshouses, Salmon Lane, Limehouse, 1851.

Stepney Meeting House, White Horse Street (White Horse Road), Stepney, "Stepney Charity School at the north end of White Horse Street from the Commercial Road" (Lockie).

Stepney New Square, Stepney, early name of Trafalgar Square (Trafalgar Gardens).

Stepney Old Road (aka Old Road), Stepney, renamed Ben Jonson Road.

Stepney Old Square, Mile End Road, Mile End, "$\frac{1}{3}$ of a mile on the left from Mile End Road and near the north side the church yard" (Lockie).

Stepney Orthodox Synagogue, 53 Stepney Green, Stepney, 1979.

Stepney Rents, Hackney Road, Bethnal Green, 1841, between Austin Street and Bakers Rents.

Stepney Scattered Homes, 14-17 Cottage Grove (Rhondda Grove), Bromley and Bow.

Stepney Square, Stepney High Street, Stepney, 1891.

Stepney Temple, Commercial Road, Stepney, 1895, between Portland Street and Bromley Street site of later Wesleyan Seamens Chapel then Wesleyan Central Hall.

Stepney Union Receiving Home, York Street West, Bromley and Bow.

Stepney Union School Poor Law Home, Ropemakers Fields, Limehouse.

Stepney Workhouse, Alderney Place (Alderney Road), Mile End, Globe Road.

Stevens Acre, Brunswick Street, Poplar, 1851.

Stevens Buildings, Narrow Street, Limehouse, 1851.

Steward Street, Off Union Street (Brushfield Street), Spitalfields, "the second on both the right and the left in Union Street from 69 Bishopsgate Street Without" (Lockie).

Stewarts Buildings, Devons Lane (Devons Road), Bromley and Bow, 1851.

Stewarts Buildings & Cottages, Back Alley (Bromley High Street), Bromley and Bow, 1891, Bromley High Street.

Still Alley, Blue Gate Fields (The Highway), Shadwell, "the second on the right about eight doors from 245 High Street Shadwell" (Lockie).

Stock Street, 1891, became part of Burcham Street.

Stocker Street, Bethnal Green, renamed Hocker Street.

Stockmar Road, Off Morning

Lane, Hackney, 1891, continued south in Frampton Park Road.

Stocks Almshouses, Bow Lane (Bazely Street), Poplar, 1862, earlier name for Esther Awes Almshouses.

Stocks Weavers (or Framework Knitters) Almshouses, Kingsland Road, Hackney, 1895, immediately north of Ironmongers Almshouses.

Stone Alley, Broad Street (The Highway), Ratcliffe, 1746.

Stone Court, St. Catherines (St. Katharines Dock), East Smithfield, 1746, St. Katharine Dock is on the site.

Stone Stairs, Broad Street (The Highway), Ratcliffe, "at 94 on the west side the India Companys warehouse and nearly facing Globe stairs Rotherhithe" (Lockie).

Stonebridge Common, Stonebridge Road (Haggerston Road), Hackney, 1895, immediately north of present-day Stonebridge Gardens.

Stonebridge House, Stean Street, Hackney, 1950, corner with Dunston Road.

Stonebridge Lane, Kingsland Road, Hackney, 1851, renamed Haggerston Road.

Stonebridge Place & Terrace, Stonebridge Road (Haggerston Road), Hackney, 1851.

Storer Street, Off Philpot Street, Whitechapel, 1860, renamed Nelson Street.

Storers Wharf, Saunders Ness Road, Isle of Dogs, 1950, present-day street, Caledonian Wharf, is on its site.

Stow Cottages, Myrtle Street (Mapledene Road), Hackney, 1851.

Stracey Street, Stepney, renamed Jamaica Street.

Strafford Houses, Wentworth Street, Spitalfields, 1950.

Strafford Place, Westferry Road, Isle of Dogs, 1851, between Strafford Street and Thomas Street.

Strafford Villas, Strafford Street, Isle of Dogs, 1870, also known as 1-17 St. Lukes Square.

Strangers Home, West India Dock Road, Limehouse, 1891.

Stratfield Road, Off Love Lane (Talwin Street), Bromley and Bow, 1891.

Stratford Place, Richmond Road, Hackney, 1851, at its corner with Holly Street.

Stratford Terrace, 1. Hardinge Street, Shadwell, 1851. 2. Thomas Street, Stepney, 1871.

Strathmore Terrace, Back Road (Cable Street), St. George in the East, 1851.

Streatfield Street, Off Burdett Road, Limehouse, 1891.

Strongs Buildings, 184-196 East India Dock Road, Poplar, 1851.

Strouds or Strouts Place, Smiths Place (Hackney Road), Bethnal Green, 1891, Hackney Road.

Stuart Street, Spitalfields, renamed Stewart Street.

Suffolk Arms Public House, 76 Boston Street (Hackney Road), Bethnal Green, 1874, Hackney Road.

Suffolk Brewery (Tap) Public House, 91 New Road, Whitechapel.

Suffolk Cottages, James Street (Vesey Street), Poplar, 1851, James Street and East India Dock Road.

Suffolk Place, 1. Commercial Road, Limehouse, 1851, close to corner of White Horse Street. 2. Hackney Road, Bethnal Green, 1841, between Minerva Street and Cambridge Heath Road. 3. Holly Street, Hackney, 1851. 4. Stonebridge Lane (Haggerston Road), Hackney, 1851.

Suffolk Road, Off Ipswich Road (Pownall Road), Hackney, 1950.

Suffolk Street, 1. Limehouse, 1891, renamed Ellerman Street, Bartlett Park is on the site. 2. Off Three Colts Lane, Bethnal Green, 1891, renamed Coventry Street. 3. Whitechapel, renamed Walden Street.

Sugar Loaf Court, 1. Back Church Lane, St. George in the East. 2. Essex Street

(Commercial Street), Spitalfields, "Essex Street, the first on the right from 105 Whitechapel High Street" (Lockie). 3. George Street (Code Street), Whitechapel. 4. 1851, Goodmans Yard to Swan Street.

Sugar Loaf Public House, 1. 155 Back Church Lane, St. George in the East. 2. 34 Betts Street, St. George in the East, 1874. 3. 37 Great Hermitage Street (Hermitage Wall), Wapping, address also 41 Great Hermitage Street. 4. 187 Hanbury Street, Spitalfields.

Sultans Public House, 1. 45 Wellington Road, Bethnal Green. 2. Wood Street (Wilkes Street), Spitalfields, 1874.

Summer Place, Ocean Street, Mile End, "the first east parallel to Ocean Street on the north side the Church Yard" (Lockie).

Summer Street, Off Old Ford Road, Bromley and Bow, 1895, opposite Blondin Street A12 is on the site.

Sumners Row & Buildings or Cottages, Upper North Street, Poplar, 1851.

Sun & Half Moon Public House, 35 Broad Street (The Highway), Ratcliffe.

Sun & Sawyers Court, 241 Poplar High Street, Poplar, 1874.

Sun & Sawyers Public House & Court, 241 Poplar High Street, Poplar, 1874, aka

Exchange Tavern, aka Rising Sun.

Sun & Sword Public House, 31 Cable Street, St. George in the East, 1874, aka Rising Sun & Sword.

Sun Court, 1. Mile End Road, Mile End, "two doors east of the Vintners Almshouses about ⅛ of a mile on the left below the turnpike" (Lockie). 2. Upper East Smithfield, East Smithfield, 1851. 3. Stepney, renamed Yule Court (Sutton Street).

Sun Public House, 1. 441 Bethnal Green Road, Bethnal Green. 2. Globe Street (Globe Road), Mile End, 1874. 3. 92 Sclater Street, Whitechapel. 4. 54 Upper East Smithfield, East Smithfield.

Sun Tavern Court, King David Lane, Shadwell, "Sun Tavern Fields on the south side the Rope walk entering by the first on the right in King David Lane from 198 Shadwell High Street" (Lockie).

Sun Tavern Fields, Shadwell High Street (The Highway), Shadwell, "on the north side Shadwell High Street say from 117 to 193 or from King David Lane to Love Lane" (Lockie).

Sun Tavern Gap, Back Road (Cable Street), St. George in the East, 1851, renamed Glamis Road.

Sun Tavern Place & Yard, Juniper Row (Juniper Street), Shadwell, 1891.

Sun Yard, Off Nightingale Lane (Thomas More Street), East Smithfield, 1800, St. Katharine Dock is on its site.

Sunderland Bridge Public House, 19 Wapping Wall, Wapping, aka Ship and Whale.

Surat Court, Place & Street, Off Preston Street (Roman Road), Bethnal Green, 1891, became part of Surat Street.

Surrey Court, Surrey Place (Poplar High Street), Poplar, rear of Surrey Place.

Surrey Place, 1. Bow Lane, Poplar, 1851, close to Poplar High Street. 2. Tredegar Road, Bromley and Bow.

Susannah Row, Dorset Street (Pitsea Street), Ratcliffe, 1891.

Sussex Arms Public House, 71 Upper North Street, Poplar, 1874.

Sussex Street, 1. Off Gainsborough Road (Eastway), Hackney, renamed Daintry Street. 2. Limehouse, 1860, renamed Lindfield Street.

Suther Street, Off Wallis Road, Hackney, 1891.

Sutton Model Dwellings, Braintree Street, Mile End, 1921.

Swale Street, Off Upper North Street, Poplar, 1891, Nankin Street is on the site.

Swallow Gardens, Royal Mint Street, East Smithfield, 1870, rear of Royal Mint Street, opposite Cartwright Street.

Swan & Lamb Public House, 3 New Gravel Lane (Garnet Street), Wapping, aka Grapes.

Swan Alley, 1. Off Nightingale Lane (Thomas More Street), East Smithfield, 1800, St. Katharines Dock is on its site. 2. Ratcliffe Cross (Narrow Street), Ratcliffe, 1746.

Swan Brewhouse, Brewhouse Lane, Wapping.

Swan Court, 1. Church Street (Bethnal Green Road), Bethnal Green, "Swan Street, four doors on the right from 154 Church Street near Brick Lane" (Lockie). 2. Mansell Street, Whitechapel, "at 9 two doors north of Swan Street" (Lockie). 3. Petticoat Lane (Middlesex Street), Spitalfields.

Swan Inn Public House, 20 Whitechapel High Street, Whitechapel, 1874, "at 20 ten doors west of Red Lion Street" (Lockie), aka White Swan.

Swan Place, Mile End Road, Mile End, "Mile End Green, opposite Epping Place being a few doors south from Mile End turnpike" (Lockie).

Swan Public House, 1. 13 Bethnal Green Road, Bethnal Green. 2. 21 Great Alie Street (Alie Street), Whitechapel, 1874, aka White Swan. 3. 438 Kingsland Road, Hackney. 4. 43 Lower Shadwell (Shadwell Park), Shadwell, aka White Swan, aka Half Moon. 5. 94 Mansell Street, Whitechapel, address also 5 Mansell Street. 6. 229 Mile End Road, Mile End, 1874, aka White Swan. 7. 161 Old Gravel Lane (Wapping Lane), Wapping, 1874, aka White Swan. 8. 57 Royal Mint Street, East Smithfield, 1874, aka White Swan. 9. 3 Swan Street (Cygnet Street), Bethnal Green, 1874, aka White Swan. 10. 211 Well Street, Hackney.

Swan Street, Off Church Street (Bethnal Green Road), Bethnal Green, "at 154 ten doors west of Brick Lane extending to Sclater Street" (Lockie), renamed Cygnet Street.

Swan Tavern Public House, 1. Church Street (Bethnal Green Road), Bethnal Green, 1891. 2. 94 Mansell Street, Whitechapel.

Swan Yard, 1. Bethnal Green Road, Bethnal Green, 1860, part of the westernmost section of Bethnal Green Road. 2. Hackney, renamed London Lane. 3. Mile End Road, Mile End, "the third on the left east from the Old Globe about ½ of a mile below the turnpike" (Lockie). 4. Osborn Street, Whitechapel, 1851. 5. Whitechapel High Street, Whitechapel, "at 20 about ten doors west of Red Lion Street" (Lockie).

Swattons Place, Cologne Street (Harford Street), Mile End, 1860, west side south of East London Cemetery.

Swedenborg Square, now Swedenborg Gardens, St. George in the East.

Swedish Church, Swedenborg Square (Swedenborg Gardens), St. George in the East, 1729-1911.

Swedish Flag Public House, 146 St. George Street (The Highway), St. George in the East, 1874, address also 2 Princes Street, 2 Swedenborg Street.

Sweet Apple or Sweetapple Court & Square, Old Castle Street, Bethnal Green, 1841.

Swiston Road, Off Approach Road, Bethnal Green, 1862, renamed Sewardstone Road.

Sydney Arms Public House, 1. 29 Arcadia Street, Poplar, 1874. 2. 474 Bethnal Green Road, Bethnal Green.

Sydney Buildings, 21 East India Dock Road, Limehouse.

Sydney or Sidney Street, Off Upper North Street, Poplar, renamed Arcadia Street.

Sydney Place, Sydney Street (Lidgett Street), Poplar, 1851.

Sydney Street, Off Wells Street (Cotton Street), Poplar, 1851, Wells Street to Woolmore Street, renamed Lidgett Street.

Sykes Buildings, Fieldgate Street, Whitechapel.

Sykes Terrace, Mile End Road, Mile End, Greenwood Street to Jubilee Street.

Sylvester (or Silvester) Row, Grove Place (Reading Lane), Hackney, 1891, renamed Sylvester Road.

T

Tabard Public House, 52 Cambridge Road (Cambridge Heath Road), Mile End.

Tabernacle Yard, Spitalfields, renamed Church Passage, and later renamed Nantes Passage.

Tabers Cottages, Devons Lane (Devons Road), Bromley and Bow, 1851.

Tagg Street, Off Bonner Street, Bethnal Green, 1891, Cranbrook Estate is on the site.

Talbot (Inn) Public House, 25 Whitechapel High Street, Whitechapel, 1874.

Talbot Tavern Public House, 208 Poplar High Street, Poplar, 1780, renamed Spotted Dog.

Tall House, Commercial Road, Stepney, 1851.

Talmud Torah Synagogue, Pinchin Street, St. George in the East, 1950.

Tamar Street, renamed Lefevre Road (Lefevre Walk), Bromley and Bow.

Tan Alley, Wheler Street, Spitalfields.

Tap House Public House, 2 Bath Street (Darling Row), Whitechapel.

Tap Street, Off Somerford Street, Whitechapel, 1851, renamed Tapp Street.

Tapley Street, Off St. Leonards Road, Poplar, 1891.

Tavern Court Row & Terrace, Quay Lane (Brunswick Road), Poplar, 1891.

Taverners Place, Cow Lane (Ben Jonson Road), Stepney, 1851.

Tavistock Street, Off Derbyshire Street, Bethnal Green, renamed Saltash Street.

Taylor Place, Ben Jonson Road, Mile End, 1891.

Taylors Buildings, Old Ford Road, Bromley and Bow, 1851.

Taylors Court, Farmer Street (Shadwell Basin), Shadwell, "at 58 the third on the left from 38 Shadwell High Street" (Lockie).

Taylors Place, Rhodeswell Road, Limehouse, 1851.

Taylors Rents, Broad Street (The Highway), Ratcliffe, 1891.

Tchechanover Synagogue, 1. 18 Fieldgate Street, Whitechapel, later address, sometimes spelled Chechenover. 2. Tchechanover Synagogue, 26 Old Montague Street, Whitechapel, sometimes spelled Chechenover.

Teal Street, Off Mape Street, Bethnal Green, 1891, became part of Cheshire Street.

Teal(s) Terrace, Seabright Place (Seabright Street), Bethnal Green, 1851.

Telegraph Public House, 1. 19 Hawkins Street (Sidney Street), Stepney, 1874. 2. 194 Westferry Road, Isle of Dogs, 1874, brief name of Magnet & Dewdrop.

Temperance Cottages, North Street (Brady Street), Whitechapel, 1851.

Temple Place, Hackney Road, Bethnal Green, 1841.

Temple Street, Off Queensbridge Road, Hackney, 1895, renamed Myrtleberry Street.

Temple Street Tap Public House, Hackney Road, Bethnal Green, 1950.

Temple Terrace, Collingwood Street, Whitechapel, 1841.

Ten Bells Public House, 84 Commercial Street, Spitalfields, 1874.

Tenbury Place, Commercial Road, Limehouse, "a few doors on the right in Jamaica Place towards Gun Lane" (Lockie).

Tennant House, Coventry Cross Estate, Bromley and Bow, St. Leonards Street.

Tenter Buildings, St. Marks Street, Whitechapel, 1891, Great Prescot Street.

Tenter Court, Tenter Street, Whitechapel, 1851.

Tenter Ground, Goodmans Fields (Prescot Street),

Whitechapel, "entrance by 39 Prescot Street about six doors on the left from Mansel Street" (Lockie).

Tenter House, St. Marks Street, Whitechapel, 1891, Great Prescot Street.

Tenterden Arms Public House, 224 Devons Road, Bromley and Bow.

Terrace Place, Stepney Green, Stepney, "the south end of Stepney Green terrace, about $^1/_5$ of a mile on the right from Mile End Road" (Lockie).

Terrace Road West, Hackney, renamed Elsdale Street.

Tethorn Place, New Gravel Lane (Garnet Street), Wapping, New Gravel Lane to Ship Street, north of gasworks.

Tetley Street, Off Chrisp Street, Poplar, 1851, Chrisp Street to St. Leonards Road.

Tewkesbury Buildings, Whitechapel High Street, Whitechapel, 1851.

Tewkesbury Court, Whitechapel High Street, Whitechapel, "at 100 nearly opposite Red Lion Street", (Lockie).

Tewsons Court, Sandys Row, Spitalfields, 1891, east of Sandys Row, and north of Wentworth St.

Thames Place, Emmett Street, Limehouse, 1950, between Emmett Street and Limehouse Stairs.

Theresa Place, Mare Street, Hackney, 1860, at corner with Well Street.

Thirza Street, Off Hardinge Street, Shadwell, 1891, immediately south of railway line.

Thistle & Crown Public House, 106 Wapping High Street, Wapping, 1874, address also 21 Wapping High Street.

Thomas Cottages, Ben Jonson Road, Mile End, 1891.

Thomas Cottages & Rents, Nightingale Lane (Thomas More Street), Wapping, 1851, renamed Willow Row.

Thomas Court or Place, 1. Old Nichol(s) Street (Boundary Estate), Bethnal Green, "the first on the right from Nichols Row" (Lockie). 2. Pell Street (Wellclose Square), St. George in the East, 1891, rear of west side of Pell Street, renamed Day Place.

Thomas Jackson House, Maples Place, Whitechapel.

Thomas Passage, Merceron Street, Whitechapel.

Thomas Place, 1. Bethnal Green Road, Bethnal Green, "a few doors on the left in Abbey Street from the said road" (Lockie). 2. Brady Street, Whitechapel, 1891. 3. Crab Tree Row (Columbia Road), Bethnal Green, "part of the right side a few doors from the Hackney Road" (Lockie). 4. Old Ford Road, Bromley and

Bow, 1851. 5. Old Nichol(s) Street (Boundary Estate), Bethnal Green, 1841. 6. Pell street (Swedenborg Gardens), St. George in the East, "Pell Street, Ratcliffe, about the middle of the west side, entering by 194 Ratcliffe Highway" (Lockie). 7. St. Leonards Avenue (St. Leonards Road), Poplar, renamed Layfield Place.

Thomas Rents, Ropemakers Fields, Limehouse, Ropemakers Fields to Narrow Street.

Thomas Row, Bethnal Green Road, Bethnal Green, "the second on the right in Charles Street from opposite Wilmot Square" (Lockie).

Thomas Street, 1. Off Brick Lane, Whitechapel, became part of Bacon Street. 2. Off Burdett Road, Limehouse, renamed Thomas Road. 3. Off Cambridge Road (Cambridge Heath Road), Mile End, 1841, renamed Faith Street. 4. Off Devas Street, Bromley and Bow, 1891, renamed Donald Street. 5. Off Fulbourne Street, Whitechapel. 6. Off Hardinge Street, Shadwell, Hardinge Street to Devonport Street, immediately south of Ronald Street. 7. Off Kingsland Road, Hackney, 1868, renamed Harwar Street later Cremer Street. 8. Off Mary Street (Waley Street), Mile End, "the first on the left from Ocean Street to Cow Lane" (Lockie). 9. Off Stainsby Road, Limehouse, renamed Gough Street. 10. Thomas Street, Poplar, renamed Thomas Road. 11. Off Twig Folly Bridge (Roman Road), Bethnal Green, 1851, Green Street. 12. Off Water Lane (Morning Lane), Hackney, renamed Ribstone Street. 13. Off Westferry Road, Isle of Dogs, renamed Havannah Street. 14. Off Whitechapel Road, Whitechapel, "the second on the right from 94 Whitechapel Road along Bakers Row and Charles Street" (Lockie), renamed Fulbourne Street.

Thomas(s) Passage, 1. Bethnal Green Road, Bethnal Green, "the first on the right in Charles Street from opposite Wilmot Square" (Lockie). 2. Brady Street, Whitechapel, 1891, route followed more or less by Merceron Street. 3. Mape Street, Bethnal Green. 4. Thomas Street (Granby Street), Bethnal Green, 1851. 5. Voss Street, Bethnal Green, became part of Voss Street.

Thompson Buildings, Old Nichol(s) Street (Boundary Estate), Bethnal Green, 1851.

Thompson Cottages, Grundy Street, Poplar, 1851.

Thompsons Place, Wilmot Street, Bethnal Green, "near the south end towards Dog Row" (Lockie).

Thorold Square, Turin Street, Bethnal Green, 1891, north west corner of Turin Street and Bethnal Green Road.

Thorps Wharf, Wapping Wall, Wapping, 1859, west of The Prospect of Whitby.

Thrall Street, Spitalfields, renamed Thrawl Street.

Thrasher House, Clarissa Street, Hackney, 1950.

Three Colt Court, Three Colt Street, Limehouse, "at 15, also called New Court" (Lockie).

Three Colts Alley, King Street (Prusom Street), Wapping, "the first on the right from Old Gravel Lane near Wapping" (Lockie).

Three Colts Corner, Hare Street (Cheshire Street), Whitechapel, 1841.

Three Colts Public House, 1. 205 Dog Row (Cambridge Heath Road), Bethnal Green, 1874. 2. 128 Lauriston Road, Hackney, 1874. 3. 58 Three Colt Street, Limehouse, close to corner with Grenade Street.

Three Colts Yard, Mile End Road, Mile End, "the second on the left below the Old Globe about ½ a mile east from the turnpike" (Lockie).

Three Compass(es) Court, Stepney Causeway, Ratcliffe, 1851.

Three Compasses Public House, 1. 14 Anchor Street (Boundary Street), Bethnal Green, 1874. 2. 2 Brick Lane, Spitalfields. 3. 99 Dalston Lane,

Hackney. 4. 9 Glasshouse Street (John Fisher Street), East Smithfield, Royal Mint Street. 5. 15 Harrow Alley (Harrow Place), Whitechapel. 6. 79 Old Montague Street, Wapping, 1874, address also 9 Glasshouse Street. 7. 44 Raven Row, Mile End, 1874, Mile End Road. 8. 49 Sclater Street, Spitalfields.

Three Cranes Public House, 1. 194 Brick Lane, Spitalfields, 1874, address also 39 Brick Lane. 2. Church Street (Mare Street), Hackney, 1874, address also 359 Mare Street. 3. 45 Mile End Road, Mile End, 1874, Park Place.

Three Crown Court, Wheler Street, Spitalfields.

Three Crowns Public House, 1. 1 Dunk Street (Hanbury Street), Spitalfields, 1874, aka Halifax Head. 2. 45 Mile End Road, Mile End, 1874. 3. 27 New Castle Street (Tyne Street), Whitechapel, 1874. 4. 6 Oakley Street (Granby Street), Bethnal Green. 5. 3 Shorter Street (Fletcher Street), St. George in the East. 6. 6 Smart Street, Bethnal Green. 7. 60 Upper East Smithfield, East Smithfield.

Three Cups Alley, Lower Shadwell (Shadwell Park), Shadwell, 1874, close to Broad Bridge.

Three Cups Court, Lower Shadwell (Shadwell Park), Shadwell, 1874.

Three Cups Public House, 1. 156 Bow Road, Bromley and Bow, 1874. 2. 21 Lower Shadwell (Shadwell Park), Shadwell, 1874.

Three Fox Court, Ratcliffe, 1895, behind Three Fox(es) public house.

Three Foxes Public House, 37 Narrow Street, Ratcliffe, 1874.

Three Loggerheads Public House, 57 Virginia Road, Bethnal Green, 1874, aka Loggerheads Arms, Two Loggerheads (1722).

Three Mariners Public House, 1. 132 Cassland Road, Hackney, 1874. 2. 34 Ropemakers Fields, Limehouse, 1874. 3. 30 Wapping Wall, Wapping, address also 33 Wapping Wall.

Three Neats Tongues Public House, 3 Great Pearl Street (Calvin Street), Spitalfields.

Three Queens Public House, 27 Mape Street, Bethnal Green.

Three Suns Public House, 61 New Gravel Lane (Garnet Street), Wapping, 1869.

Three Swedish Crowns Public House, 83 Old Gravel lane (Wapping Lane), Wapping, opposite Watts Street.

Three Tuns Alley, Wentworth Street, Whitechapel, "Whitechapel, the first south parallel to part of it extending from Petticoat Lane to Old Castle Street" (Lockie).

Three Tuns Court, Bow High Street (Bow Road), Bromley and Bow, 1851.

Three Tuns Public House, 1. Bow High Street (Bow Road), Bromley and Bow, 1851. 2. 121 Broad Street (The Highway), Ratcliffe, 1874. 3. 39 Pennyfields, Limehouse, 1874. 4. 1 Whitechapel High Street, Whitechapel.

Throwsters Arms Public House, 16 Essex Street (Commercial Street), Spitalfields.

Thurlow Place, 1. Bethnal Green, Bethnal Green, "on the east side of the green near the Rising Sun" (Lockie), Burnham Estate is on the site. 2. Hackney Road, Bethnal Green, 1827, Queen Elizabeth Hospital for Children was built on the site.

Thurlow Square, Green Street (Roman Road), Bethnal Green, 1851.

Tiger Public House, 1. 79 Kerbey Street, Poplar. 2. 14 Longnor Road, Mile End, 1874.

Tiger Tavern Public House, 245 Wick Road, Hackney.

Tilley Street, Shepherd Street (Commercial Street), Spitalfields, 1891, Brune House was built on the site.

Tillotson Street, 1. Off Diggon Street, Stepney, 1891. 2. Off Oley Place (Stepney Green School), Stepney, 1950, Oley Place to Latimer Street, Stepney

Green football pitch is on the site.

Timothys Wharf, Westferry Road, Isle of Dogs, 1950, south of Arnhem Place.

Tites Alley, Narrow Street, Limehouse, "Limehouse, the first on the left below Mr Turners house leading to Risbys rope walk" (Lockie).

Titmouse or Tittymouse or Tetemouse Alley, Farmer Street (Shadwell Basin), Shadwell, "at 54 about the middle of the east side" (Lockie).

Tobacco Pipe Alley, Nightingale Lane (Thomas More Street), Wapping, Sun Lane, Rocque 2F5.

Tomlins Grove, 1. Bow Road, Bromley and Bow, 1891. 2. Parnham Street, Stepney, 1891.

Tomlins Terrace, Chrisp Street, Poplar, 1851.

Tongue Yard, Whitechapel Road, Whitechapel, "at 247 the third on the right about thirty six doors east of the church" (Lockie), just east of the corner of Fieldgate Street and Whitechapel Road.

Tooke Street, Off Westferry Road, Isle of Dogs, 1851.

Tookes Place, Westferry Road, Isle of Dogs, 1851, between Maria Street and Janet Street.

Toplis Court, East Street (Bishops Way), Bethnal Green.

Toronto Buildings, Cotton Street, Poplar, 1900.

Torrington Arms Public House, 34 Westferry Road, Isle of Dogs, 1874.

Torrington Causeway, Westferry Road, Isle of Dogs, ran from Westferry Road to the Thames via Torrington Wharf close to Strafford Street.

Torrington Street, Off Pennington Street, St. George in the East, 1790, Pennington Street to Shard Street.

Torrington Wharf & Yard, Westferry Road, Isle of Dogs, 1891, on the riverfront close to Strafford Street.

Totnes (or Totness) Cottages, Westferry Road, Isle of Dogs, close to Harbinger School on the river side of Westferry Road.

Totten Street, Stepney, renamed Belgrave Street.

Totty Street, Off Roman Road, Bromley and Bow, Mile End Park is on site.

Tower Buildings, Brewhouse Lane, Wapping, 1891, Wapping High Street.

Tower Hamlets Association for Rescue & Preventive Work, Bow Road, Bromley and Bow.

Tower Hamlets Dispensary, Old Gravel Lane (Wapping Lane), Wapping, "Established in 1792 for diffusing the benevolent services of a dispensary in the district" (Elmes).

Tower Hamlets Hostel, 43 Hardinge Street, Shadwell.

Tower Hamlets Prison, Wellclose Square, St. George in the East, 1799.

Tower House Asylum, London Fields, Hackney, 1841.

Tower of London Public House, 14 Cable Street, St. George in the East.

Tower Public House, 19 Artillery Street (Artillery Lane), Spitalfields.

Tower Stores Public House, 80 Rhodeswell Road, Limehouse.

Tower Street, 1. Off London Fields, Hackney, renamed Martello Street. 2. Off Stonebridge Lane (Haggerston Road), Hackney, 1827, just north of the canal.

Tower Terrace, Hackney, renamed Martello Terrace (Wadeson Street).

Town of Leith Public House, 1 Lower East Smithfield (St. Katharines Way), East Smithfield, 1874, address also 35 St. Katharines Way.

Toy(e)s Buildings, Bethnal Green Road, Bethnal Green, 1891, corner of Mansford Street; and further south in Mansford Street.

Tracey Cottages, Chisenhale Road, Bromley and Bow.

Trader Street, Off Durham Row, Stepney.

Trafalgar Place, 1. Brady Street, Whitechapel, renamed Neath Place Collingwood Estate is now on the site. 2. Hackney Road, Bethnal Green, 1827, either side of Great Cambridge Street. 3. Pleasant Row (Redmans Road), Mile End, "a few small houses behind 16 the first on the left from Redmans Row" (Lockie).

Trafalgar Public House, 28 West India Dock Road, Limehouse.

Trafalgar Square, Stepney Green, Stepney, Mile End renamed Trafalgar Gardens; "Stepney entrance about 1/3 of a mile on the left along Stepney Green from Mile End Road" (Lockie).

Trafalgar Street, Off Half Nichol(s) Street (Boundary Street), Bethnal Green, 1851.

Trafalgar Terrace, 1. Cow Lane (Ben Jonson Road), Stepney, "part of the north side of Cow Lane, by Ocean Street near the church" (Lockie). 2. 217-223 East India Dock Road, Poplar, 1902. 3. Hackney Road, Bethnal Green, 1841, opposite Nelson Street.

Tranquil Place, Abbot Street, Hackney, 1841, Kingsland Road.

Tredegar Arms Public House, 155 Tredegar Road, Bromley and Bow.

Tredegar House, Bow Road, Bromley and Bow, 1851.

Tredegar Square & Mews, Tredegar Street, Bromley and Bow, 1891.

Tredegar Works, Ordell Road, Bromley and Bow, 1891.

Trego Road, Off Wansbeck Road, Bromley and Bow, 1891.

Trelawney Road, Off Paragon Road, Hackney, 1891.

Trellis Street, Off Malmesbury Road, Bromley and Bow, 1891.

Trevor Terrace, Cubitt Town, Isle of Dogs, 1888.

Trewint Industrial Home, 201 Mare Street, Hackney.

Triangle (Place), 1. Cambridge Road (Cambridge Heath Road), Bethnal Green, 1851. 2. Triangle Road, Hackney, 1895, became part of Warburton Street.

Triangle Terrace, West Street (Westgate Street), Hackney, 1891.

Triggs Cottage or Place, Nightingale Lane (Thomas More Street), Wapping, renamed Chivers Court.

Triggs Place, Northey Street, Limehouse, 1860, close to its corner with Nightingale Lane.

Trinity Arms Public House, 45 Orchard Place, Poplar, 1874.

Trinity Chapel, Devonshire Road (Brenthouse Road), Hackney, 1895.

Trinity Chapel Day Schools, Upper North Street, Poplar.

Trinity Congregational Church & Schools, Hanbury Street, Spitalfields.

Trinity Congregational Chapel, East India Dock Road, Poplar, Trinity Methodist Mission built on site.

Trinity Cottages, Orchard Street (Orchard Place), Poplar, 1851.

Trinity Episcopal Chapel, Cannon Street Road, St. George in the East, 1831.

Trinity Ground Almshouses, Cambridge Road (Cambridge Heath Road), Mile End, 1841.

Trinity Hall Sunday School, Augusta Street, Poplar, 1921.

Trinity Market, Grundy Street, Poplar, early name for Randalls Market.

Trinity Road & Row, Orchard Place, Poplar, 1891.

Trinity Stairs, Ship Alley (The Highway), Ratcliffe, Broad Street.

Trinity Terrace, East India Dock Road, Poplar, 1851.

Tripe(s) Yard, Sandys Row, Spitalfields, 1891, east of Sandys Row, and north of Wentworth St.

Trotters Court, New Gravel Lane (Garnet Street), Wapping, 1851.

Trout Road, Bromley and Bow, renamed Stour Road.

Trowbridge Place, Trowbridge Road, Hackney, Trowbridge Road to Wick Road.

True Briton Public House, 28 Gill Street, Limehouse.

True Friends Public House, 53 Fieldgate Street, Whitechapel.

Trumans Fields, Charles Street (Vallance Road), Whitechapel, Also known as Coverley Fields site of Trumans Brewery eastern stores, Osmani primary school is on part of the site.

Trump or Trumpet Court, Whitechapel Road, Whitechapel, "at 43 a few doors on the left east from the church" (Lockie).

Tryon or Tyones Place, Mare Street, Hackney, 1827, renamed Tudor Road.

Tryphena Place, Bow Common Lane, Bromley and Bow, 1851, north of St. Pauls Way.

Tuckers Court, Dingles Lane (Dingle Gardens), Poplar, 1851, Poplar High Street.

Tuckers Row, Dingles Lane (Dingle Gardens), Poplar, 1851, Poplar High Street.

Tudor Cottages, Bow Common Lane, Bromley and Bow, 1851.

Tufton Buildings, Poplar High Street, Poplar, "nearly opposite North Street about $\frac{1}{8}$ of a mile on the right from the Commercial Road" (Lockie).

Tuilerie Street, Off Hackney Road, Bethnal Green, 1891, east of Yorkton Street.

Tunnel Gardens, Robin Hood Lane, Poplar, public gardens at original entrance to Blackwall Tunnel.

Turk Court, Virginia Row (Virginia Road), Bethnal Green, 1841.

Turk Street, Off Virginia Row (Brick Lane), Bethnal Green, "the continuation of Tyson Street opposite Brick Lane to Virginia Street behind Shoreditch Church" (Lockie), became the northernmost part of Brick Lane.

Turkish Slave Public House, 157 Brick Lane, Whitechapel, aka Jolly Butchers, aka Turk and Slave, aka Turkish Head.

Turks Head Public House, 1. 308 Brick Lane, Bethnal Green, 1874, address also 1 Turk Street. 2. 20 Tench Street, Wapping. 3. 326 Wapping High Street, Wapping, Thames riverfront.

Turn Again Lane, Whitechapel, later Charles Street, now part of Vallance Road.

Turner Place, West Street (Usk Street), Bethnal Green, 1851.

Turner Square, Whitechapel Road, Whitechapel, "at 219 about seven houses which stand back from the line of the pavement near $\frac{1}{4}$ of a mile east of the church" (Lockie), just west of corner of Whitechapel Road and New Road.

Turners Buildings, Grove Street (Golding Street), St. George in the East, 1891, Grove Street to Christian Street, opposite Ellen Street.

Turners Buildings, Pennyfields, Limehouse, 1890.

Turners Cottages, 1. Rhodeswell Road, Limehouse, 1851. 2. Risbies Ropewalk (Narrow Street), Limehouse, 1851.

Turners Court, 1. Church Lane (Back Church Lane), St. George in the East, "Church Lane, the first on the right from the Commercial Road towards Wellclose Square" (Lockie). 2. Robin Hood Lane, Poplar, 1851.

Turners Place or Row, Northey Street, Limehouse, 1891.

Turville Buildings, Court & Place, Turville Street, Bethnal Green, 1841.

Tuscan Street, Off Knottisford Street, Bethnal Green, 1891, diagonally opposite Butler Street.

Tuson(s) or Tewsons Court, Petticoat Lane (Middlesex Street), Spitalfields, 1851, Petticoat Lane.

Tusons Buildings, Castle Lane (Old Castle Street), Whitechapel, "the continuation of Barns Buildings being the first on the left from 124 Whitechapel" (Lockie).

Tusons Court, Tripe Yard (Sandys Row), Spitalfields, 1891.

Twemloe or Twemlow Terrace, West Street (Westgate Street), Hackney, 1851, became part of Westgate Street.

Two Beehives Public House, 89 Devas Street, Bromley and Bow.

Two Bells Public House, 11-13 Whitechapel Road, Whitechapel.

Two Black Boys Public House, 171 Well Street, Hackney.

Two Brewers Public House, 1. 154 Brick Lane, Spitalfields, address also 1 Brick Lane, aka Old Two Brewers Public House. 2. 26 Glasshouse Street (John Fisher Street), East Smithfield, 1874, address also Whites Yard. 3. 35 Globe Road, Mile End. 4. 98 Narrow Street, Limehouse, 1874, next to Duke Shore Stairs. 5. 7 Skidmore Street (Harford Street), Stepney, address also 1 John Street. 6. 11 Spital Street, Spitalfields, 1874.

Two Friends Public House, 53 Fieldgate Street, Whitechapel.

Two Loggerheads Public House, Virginia Row (Virginia Road), Bethnal Green, 1722, aka Three Loggerheads Arms, Two Loggerheads (1722).

Two Mariners Public House, 15 Hardinge Street, Shadwell, 1874.

Tye Street, Off Rhodeswell Road, Limehouse.

Tynemouth Castle Public House, 193 New Crane (New Crane Place), Wapping, address also 192 Wapping High Street.

Type Passage, Type Street, Bethnal Green, Cranbrook Estate is on the site.

Tyrell Place, Tyssen Street, Bethnal Green, 1841.

Tyrell Street, Off Bethnal Green Road, Bethnal Green, "at the north-east corner of Thorold Square" (Lockie).

Tyres Alley, Narrow Street, Limehouse, 1851.

Tyrone or Tryons Place, Mare Street, Hackney, 1827, renamed Tudor Road.

Tyrrell Street, Off Turin Street, Bethnal Green, 1891.

Tyssen Arms Public House, 27 Dalston Lane, Hackney, 1874.

Tyssen Cottages, Passage, Pavement & Terrace, Dalston Lane, Hackney, close to Dalston Junction.

Tyssen or Tyson Street, Off Church Street (Bethnal Green Road), Bethnal Green, "at 52 opposite Brick Lane about ¼ of a mile on the left from 65 Shoreditch" (Lockie), became part of Brick Lane.

U

Ulmar Place, Ming Street, Limehouse, 1950, behind Blue Posts public house.

Unanimous Row, 1. Church Street (Fournier Street), Spitalfields, "a few yards behind 27 Church Street entering opposite King Street" (Lockie). 2. Queen Street (Coverley Close), Whitechapel, Coverley Close is on the site.

Underwood Street, Off Vallance Road (Whitechapel), Spitalfields, now Underwood Road.

Unicorn Street, Off Guildford Road (Upper North Street), Poplar, 1891, renamed Alton Street.

Union (Tavern) Public House, 17 Emmett Street, Limehouse, 1874.

Union Arms Public House, Union Road (Westferry Road), Isle of Dogs, aka Pin & Cotter.

Union Brewery, Wapping High Street, Wapping, "about ⅛ of a mile below Hermitage Bridge" (Lockie).

Union Buildings, 1. Garden Street (Poplar High Street), Poplar, 1851. 2. Union Street (Boston Street), Bethnal Green, 1868, part renamed Long Street. 3. renamed Union Walk, Bethnal Green, 4. Whitehead Street (Cleveland Way), Mile End, 1891.

Union Chapel, Bow Lane (Newby Place), Poplar, 1845, east side of All Saints church yard.

Union Cottage, Wrights Place (Cotton Street), Limehouse, 1891, Providence Place.

Union Court, Osborn Place (Osborn Street), Whitechapel, 1851.

Union Court & Place, 1. Fashion Street, Spitalfields, 1851. 2. Whitehead Street (Cleveland Way), Mile End,

1891. 3. Ming Street, Limehouse, renamed Ulmar Place. 4. Fashion Street, Spitalfields, north of and parallel with the east end of Fashion Street

Union Court, Place & Terrace, Eastfield Street, Limehouse, 1891.

Union Crescent, Union Street (Boston Street), Bethnal Green, 1868.

Union Flag (& Punchbowl) Public House, 64 Wapping High Street, Wapping, 1874.

Union Flag Public House, 8 Union Street (Whitehead Street), Mile End, 1874.

Union Jack Shoeblack Society, 8 Three Colt Street, Limehouse.

Union Passage, Shadwell, renamed Watney Passage.

Union Place, 1. Stepney Way, Mile End, 1851, renamed Cressy Place. 2. Wheler Street, Spitalfields, 1891, behind the premises at the corner of Wheler Street and Quaker Street. 3. Mile End, renamed Whitehead Place (Cleveland Way). 4. Wilmot Street, Bethnal Green, 1851. 5. 4 Henrietta Street (Allgood Street), Bethnal Green.

Union Road, 1. Off Westferry Road (river side), Isle of Dogs, became part of Mellish Street. 2. Off Wick Road, Hackney, renamed Bradstock Road.

Union Row, 1. Bethnal Green Road, Bethnal Green, "the continuation of the west side of Wilmot Street" (Lockie). 2. Fashion Street, Spitalfields, "a few doors on the right from 193 Brick Lane" (Lockie). 3. Mile End Road, Mile End, "forms part of the south side near the Plough about two miles from Aldgate" (Lockie). 4. Morning Lane, Hackney, 1851, east of Stevens Avenue. 5. Morpeth Street, Bethnal Green, 1841. 6. Mile End, "9 Stepney Green, the first on the right in Union Place from the green" (Lockie), renamed Mulberry Street.

Union Row or Road, Off Union Street (Adler Street), Whitechapel, "the first on the left from the said road facing Sion Chapel" (Lockie), Mulberry Street is on the site.

Union Stairs, Wapping High Street, Wapping, "at 326 about 1/6 of a mile below Hermitage Bridge" (Lockie).

Union Street, 1. Whitechapel, renamed Adler Street. 2. Off Bethnal Green Road, Bethnal Green, "three doors west of the turnpike near 1/2 a mile on the left from 65 Shoreditch" (Lockie), renamed Turin Street. 3. Spitalfields, renamed Brushfield Street. 4. Off Cleveland Street (Cleveland Way), Mile End, 1891, renamed Whitehead Street. 5. Off East India Dock Road, Poplar, renamed Bullivant Street. 6. Off Hackney Road, Bethnal Green, renamed Boston Street. 7. Off Hackney Road, Bethnal

Green, renamed Waterson Street. 8. Off Shadwell High Street (The Highway), Shadwell, "at 227 opposite New Gravel Lane extending to Back Lane" (Lockie). 9. Off Watney Street, Shadwell, 1929, renamed Dunch Street.

Union Tavern Public House, 15-17 Emmett Street, Limehouse.

Union Walk, Union Street (Boston Street), Bethnal Green, 1868.

Union Wharf, 1. Orchard Place, Poplar, 1950. 2. Wapping Wall, Wapping, 1859, absorbed into Metropolitan Wharf.

Unitarian Chapel, Chatham Place, Hackney, 1858-1950, close to corner with Paragon Road.

Unitarian College Chapel, Stepney Green, Stepney, corner of Garden Street.

United Workmens Synagogue, Spital Square, Spitalfields.

United Brothers Public House, 1. 12 Emmett Street, Limehouse. 2. 20 Hale Street, Poplar.

United Charity School of Poplar & St. Anne Limehouse, Poplar High Street, Poplar, 1806, built on Poplar Workhouse site.

United Friends Synagogue, 16 Fashion Street, Spitalfields.

United Methodist Free Church, 1. Cheval Street, Isle of Dogs, 1868, between Thomas Street

and Tooke Street. 2. East India Dock Road, Poplar, renamed King Georges Hall, fire station is on the site.

United States Public House, 69 St. George Street (The Highway), St. George in the East, aka Bunch of Grapes Public House.

Up Court, Church Row (Newell Street), Limehouse, 1851.

Upper & Lower Keate Street, Off Keat(e) Street (Thrawl Street), Spitalfields.

Upper Baker Street, Off Russell Street (Halcrow Street), Whitechapel.

Upper Berner Street, Off Commercial Road, St. George in the East, joined with Lower Berner Street to become Berner Street, northern section later renamed Henriques Street.

Upper Chapman Street, Off Cannon Street Road, St. George in the East, "is the first turning on the right hand going from the Commercial Road towards Back Lane and extending to Duke Street" (Elmes), renamed Chapman Street.

Upper Charles Street, Poplar, renamed Donald Street (Devas Street).

Upper Chrisp Street, Poplar, became part of Chrisp Street.

Upper Cornwall Street, Off Lower Cornwall Street (Cornwall Street), St. George in the East, combined with Lower Cornwall

Street in the east to form Cornwall Street.

Upper Felix Street, Off Cambridge Crescent, Bethnal Green, 1841.

Upper Fenton Street, Off Commercial Road, St. George in the East, 1891, renamed Fenton Street.

Upper George Street, Bromley and Bow, renamed Empson Street.

Upper Grove Street, Off Grove Street (Golding Street), St. George in the East, southern section of what would become, along with Middle Grove Street and Lower Grove Street.

Upper Gun Alley, Wapping High Street, Wapping, "at 104 opposite Gun Dock about seven doors on the left below the London Docks" (Lockie).

Upper John Street, Off Lower John Street (Sutton Street), Shadwell, combined with Lower John Street and renamed Blakesley Street.

Upper King Street, Off Christian Street, St. George in the East, combined with Lower King Street to form Christian Street.

Upper Montague Street, Bromley and Bow, renamed Tredegar Terrace.

Upper North Street, Whitechapel, became part of Brady Street.

Upper Queens Row, Cambridge Road (Cambridge Heath Road), Bethnal Green, 1851.

Upper Randall Street, renamed Augusta Street.

Upper Shadwell, alternative name for Shadwell High Street (The Highway), Shadwell.

Upper Stainsby Road, Limehouse, renamed Stainsby Road.

Upper Turning, Great Spring Street (Shadwell Basin), Shadwell, northernmost road connecting Shakespeares Walk and Great Spring Street, above Middle Turning and Lower Turning Shadwell Basin is on the site.

Upper Well Alley, Green Bank, Wapping, 1891, renamed Dundee Street.

Upton Place, Commercial Road, Stepney, 1868, Sidney Street to Bromehead Street.

Upton Terrace, Commercial Road, Limehouse, 1871.

Urban Place, Sheep Lane, Hackney, 1851.

V

Valentine Corner, Grove Street (Ellsworth Street), Bethnal Green, 1841.

Valentine Terrace, Mill Street (Old Ford Road), Bromley and Bow, 1851.

Valley Place, Orange Street (Satchwell Road), Bethnal Green, 1851.

Van Tromp Public House, 121 Bethnal Green Road, Bethnal Green, 1874.

Vanes Wharf, 36 Narrow Street, Ratcliffe, 1895.

Vaughan Estate, Diss Street, Bethnal Green, 1950, corner of Diss Street and Baroness Road.

Vectus Cottages, Henry Street (Carr Street), Stepney, 1871.

Venice Street, Off Somerford Street, Whitechapel, 1950.

Venour Road or Street, Off Maidman(s) Street (Burdett Road), Bromley and Bow, 1891.

Venue Street, Off Teviot Street, Poplar, renamed Celtic Street.

Vesey Street, Off East India Dock Road, Poplar, 1891, Vesey Path opposite Poplar Baths is to the west of its path.

Veteran Public House, 78 Whitechapel Road, Whitechapel.

Vicar of Wakefield Public House, 83 Coventry Street (Coventry Road), Bethnal Green, 1874, Three Colts Lane.

Victoria & Albert Cottages, Devonshire Street (Colebert Avenue), Mile End, immediately east of Globe Road.

Victoria Arms Public House, 1. 77 Lower Chapman Street (Bigland Street), St. George in the East. 2. 39 Warley Street, Bethnal Green.

Victoria Buildings, Emmott Street (Essian Street), Mile End, 1891.

Victoria Cottage(s), 1. Hackney Road, Bethnal Green, 1851. 2. Mill Street (Old Ford Road), Bromley and Bow, 1851. 3. Victoria Park Bromley and Bow, 1851.

Victoria Gardens, Grove Road, Bromley and Bow, 1851.

Victoria Grove, 1. Cambridge Road (Cambridge Heath Road), Bethnal Green, 1851. 2. Morpeth Road, Hackney, 1868, renamed Morpeth Grove. 3. Victoria Park Road, Hackney, 1891, renamed Earlston Grove.

Victoria Hotel & Public House, 171 Burdett Road, Bromley and Bow, 1874, address also Victoria Road.

Victoria Mews, Old Ford Road, Bromley and Bow, north of Cyprus Place, renamed Elsden Mews.

Victoria Park Congregational Hall, Approach Road, Bethnal Green.

Victoria Place, 1. Brunswick Street (Haggerston Road), Hackney, 1868, between Brunswick Street and Hertford Place, became part of Haggerston Road. 2. Coopers Gardens (Hackney Road), Bethnal Green, 1841. 3. George Gardens (Bethnal Green Road), Bethnal Green, 1851. 4. Hackney Road, Bethnal Green, 1891, behind

Methodist Chapel opposite Minerva Street. 5. Martha Street (Wadeson Street), Hackney, 1851. 6. Oval Cottages (Hackney Road), Bethnal Green, 1841. 7. Queens Road (Queensbridge Road), Hackney, 1841. 8. Victoria Street (Dellow Street), Shadwell, 1851. 9. Westferry Road, Isle of Dogs, 1851, between Charles Street and Maria Street.

Victoria Place or Buildings, James Street (Chilton Street), Bethnal Green, 1891, renamed Entick Street.

Victoria Public House, 1. 8 Casket Street (Gascoigne Place), Bethnal Green, Casket Street was south of Columbia Road and west of Gascoigne Place. 2. 110 Grove Road, Bromley and Bow, 1874. 3. 37 Hassard Street, Bethnal Green. 4. 55 Hind Grove, Limehouse. 6. 451 Queensbridge Road, Hackney. 7. 46 Three Colt Street, Limehouse, 1874. 8. 359 Wick Road, Hackney.

Victoria Road, 1. Hackney, renamed Brougham Road. 2. Bromley and Bow, renamed Usher Road. 3. Off Wick Road, Hackney, 1950, became the easternmost section of Wick Road from Eastway to Berkshire Road section no longer exists.

Victoria Street, 1. Off Back Road (Cable Street), St. George in the East, 1851, renamed Dellow Street. 2. Poplar,

renamed Cording Street. 3. Off Gascoigne Place, Bethnal Green, 1841, renamed Casket Street. 4. Off King Edwards Road, Hackney, became part of Warneford Street.

Victoria Tavern, 47 Morpeth Road, Hackney, 1874.

Victoria Terrace, Russia Lane, Bethnal Green, 1851.

Victoria Villas, Queens Road (Queensbridge Road), Hackney, 1862, between Laurel Street and Temple Street.

Victoria Wharf, 1. Westferry Road, Isle of Dogs, 1950, Homer Drive is on its site. 2. Lower Shadwell (Shadwell Park), Shadwell, 1895. 3. Narrow Street, Limehouse, 1950, between Regent's Canal and Limehouse Cut entrances.

Victorias Head Public House, 278 Cambridge Heath Road, Bethnal Green.

Victory Public House, 1. 144 Ben Jonson Road, Mile End. 2. 39 Cadiz Street (Masters Street), Mile End. 3. 39 Collingwood Street, Whitechapel, aka Lord Napier. 4. 266 Commercial Road, Shadwell. 5. 272 Devonshire Street (Colebert Avenue), Mile End. 6. 65 Fournier Street, Spitalfields. 7. 7 Great Cambridge Street (Queensbridge Road), Bethnal Green, 1874, Hackney Road. 8. 160 Mare Street, Hackney. 9. 27 Nelson Street (Boundary Estate),

Bethnal Green, 1874. 10. 6 Providence Place (West India Dock Road), Limehouse. 11. Rhodeswell Road, Limehouse, 1874. 12. 169 St. Leonards Road, Poplar, aka Carpenters Arms. 13. 27 Vyner Street, Bethnal Green.

Vincent Place, Glasshouse Street (John Fisher Street), East Smithfield, Royal Mint Street.

Vincent Street, Off Boundary Street, Bethnal Green, 1891, Boundary Estate is on the site.

Vincent Street, 1. Off Carr Street, Limehouse, renamed Halley Street. 2. Off Charles Street (Aylward Street), Stepney, renamed Perth Street.

Vine (Tavern) Public House, 1. 85 Broad Street (The Highway), Ratcliffe, 1874, address also 471 The Highway. 2. 31 Mile End Road, Mile End, was free-standing on the pavement close to the corner with Cambridge Heath Road.

Vine Cottage, 1. Hollybush Gardens, Bethnal Green. 2. Navarino Road, Hackney, 1891, Dalston Lane.

Vine Court, Lamb Street, Spitalfields, 1746.

Vine Court Place, Commercial Street, Spitalfields.

Vine Court Synagogue, Vine Court, Spitalfields, 1960.

Vine Passage, Broad Street (The Highway), Ratcliffe, "at 84 about the middle of the north side" (Lockie).

Vine Public House, 452 Commercial Road, Shadwell.

Vine Street, Off King Street (Brick Lane), Spitalfields, 1851.

Vine Yard or Vineyard, Little Pearl Street (Calvin Street), Spitalfields, 1891.

Vine Yard Place, Brook Street (Cable Street), Ratcliffe, 1851.

Vintners Almshouses, Mile End Road, Mile End, "opposite Mutton Lane and were erected after the fire of London in lieu of those which were then destroyed in Upper Thames Street" (Elmes), just east of Trinity Almshouses.

Violet Cottages, West Street (Usk Street), Bethnal Green.

Violet Row, Braemar Street (Usk Street), Bethnal Green.

Violet Row, 1. Moss Street (Smart Street), Bethnal Green, 1891. 2. Roman Road, Bethnal Green, opposite the Cranbrook Estate.

Violet Street, 1. Off Braemar Street (Usk Street), Bethnal Green. 2. Bromley and Bow, renamed Violet Road.

Virgin Court, Upper Well Alley (Green Bank), Wapping, 1851.

Virginia Court or Place, Lower Chapman Street (Bigland Street), St. George in the East, 1891.

Virginia Planter Public House, 1. 80 Shadwell High Street (The Highway), Shadwell. 2. 124

Virginia Road, Bethnal Green, 1874.

Virginia Row, Bethnal Green, renamed Virginia Road.

Virginia Street, 1. Off (Old) Castle Street (Virginia Road), Bethnal Green, "the continuation of Castle Street behind Shoreditch Church to the Bird cage" (Lockie). Old Castle Street became westernmost part of Virginia Road. 2. Off Ratcliffe Highway (The Highway), St. George in the East, "at 50 near Ratcliffe Highway extending to the London Docks" (Lockie), south of Wellclose Square, opposite side of The Highway.

Vittoria Place, 1. Cambridge Road (Cambridge Heath Road), Bethnal Green, 1851. 2. Commercial Road, Limehouse, 1860, between Margaret Street and Dalgleish Street. 3. Mile End Road, Mile End, immediately east of Beaumont Street (later Grove).

Volunteer Public House, 1. 238 East India Dock Road, Poplar, corner of Robin Hood Lane. 2. 494 Old Ford Road, Bromley and Bow. 3. 43 Watney Street, Shadwell.

Volunteers Arms Public House, 7 Mill Place (Bowen Street), Limehouse, 1874, Commercial Road.

Von Tromp Public House, 121 Bethnal Green Road, Bethnal Green.

Vulcan Public House, 1. 20 Brunswick Street, Poplar. 2. 178 Rhodeswell Road, Limehouse, corner of Parnham Street. 3. 240 Westferry Road, Isle of Dogs.

Vulcan Street, Off Castor Street (Birchfield Street), Limehouse, 1891, Castor Street connected Birchfield Street to Church Path.

Vyner Street, Off Cambridge Road (Cambridge Heath Road), Bethnal Green, 1891.

W

Wade Street & Terrace, East India Dock Road, Poplar, 1851, East India Dock Road west of and parallel with Wades Place.

Wades Arms Public House, 15 Jeremiah Street, Poplar, 1874.

Wades Place, Mile End Road, Mile End, "nearly opposite Bencrofts Almshouses about 1¾ of a mile on the right from Aldgate" (Lockie), opposite St. Benets Church.

Wadham House, Wentworth Street, Whitechapel, 1891.

Wageners Buildings, Gowers Walk, Whitechapel, 1851.

Waggoners Place, Wapping Wall, Wapping, 1851.

Walburgh Court, St. George in the East, 1895, renamed Walburgh Place.

Walcot Cottages & Place, London Lane, Hackney, 1841.

Wales Place, Hackney Road, Bethnal Green, 1860, opposite its south corner with the present-day Columbia Road.

Walk Place Road, Off Mile End Road, Mile End, 1950, opposite Queen Mary College.

Walker Street, 1, Off Morris Road, Poplar, part renamed Fawe Street part renamed Brabazon Street. 2. Off St. Pauls Way, Bromley and Bow, south towards canal.

Walmsleys Maltings, St. Leonards Street, Bromley and Bow, 1891.

Walnut Tree Court, Globe Alley (Narrow Street), Limehouse, "the third turning on the left hand side of Nightingale Lane going from Fore Street" (Elmes).

Walnut Tree Public House, 18 Ben Jonson Road, Mile End.

Walsby Place, Coopers Gardens (Hackney Road), Bethnal Green, 1841.

Walter Court, Bromley High Street, Bromley and Bow, 1891.

Walter Street, Stepney, 1895, renamed Walter Terrace.

Walter(s) Terrace, 1, Essex Street (Blythe Street), Bethnal Green, 1891. 2. Wick Road, Hackney, 1862.

Walters Cottages, Westferry Road, Isle of Dogs, 1891.

Waltons Court, 1. Cartwright Street (Royal Mint Street), East Smithfield, 1851, Royal Mint Street. 2. Poplar High Street, Poplar, south west corner of Recreation Ground.

Wapping Dock Stairs, Wapping High Street, Wapping, "at 230 Wapping Street near Old Gravel Lane and opposite Rotherhithe church" (Lockie).

Wapping New Stairs, Wapping High Street, Wapping, "at 261 Wapping Street near Red Lion Street and opposite King Stairs Rotherhithe" (Lockie).

Wapping Old Stairs, Wapping High Street, Wapping, "at 290 Wapping Street, west side of the church and nearly opposite Cherry Garden Stairs" (Lockie).

Wapping Recreation Ground, Wapping, renamed Wapping Gardens.

Wapping Street, Wapping High Street, Wapping, "parallel to the Thames extending from Hermitage Bridge where the numbers begin and end, viz 1and 365 to New Gravel Lane about $^3/_4$ of a mile in length" (Lockie), also called Wapping High Street.

Wapping Workhouse, Off Upper East Smithfield, East Smithfield, 1800, just east of Nightingale Lane.

Warburton Arms Public House, 138 Mare Street, Hackney, 1874.

Warburton Square, Triangle Road, Hackney, 1891.

Ward(e)s Row, Bethnal Green Road, Bethnal Green, "is part of the left hand side of the road" (Elmes), between Harts Lane and Pollards Place.

Warkworth Terrace, Commercial Road, Limehouse, 1860, north side of Commercial Road, straddling Margaret Street.

Warrens Court, Ropemakers Fields, Limehouse, 1851.

Warrington Place, Yabsley Street, Poplar, 1891.

Warrior Public House, 1. 246 Commercial Road, St. George in the East. 2. 32 Limehouse Causeway, Limehouse.

Warton Place, Schoolhouse Lane, Shadwell, 1851.

Warwick Place, 1. Stepney, renamed Durning Place (Elsa Street). 2. Kingsland Road, Hackney, 1868, north of Grange Road.

Warwick Villas, Shepherds Lane, Hackney, 1862.

Washington Street, 1. Off Bow Common Lane, Bromley and Bow, 1891, renamed Single Street. 2. Off St. Leonards Street, Bromley and Bow, 1891, renamed Washington Close.

Water Lane, Morning Lane, Hackney, became part of Morning Lane.

Waterloo (Tavern) Public House, 64 Samuel Street (Wicker Street), St. George in the East.

Waterloo Buildings, Three Colts Lane, Bethnal Green, 1891, Cambridge Road.

Waterloo Cottages & Street, Off Commercial Road, Limehouse, 1851, Sailors Home is on the site.

Waterloo Court, Poplar High Street, Poplar, 1851.

Waterloo Court or Place, St. George in the East, 1929, renamed Wicker Terrace.

Waterloo Hero Public House, 19 Gough Street (Gough Walk), Limehouse, 1874.

Waterloo Place, 1. Commercial Road, Ratcliffe, 1851. 2. Coventry Street (Coventry Road), Bethnal Green, 1841. 3. Cyprus Street, Bethnal Green, Globe Road.

Waterloo Street, Off Haggerston Road, Hackney, 1895, renamed Pamela Street.

Waterloo Terrace, 1. Commercial Road, Ratcliffe, 1860, Ratcliffe Street to White Horse Street. 2. Selby Street, Whitechapel, 1841.

Watermans Arms Public House, 1. 1 Glenaffric Avenue, Isle of Dogs, renamed the Great Eastern. 2. 2 Lower Shadwell (Shadwell Park), Shadwell. 3. 44 Maroon Street, Limehouse. 4. 92 Narrow Street, Limehouse, 1874. 5. 21 Old Castle Street, Bethnal Green, 1874. 6. 290 Poplar High Street, Poplar. 43 Virginia Road, Bethnal Green. 7. 261 Wapping

High Street, Wapping. 8. 22 Wapping Wall, Wapping, 1874. 9. 6 Westferry Road, Isle of Dogs, 1815, corner of Robert Street.

Watermans Lodge Beer House, Totnes Terrace (Westferry Road), Isle of Dogs, 1870, Westferry Road.

Watermans Row, Upper Well Alley (Green Bank), Wapping, "at the north end of Upper Well Alley entering by 110 Wapping Street" (Lockie).

Watkins Terrace, St. Leonards Road, Poplar, 1862, between Tapley Street and Burcham Street.

Watney Passage, Watney Street, Shadwell, 1891, Watney Street to Morris Street.

Watsons Buildings, 1. Ducking Pond Row (Durward Street), Whitechapel, "the second turning on the left hand from North Street" (Elmes). 2. Pennyfields, Limehouse, "behind the Silver Lion at Poplar" (Elmes).

Watsons Wharf, Wapping High Street, Wapping, 1895, south of Sampson Street.

Watts Place, Bow Lane, Poplar, 1851.

Weathered Gardens, Crab Tree Row (Columbia Road), Bethnal Green, 1841.

Weaver(s) Street, 1. Off Fleet Street Hill (Pedley Street), Whitechapel, 1841. 2. Off New

Castle Street (Tyne Street), Whitechapel, 1891

Weavers Alley, Spicer Street (Buxton Street), Whitechapel, 1746.

Weavers Arms Public House, 1. 57 Back Church Lane, St. George in the East, 1874. 2. 69 Bethnal Green Road, Bethnal Green. 3. Green Street (Roman Road), Bethnal Green. 4. 17 Hanbury Street, Spitalfields, 1874. 5. 68 Pelham Street (Wheler Street), Spitalfields, 1874. 6. 13 Vallance Road, Whitechapel. 7. 1 Warley Street, Bethnal Green.

Webb Place, Narrow Street, Limehouse, 1851.

Webbs Buildings, 1. Risbies Ropewalk (Narrow Street), Limehouse, "the first on the right from behind Mr Goodharts Sugar house" (Lockie). 2. St. John Street (Grimsby Street), Bethnal Green, "about twenty doors on the left from 105 Brick Lane" (Lockie).

Webbs Place, Gowers Walk, Whitechapel, 1851.

Welcome Institute Coffee Tavern & Club Rooms for Factory Girls, 333 Westferry Road, Isle of Dogs, 1899, before moving to East Ferry Road, premises of later Dockland Settlement.

Weldon Place, Viaduct Street, Bethnal Green, 1950, Weavers Fields are on the site.

Well & Bucket Public House, 143 Bethnal Green Road, Bethnal Green.

Well Alley, Ropemakers Fields, Limehouse, "at 63 about the middle of the north side" (Lockie).

Well Court, 1. Hackney Road, Bethnal Green, "about ¼ of a mile on the right from Shoreditch Church and opposite Middlesex Place" (Lockie). 2. Well Street (Ensign Street), St. George in the East.

Well Street, 1. St. George in the East, renamed Ensign Street. 2. Off Hanbury Street, Spitalfields, became part of Hanbury Street, the section between Spital Street and Greatorex Street.

Well Yard, 1. Cartwright Street (Royal Mint Street), East Smithfield, Royal Mint Street. 2. Goodmans Fields (Leman Street), Whitechapel, "Leman Street the second on the right in Hooper Square from 82 Leman Street" (Lockie).

Wellclose Place, New Road, Whitechapel, "the entrance to Princes Square" (Lockie).

Wellington Alley, Wells Street (Cotton Street), Poplar, 1851.

Wellington Arms Public House, 1. 145 St. Leonards Road, Poplar. 2. 32-34 Wellington Street (Cyprus Street), Bethnal Green.

Wellington Buildings, Samuel Street (Wicker Street), St. George in the East, 1891.

Wellington Place, 1. Back Road (Cable Street), St. George in the East, 1860, north side of Back Road, between Charles Street and Cross Street. 2. Bonner Street, Bethnal Green, renamed Royston Street. 3. Brook Street (Cable Street), Ratcliffe, 1851. 4. King Street (Mace Street), Bromley and Bow, 1841, Harts Lane. 5. Old Bethnal Green Road, Bethnal Green, renamed Kite Place. 6. Stracey Street (Jamaica Street), Stepney, 1862, Stracey Street to Heath Street, became part of Oxford Street. 7. Bethnal Green, renamed Waterloo Gardens.

Wellington Place & Terrace, West India Dock Road, Limehouse, 1851.

Wellington Pond, Elizabeth Street (Mansford Road), Bethnal Green, 1841.

Wellington Public House, 14 Cannon Street (Cannon Street Road), St. George in the East, also known as Duke of Wellington.

Wellington Road, Off Bow Road, Bromley and Bow, 1891, renamed Wellington Way.

Wellington Row, Bird Cage Walk (Columbia Road), Bethnal Green, 1860, renamed Quilter Street.

Wellington Street, 1. Off Artillery Street (Peace Street), Whitechapel, 1841. 2. Off Bath Street (Darling Row), Whitechapel, 1851. 3. Off Cobden Street (Langdon Park School), Poplar, 1891, Langdon Park School is on the site. 4. Off Globe Road, Bethnal Green, renamed Cyprus Street. 5. Off Merceron Street, Whitechapel, renamed Pereira Street. 6. Bethnal Green, became part of Vallance Road. 7. Off Wellington Place, Stepney, 1862, renamed Pole Street.

Wellington Terrace, 1. St. Leonards Road, Poplar, 1862, between Byron Street and St. Leonards Avenue. 2. Stonebridge Lane (Haggerston Road), Hackney, 1851.

Wells Court, Hackney Road, Bethnal Green, 1841.

Wells Court, Place, Row & Yard, Gowers Walk, Whitechapel, 1851.

Wells Street, Off Cotton Street, Poplar, 1891, Cotton Street to Robin Hood Lane.

Welsh Calvinistic Mission, Augusta Street, Poplar, 1921.

Wentworth Arms Public House, 54 Wentworth Road (Eric Street), Bromley and Bow, 1874, Bow Road, address also 127 Eric Street.

Wentworth Court West & East, Wentworth Street, Spitalfields, 1891, north of Wentworth Street, just west of Commercial Street.

Wentworth Lodge, Coborn New Road (St. Stephens Road), Bromley and Bow, 1851, Roman Road.

Wentworth Place, Mile End Road, Mile End, "part of the left side about $1/5$ of a mile below the turnpike adjoining Red Cow Lane" (Lockie).

Wentworth Road, Off Bridge Street (Hamlets Way), Bromley and Bow, 1891, renamed Brantridge Street.

Wesleyan Chapel, Hale Street, Poplar, 1807, moved to East India Dock Road corner with Woodstock Terrace.

Wesleyan Methodist Chapel, Richmond Road, Hackney, 1895.

Wesleyan Seamens Mission, Jeremiah Street, Poplar, 1888, briefly used for original Queen Victoria Seamens Rest.

Wesleyan Terrace, 158-162 East India Dock Road, Poplar, Poplar Recreation Ground is on the site.

Wesleyan Chapel, Alpha Road (Alpha Grove), Isle of Dogs, also known as Alpha Hall or later Alpha Grove Community Centre.

Wesleyans Seamens Chapel, Commercial Road, Stepney, 1868, immediately east of Portland Street later Wesleyan Central Hall.

West Alpha Place, Chrisp Street, Poplar, 1851.

West Arms Public House, 26 Birchfield Street, Limehouse.

West Durham Place, Hackney Road, Bethnal Green, 1851.

West Ferry Road, Isle of Dogs, spelling of Westferry Road until c1950.

West Folly, Langdale Street, St. George in the East, 1891.

West Ham Water Works, Mile End Road, Mile End, "on the north side about 2 miles from Aldgate and opposite Ewings Buildings" (Lockie).

West House Asylum, Helmsley Street, Hackney, 1841, Mare Street.

West India Dock Company Library & Reading Room, Dolphin Lane, Poplar, 1860.

West India Dock Cottages, Dolphin Lane, Poplar, 1862, Poplar High Street.

West India Dock Railway Station, West India Dock Road (Aspen Way), Poplar, 1840-1926, immediately north of entrance to West India Docks.

West India Dock Tavern Public House, 4 Cold Harbour, Poplar.

West Patriot Row, Cambridge Road (Cambridge Heath Road), Bethnal Green, 1851.

West Place, Patriot Square, Spitalfields, "the first on the left from Patriot Square towards the Hackney Road" (Lockie).

West Row, St. Ann Street, Limehouse, 1851.

West Seabright Place, Hackney Road, Bethnal Green, 1851.

West Street, 1. Off Crispin Street, Spitalfields, "at 10 leading to the west side of market" (Lockie). 2. Off Devonshire Street (Cephas Street), Mile End, part renamed Braintree Street part renamed Malcolm Road. 3. Off Gill Street, Limehouse, renamed Lance Street. 4. Off Green Street (Roman Road), Bethnal Green, 1891, renamed Usk Street. 5. Off Loddiges Road, Hackney, 1868, became part of Elsdale Street. 6. Off Mare Street, Hackney, renamed Westgate Street. 7. Off Martha Street (Wadeson Street), Hackney, 1868, renamed Mowlem Street. 8. Off Orchard Place, Poplar, 1890. 9. Off Spitalfields Market (Commercial Street), Spitalfields, 1851. 10. Off Spread Eagle Street (Gill Street), Limehouse, 1851. 11. Off West India Dock Road, Limehouse.

West Tap Street, Off Somerford Street, Whitechapel, 1851.

Westbury Street, Off Quaker Street, Spitalfields.

Western Cottages, Sage Street, Shadwell, 1891, Cable Street.

Westferry Arms Public House, 43 West India Dock Road, Limehouse, aka Oporto (Tavern).

Westminster Arms Public House, 1. 163 Gosset Street, Bethnal Green. 2. Warner Place, Bethnal Green, 1874, Hackney Road.

Westmoreland Street, Off Dunloe Street, Bethnal Green, 1895, became the western end of Dunloe Street.

Weston Cottage, 1. Durham Grove (Morning Lane), Hackney, 1891, Morning Lane. 2. Westferry Road, Isle of Dogs, 1851, close to Gaverick Street river end.

Weston Place, Mare Street, Hackney, 1895, renamed Weston Walk.

Weston Street, Off Devons Road, Bromley and Bow, 1891, renamed Watts Grove.

Westover Street, Off Ben Jonson Road, Mile End, 1891, renamed Ocean Street.

Westrup Mews, Brady Street, Whitechapel, 1891.

Wests Brewery Public House, 313 Hackney Road, Bethnal Green.

Weymouth Mews, Hackney Road, Bethnal Green, 1874, renamed Weymouth Terrace.

Weymouth Street, Off Dunloe Street, Bethnal Green, 1895, became part of Dunloe Street.

Weymouth Terrace British School, Weymouth Terrace, Bethnal Green, 1863-1891, Hackney Road.

Wharf Cottage, Old Ford Road, Bromley and Bow.

Wharf Road, 1.Isle of Dogs, west section became part of Ferry Street, east section renamed Saunders Ness Road. 2. Off Pritchards Road, Bethnal Green, 1895, renamed Wharf Place. 3. Off Wharf Place, Bethnal Green, renamed Wharf Place.

Wharncliff(e) Street, Off Royston Street, Bethnal Green, Brierly Gardens part on the site.

Wheatsheaf Public House, 1. 119 Mare Street, Hackney. 2. 13 Mauve Street (Burcham Street), Poplar. 3. 39 Middleton Street, Bethnal Green. 4. 23 Philip Street (Ellen Street), St. George in the East. 5. 15 Star Street (Planet Street), Shadwell. 6. 38 Upper Chapman Street (Chapman Street), St. George in the East, 1874. 7. 219 Wapping High Street, Wapping, 1874. 8. 71 Wapping Wall, Wapping.

Wheatsheaf Tavern Public House, 2 Commercial Road, Whitechapel.

Wheeler Street, Spitalfields, common misspelling of Wheler Street.

Wheelers Buildings, Wentworth Street, Whitechapel, "three houses on the right hand side of George Yard going from Wentworth Street" (Elmes).

Whiston Street, Bethnal Green, renamed Whiston Road.

Whitaker Buildings, The Highway, Shadwell, 1950, corner of The Highway and Brodlove Lane.

White Bear Court, Lambeth Street (Alie Street), Whitechapel, 1851.

White Bear Public House, 1. Kingsland Road, Hackney, 1874. 2. 26 Lambeth Street (Alie Street), Whitechapel. 3. 96 Little Alie Street (Alie Street), Whitechapel, 1874. 4. Ratcliffe Cross (Narrow Street), Ratcliffe. 5. 1 St. George Street (The Highway), St. George in the East, 1874.

White Cottages, Homerton Terrace, Hackney, 1841.

White Cross Street, Whitechapel, now the northern end of Spelman Street.

White Hart & Fountain Public House, 139 Royal Mint Street, East Smithfield, 1874, aka Old Fountain.

White Hart Place, 1. Sugar Loaf Alley, Bethnal Green, 1841. 2. Wells Street (Cotton Street), Poplar, 1851.

White Hart Public House, 1. 4 Alfred Street, Bromley·and Bow. 2. 359 Bethnal Green Road, Bethnal Green. 3. 101 Brook Street (Cable Street), Ratcliffe, 1874, address also 531 Cable Street. 4. 10 Greenfield Street (Greenfield Road), Whitechapel. 5. 4 Hooper Street (Hooper Square), Whitechapel. 6. 74 Kingsland Road, Hackney, 1874. 7. 43 Leman Street, Whitechapel. 8. 1 Little Pearl Street (Calvin Street), Spitalfields. 9. 65 Medland Street (Horseferry Road), Ratcliffe, address also 505 The Highway. 10. 115 Narrow Street, Limehouse, 1874, close to corner of Ropemakers Fields. 11. 118 Old Church Road, Stepney. 12. 413 Old Ford Road, Bromley and Bow. 13. 96 Pennington Street, St. George in the East. 14. 307 Poplar High Street, Poplar, 1874. 15. Queen Street (Horseferry Road), Ratcliffe, 1874. 16. 32 Shadwell High Street (The Highway), Shadwell. 17. Suffolk Street, Mile End, 1874. 18. 47 Turner Street, Whitechapel. 19. Vine Court, Spitalfields, 1874.

White Horse & Leaping Bar Public House, 58 Whitechapel High Street, Whitechapel, 1874, aka Horse & Leaping Bar.

White Horse & Woolpack Public House, 443 Old Ford Road, Bromley and Bow, 1874.

White Horse Court, 1. Little Prescot Street (Prescot Street), Whitechapel, 1851, Royal Mint Street. 2. Wheler Street, Spitalfields, 1792, just south of Great Pearl Street.

White Horse Lane, New Road, St. George in the East, 1837, now the section of Commercial Road heading west from New Road to almost Back Church Lane.

White Horse Place, Commercial Road, Shadwell, "the third on the right about $^1/_8$ of a mile east of the halfway house" (Lockie) renamed Hardinge Street.

White Horse Public House, 1. Bow Common Lane, Bromley and Bow, 1874. 2. 214 Bow Road, Bromley and Bow, 1874. 3. 106 Burdett Road, Bromley and Bow. 4. 12 Buxton Street, Whitechapel. 5. 44 Hare Street (Cheshire Street), Whitechapel. 6. 150 Mile End Road, Mile End, 1874. 7. 9-11 Poplar High Street, Poplar, 1874. 8. 163 Roman Road, Bethnal Green, 1874. 9. 13 Sandys Row, Spitalfields. 10. Spital Street, Spitalfields, 1874. 11. Stepney Green, Stepney, 1874. 12. 37 The Grove (Reading Lane), Hackney, Mare Street. 13. 69 Wapping Wall, Wapping. 14. 21 Wheler street, Spitalfields. 15. 94 White Horse Lane, Mile End. 16. 48 White Horse Street (White Horse Road), Stepney, 1874.

White Horse Street, Off Commercial Road, Stepney, previously extended to south of Commercial Road The road north of Commercial Road was renamed White Horse Road, southernmost section became part of Butcher Row.

White Horse Tavern Public House, 94 White Horse Lane, Mile End.

White Horse Terrace, White Horse Street (White Horse Road), Stepney, 1851.

White Lion Brewery, 35 Folgate Street (Spitalfields), Spitalfields, aka Hopes Brewery.

White Lion Court, Blossom Street, Spitalfields, 1746.

White Lion Public House, 1. 37 Fashion Street, Spitalfields, 1874. 2. 49 Green Bank, Wapping, 1874, aka Old White Lion. 3. 19 King Street (Prusom Street), Wapping. 4. 30 Old Gravel Lane (Wapping Lane), Wapping, 1874. 5. 27 Raven Row, Mile End. 6. 68 Shadwell High Street (The Highway), Shadwell, 1874. 7. 331 Wick Road, Hackney.

White Lion Street, 1. Off Folgate Street, Spitalfields, 1891, renamed Folgate Street. 2. Off Goodmans Fields (Leman Street), Whitechapel, "the continuation of Leman Street to 76 Rosemary Lane" (Lockie), the southern end of the present-day Leman Street.

White Raven Public House, 38 Raven Street (Cavell Street), Whitechapel, Raven Street became part of Bedford Street.

White Raven Terrace, Raven Street (Cavell Street), Whitechapel, 1851, Raven Street became part of Bedford Street.

White Street, Off Bethnal Green Road, Bethnal Green, 1891, became part of Vallance Road.

White Street or Row, Fashion Street, Spitalfields, "the

continuation of Fashion Street from 194 Brick Lane" (Lockie).

White Swan Public House, 1. 30 Brunswick Street, Poplar. 2. 9 Cinnamon Street, Wapping. 3. 556 Commercial Road, Ratcliffe. 4. 121 Devons Road, Bromley and Bow. 5. 36 Great Alie Street (Alie Street), Whitechapel, address also 21 Great Alie Street. 6. 48 Ida Street, Poplar. 7. 6-7 Lower Keate Street (Thrawl Street), Spitalfields, 1874. 8. 229 Mile End Road, Mile End, 1874, aka Swan. 9. 161 Old Gravel Lane (Wapping Lane), Wapping, 1874, aka Swan. 10. Rose Lane (Ratcliffe Lane), Ratcliffe, 1874, Commercial Road. 11. 57 Royal Mint Street, East Smithfield, 1874, aka Swan. 12. 225 Shadwell High Street (The Highway), Shadwell, 1874, address also 43 Lower Shadwell, aka Swan, aka Half Moon. 13. 124 St. George Street (The Highway), St. George in the East, 1874. 14. 3 Swan Street (Cygnet Street), Bethnal Green, 1874, aka Swan. 15. 141 Wapping High Street, Wapping, 1874, address also 101 Wapping High Street. 16. 24 Wapping Wall, Wapping, 1874. 17. 20 Whitechapel High Street, Whitechapel, aka Swan Inn.

White Swan Yard, Whitechapel Road, Whitechapel, 1860, immediately east of Half Moon Passage.

Whitechapel Boys & Girls Shelter, George Yard (Gunthorpe Street), Whitechapel, Whitechapel High Street.

Whitechapel County Court, Great Prescot Street (Prescot Street), Whitechapel, 1891.

Whitechapel Foundation School, Leman Street, Whitechapel, 1891.

Whitechapel or Aldgate Bars, Whitechapel Road, Whitechapel, "at the end of Middlesex and Somerset Street and mark the eastern boundaries of the city liberties in that direction" (Elmes).

Whitechapel Lane, Whitechapel Road, renamed Brick Lane.

Whitechapel Public Baths & Wash Houses, Goulston Street, Whitechapel, 1895.

Whitechapel Road Synagogue, 192 Whitechapel Road, Whitechapel, 1930.

Whitechapel School, Whitechapel Road, Whitechapel, "a free school founded by the Rev Ralph Davenant in 1680" (Elmes).

Whitechapel Union Receiving Home, 403-409 Mile End Road, Mile End, site of later Odeon Cinema.

Whitechapel Union Scattered Homes, Whitehall Cottages, Whitehall Lane, Whitechapel

Whitechapel Union Workhouse, 1. Fulbourne Street,

Whitechapel, 1930-1944, aka Spitalfields Workhouse aka St. Peters Hospital. 2. South Grove (Southern Grove), Bromley and Bow.

Whitechapel Workhouse, Whitechapel Road, Whitechapel, close to St. Marys Street.

Whitehall Court & Place, Three Colt Street, Limehouse, 1851.

Whitehead Place & Street, Off Cleveland Street (Cleveland Way), Mile End, 1891, formerly Union Street.

Whites Buildings, Code Street, Whitechapel, 1890.

Whites Cottages, Tooke Street (Westferry Road), Isle of Dogs, 1851.

Whites Grounds, Bethnal Green Road, Bethnal Green, "at 95 the first on the right east of the turnpike" (Lockie).

Whites Rents, Ropemakers Fields, Limehouse, 1891, Ropemakers Fields to Narrow Street.

Whites Row, Durward Street, Whitechapel, now the western section of Durward Street.

Whites Street, Off Fashion Street, Spitalfields, "the continuation of Fashion Street" (Elmes).

Whites Yard, 1. Belgrave Street, Stepney, 1891. 2. Mile End Road, Mile End, "about ⅛ of a mile on the right east of Stepney

Green and opposite the Old Globe" (Lockie).

Whitesmiths Arms Public House, 47 Chicksand Street, Whitechapel, address also 37 Chicksand Street.

Whitethorn Court & Place, Prusom Street, Wapping, 1891, between Prusom Street and Boarded Entry.

Whitethorn Public House, 30 Whitethorn Street, Bromley and Bow, 1874.

Whitmores Buildings, Mansford Street, Bethnal Green, 1891.

Whittington & Cat Public House, 1. 12 Church Row (Bethnal Green Road), Bethnal Green, 1874. 2. 35 Whitechapel High Street, Whitechapel.

Whittington Club & Chambers for Working Youths, 86 Leman Street, Whitechapel.

Wick Lane, Wick Road, Hackney, 1862, east end of, and became part of, Wick Road.

Wick Street, Off Well Street, Hackney, 1841, renamed Cassland Road.

Wickers Court, Glasshouse Fields, Shadwell, 1851.

Widows Retreat (aka Retreat or Robinsons Retreat Almshouses), Retreat Place, Hackney, 1841.

Widows Son Public House, 75 Devons Road, Bromley and Bow, 1841.

Wil(l)mot Road, Hackney, 1862, renamed Greenwood Road,.

Wilders Buildings, Milk Yard, Shadwell.

Wildmans Cottages, Cuba Street, Isle of Dogs.

Wilk Court, Great Pearl Street (Calvin Street), Spitalfields, 1891, north of corner of Great Pearl Street and Little Pearl St.

Wilk(e)s Street, Off Quaker Street, Spitalfields, "the second on the left from 173 Brick Lane behind Hanburys brewery" (Lockie).

Wilkes Court, Great Pearl Street (Calvin Street), Spitalfields, 1851.

Wilkes Street Synagogue, 93 Wilkes Street, Spitalfields.

Wilkinson House, Blount Street, Poplar, 1950.

Will Somers Public House, 25 Crispin Street, Spitalfields, aka Old Will Somers.

Willey Court, Pinchin Street, St. George in the East, 1891.

William Cottages, Powis Road, Isle of Dogs, 1891.

William Court, Teal Street (Cheshire Street), Whitechapel, 1891.

William IV Public House, 1. 309 Poplar High Street, Poplar, 1874, aka Coopers Arms. 2. 52 Warley Street, Bethnal Green. 3. William Street (Ivimey Street), Bethnal Green, 1874.

William Street, 1. Off Barnet Grove, Bethnal Green, renamed Ivimey Street. 2. Off Buxton Street, Whitechapel, 1891, renamed Eckersley Street. 3. Off Cannon Street Road, St. George in the East, renamed Ponler Street. 4. Off Devonport Street, Shadwell, renamed Ronald Street. 5. Off East India Dock Road, Poplar, 1851, opposite Poplar Baths renamed Woollett Street. 6. Off Green Street (Roman Road), Bethnal Green, 1841, renamed Warley Street. 7. Off Hardinge Street, Shadwell, 1851. 8. Off Locksley Street, Limehouse, renamed Dixon Street. 9. Off Maroon Street, Limehouse, renamed Dakin Street. 10. Off New Road, Whitechapel, renamed Fordham Street. 11. Off Nye Street (Susannah Street), Poplar. 12. Off Oxford Street (Stepney Way), Whitechapel, 1891, renamed Gold Street. 13. Off Pedley Street, Whitechapel, renamed Eckersley Street. 14. Off Spicer Street (Buxton Street), Whitechapel, 1851.

William Terrace, 1. 173-177 East India Dock Road, Poplar, 1851. 2. Hardinge Street, Shadwell, 1871. 3. Sewardstone Road, Bethnal Green, 1895.

Williams Buildings, 1. Braintree Street, Mile End, 1921. 2. West Street (Braintree Street), Mile End, 1891, part renamed

Braintree Street part renamed Malcolm Road.

Williams Cottages, Grove Lane (Reading Lane), Hackney, 1891.

Williams Court, The Highway, St. George in the East, 1878, north of Wellclose Square.

Williams Court & Place, Teal Street (Cheshire Street), Whitechapel.

Williams House, Dupont Street (Shaw Crescent), Stepney, 1950, Limehouse Fields Estate.

Williams Place Street & Terrace, Salmon Lane, Limehouse, renamed Raby Street.

Williams Rents, 1. Back Church Lane, St. George in the East, 1851, north end and west side of Back Church Lane. 2. Providence Place (Darling Row), Whitechapel.

Willow Cottage, Wick Road, Hackney, 1862.

Willow Row, Nightingale Lane (Thomas More Street), Wapping, 1851.

Willow Street, Off Nicholas Road, Mile End, renamed Osier Street.

Willow Tree Alley, Nightingale Lane (Thomas More Street), Wapping, 1746.

Willow Tree Court, New Market Street (Wapping Lane), Wapping, 1851, "ten doors on the left from 157 Wapping

Street" (Lockie), later Brewhouse Lane.

Willow Walk, 1. Barnet Grove, Bethnal Green, 1851, renamed Baxendale Street. 2. Hackney Road, Bethnal Green, "opposite Middlesex Place, about ¼ of a mile on the right from Shoreditch Church" (Lockie). 3. King Street (Pelter Street), Bethnal Green, renamed Pelter Street.

Willson Place, Flower and Dean Street, Spitalfields, Flower and Dean Street.

Wilman Grove & Cottages, Lansdowne Road (Lansdowne Drive), Hackney, 1891.

Wilmot House, Mansford Street, Bethnal Green, 1950, east side north of Florida Street.

Wilmot Square, Bethnal Green Road, Bethnal Green, "about ¾ of a mile on the left from 65 Shoreditch" (Lockie), became part of Mansford Street, opposite Derbyshire Street.

Wilmot(s) Grove, Bethnal Green Road, Bethnal Green, "on the north side of Wilmot Square" (Lockie), became the southern half of Mansford Street.

Wilmot's Folly, Bethnal Green Road, Bethnal Green, "at the north end of Marys Row entering on the east side of Wilmot Square" (Lockie).

Wilson Place, Flower and Dean Street, Spitalfields, 1851.

Wilson Street, 1. Off Dewberry Street, Poplar, 1891, renamed

Mills Grove. 2. Off Lansdowne Road (Lansdowne Drive), Hackney, 1868. 3. Bromley and Bow, renamed Wager Street. 5. Off White Horse Street (White Horse Road), Stepney, 1868, renamed Matlock Street.

Wilson Terrace, 1. Bow Lane, Poplar, 1851. 2. Four Mills Street (St. Leonards Street), Bromley and Bow, 1851.

Wilson(s) Arms Public House, 29 Campbell Road, Bromley and Bow, 1874.

Wilsons Court, Half Nichol(s) Street (Boundary Street), Bethnal Green.

Wilsons Place, Salmon Lane, Limehouse, 1851, diagonally opposite Copenhagen Place.

Wilton Road, Off Parkholme Road, Hackney, 1891, renamed Wilton Way.

Wilton Terrace, Park Road (Parkholme Road), Hackney, 1851, south of Wilton Road.

Wiltshire Brewery Public House, 505 Hackney Road, Bethnal Green.

Wiltshire Lane, Ratcliffe Highway (The Highway), St. George in the East, "at 40 a few doors west of Ratcliffe Highway" (Lockie), south of Wellclose Square, opposite side of The Highway.

Wiltshire Stores Public House, 118 Vallance Road, Whitechapel.

Wiltshire Villas, Strattondale Street, Isle of Dogs, 1891.

Winchester Crescent, Winchester Street (Dunbridge Street), Bethnal Green, 1841.

Winchester Place, 1. Bethnal Green, renamed Dunbridge Place (Dunbridge Street). 2. Hackney Road, Bethnal Green, "near the end of Willow walk or Green gate Gardens" (Lockie).

Winchester Row, Hackney Road, Hackney, "a few small houses behind Wells Row near the last street" (Lockie).

Winchester Street, Off Cheshire Street, Whitechapel, 1841, part renamed Dunbridge Street.

Windmill Court, Royal Mint Street, East Smithfield, 1851.

Windmill Public House, 1. 8 Robert Place (Salter Street), Limehouse, 1874, corner of Salter Street and Robert Street last renamed Mandarin Street. 2. 55 Royal Mint Street, East Smithfield. 3. Windmill Public House, Westferry Road, Isle of Dogs, near Millwall Pier (river end of Powis Road, formerly close to St. Pauls Church).

Windmill Street, Off Herbert Street (Haggerston Park), Hackney, 1862, Haggerston Park is on the site.

Windsor Castle Public House, 1. 119 Bishops Road (Bishops Way), Bethnal Green, 1874. 2. 8 Bowen Street (Chrisp Street), Poplar. 3. 265 Mile End Road,

Mile End. 4. 52 Oxford Street (Stepney Way), Whitechapel, aka Coopers Arms.

Windsor Road, Hackney, renamed Berkshire Road.

Windsor Terrace, Osborne Road, Hackney, renamed Berkshire Terrace.

Windward House, Limehouse Causeway, Limehouse, St. Vincent Estate, demolished in 1993.

Wine Street, Off Lamb Street, Spitalfields, "at 24 the second on the left from Spital Square" (Lockie).

Winford Court, Wentworth Street, Whitechapel, "about six doors west of Rose Lane" (Lockie).

Winford or Wentford Street, Off Wentworth Street, Whitechapel, 1650, misspelling of Wentworth Street on early maps.

Winifred House, Thrawl Street, Spitalfields, 1950.

Winkleys Wharf, Westferry Road, Isle of Dogs, 1950, river end of Crews Street.

Winnipeg Buildings, Prestons Road, Poplar, 1900.

Wint Terrace, Manchester Road, Isle of Dogs, 1860, opposite the Queen Public House.

Winter Place, Brownlow Road, Hackney, 1868.

Winterton Buildings, Anthony Street, St. George in the East, 1891.

Winterton Street, Off Commercial Road, Shadwell, 1950, parallel with Watney Street.

Winwood Street, Off Lindley Street, Limehouse, Sidney Street.

Wise Court, Wheler Street, Spitalfields, "the first on the left from 31 Lamb Street" (Lockie).

Wiskers Gardens, Bonner Street, Bethnal Green, 1851.

Wiskins Cottages, Isle of Dogs, 1851, precise location unknown.

Wlodowa Synagogue, Spital Square, Spitalfields.

Wolsey Street, Off Sidney Street, Whitechapel, 1895, Sidney Street to Jubilee Street, south of Hawkins Street.

Wolverley Arms Public House, 62 Viaduct Street, Bethnal Green, 1874.

Wolverly Street, Off Seabright Place (Seabright Street), Bethnal Green, 1827, Hackney Road opposite Durham Street.

Wombwells Yard, Warkworth Terrace (Commercial Road), Limehouse, 1851.

Wood Cottages, Westferry Road, Isle of Dogs, demolished to make room for Millwall Dock entrance lock.

Wood Street, Off Church Street (Fournier Street), Spitalfields,

Southern section of present day Wilkes Street.

Wood Street, Off Hare Street (Cheshire Street), Whitechapel, "on the south side the Church Yard or the last on the left in Hare Street from 110 Brick Lane" (Lockie), renamed Wood Close.

Woodbine Cottages, 1. Holly Street, Hackney, 1851, Dalston Lane. 2. Homerton Terrace, Hackney, 1891, renamed Woodbine Terrace.

Woodin Street, Off Chadbourn Street, Poplar, Langdon Park School is on the site.

Woodison Street, Off Canal Road (Mile End Road), Bromley and Bow, 1891, west of canal.

Woodland Street, Off Dalston Lane, Hackney, 1895, Dalston Lane to Richmond Road, southern section renamed Forest Grove.

Woodman Public House, 1. 148 Betts Street (St. Leonards Street), Bromley and Bow. 2. 20 Woodland Street, Hackney.

Woods Buildings, Whitechapel Road, Whitechapel, "at 124 opposite the London Hospital leading to Ducking pond Row" (Lockie).

Woods Close, Church Row (Bethnal Green Road), Bethnal Green, "on the south side the church near Hare Street" (Lockie).

Woods Place, Mill Street (Old Ford Road), Bromley and Bow, 1851.

Woods Yard, 1. Quaker Street, Spitalfields, 1792, between Quaker Street and Phoenix Street.

Woods Yard, Wheler Street, Spitalfields, "the second on the right from 38 Wheler Street" (Lockie).

Woodstock Road, Off Poplar High Street, Poplar, 1937, renamed Woodstock Terrace.

Wooldrichs Gardens, Fleet Street (Pedley Street), Whitechapel, "a number of small houses at the east end of it" (Lockie).

Woolfords Ways, Wapping Wall, Wapping, "on the east side of King James stairs opposite Star Street Shadwell" (Lockie).

Woollett Street, Off East India Dock Road, Poplar, 1891, opposite Poplar Baths.

Woolmore Place, Woolmore Street, Poplar, 1851.

Woolmore Street School, Woolmore Street, Poplar, 1816, former Poplar and Blackwall Free British School.

Woolpack (Inn) Public House, 8 Morning Lane, Hackney.

Woolpack or Woolsack Place, Water Lane (Morning Lane), Hackney, 1841.

Woolpack Public House, 1. 9 James Street (Cadiz Street), Mile

End. 2. Kingsland Road, Hackney, 1874. 3. 89 Sceptre Road, Bethnal Green.

Woolsack Public House, 43 Willis Street, Poplar.

Woolsley Terrace, Cubitt Town Isle of Dogs, 1888.

Worcester Court & Street, Off Old Gravel Lane (Wapping Lane), Wapping, 1891, part renamed Reardon Street.

Worcester Street, Off Old Gravel Lane (Reardon Street), Wapping.

Wordsworth House, Wordsworth Road, Bethnal Green, 1891.

Working Lads Institute & Home, 279 Whitechapel Road, Whitechapel.

Worlds End, Stepney Green, Mile End, became the western end of Ben Jonson Road.

Worlds End Public House, 47 Ben Jonson Road, Mile End, 1874.

Wormills Rents, Periwinkle Street (Ratcliffe Cross Street), Ratcliffe, 1851.

Wormwood Rents, Ratcliffe Square (Ratcliffe Cross Street), Ratcliffe, 1871.

Wray Terrace, Old Bethnal Green Road, Bethnal Green, 1868, opposite Temple Street.

Wrights Buildings, Tagg Street (Cranbrook Estate), Bromley and Bow, 1891.

Wrights Buildings & Cottage, Salmon Lane, Limehouse, 1891, opposite south end of Brenton Street.

Wrights Place, Cotton Street, Poplar, 1851.

Wrights Rents, Pell Street (Wellclose Square), St. George in the East, "the first turning on the left hand side of Pell Street, from the New Road" (Elmes).

Wrights Road, Off Libra Road, Bromley and Bow, 1891.

Wrights Row, Pell Street (Wellclose Square), St. George in the East, 1891.

Wycliffe Congregational Church, Philpot Street, Whitechapel, 1831-1907.

X

XX Place, Globe Road, Mile End, 1891, alternative spelling for Double X Place, Globe Road opposite the Horn of Plenty public house.

Y

Yalford Street, Off Fieldgate Street, Whitechapel, 1891.

Yanover Synagogue, 45 Fashion Street, Spitalfields.

Yarmouth Arms Public House, 1. 85 Green Street (Roman Road), Bethnal Green. 2. 170 Wapping High Street, Wapping. 3. 20 Willis Street, Poplar.

Yarmouth Town Public House, 168 Old Gravel Lane (Wapping Lane), Wapping, 1874.

Yattan Street, Off Teviot Street, Poplar.

Yatton Street, Off St. Leonards Road, Poplar, 1891.

Ye Old Victory Public House, 213 Old Ford Road, Bromley and Bow.

Ye Olde Angel Public House, 85 Whitechapel High Street, Whitechapel, aka Angel Public House.

Yoakleys Almshouses, Hope Court (Wentworth Street), Spitalfields, Wentworth Street.

Yoakleys Buildings, Mile End Road, Mile End, "Mile End Green, Nine houses eastward of the London Hospital" (Elmes).

York (Tap) Tavern Public House, 647 Commercial Road, Limehouse, aka Star Tavern.

York Buildings, Old Gravel Lane (Wapping Lane), Wapping, 1891.

York Minster Public House, 44 Philpot Street, Mile End, 1874.

York Passage, Knott Street (Cadiz Street), Mile End, 1891.

York Place, 1. Brookfield Road, Hackney, 1862, became part of Wick Road. 2. Grove Street (Ellsworth Street), Bethnal Green, 1841. 3. Little Collingwood Street (Collingwood Street), Whitechapel, 1841. 4. Lower Chapman Street (Bigland Street), St. George in the East, renamed Goodhart Place. 5. Maroon Street, Limehouse. 6. Mile End Road, Mile End, "part of the south side, by Saville Place about 2½ miles from Aldgate" (Lockie). 7. Mile End Road, Mile End, Mile End "the first on the left in York Street from the Commercial Road, leading into Thomas Street" (Lockie). 8. Old Gravel Lane (Wapping Lane), Wapping, renamed Lowder Street. 9. York Street (Commercial Road), Limehouse, "the first on the left in York Street from the Commercial Road leading into Thomas Street" (Lockie).

York Place or Row, Hackney Road, Bethnal Green, 1860, at its corner with the later Angela Street.

York Road, 1. Off Commercial Road, Limehouse, 1890, renamed Yorkshire Road. 2. Mile End, renamed Harford Street.

York Row, Pearson Street, Bethnal Green, Pearson Street to Hows Street.

York Street, 1. Off Church Street (Bethnal Green Road), Bethnal Green, renamed Ebor Street. 2. Off Commercial Road, Whitechapel, "the second on the right from Cannon Street Road towards Whitechapel Church extending to 45 Charlotte Street" (Lockie), renamed Myrdle Street. 3. Ratcliffe, renamed

Flamborough Street. 4. Off
Globe Road, Mile End, renamed
Leatherdale Street. 5. Off
Hackney Road, Bethnal Green,
renamed Yorkton Street. 6. Off
Kingsland Road, Hackney, 1868,
renamed Hows Street.

York Street East, Commercial
Road, Limehouse, 1891, renamed
Flamborough Street in 1905.

York Street West, Commercial
Road, Limehouse, 1891, renamed
Barnes Street.

York Terrace, 1. Kingsland
Road, Hackney. 2. York Street
West, Limehouse, 1871.

Yorkshire Grey Public House,
1. 180 Brady Street,
Whitechapel. 2. 48-49
Whitechapel High Street,
Whitechapel, 1874.

Young Prince Public House, 1.
81 Cambridge Road (Cambridge
Heath Road), Whitechapel. 2. 77
Chrisp Street, Poplar. 3.
Elizabeth Street (Mansford
Road), Bethnal Green, 1874. 4.
164 Roman Road, Bethnal
Green.

Yule Court, Sutton Street,
Shadwell.

Z

Zangwill House, Carr Street,
Limehouse, 1950, Limehouse
Fields Estate.

Zetland Hall, Mansell Street,
Whitechapel, 1870.

Printed in Great Britain
by Amazon

71703520R00173